BlockPrint

Quarto.com

First published in 2016 by Rockport Publishers,
an imprint of The Quarto Group,
100 Cummings Center, Suite 265-D,
Beverly, MA 01915, USA.
T (978) 282-9590 F (978) 283-2742

EEA Representation, WTS Tax d.o.o.,
Žanova ulica 3, 4000 Kranj, Slovenia.
www.wts-tax.si

Rockport Publishers titles are also available at discount for retail, wholesale, promotional, and bulk purchase. For details, contact the Special Sales Manager by email at specialsales@quarto.com or by mail at The Quarto Group, Attn: Special Sales Manager, 100 Cummings Center, Suite 265-D, Beverly, MA 01915, USA.

ISBN: 978-1-63159-113-6

Digital edition published in 2016
eISBN: 978-1-63159-181-5

Library of Congress
Cataloging-in-Publication Data available.

Design: Timothy Samara
Photography: Andrea Lauren

Everything you need to know for printing with lino blocks, rubber blocks, foam sheets, and stamps

BlockPrint

ANDREA LAUREN

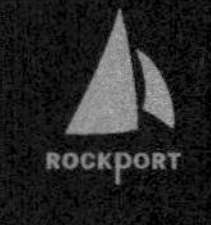

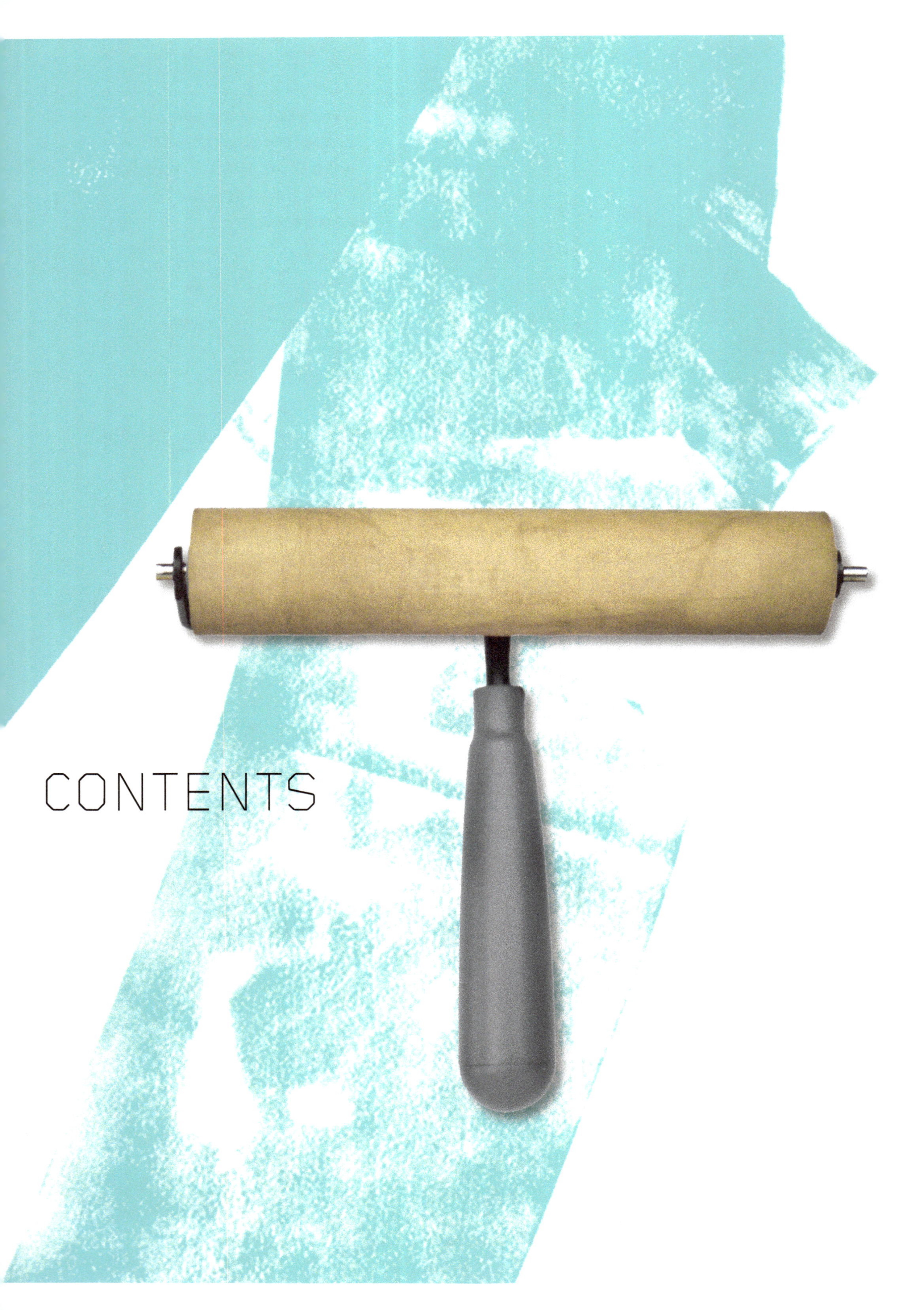

CONTENTS

INTRODUCTION

First you'll notice the intoxicating aroma of ink. Then there's the excitement that builds as you prepare to make your initial cut into a fresh printing block. That's just the start. You'll see. The joy you'll experience when you pull your first print off the carved block is pure magic. It can inspire a lifelong passion for designing, carving, and printing images, as it has for me.

Relief printmaking is one of the most versatile of arts—it's available to artists of all skill levels and lends itself to virtually every design and drawing style. It's also one of the most flexible of art forms: From the woodblock prints of Japan's ukiyo-e artists and Europe's old masters, to the early twentieth-century linoleum prints of Picasso and Matisse, relief printing has adapted effortlessly to new mediums and technologies. Today, artists can also make prints from rubber, foam, and precut stamps.

In *Block Print* you'll find a range of techniques and inspiring project ideas for the beginning printmaker as well as for experienced artists. The step-by-step how-tos take you through the basics of single-color printing, show you how to master registration for multicolor prints, and explore ways to combine materials and techniques for variety in your printmaking.

Building on the classic tradition, combining it with all that's new, *Block Print* will guide you to success—and joy—in creating your own original art prints.

ANDREA LAUREN

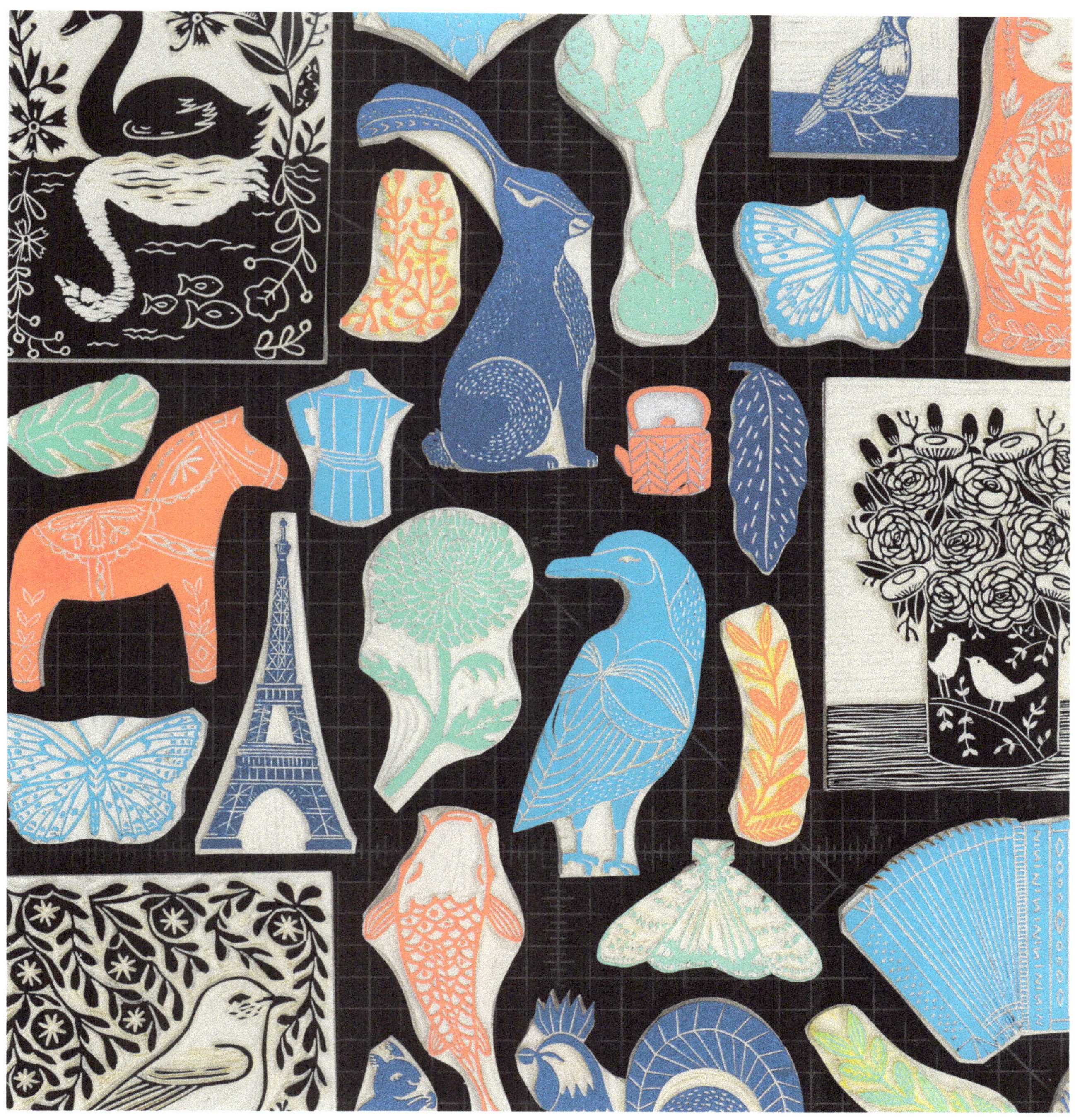

BLOCKS FROM
THE AUTHOR'S
STUDIO

MATERIALS

The materials you'll need to start block printing—blocks, ink, and paper—can all be sourced at art supply shops and online. As detailed in this section, the carving blocks you choose will vary depending on your experience, your tools, and the type of ink you use. The recommended inks for each of the projects in this book clean up with soap and water. For paper, I suggest Japanese-style printing papers; they are thin, yet very strong, and are specifically designed for printing by hand.

CARVING BLOCKS

There are a number of types of linoleum and rubber carving blocks available. To an extent, they're interchangeable, but there are times when one is a better choice than another. Each type handles differently and some carving tools work better with certain types of blocks. If you're working on a project with multiple blocks that will require careful registration, make sure all your blocks are the same height.

NOTE

Before carving, warm your linoleum block with a hair dryer or by sitting on it for a few minutes. You'll notice a softer and more pliable surface.

Linoleum Blocks

The standard linoleum block is gray and is often referred to as battleship linoleum. The printing techniques in this book primarily call for unmounted linoleum. This material is flexible, has a jute backing, and can be cut through with a craft knife. Beginner gouges with interchangeable blades are not the best choice for carving this type of linoleum: It's made from ground limestone and dulls blades fairly quickly. If you plan to work with battleship linoleum blocks often, you'll need a set of higher-quality blades kept consistently sharp with a honing tool.

—

Another consideration is the freshness of the linoleum: It dries out over time and becomes harder to work with. It's difficult to judge the freshness of linoleum, so it's worthwhile to buy your blocks from a source that sells through its stock regularly.

Rubber-Vinyl Carving Block

This is a new material, somewhat denser than rubber carving blocks. It's easy to carve, like rubber. It can hold fine lines like linoleum, but it doesn't dry out and crumble like linoleum, and it doesn't dull carving blades as quickly. Rubber-vinyl blocks can be used with water-soluble printing inks as well as soy-based or safe-wash inks.

Dense Rubber Blocks

Rubber carving blocks come in a variety of thicknesses and colors. Each type handles slightly differently and you may find that you have a preference once you begin developing your own carving technique. These blocks are easy to carve and are suited for a beginner's set of gouges. As always, the sharpness of your gouges is important. Rubber blocks are easily trimmed to a custom size with a craft knife and are designed for use *only* with water-soluble printing inks. Be sure to store your rubber blocks flat. If you need to stack them in storage, separate them with cardboard to prevent them from sticking together.

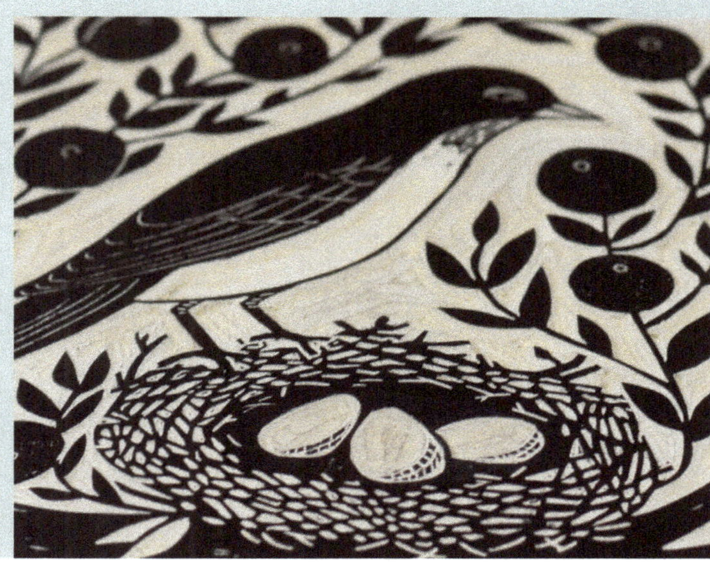

MATERIALS

STAMPS AND SHEETS

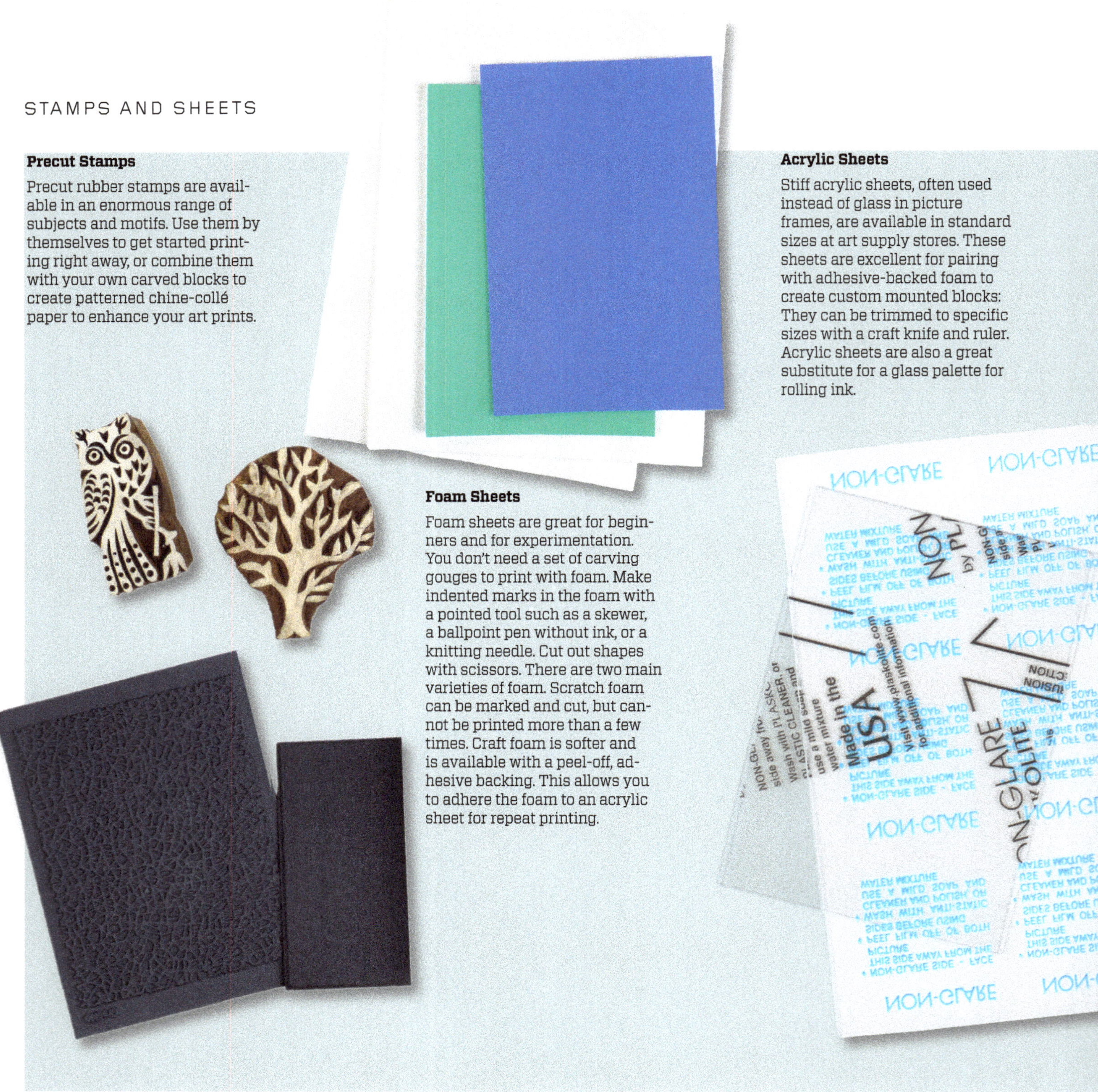

Precut Stamps

Precut rubber stamps are available in an enormous range of subjects and motifs. Use them by themselves to get started printing right away, or combine them with your own carved blocks to create patterned chine-collé paper to enhance your art prints.

Acrylic Sheets

Stiff acrylic sheets, often used instead of glass in picture frames, are available in standard sizes at art supply stores. These sheets are excellent for pairing with adhesive-backed foam to create custom mounted blocks: They can be trimmed to specific sizes with a craft knife and ruler. Acrylic sheets are also a great substitute for a glass palette for rolling ink.

Foam Sheets

Foam sheets are great for beginners and for experimentation. You don't need a set of carving gouges to print with foam. Make indented marks in the foam with a pointed tool such as a skewer, a ballpoint pen without ink, or a knitting needle. Cut out shapes with scissors. There are two main varieties of foam. Scratch foam can be marked and cut, but cannot be printed more than a few times. Craft foam is softer and is available with a peel-off, adhesive backing. This allows you to adhere the foam to an acrylic sheet for repeat printing.

NOTE

Water-soluble inks are different from water-clean-up paints such as acrylics. Acrylic paint will dry out your brayers and ruin your blocks. Avoid using acrylic paint as a substitute for water-soluble printing inks.

Traditional oil-based printing inks, although beautiful, can be problematic for use in the home studio.

Most require chemical clean-up and proper ventilation. They are not used for any of the projects in this book.

INKS

Water-Soluble Block-Printing Ink

With their easy soap-and-water cleanup, water-soluble inks are great for beginners and for use at home. These inks come in a variety of colors as well as metallic options. They have a short open time; this means they dry quickly and require efficient work habits.

Soy-Based Ink

Soy-based inks are designed to mimic traditional, oil-based, printmaking ink, with the advantage of easy cleanup with soap and water. Soy-based inks have long open times, rich colors, deep blacks, and permanence; this makes them a desirable alternative to water-soluble options.

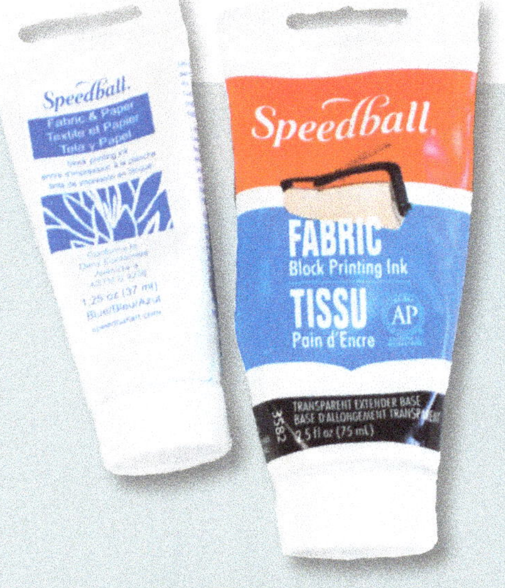

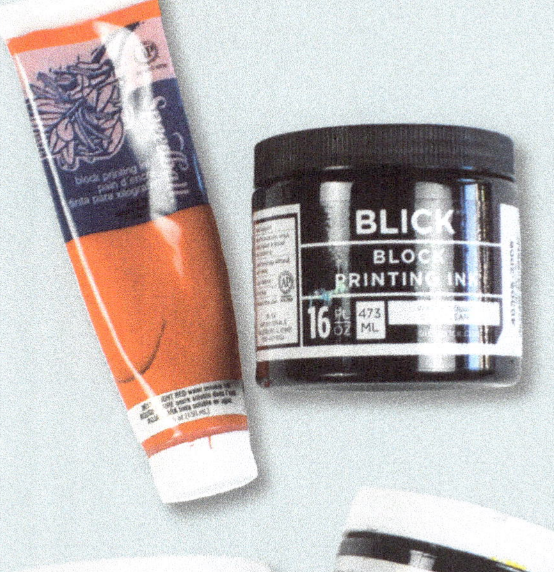

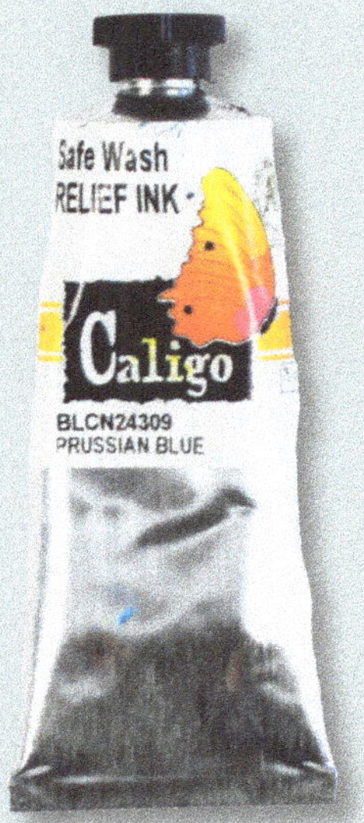

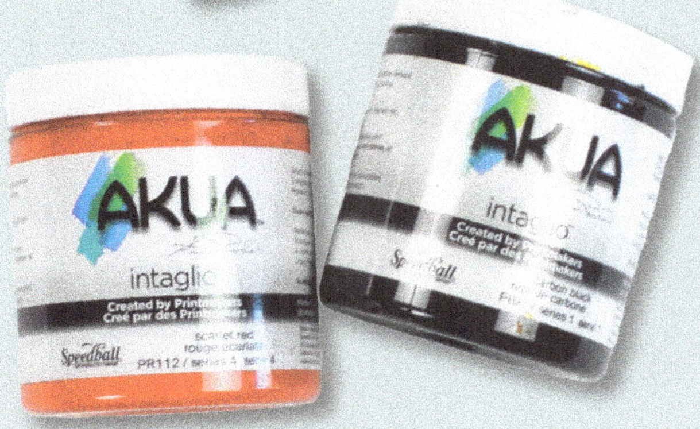

Safe-Wash Inks

Safe-wash inks, made with vegetable oil, are also designed as a nontoxic alternative to traditional oil-based printmaking ink. As with the soy-based inks, the colors are high strength and lightfast.

Fabric Inks and Modifiers

Some printing inks designed for use on fabric can also be applied on paper. Check the manufacturer's instructions for proper use.

—

There are a number of special products available that can be combined with printing ink for specific purposes. Ink modifiers, such as extenders and retarders, are mixed with ink to lengthen the open time—the amount of time it takes the ink to dry. Transparent bases are mixed with printing ink to control the ink's opacity. These products are available wherever printing inks are sold.

MATERIALS

PAPER

There are two families of printmaking paper: Western papers made from cotton and Japanese-style papers made from plant fibers such as mulberry, gampi, and mitsumata. The thicker, Western printmaking papers are best suited for use with a printing press. The focus of this book is hand printing, and I recommend using a Japanese-style washi paper for your prints.

Washi Paper

Japanese papers are thin, but strong, and they have been developed over many hundreds of years as part of the hand-printed, woodcut tradition. Get started using washi paper by purchasing a pack of affordable mulberry paper cut to standard sizes. These come in a range of natural colors. They also come in bright reds, yellows, and black, which are great for chine-collé or for use with white ink. As you increase your printing experience, explore some of the many beautiful, fine-art, Japanese printmaking papers.

Decorative Papers

Decorative printing papers are used for making chine-collé prints. In this technique, the decorative papers are glued to the printing paper. The selections shown are Japanese chiyogami papers. They are acid-free and come in a variety of beautiful patterns and metallic finishes.

NOTE
It's best to avoid using drawing paper, card stock, watercolor paper, or glossy papers when block printing by hand.

Indispensable Papers and Acetate

NEWSPRINT

A large pad or roll of newsprint is indispensable in the printmaking studio. You'll need it for pulling test prints and also for protecting your work surface.

TRANSPARENCY SHEETS

Printing with multiple blocks and colors requires registration to make sure everything prints where it should. Registration is easy when you use transparent acetate sheets. Also known as transparency film, or overhead projector film, transparent acetate comes in packs of loose sheets.

TRACING PAPER

You will need tracing paper for transferring your original drawing to a block. Tracing paper allows you to position your drawing on the block accurately, and allows easy transfer of graphite lines.

ATEGAMI PAPER

This is a thin, slick, water-resistant paper similar to the waxed paper you might have in your kitchen. It's used to protect the printmaking paper during the hand-printing process. When the printing paper is placed on top of an inked block, it can then be covered with a sheet of ategami paper. The ategami will act as a barrier, protecting the paper when you rub it with a baren to transfer the ink. A single piece of ategami paper can be used many times.

GLUES AND PASTES

When making chine-collé prints, use acid-free glues or pastes, applied with a small brush. PVA glue, nori paste, and wheat paste are archival and reversible fixatives, specifically manufactured for use on paper. Use them to avoid the wrinkling, bulging, and hard finish of craft glues.

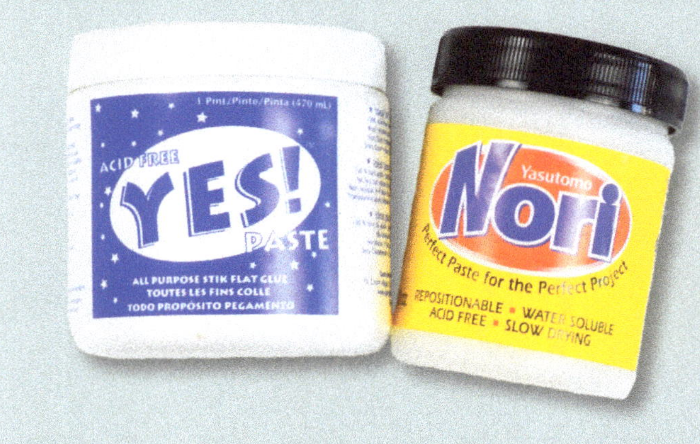

TOOLS

The tools for getting started in printmaking are quite affordable. With a basic set of gouges and brayers, you'll be on your way to pulling your first prints very quickly. As your experience grows, you'll find other tools helpful in achieving the results you desire.

CARVING TOOLS

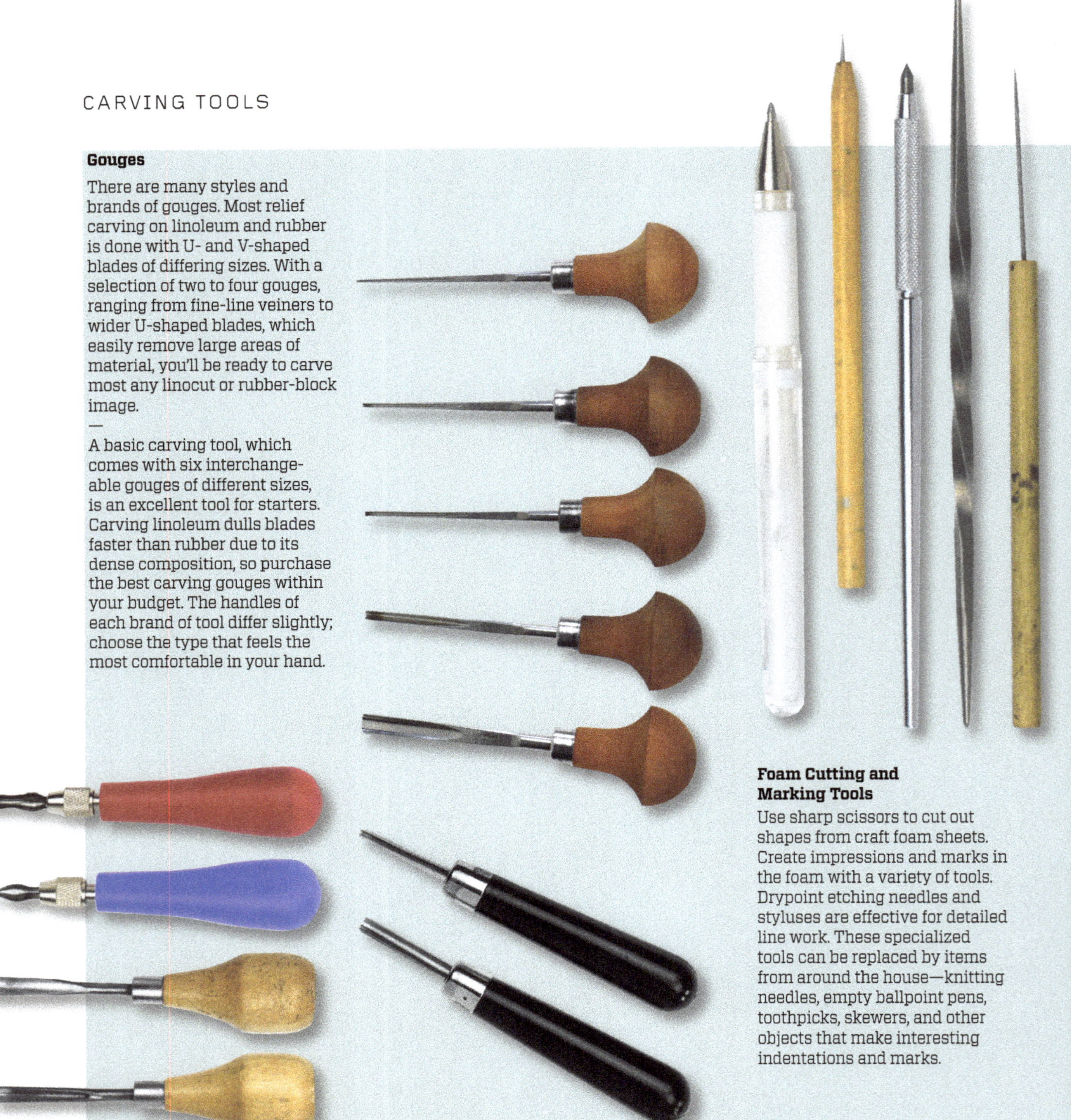

Gouges

There are many styles and brands of gouges. Most relief carving on linoleum and rubber is done with U- and V-shaped blades of differing sizes. With a selection of two to four gouges, ranging from fine-line veiners to wider U-shaped blades, which easily remove large areas of material, you'll be ready to carve most any linocut or rubber-block image.

—

A basic carving tool, which comes with six interchangeable gouges of different sizes, is an excellent tool for starters. Carving linoleum dulls blades faster than rubber due to its dense composition, so purchase the best carving gouges within your budget. The handles of each brand of tool differ slightly; choose the type that feels the most comfortable in your hand.

Foam Cutting and Marking Tools

Use sharp scissors to cut out shapes from craft foam sheets. Create impressions and marks in the foam with a variety of tools. Drypoint etching needles and styluses are effective for detailed line work. These specialized tools can be replaced by items from around the house—knitting needles, empty ballpoint pens, toothpicks, skewers, and other objects that make interesting indentations and marks.

Craft Knife

This useful tool with its interchangeable blades is perfect for carving out large shapes in rubber blocks as well as for cutting unmounted linoleum to custom sizes. The curved #10 blade is useful for slicing rubber blocks smoothly. The standard wedge-shaped #2 blade cuts linoleum very well.

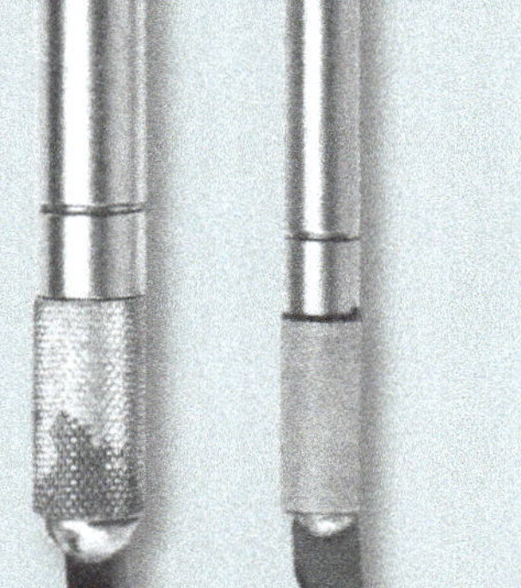

HONING TOOLS

Sharpen your gouges regularly and you'll increase your enjoyment of carving immensely. A combination sharpener, such as the Flexcut SlipStrop, combines a wood surface for deburring blade edges, a polishing compound, and a leather honing surface. It brings blades back to a high polish and a sharp cutting edge.

INKING TOOLS

Brayers

Brayers, used for rolling ink onto blocks, are available in many widths and materials. The soft rubber variety is practical for most relief printmaking applications: The subtle give of the rubber allows the ink to fully cover a block without clogging the finely carved lines of an image.

—

Having brayers of various widths on hand is useful if you do a lot of printing, but even a single 4" (10 cm) wide brayer is workable for most small projects. A larger block is most effectively inked with a brayer that is at least as wide as the block's shortest side.

—

Handle your brayers with care—clean them thoroughly before the ink dries and store them with the roller facing up to avoid dents. Your brayers are among the most important tools for creating a successful print so treat them well.

Inking Platen

A smooth, nonporous surface is essential for inking with a brayer and for mixing ink colors. A sheet of safety glass with a beveled edge is a fine choice. Other options include plexiglass, mirror, disposable palette pads, or glass from a picture frame. If you use the glass from a picture frame, be sure to cover the edges with masking tape and handle it with extreme care.

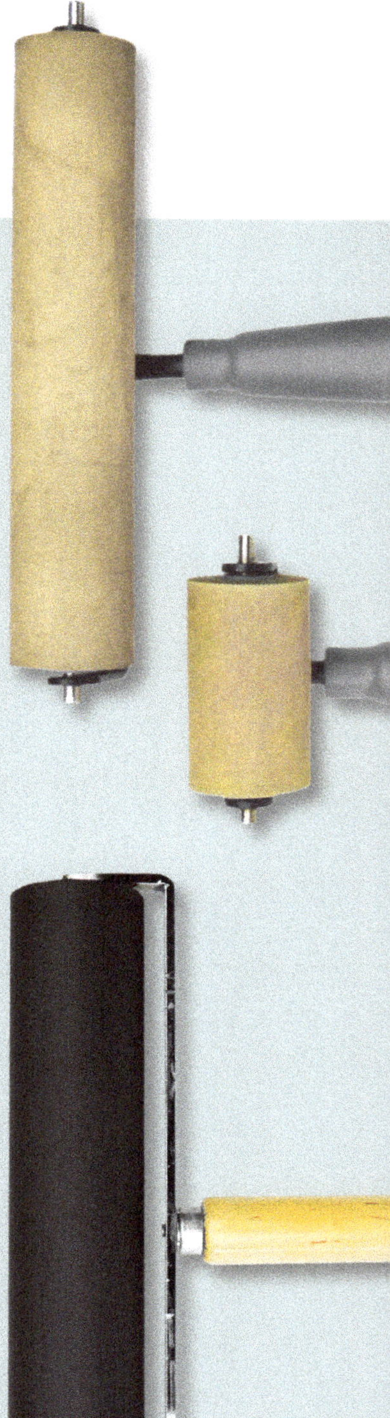

TOOLS

BURNISHING TOOLS

Barens

After your printing paper has been set down on an inked block, burnishing your paper evenly will ensure perfect printing results. The Japanese-style baren is specifically designed for hand printing. This traditional style of baren features a smooth bamboo leaf over a coil of woven rope fitted inside a wood housing.

—

Modern barens are available in plastic with a smooth surface, plastic with a pattern of raised bumps, and a metal version fitted with small ball bearings.

For small printing areas, such as spot colors, your own fingertips make very effective barens—this is especially true when you're working with rubber blocks.

Bone Folder

Use this smooth, dull-edged hand tool to transfer a pencil sketch onto a block by rubbing the back of the drawing. It can also be used as a burnishing tool when printing with linoleum blocks with finely carved lines.

Spoons

The round underside of a wooden spoon, a metal spoon, or a sushi paddle, makes an excellent burnisher. There are no spoons designed specifically for printmaking, so try different types to see what works for you. As an alternative, flat, wooden drawer pulls can be used the same way.

OTHER TOOLS

Bristle Brush

Use a bristle brush to remove the carving leftovers hiding in the fine-carved lines of your block. These unwanted pieces may be picked up by your brayer during inking and show up in the finished print. Bristle brushes are also useful for applying india ink to the surface of linoleum blocks before carving.

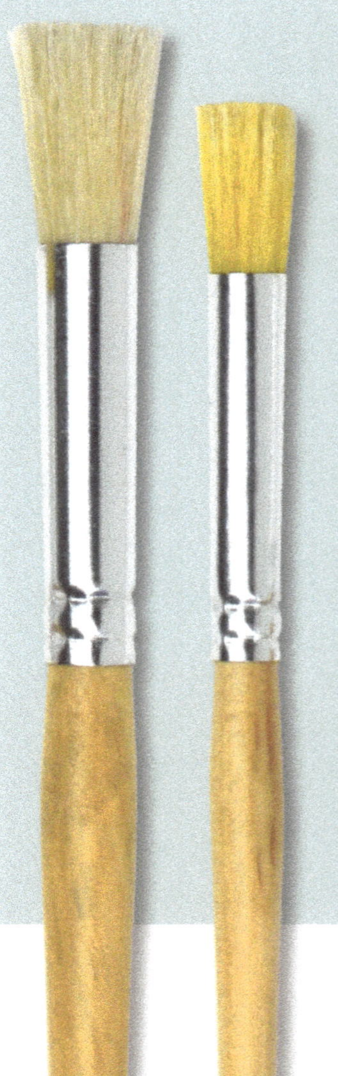

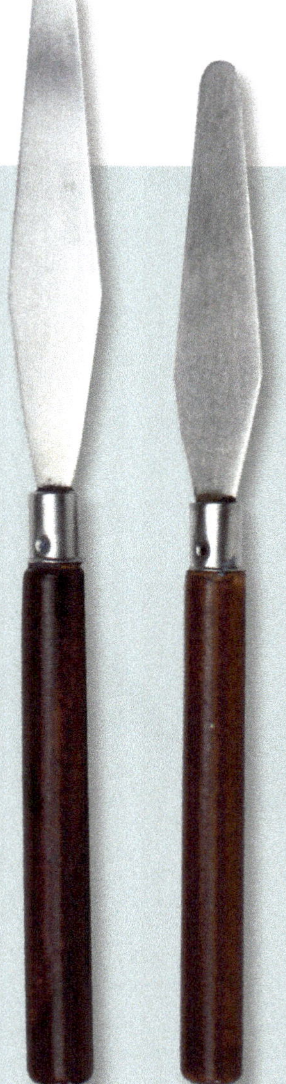

Metal Rulers

Steel or aluminum rulers provide a solid edge and guideline when you're cutting unmounted linoleum with a craft knife. They are also effective in allowing you to tear a beautiful edge on a piece of printing paper.

Acrylic Rulers

Transparent acrylic rulers are excellent guides when you are carving straight lines into rubber blocks and foam because they allow you to see where you're going. They are also indispensable when you're lining up your printing paper on a cutting mat, jig, or template.

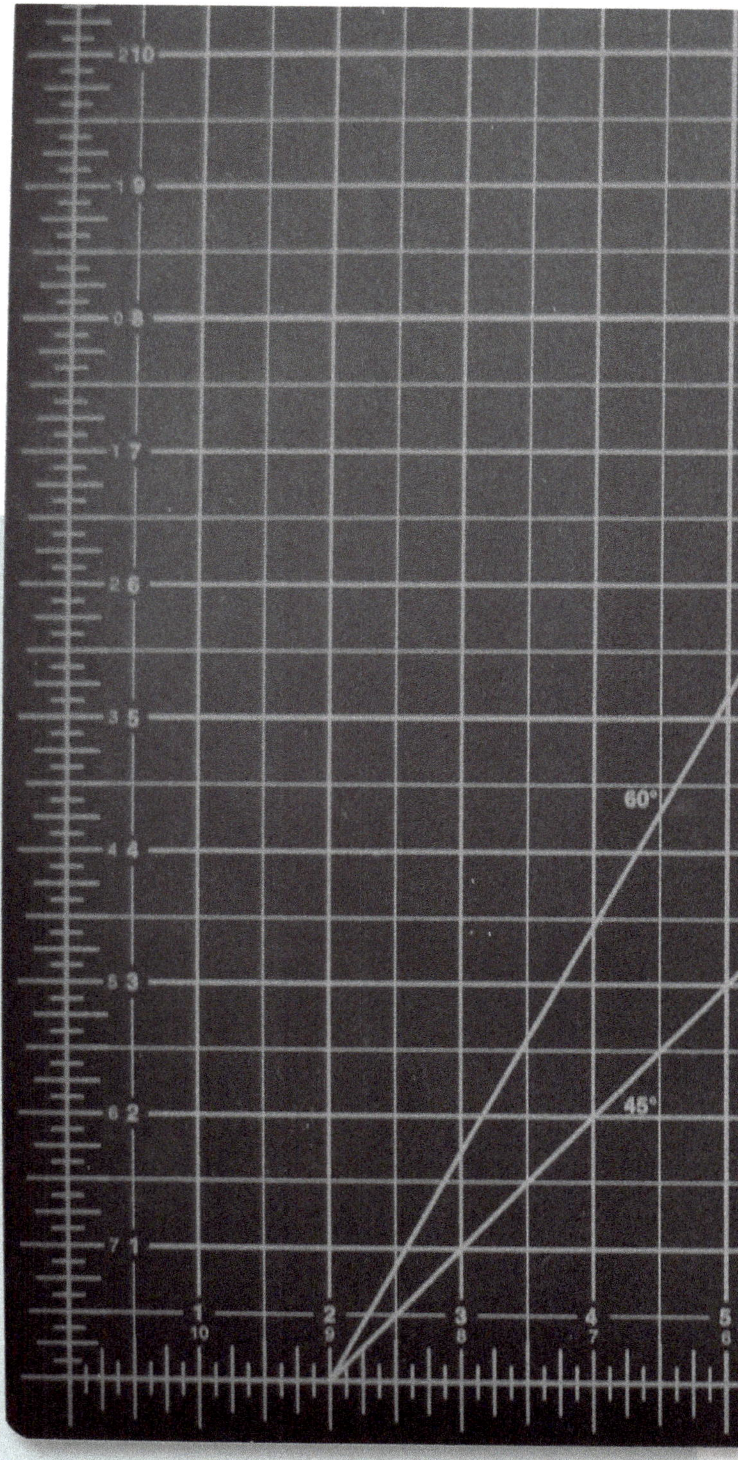

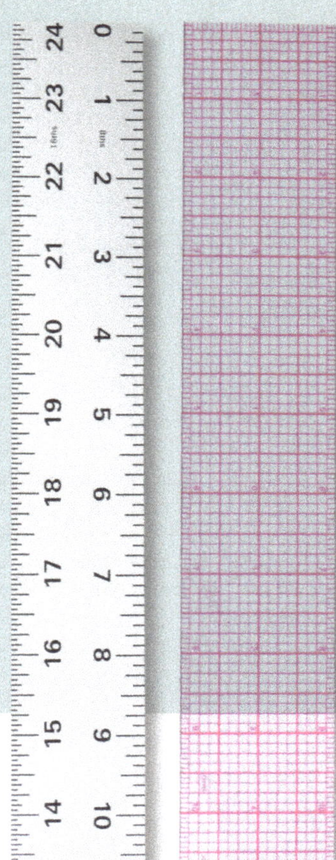

Palette Knife

Whether flexible or rigid, metal or plastic, a palette knife is useful for mixing inks and for depositing a small amount of ink on the inking platen when you're ready to roll.

Cutting Mat

Use a cutting mat to protect your work surface when you cut with a craft knife or gouge. A cutting mat with a grid is extremely useful for lining up small prints or test prints during the printing process.

Soft Lead Pencils

Transfer your image to a carving block with a soft lead pencil. 2B, 4B, and 6B pencils provide ample graphite to transfer an image easily.

RULES

The rules detailed in this section are the basic techniques used in all types of block printing. You might want to keep a bookmark here, because you'll be referring back to the basics as you work your way through the projects in this book.

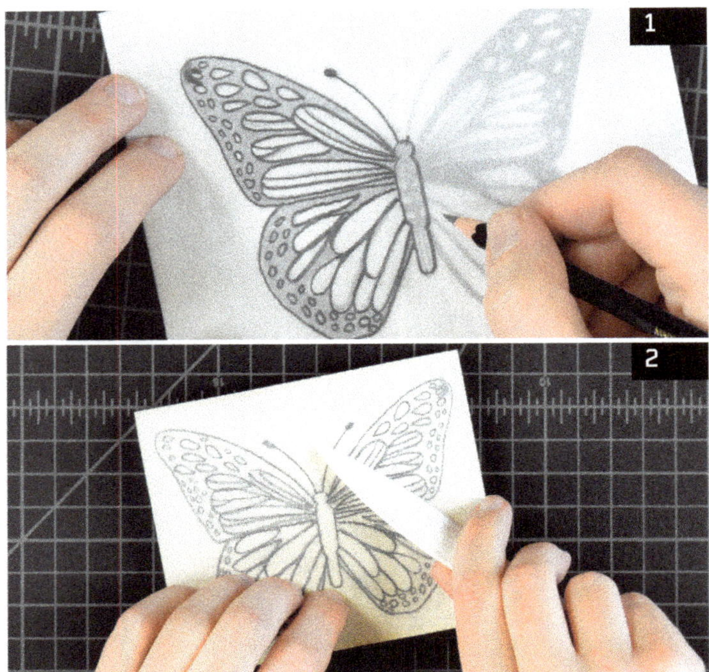

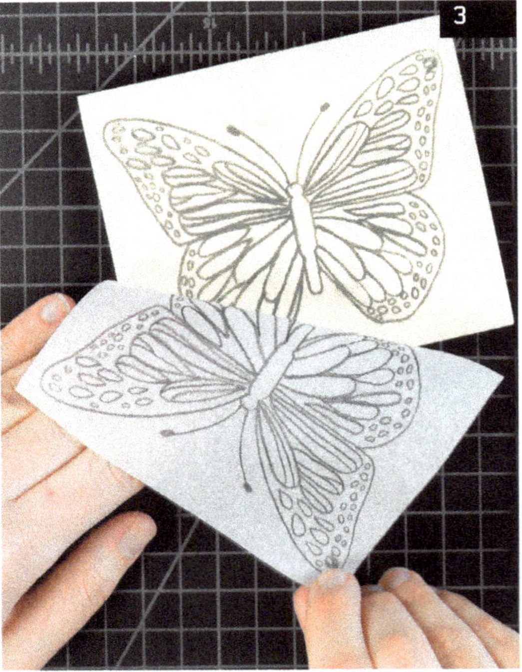

Transferring a Drawing

Once you've drawn an image for your print, you're ready to transfer the design to the surface of a carving block. There are a number of ways to do it. Both of the methods described are effective. The tracing-paper method is easy and is perfect for small images and rubber carving blocks. For larger images and fine details, or if you are using battleship linoleum blocks, the carbon-paper transfer method is preferable.

Remember that the image on the block will print in reverse. If there is any text or if the pictorial orientation is important—for a map, for instance, or for someone playing a sport or a musical instrument—be sure to plan your drawing accordingly. If you prefer to be more spontaneous, draw directly onto the surface of the block with a pencil or a permanent marker, but keep in mind that erasing and adjusting an image directly on the block can be difficult.

Tracing-Paper Method

TOOLS AND MATERIALS

tracing paper
soft lead pencil
tape
dense rubber block
scissors
bone folder
permanent marker (optional)

1 / Draw your image on a sheet of tracing paper using a soft lead pencil. The amount of detail you choose to include is up to you. You can simply outline the drawing and use it as a rough guide or shade in areas to guide the carving process.

2 / Cut the tracing paper to the size of the block. With the pencil drawing facing downward, tape the image onto the block. (The tape is optional for smaller pieces.) Using a bone folder, burnish the back of the tracing paper, working from the center of the image to the outer edges.

3 / Lift a corner of the tracing paper to check the transfer progress. Go back over any areas that appear too faint. Remove the tape and the tracing paper. If you wish, trace over the pencil lines with a permanent marker. Use a variety of marker tip sizes to re-create the detail of the original image. The block is ready for carving.

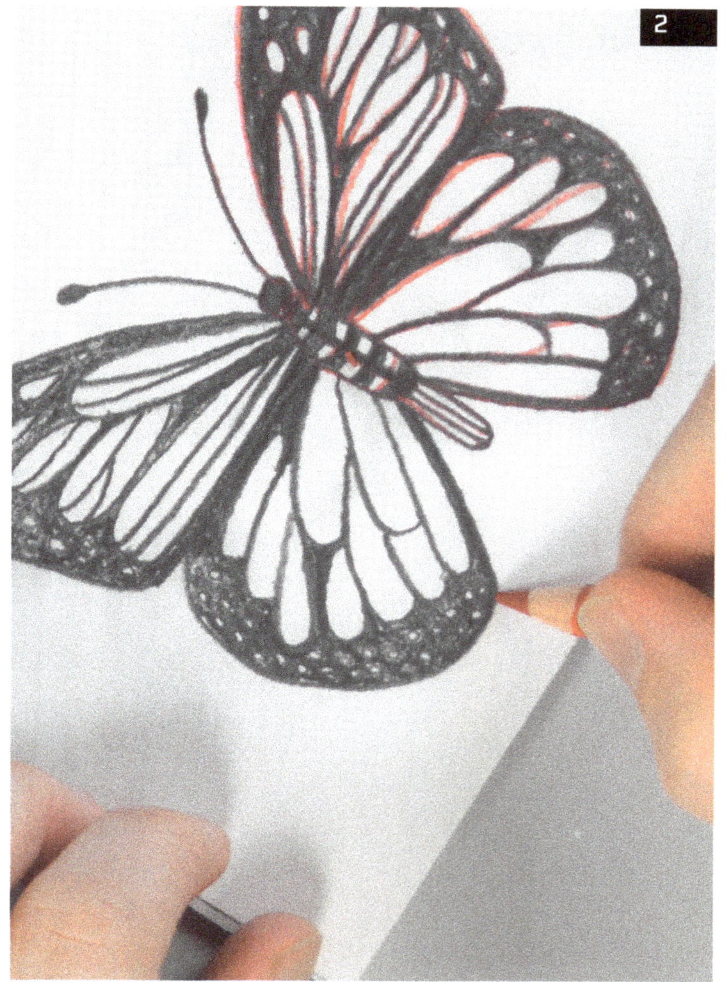

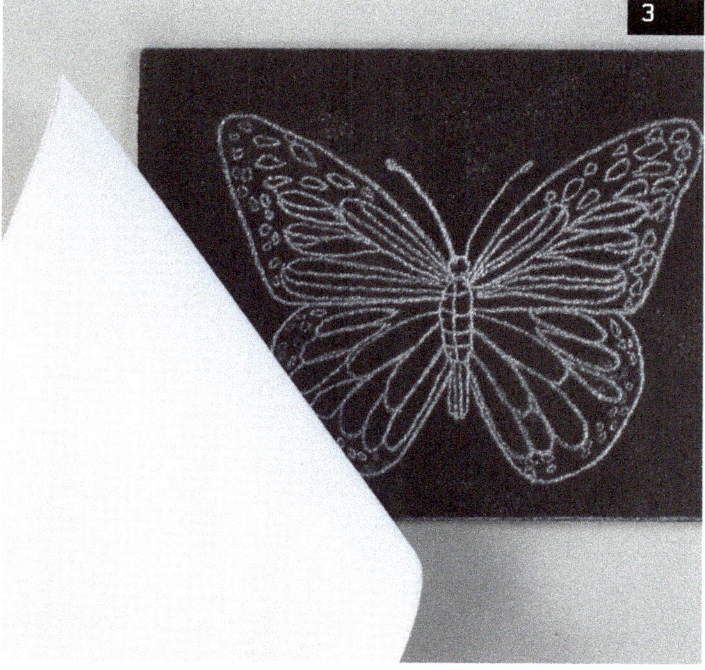

Carbon Transfer-Paper Method

TOOLS AND MATERIALS

battleship linoleum
india ink
brush
carbon transfer paper
tape
colored pencil

This method uses a sheet of carbon transfer paper sandwiched between the block and the drawing. Carbon transfer paper comes in a variety of colors, including white. When you're working on a battleship linoleum block, it's helpful to paint the surface of the block with india ink before transferring the image. Using white carbon paper will give you a high-contrast transfer. Then, when you carve away the inked surface of the block, the pale area underneath will provide a close approximation of what the finished print will look like.

1 / Coat the surface of the linoleum block with india ink. Allow it to dry.

2 / Cut the carbon paper and your drawing to the size of the block. Place the carbon paper, ink-side down, on the block. Place the drawing, pencil-side up, on top. Tape both layers to the block. Carefully trace over the image with a pencil. Using a colored pencil will allow you to see which areas have been completed and which ones remain.

3 / Check the transfer by lifting a corner of the carbon paper. When complete, remove the sheets from the block. Begin carving.

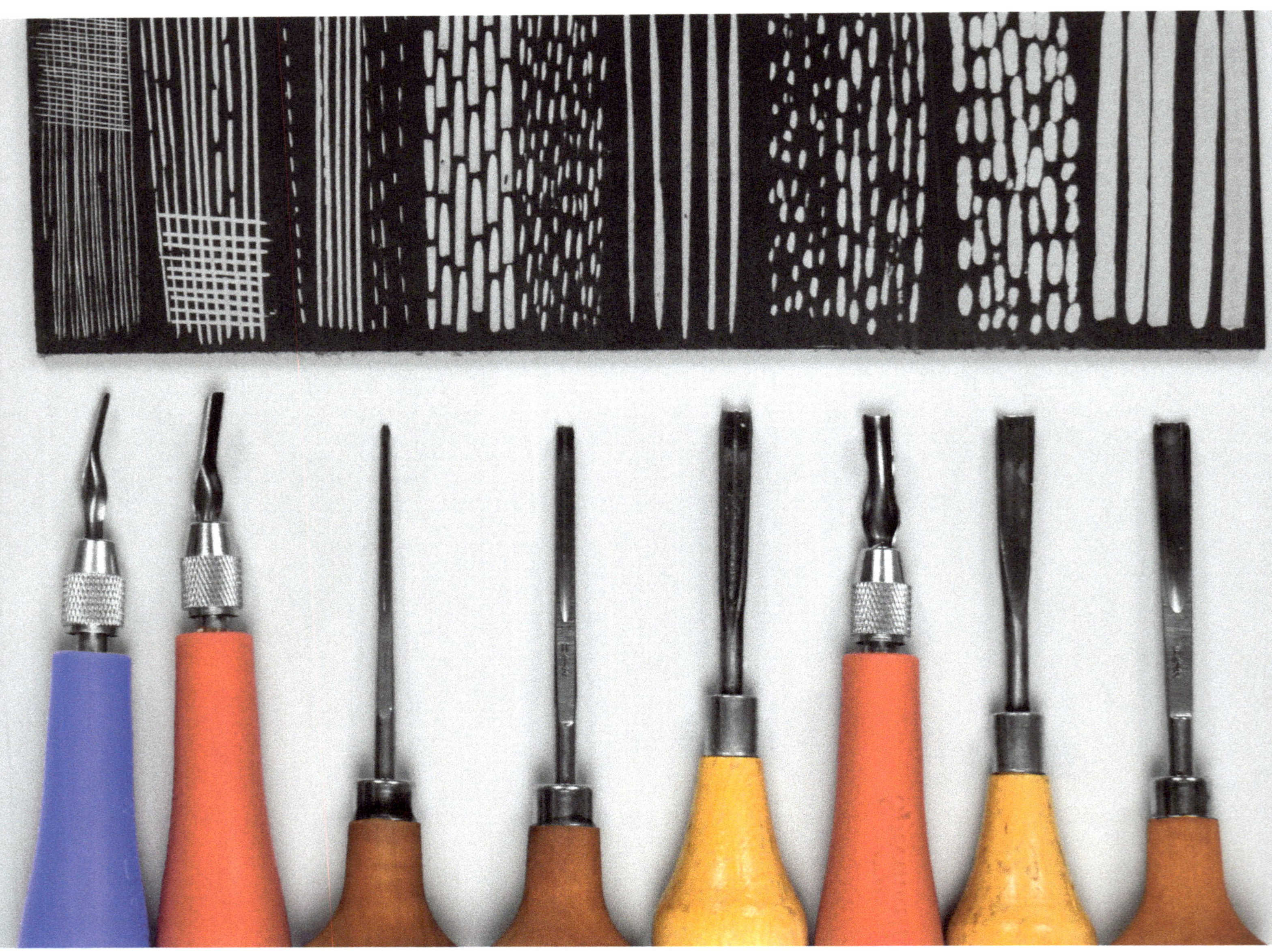

Carving

Think of carving gouges as your paintbrushes—your main tools for expression in block printing. Experiment with a variety of gouge sizes and shapes for different effects. Building up a library of your personal carving marks will help you add interest to your finished print. Consider cross-hatching, the use of positive space and negative space, experimenting with uneven or jagged lines for texture, and other interesting contrasts as possibilities in planning your image.

Carving gouges have two parts that need consideration—the blade and the handle. The gouge blades used most often in this book are U shaped or V shaped. (There are also other shapes of blades that are used more often for woodcuts.)

The handle shape varies by brand, and will be a personal choice based on its feel in your hand. Regardless of the type you choose, aim to hold the tool in a firm but relaxed way, allowing the muscles in your arm do the work of carving, not your fingers or palm.

CARVING TIPS

Always carve away from yourself.

—

Hold the block along the side. Avoid putting your hand in the path of the carving tool in case of slips.

—

Let the gouges do the carving; they should be very sharp.

—

If carving is at all difficult, hone the blade to sharpen the edge. Follow the instructions that come with your carving tools for the proper method of honing.

—

When carving, the blade does not need to go deeply into the block material. Only a very shallow top layer of the block is removed with the gouge.

—

For circles and curved lines, turn the block while the blade slowly cuts the material.

—

Go slowly. Take your time.

—

Practice carving corners, circles, and straight lines to develop your personal technique for handling the tools.

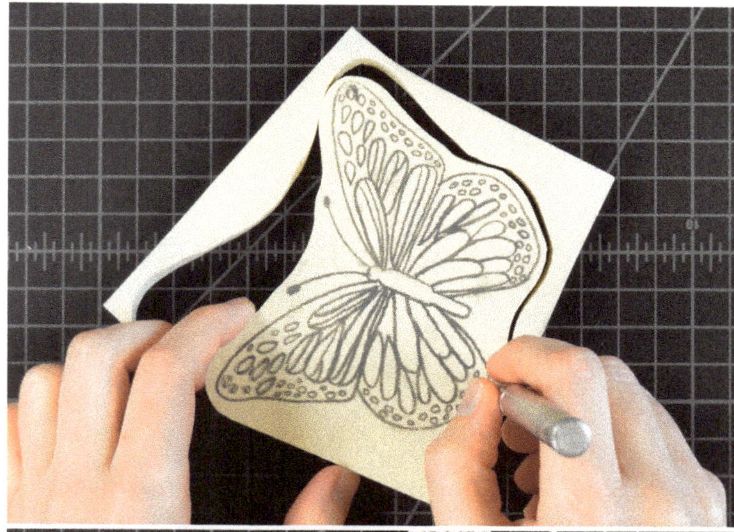

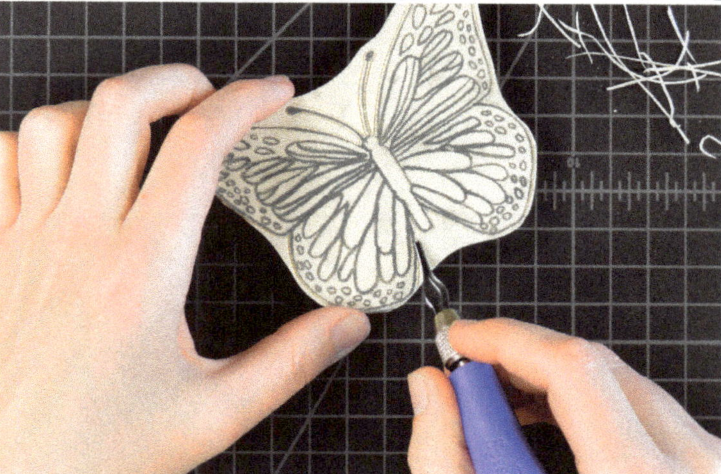

If you're using a dense rubber block, carve away the excess material outside of the image.

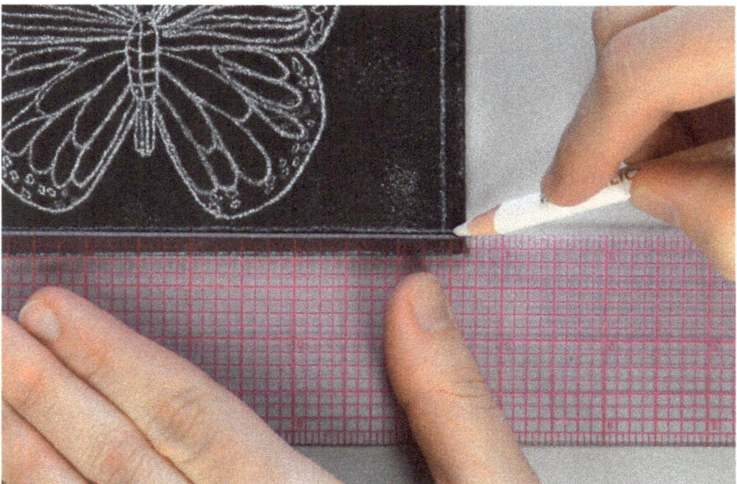

If you are using a linoleum block, consider adding a border to the image.

RULES

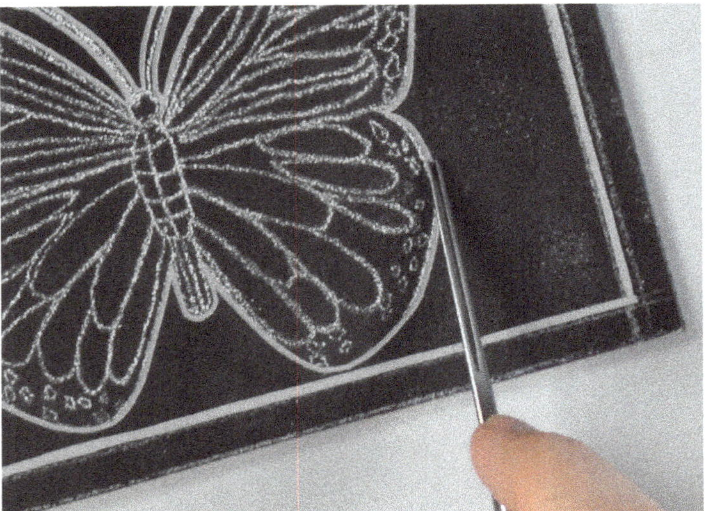

Start by carving the block space outside of the pencil image. Use a small veiner gouge to carve.

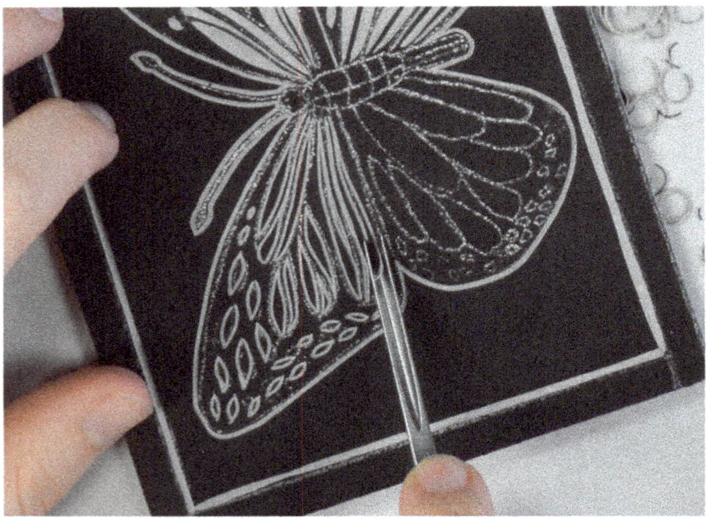

A U-shaped gouge allows you to quickly remove material from larger areas. If you have carving tools with interchangeable blades, it's useful to invest in a couple of handles so that the blades you use most often can be left in place.

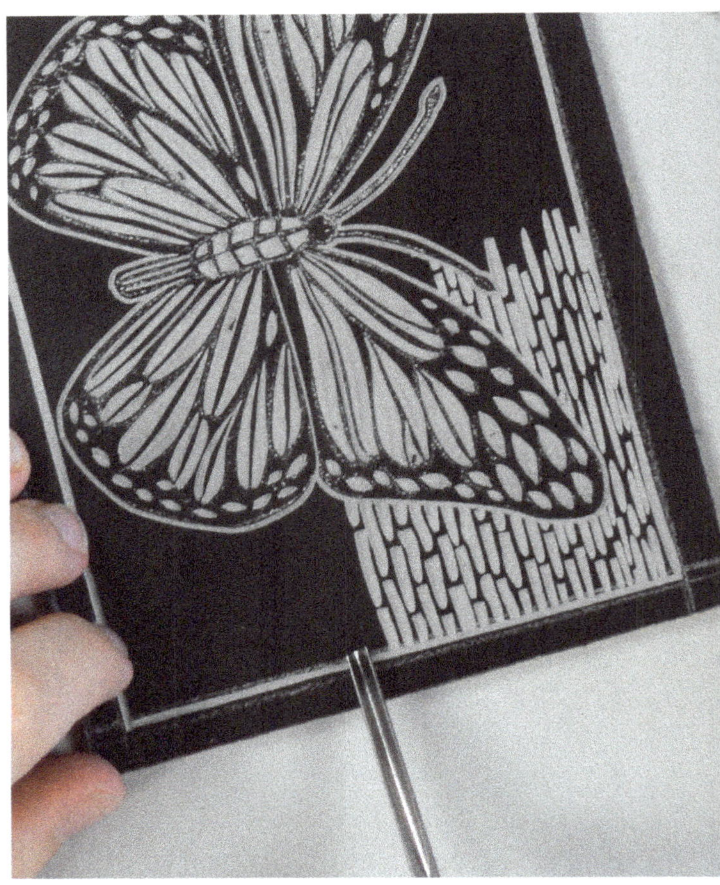

For linocuts with a border, consider carving a texture or pattern in the background of the scene for visual interest. For detailed prints, plan a combination of negative and positive spaces and make use of the growing library of expressive marks in your repertoire.

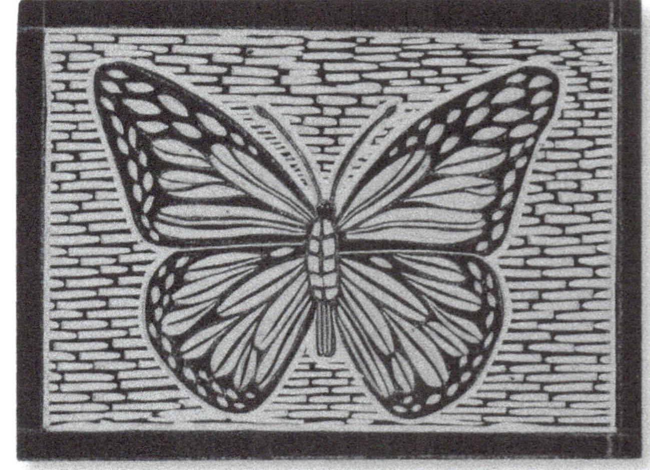

A FINISHED BLOCK

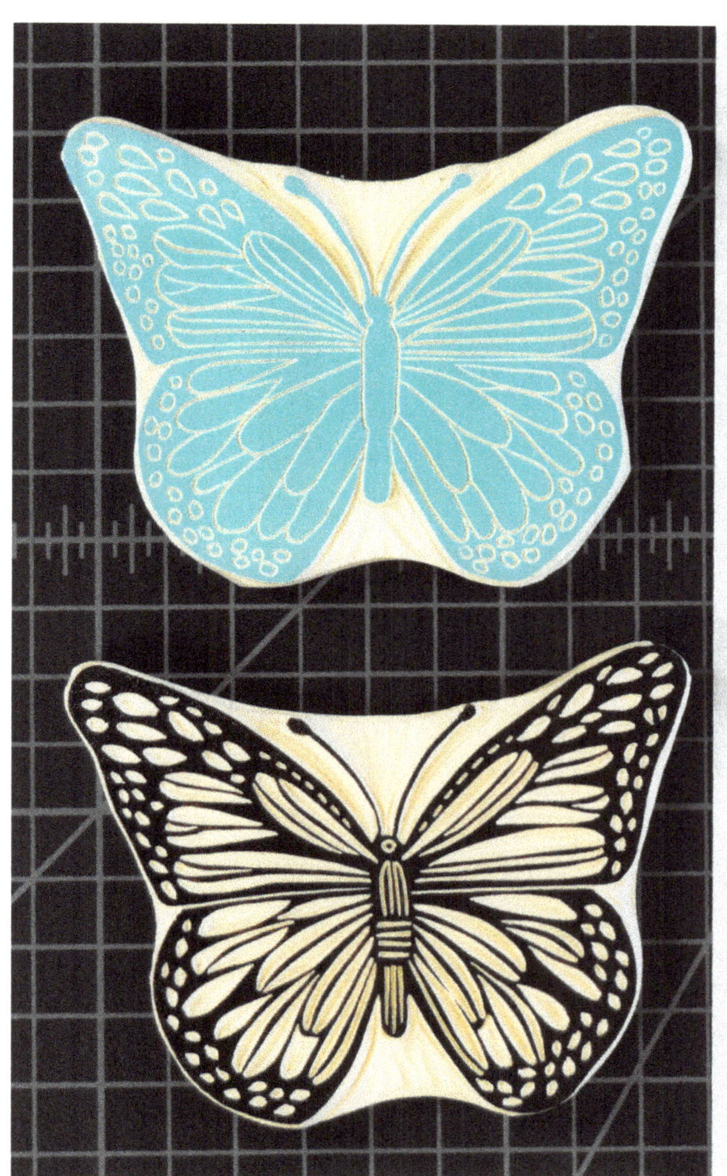

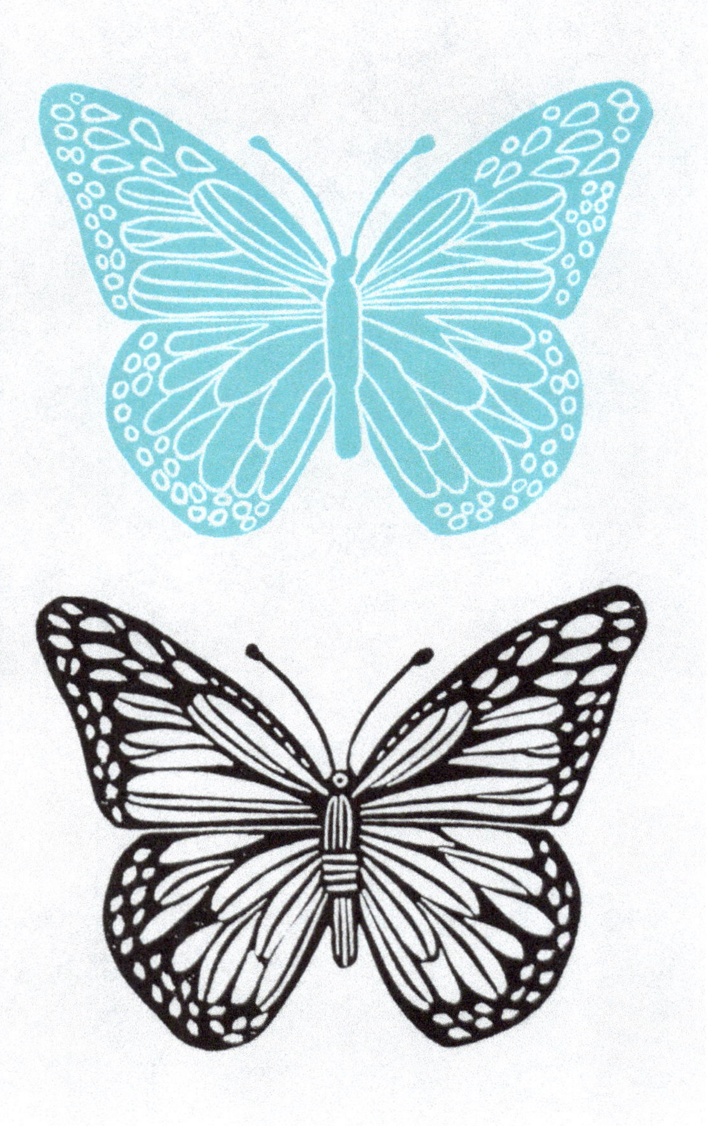

Positive and Negative Contrasts

Positive and negative contrasts are important when planning a print design. The hallmark of all relief prints—from the simplest single-color stamp to a complex multicolor block—is the interplay of the spaces removed and those that remain. Remember that the parts of the block that you carve away will be the color of the paper in your finished print.

POSITIVE AND NEGATIVE

To create a negative image [top], carve away the pencil lines of the transferred drawing. These carved lines will be the color of the paper when printed.

For a positive image [bottom], carve away all of the material *except* the pencil lines. I transferred the same image to both of these dense rubber blocks and carved them differently to achieve contrasting results.

NOTE

Water-soluble, block-printing inks are highly recommended for beginning printmakers due to their availability, easy cleanup, and affordability.

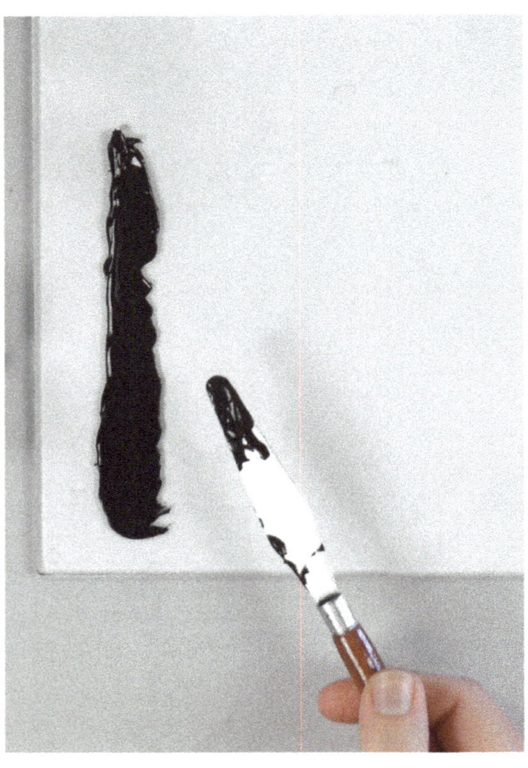

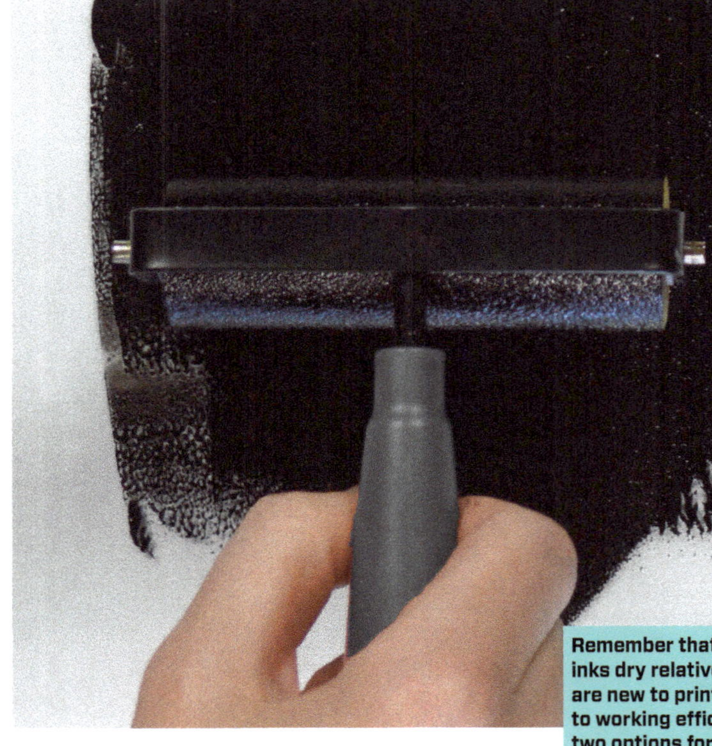

Inking

When you're ready to print, gather all your materials. The inks, inking platen, palette knife, and brayer should be close at hand. Have the printing paper precut to size. Different inks have different open times (the time it takes them to dry). Be aware of the working speed necessary for the type of ink you are using.

Squeeze a 2" (5 cm) diameter blob of ink from a tube, or use the palette knife to scoop it from a tub. Spread the ink in one corner of the inking platen.

Choose a brayer that is slightly wider than one side of your block. Pick up a small amount of ink on the brayer or use a palette knife to spread a bead of ink into the middle of the platen. Start with short, repetitive motions, rolling the brayer back and forth in the ink until it is coated.

Once the brayer is coated, smoothly and with minimal pressure, begin rolling it over a larger area of the platen. Use forward, diagonal, and side-to-side rolling motions, to form an even, opaque rectangle or square of ink. The sound of rolling will have a subtle hiss from the sticky ink. The feeling should be slightly tacky and the ink will have a tactile, orange peel–like appearance. Practice and experience will tell you what is too little or too much ink.

Remember that water-soluble inks dry relatively quickly. If you are new to printing and not used to working efficiently, there are two options for working around the ink's quick-drying time.

The first is to plan to print a short run of between two and five prints at a time, rinsing and drying the platen, brayer, and block between sessions.

Another alternative is to use an ink retarder. Retarders, mixed with water-based printing inks, lengthen the open time on the platen. If you are working with a soy-based or vegetable oil-based ink, the open times are much longer and of less concern.

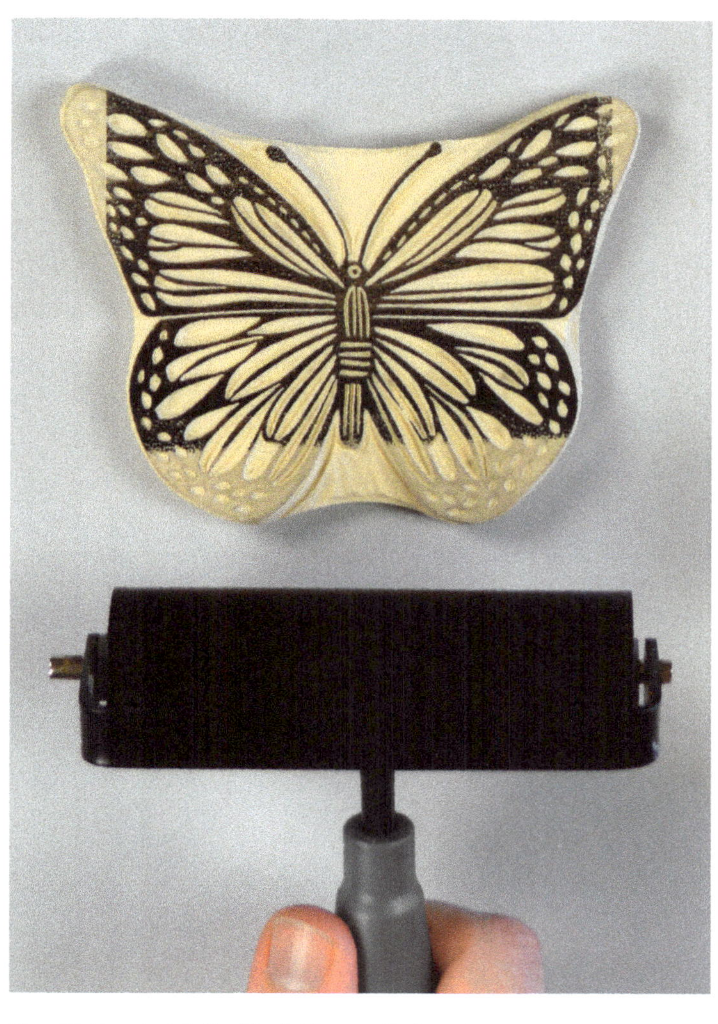

Now it's time to ink the block. Be sure that you've removed any dust or carving scraps from the block; these can be picked up by the brayer and leave unintended spots in the print. Roll the ink onto the block in smooth, even coats. Be sure to cover all areas and roll the brayer in a variety of directions. Reapply ink from the platen to the brayer, as needed. A shiny appearance to the inked block indicates you're ready to test print.

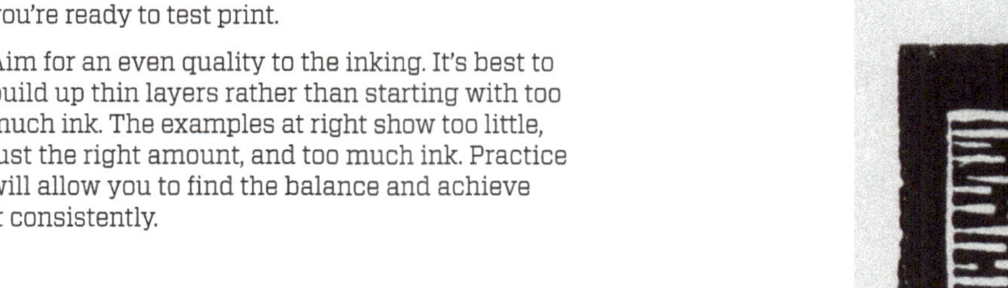

Aim for an even quality to the inking. It's best to build up thin layers rather than starting with too much ink. The examples at right show too little, just the right amount, and too much ink. Practice will allow you to find the balance and achieve it consistently.

NOTE

If your brayer is narrower than the block, you can still achieve even inking. Practice concealing the roller marks left by the edges of the brayer with carefully applied thin coats.

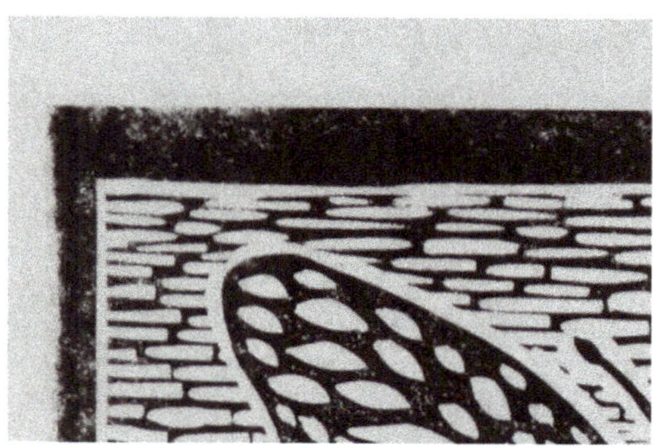

Printed block with too little ink. Notice the spotty, salt-and-pepper look.

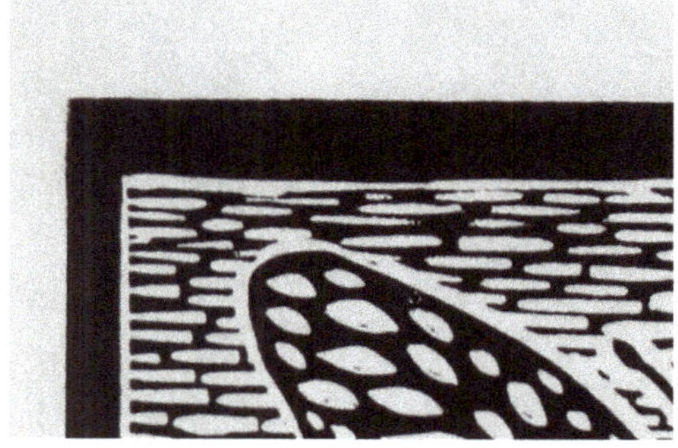

Just enough ink in this print. There is even coverage without spottiness or lines being filled in.

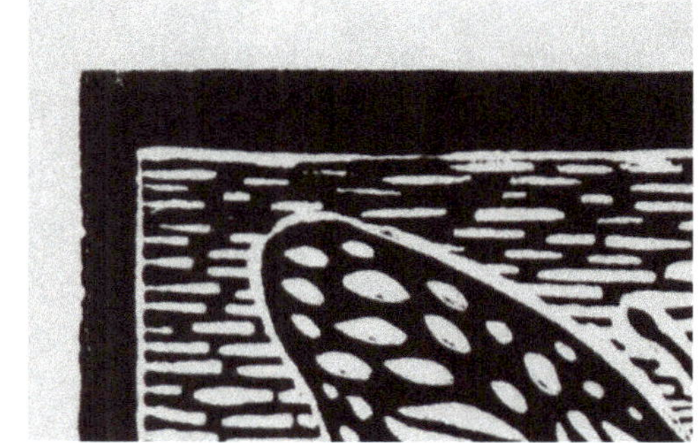

With overinking, the finely recessed lines in the block will be filled with ink. Rinse the ink from the block, let it dry, and start the inking process over again.

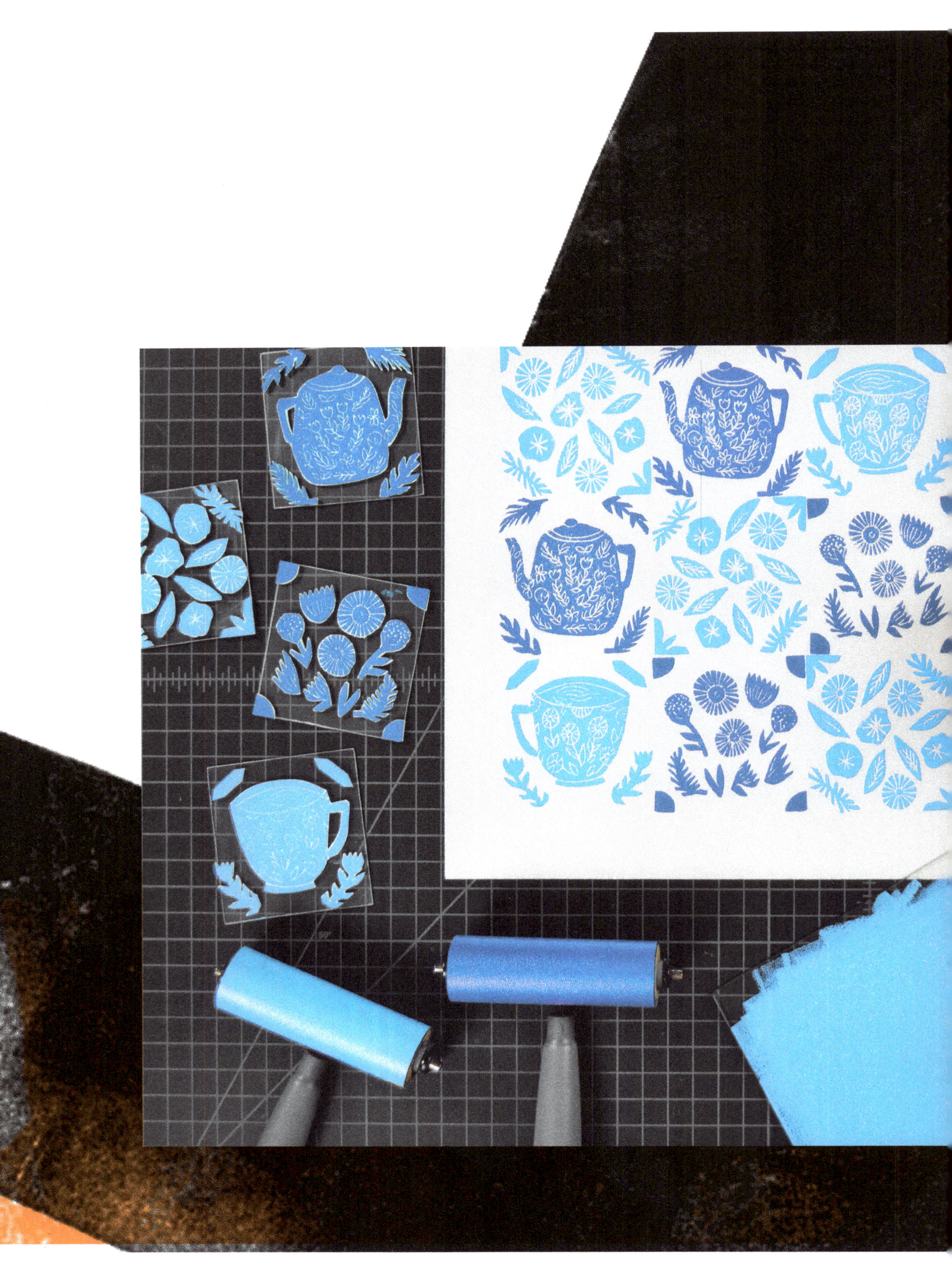

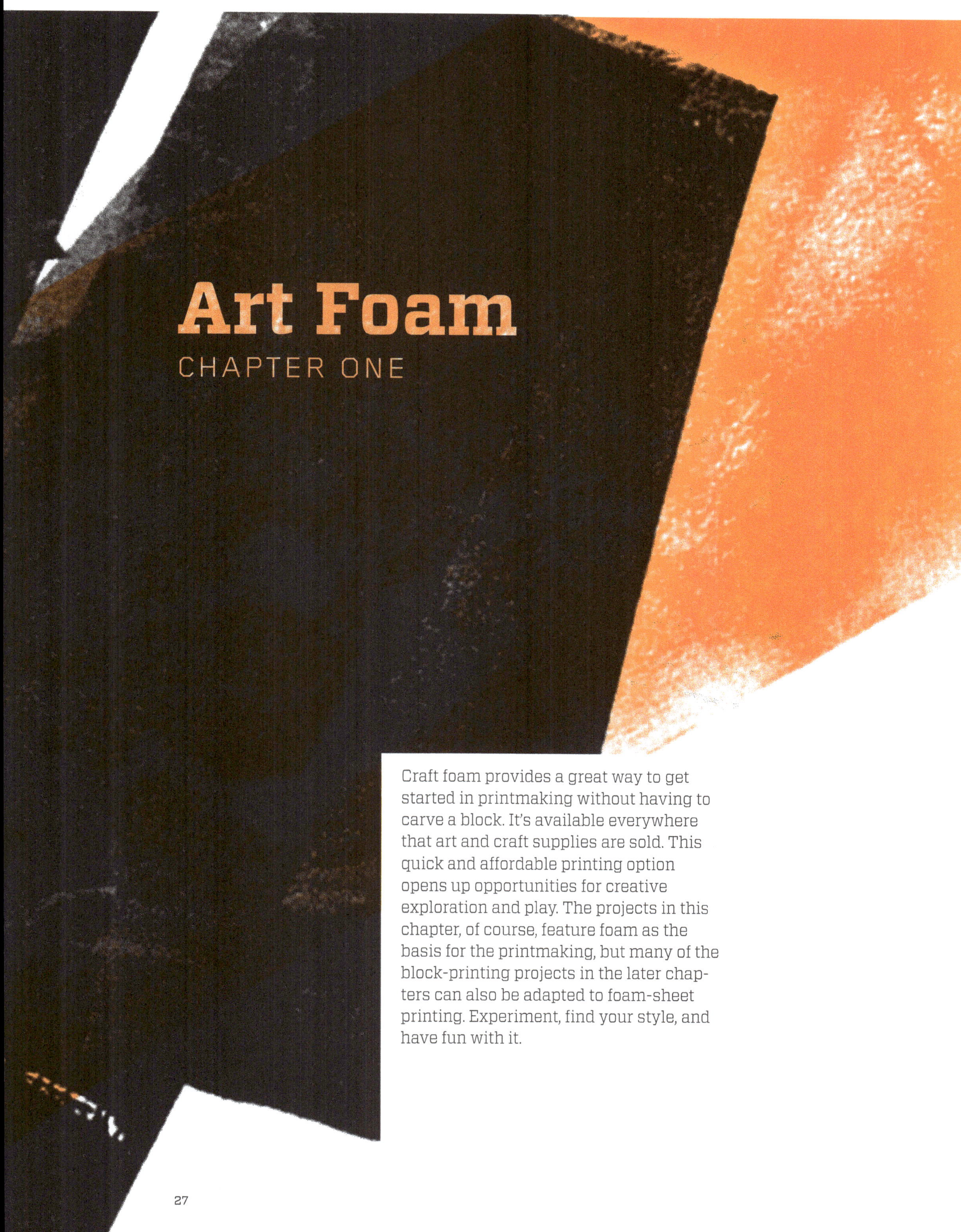

Art Foam

CHAPTER ONE

Craft foam provides a great way to get started in printmaking without having to carve a block. It's available everywhere that art and craft supplies are sold. This quick and affordable printing option opens up opportunities for creative exploration and play. The projects in this chapter, of course, feature foam as the basis for the printmaking, but many of the block-printing projects in the later chapters can also be adapted to foam-sheet printing. Experiment, find your style, and have fun with it.

The art of imitating the arrangement and repeat patterns of ceramic tiles is a familiar theme in the block-printing tradition. The prints in this group were inspired by Delft pottery. The bright blues, intricate patterns, and classic look of Delftware translates well into a foam-tile technique. Experimenting with tile blocks allows you to explore composition. As you will discover, there are a surprising number of ways that you can arrange and rotate the blocks to create the final design of your print. For this piece, I balanced two strong motifs—teapot and teacup—with decorative florals and alternating blue colors to give the print variety.

FOAM TILES: DELFTWARE

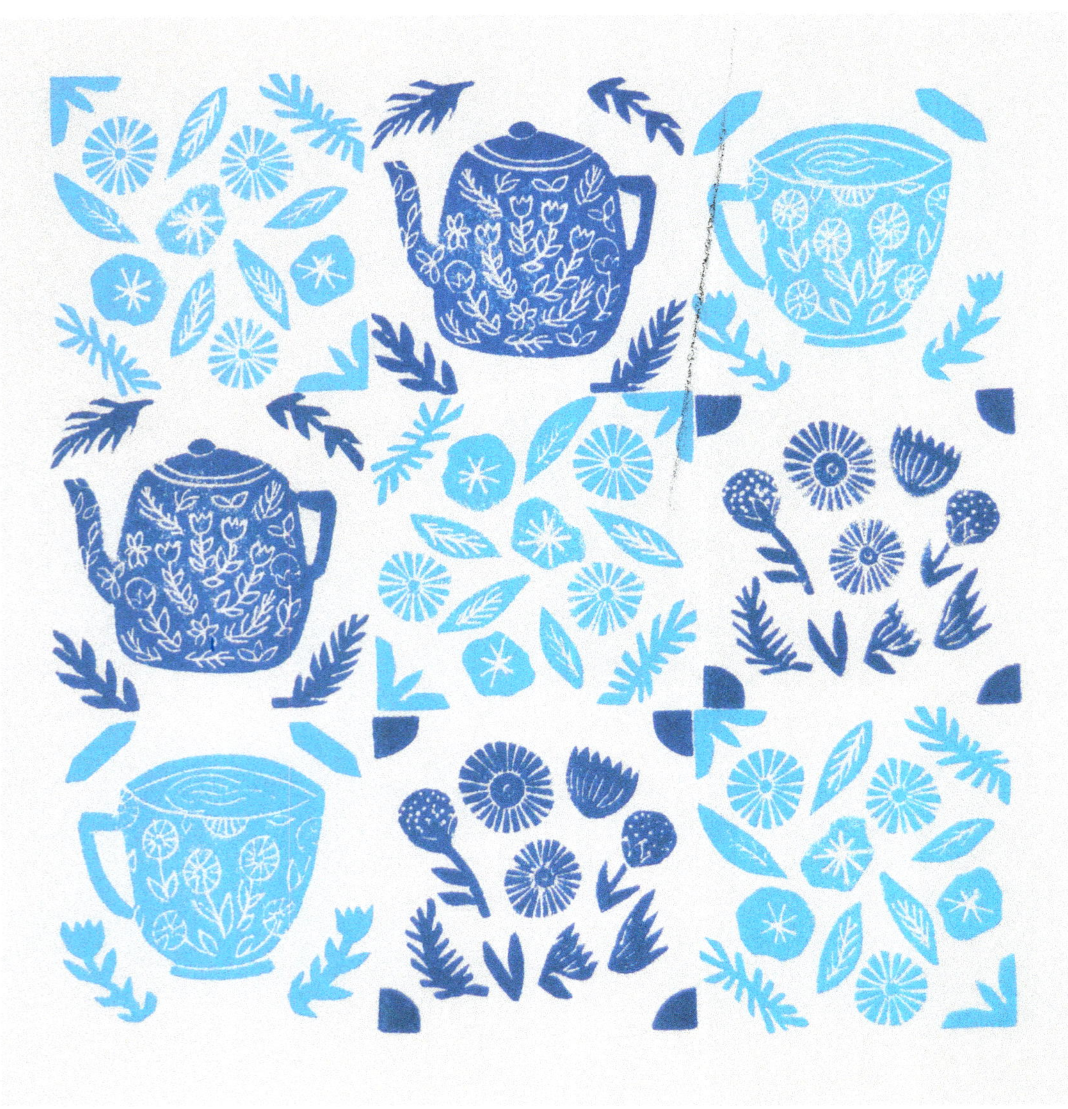

TOOLS AND MATERIALS

- soft lead pencil
- graph paper or drawing paper
- transparent acrylic ruler
- adhesive-backed foam sheets
- scissors
- craft knife
- cutting mat with grid (optional)
- pointed mark-making tool
- acrylic mounting sheets (one for each tile design, cut to size)
- water-soluble block-printing inks
- inking platen
- brayers
- newsprint or scrap paper
- printing paper

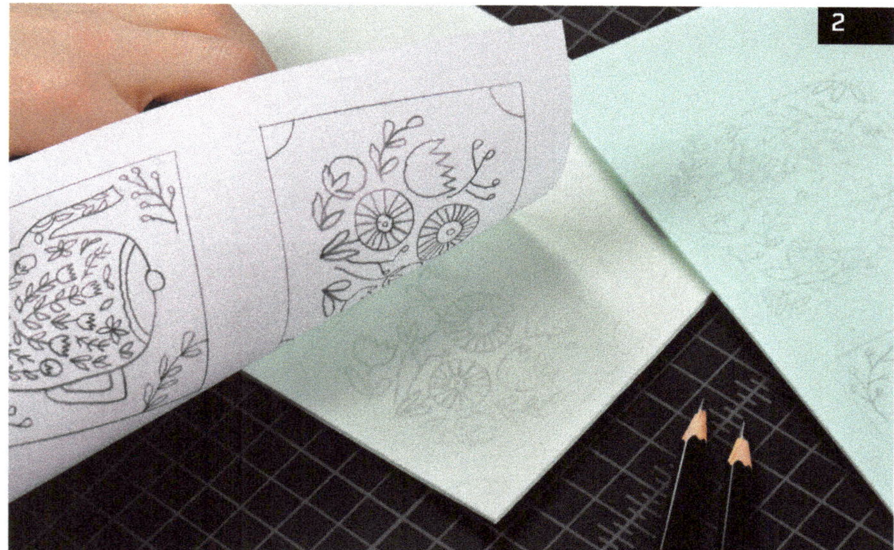

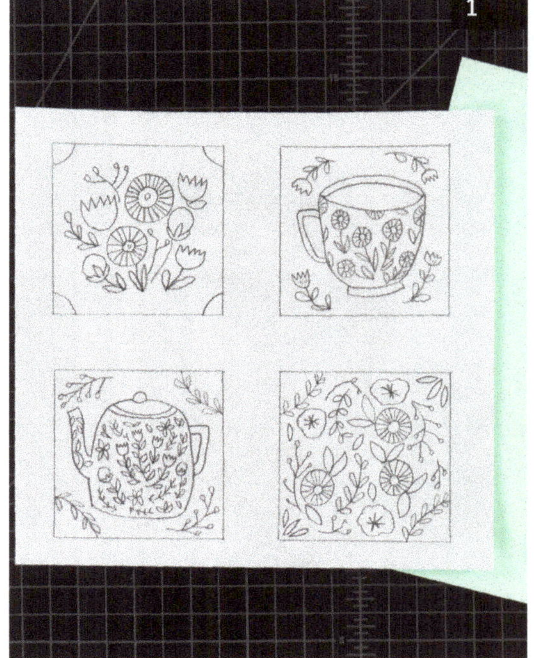

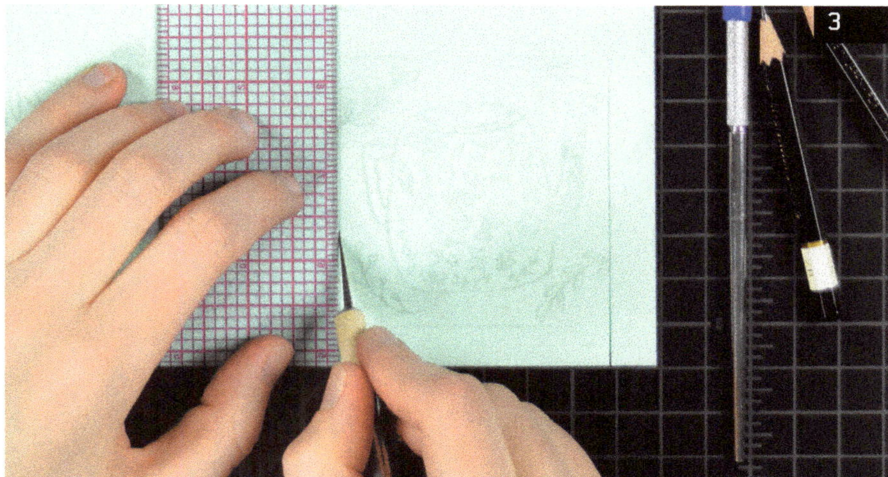

1 / Decide on the size of your tiles and the number of designs you'd like to include. My designs are each 3" (7.5 cm) square. Use the pencil and ruler to draw the squares on paper, then draw your designs on each of the tiles. Keep in mind that thicker lines and flat areas of color work best for foam sheets and that darkly penciled lines will transfer best.

2 / Transfer each drawing, one at a time, by turning it pencil-side down onto the foam sheet. Rub the back of the sheet of paper with your fingers. Avoid making scratches or dents in the foam; they will appear in your final print. Without shifting the paper, lift a corner to check the transfer process. Continue if necessary.

3 / Cut your tiles from the foam sheet with scissors or by using a clear ruler and craft knife. Protect your work surface with a cutting mat if you use a craft knife.

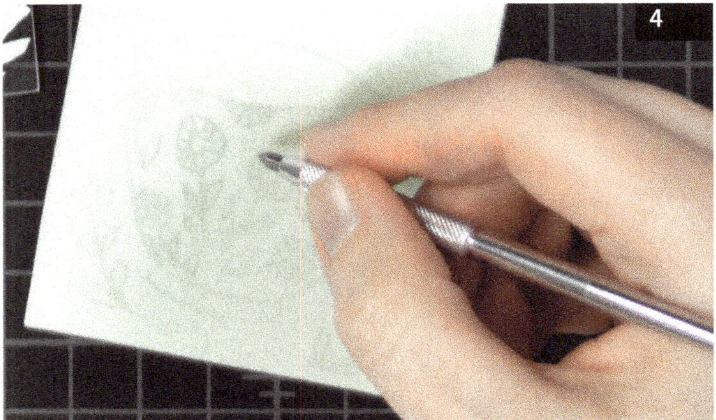

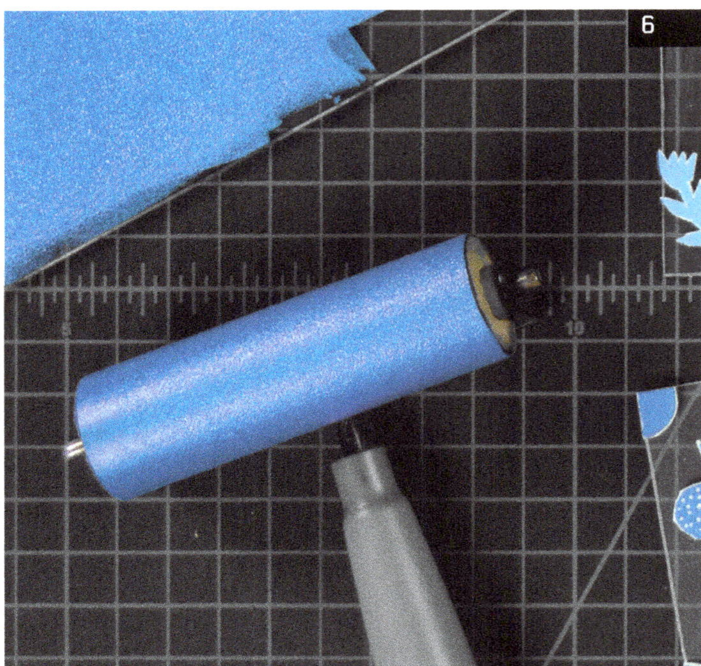

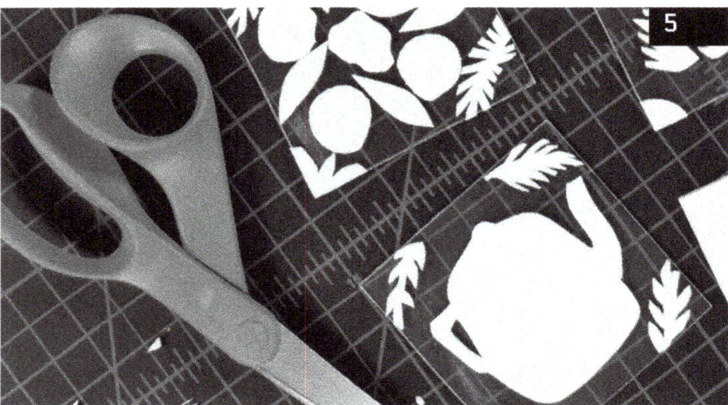

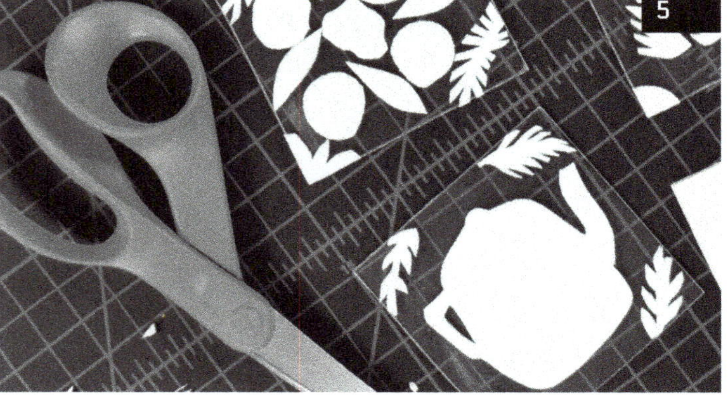

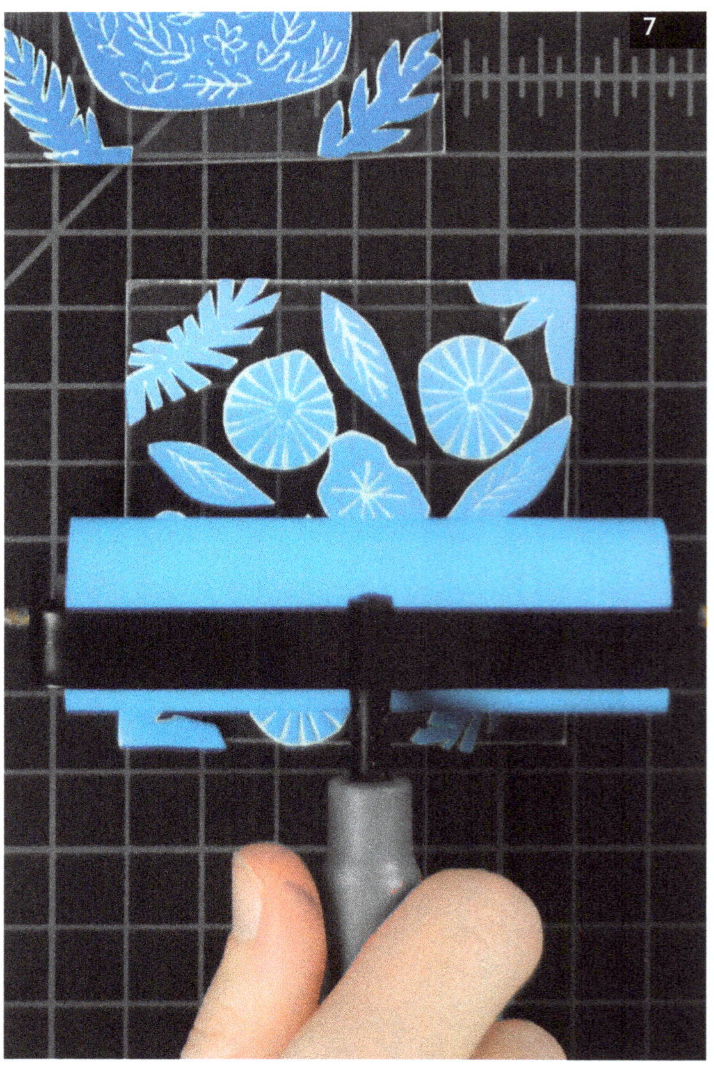

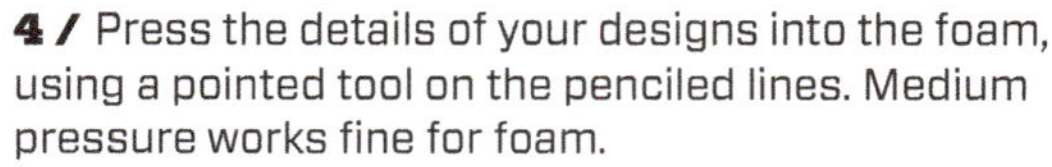

4 / Press the details of your designs into the foam, using a pointed tool on the penciled lines. Medium pressure works fine for foam.

5 / Cut out the main shapes with scissors or a craft knife. Peel off the foam sheet's backing to expose the adhesive. Arrange the components for each foam tile on individual acrylic mounting sheets.

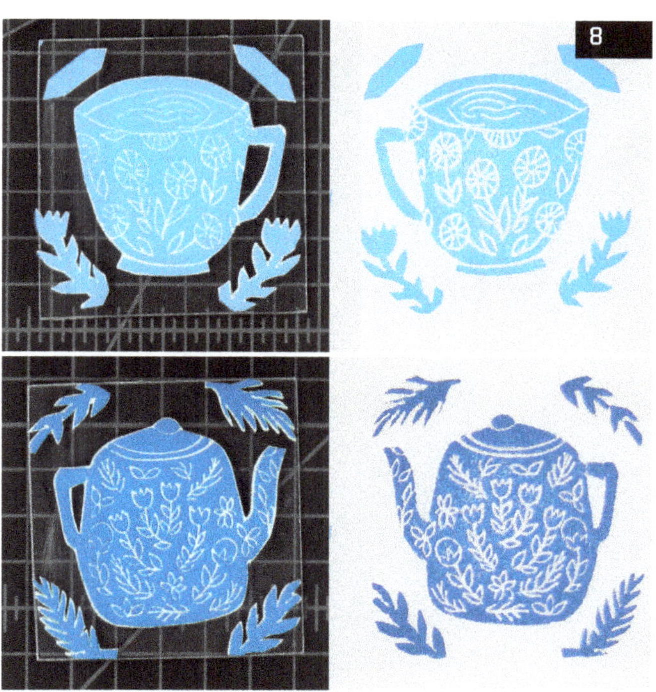

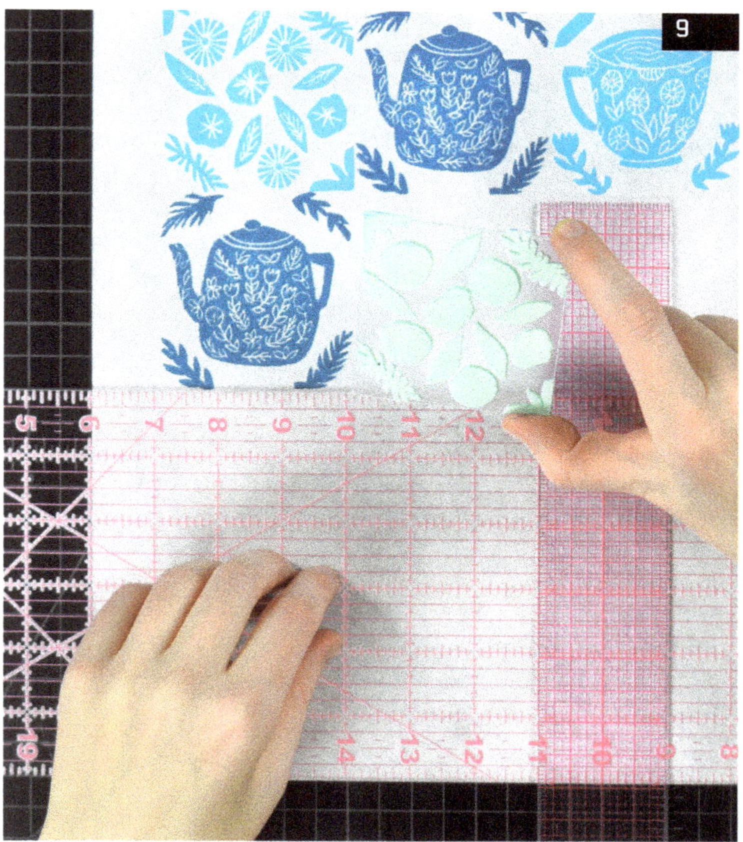

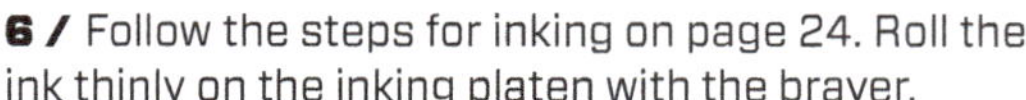

6 / Follow the steps for inking on page 24. Roll the ink thinly on the inking platen with the brayer.

7 / Apply thin, even coats of ink on your blocks. (Use different colors for each block, if you like.)

8 / Test print your tiles on scrap paper. Pick up a tile by the edges. Carefully turn it ink-side down and place it straight down on the paper. Apply even pressure on the back of the tile with your hand or with a book. Carefully lift the tile straight up and set it aside. Your test prints will give you a chance to practice applying the correct amount of ink and the correct amount of pressure.

9 / Use your test prints to determine how you would like to arrange the tiles in your finished print. Determine how many times you'll print your tiles, based on the size of your printing paper. To make sure that both the printing paper and the tiles are lined up squarely when you print, place the printing paper on a gridded cutting mat and use a transparent ruler to line up the edges of each print. Print the tiles one at a time. Repeat until your piece is complete.

10 / Set your print aside to dry. Frame or display your piece for all to enjoy!

Mounting art foam onto clear acrylic plates provides an easy means to register multiple-color prints. The two colors of citrus fruit in this print are interspersed, but because the acrylic is clear, you will need to look only at the drawing to line up the colors when printing. There are many artistic ways to explore this simple yet effective medium.

SIMPLE CUT SHAPES: ORANGES AND LEMONS

TOOLS AND MATERIALS

- drawing paper
- soft lead pencil
- tracing paper
- 2 adhesive-backed art foam sheets
- 2 acrylic mounting sheets
- bone folder
- 2 colored pencils
- ruler
- scissors
- pointed mark-making tool
- mat board or card stock
- water-soluble printing inks
- brayers
- inking platen
- palette knives
- printing paper
- baren or wooden spoon

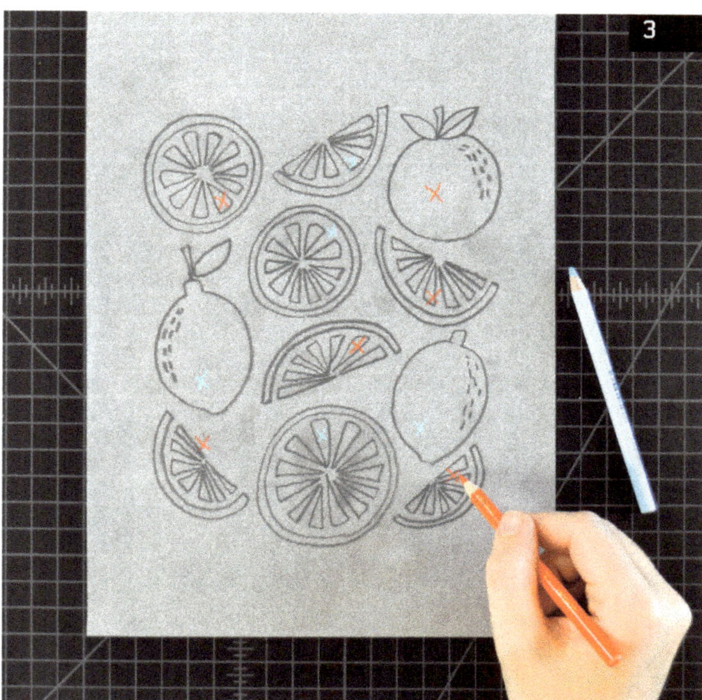

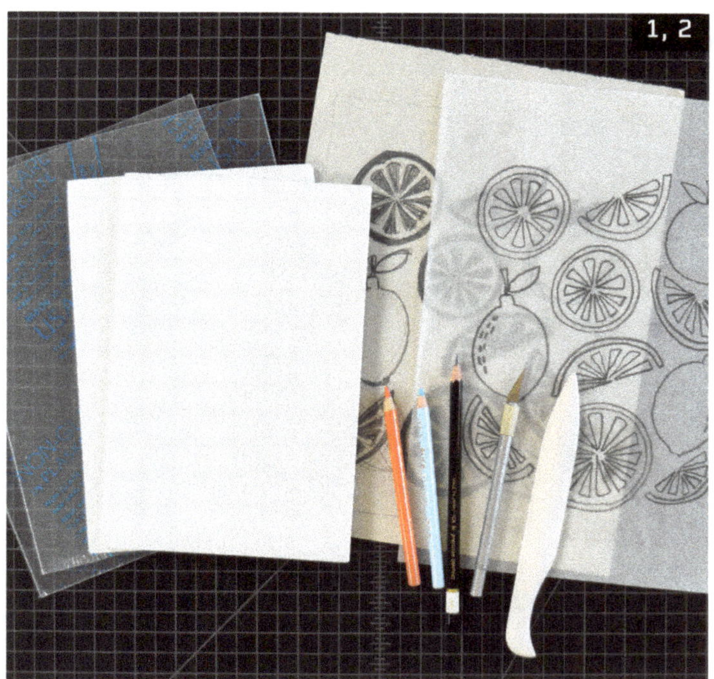

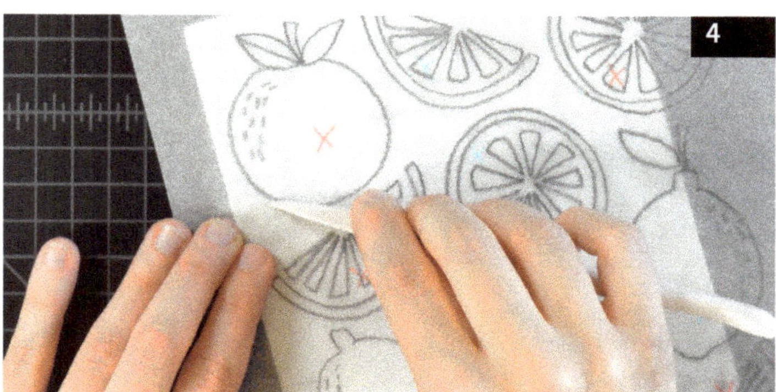

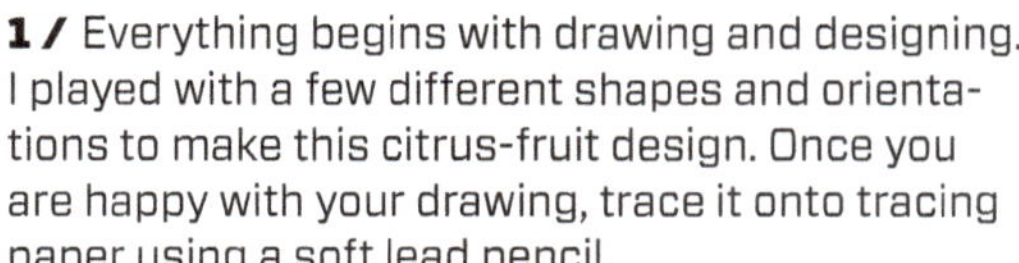
1 / Everything begins with drawing and designing. I played with a few different shapes and orientations to make this citrus-fruit design. Once you are happy with your drawing, trace it onto tracing paper using a soft lead pencil.

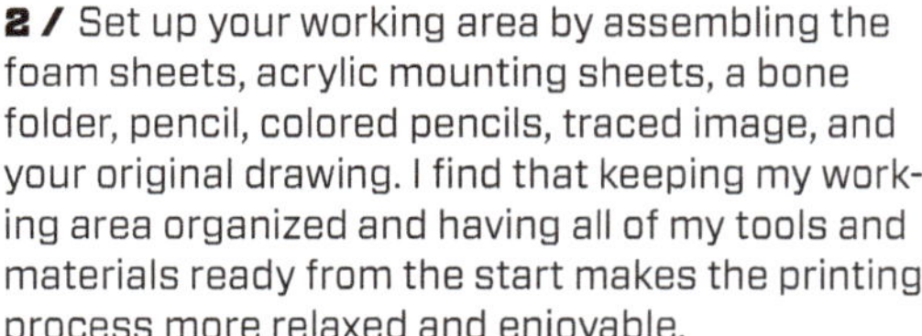
2 / Set up your working area by assembling the foam sheets, acrylic mounting sheets, a bone folder, pencil, colored pencils, traced image, and your original drawing. I find that keeping my working area organized and having all of my tools and materials ready from the start makes the printing process more relaxed and enjoyable.

3 / You will make a two-color print with two foam sheets and two acrylic mounting sheets. Use colored pencils to mark which fruit will be which color with an X on the tracing paper drawing.

4 / Place the tracing paper pencil-side down on the first foam sheet. Rub the back of the paper with a bone folder, focusing on the parts of the drawing that are all one color. Then do the same on the second foam sheet, focusing on the sections in the second color. The foam is soft, so rub gently to make sure you don't leave any unintended marks or grooves.

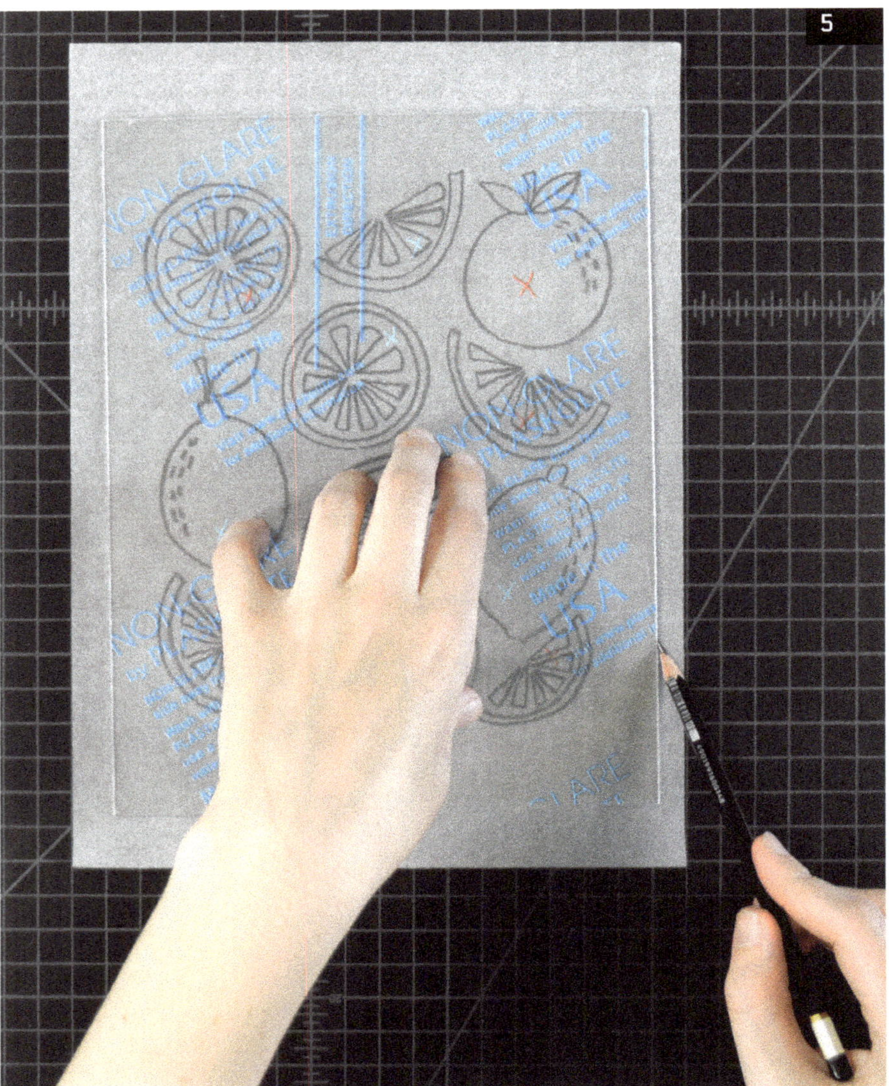

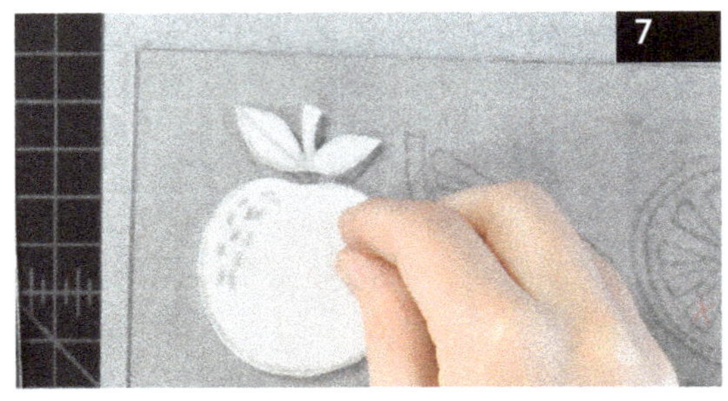

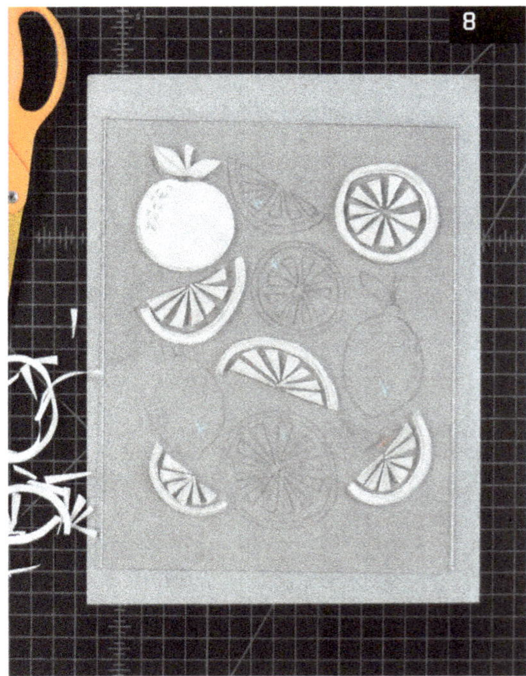

5 / Place the tracing-paper drawing face up on your work surface. Place one of the acrylic mounting sheets on top, centering it over the drawing. With your pencil, outline the edges of the acrylic mounting sheets on the tracing paper, framing the drawing.

6 / Decide which color to develop first, and select the piece of art foam with the transferred drawings for that color. Cut out the shapes with scissors.

7 / Making sure the acrylic mounting sheet stays precisely within the penciled lines on the tracing paper, position the cut-out pieces of foam directly over their equivalents in the drawing. Peel off the backing and stick the cutouts onto the acrylic mounting sheet.

8 / Set the first acrylic sheet aside. Position the second sheet within the penciled outline on the tracing paper. Repeat steps 6 and 7 for the second color.

9 / Add additional line work and details to the foam cutouts. Using a pointed tool, carefully press into the surface of the foam to make indented marks. For the oranges, I added dots and short lines to add visual interest to the large, full, fruit shapes.

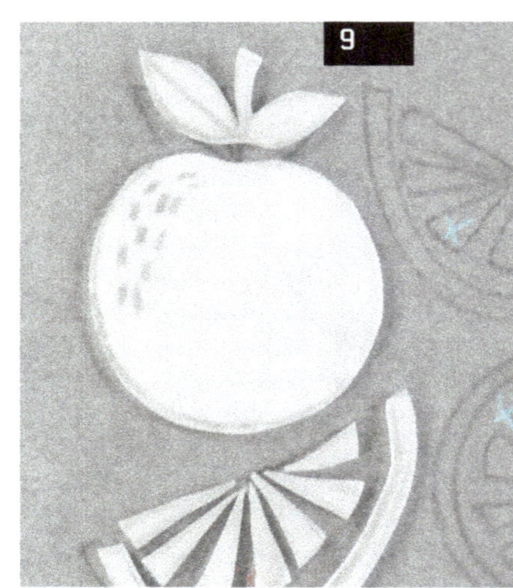

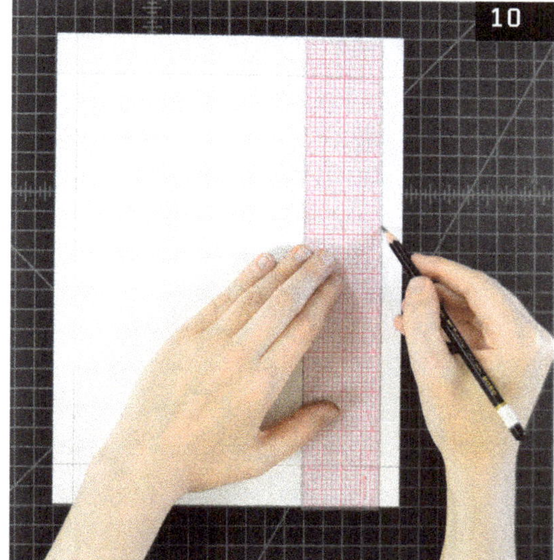

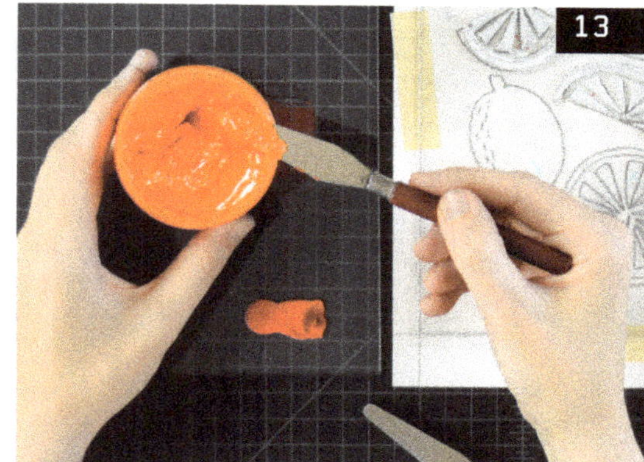

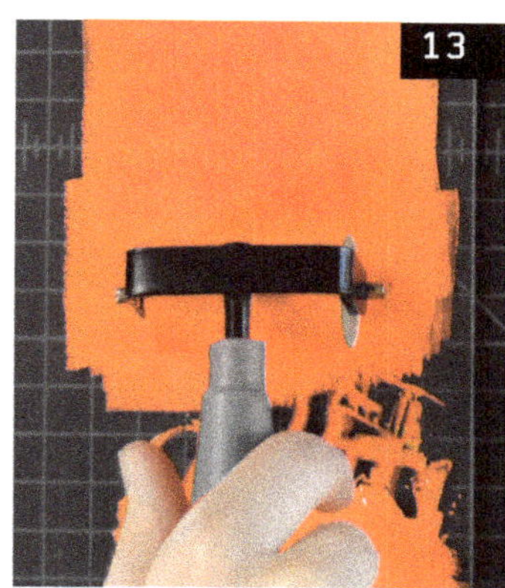

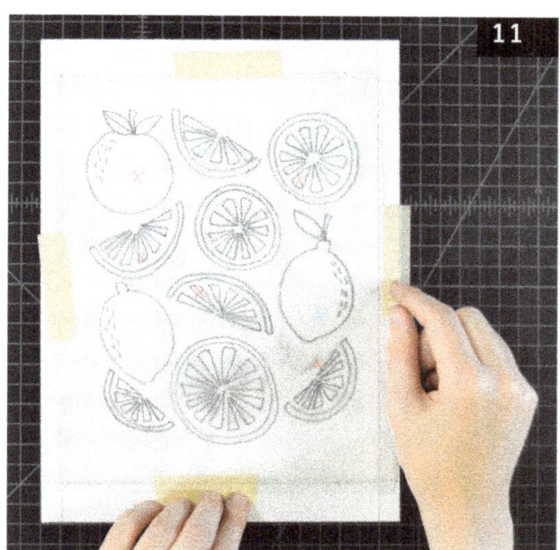

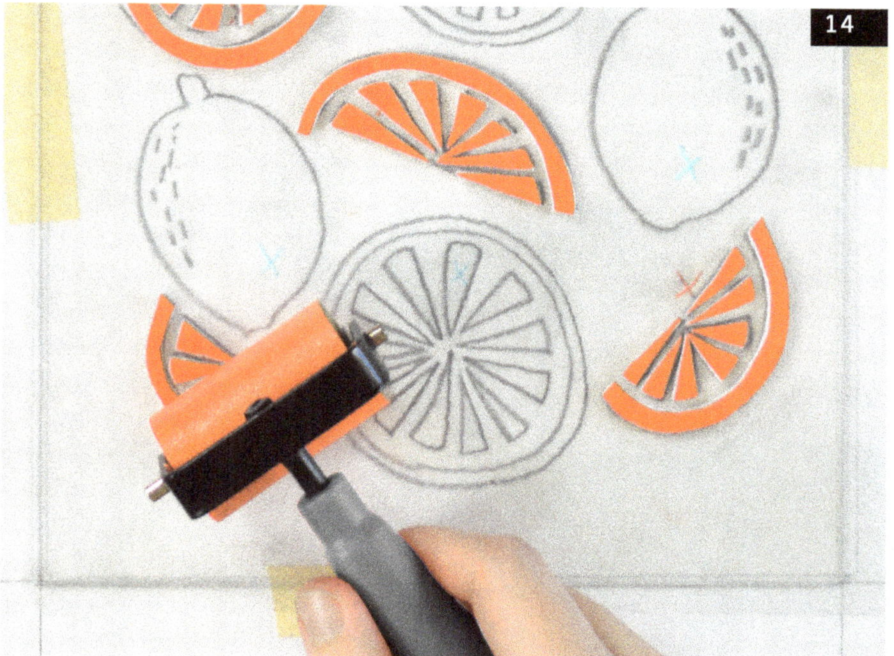

10 / You're ready to print. Prepare a printing jig by cutting a piece of mat board the same size as your printing paper. Draw a margin on the jig using a ruler and pencil. The margin is roughly determined by the size of the acrylic mounting sheet. Center the acrylic mounting sheet on the jig and trace around it.

11 / Place your tracing paper image pencil-side down on the jig. Tape the tracing paper to the jig using the pencil margin lines as a guide. This will help you determine the placement of the acrylic mounting sheets when printing.

12 / Prepare your printing area by assembling inks, brayers, palette knives, the acrylic mounting sheets, and printing paper within easy reach.

13 / Select the ink color for the first acrylic sheet. Use a palette knife to place a small amount of the ink on the platen. Use the brayer to pick up a small amount of ink and begin rolling it out for an even consistency. Look for an orange peel–like texture in the ink. Follow the inking instructions on page 24.

14 / With the brayer charged, roll the ink over the foam shapes on the first acrylic sheet. If your brayer dips onto the acrylic sheet, quickly wipe up any ink. Recharge the ink on the brayer as needed to ensure thin, even coats on the foam.

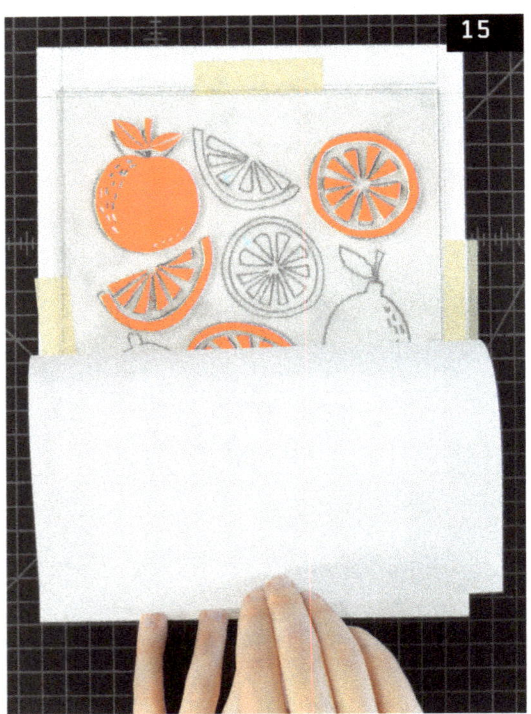

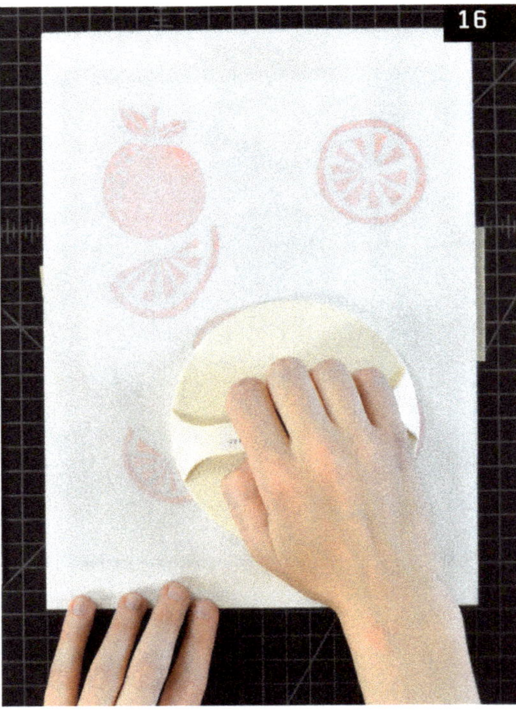

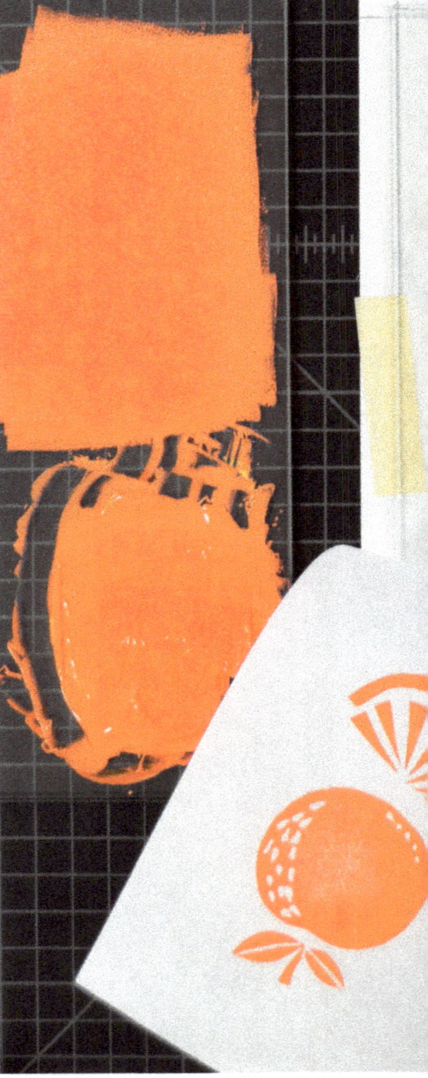

15 / Align the inked printing plate with the pencil margins on the jig. With clean hands, take a sheet of printing paper and position it by lining it up along the bottom edge of the jig. Use one hand to keep the paper in place along the bottom edge. Use your other hand to slowly and carefully roll the paper down onto the printing plate.

16 / Using your fingers, a baren, or a wooden spoon, burnish the back of the paper until the ink is transferred. Work methodically, burnishing all areas of the print.

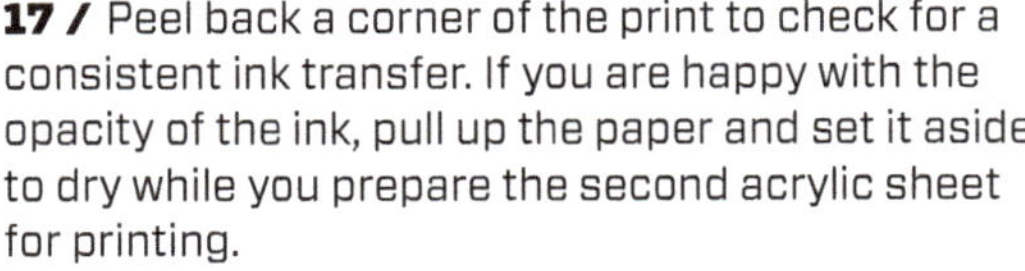

17 / Peel back a corner of the print to check for a consistent ink transfer. If you are happy with the opacity of the ink, pull up the paper and set it aside to dry while you prepare the second acrylic sheet for printing.

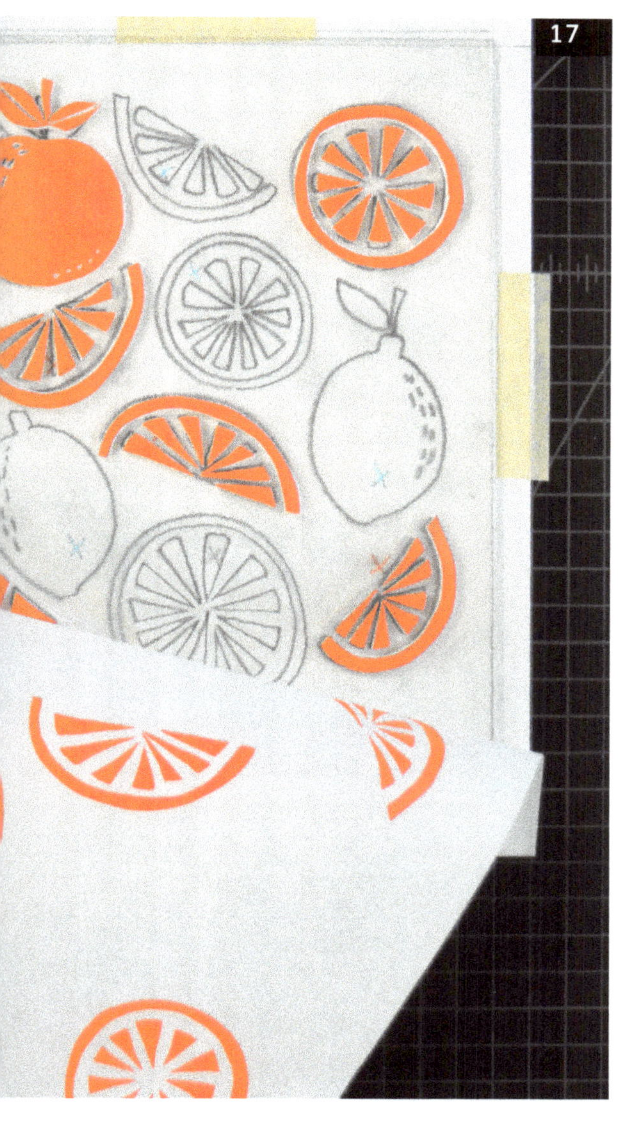

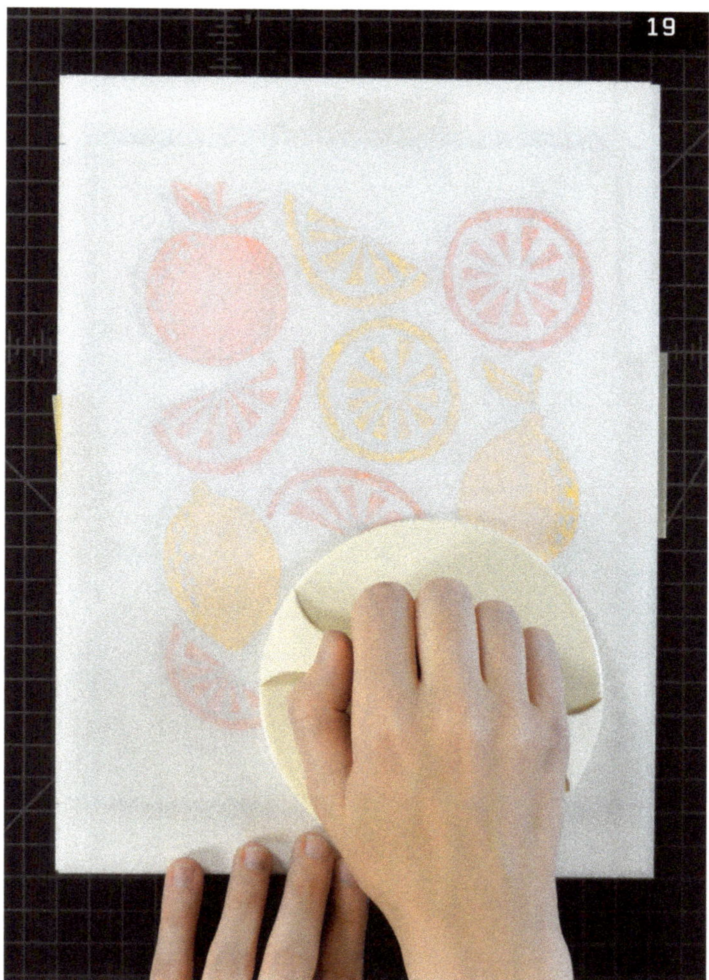

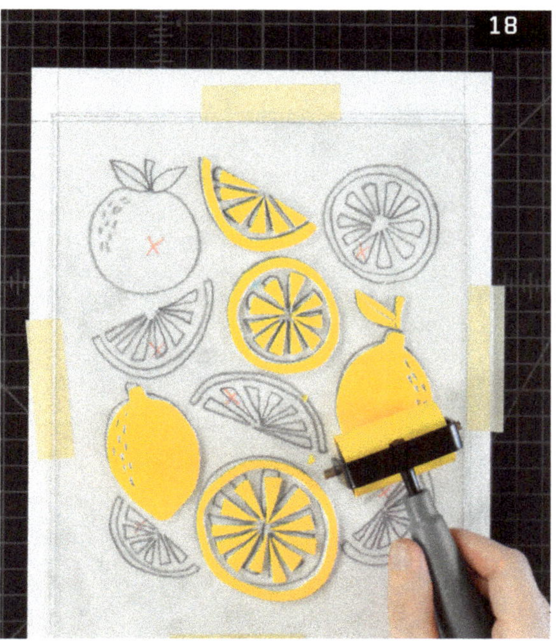

18 / Rinse the platen and brayer and allow them to dry. Roll out the second color charging the brayer with thin, even layers of ink. Set the second acrylic block onto the printing jig, lining it up with the pencil margins. Coat the foam elements with several thin, even layers of ink.

19 / Repeat steps 15 and 16 for the second acrylic sheet.

20 / Carefully lift one corner of the printing paper, checking for an even transfer. If you are happy with the transfer of ink, peel up the print and set it aside to dry. Enjoy your beautiful foam print!

It's easy to create multicolored prints when you use acrylic mounting sheets. Start with a single drawing, then make a separate plate for each color area. When you're ready to print, start with the lightest color first and work your way toward the darkest, printing one color on top of the other. The vase in this print is printed twice, the first time in blue and the second in black.

MULTICOLOR PRINTING: PALM PLANTER

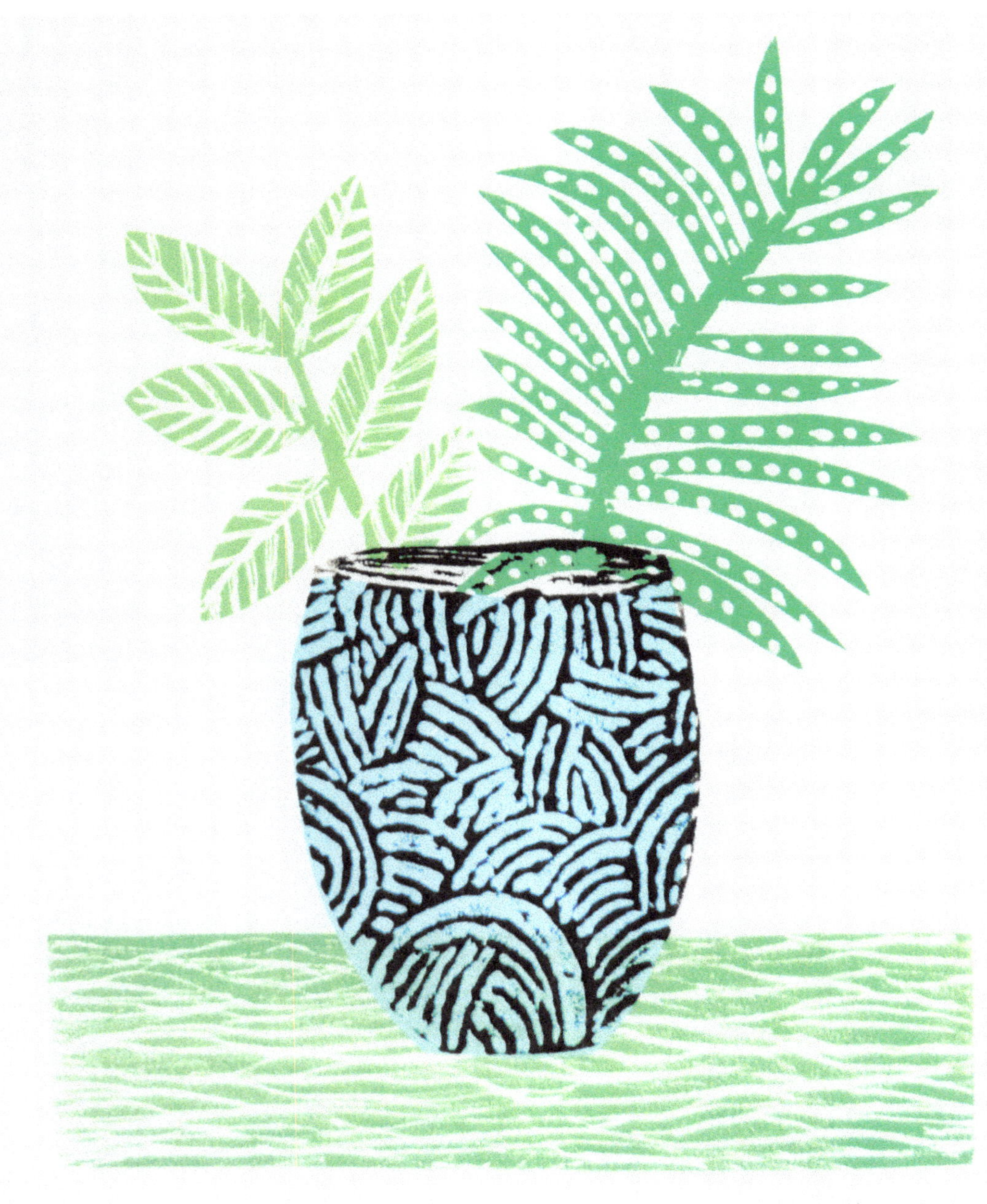

TOOLS AND MATERIALS

3 acrylic mounting sheets

tracing paper

pencil

3 to 5 adhesive-backed foam sheets

bone folder

scissors

pointed mark-making tool

mat board or card stock

masking tape

water-soluble printing inks

inking platen

brayers

palette knives

printing paper

baren or wooden spoon

washi paper

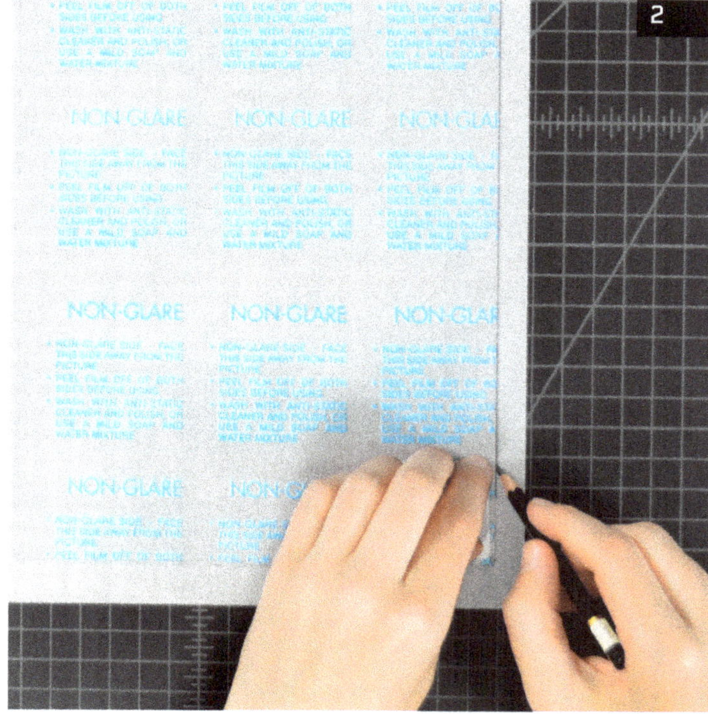

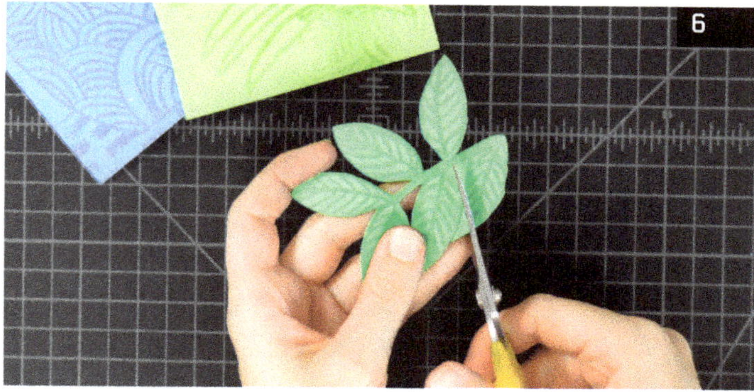

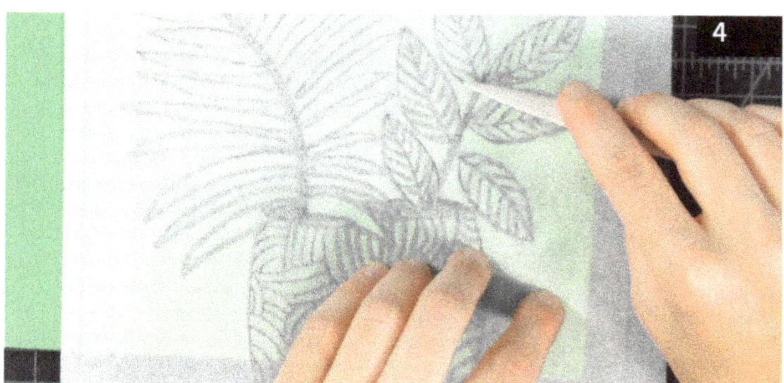

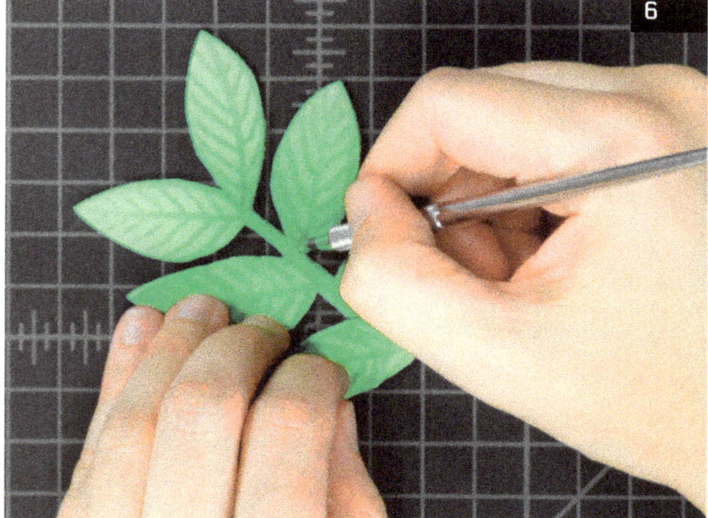

1 / Assemble the acrylic mounting sheets, tracing paper, pencil, foam sheets, and bone folder within easy reach on your work surface.

2 / Center one of the acrylic mounting sheets on a piece of tracing paper. Holding the acrylic sheet in place, trace around the edge with a soft lead pencil. Set the acrylic sheet aside.

3 / Use the pencil to draw a design for your print inside the penciled outline. I like to create a design that's the same size as my printing plate because it makes it easy to line up the plates during the printing process.

4 / Now you're ready to transfer the design to the foam sheets. Decide what section of the design you want to transfer first. Place a foam sheet on your work surface. Turn the transfer face down on top of it, making sure the section you want to transfer has adequate space. Holding the tracing paper in place with one hand, rub the back of the paper with the bone folder to transfer that section of the design. Work from the center out toward the edges so the paper doesn't shift or crease. Peel back one corner of the paper to check that the pencil lines have transferred.

5 / Repeat step 4 for each color area of your print, transferring each section onto a separate piece of foam. Because the vase in my design is printed with two colors, I transferred that section twice—once for the blue ink and once for the black.

6 / Use scissors to cut the individual pieces of the design from the foam sheets. Lay the cut-out pieces on your work surface. Use a pointed tool to make indentations in the foam to indicate the leaf veins, wood grain, and vase decoration. Remember that any indentations will be the color of your paper when you print. (For this print, I did not make any indentations in the cut-out for the blue layer of the vase.)

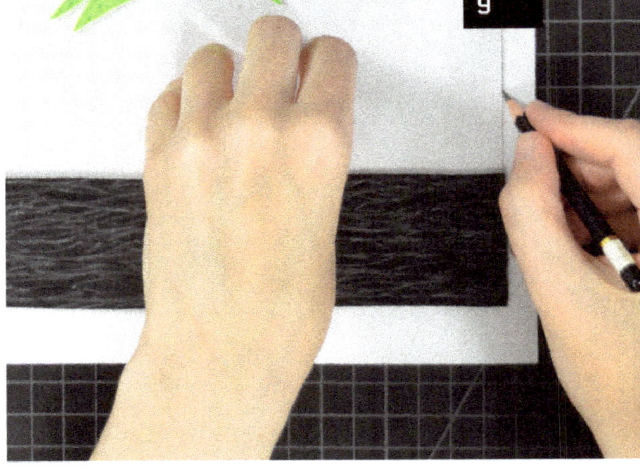

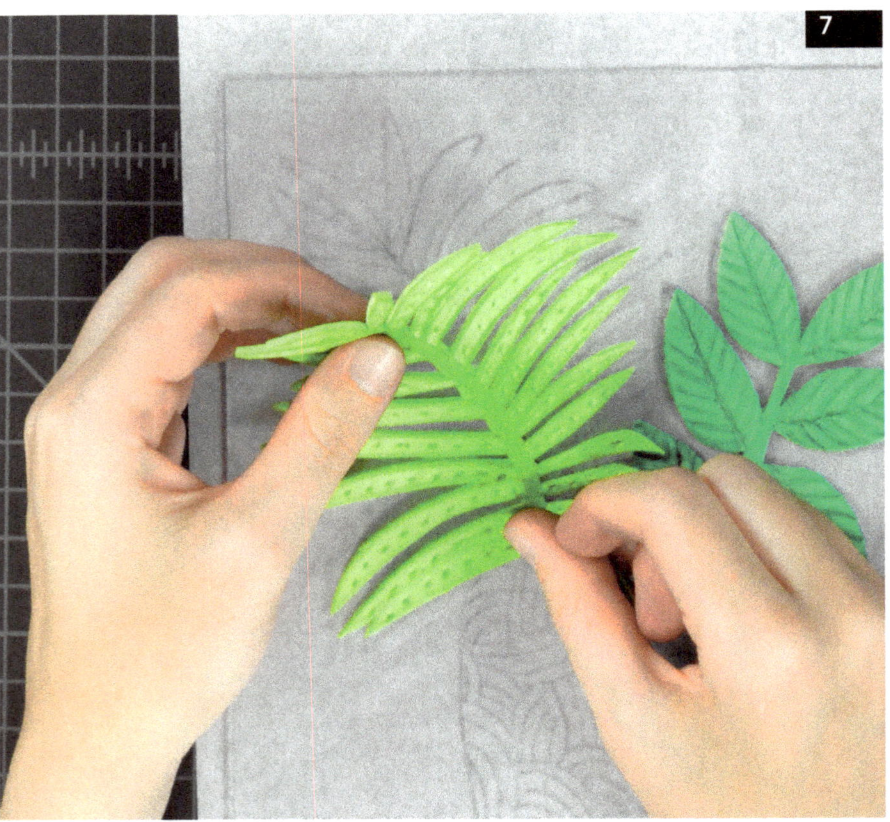

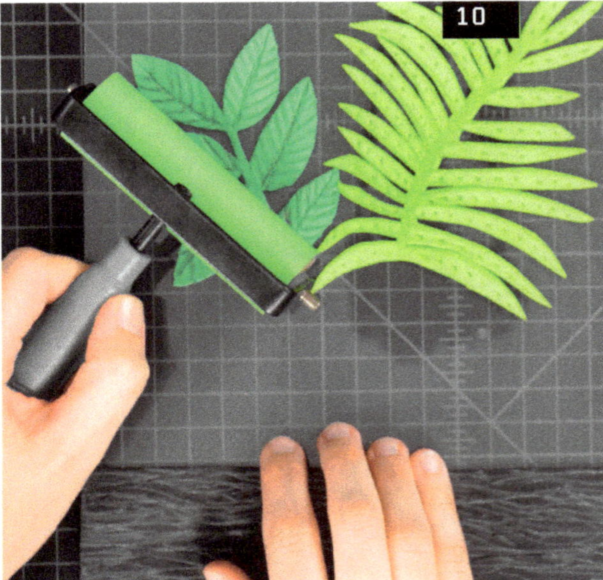

7 / Now you're ready to make your printing plates. Place the tracing paper face down on your work surface. Place one of the acrylic sheets on top of the drawing, lining up the edges of the acrylic with the outline that you drew in step 2. Select the foam element(s) you want to print first. I will be printing the two colors of green leaves, along with the wood-grain table top, together on one plate because none of the elements overlap. Peel the backing from the pieces, line them up with the drawing, and stick them on the plate.

8 / Set out your printing materials: inks, platen, brayers, and washi printing paper. Water-soluble inks will dry if left on your foam too long, so have your printing paper cut to the correct size before you begin.

9 / Prepare a printing jig by cutting a piece of mat board to the size of your printing paper and taping it to your work surface. Take the first of your prepared printing plates and center it on the jig. Trace around the edge of the plate with a pencil and remove the plate. (You will place each inked plate inside this outline with each round of printing.)

10 / Following the inking instructions on page 24, squeeze or scoop some ink onto the inking platen. Because I will be printing two shades of green for the leaves and table top at the same time, I roll out both colors on the same platen with a separate brayer for each. Once your brayers are charged with ink, roll the ink onto the foam pieces in thin even coats. The ink should be opaque when it is properly applied, meaning that you shouldn't be able to see any of the foam through the ink.

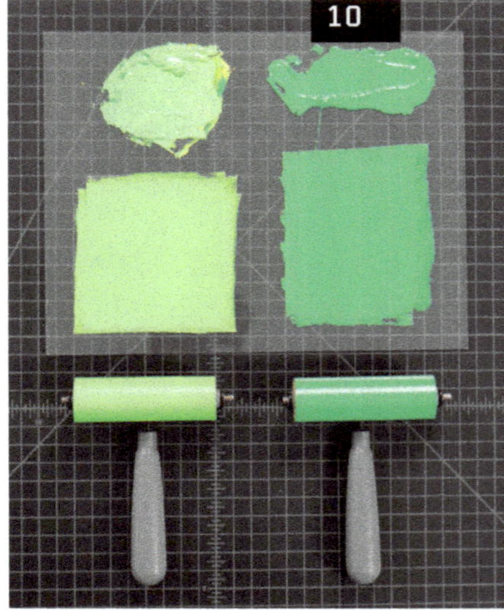

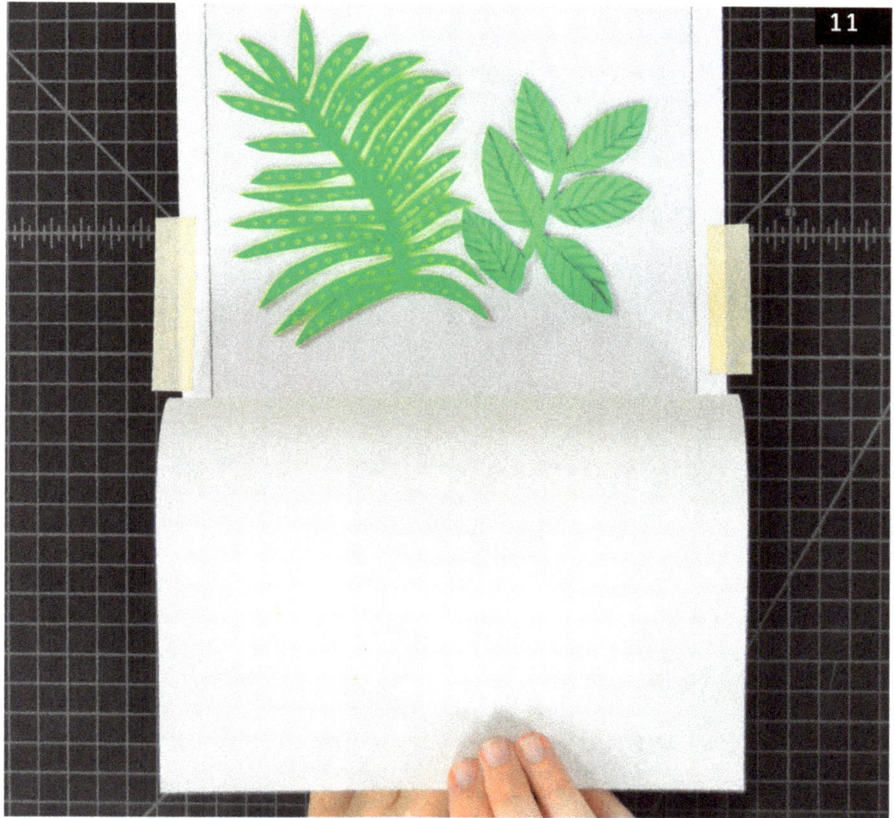

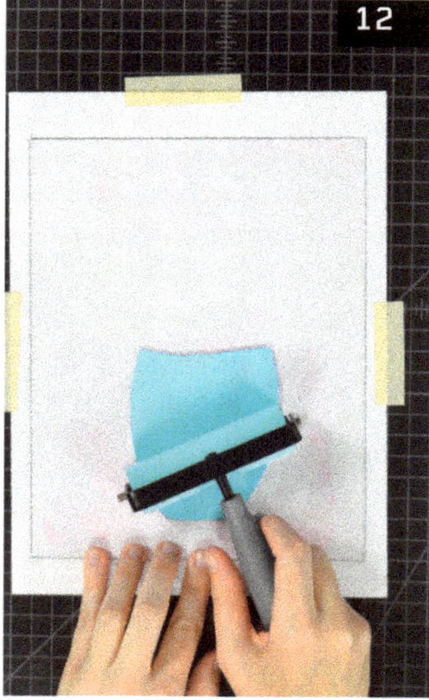

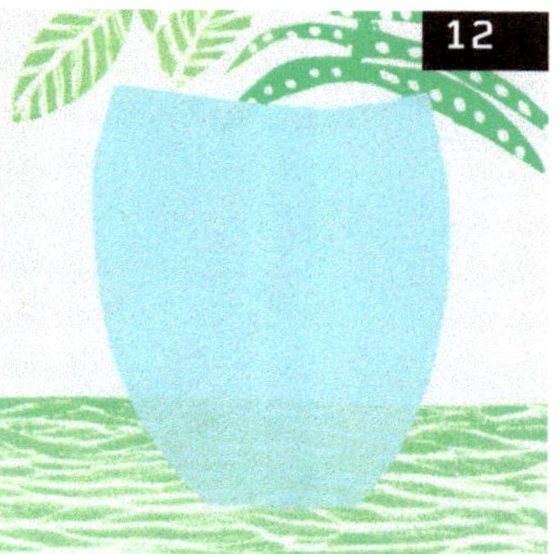

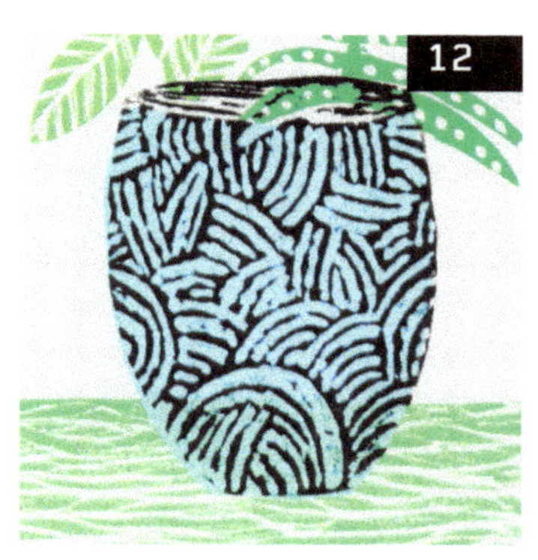

11 / Place the inked plate inside the penciled outline on the jig. Line up your printing paper with the bottom edge of the jig. Hold it in place with one hand, and carefully roll the paper down on top of the inked foam. Try to roll the paper down in one continuous motion. Burnish the back of the paper with your hand, a baren, or a wooden spoon.

Peel back one corner of the print to check the ink transfer. If the image is crisp, lift the printing paper and set it aside. If the ink is spotty, place the paper back down on the foam and continue burnishing with a little more pressure. Work quickly because you don't want your paper to dry onto the inked plate.

12 / Wash the platen and brayer, and allow them to dry. When the ink on your print is thoroughly dry, repeat step 11 with the next plate and color, saving the black for last. If you line up the edges of the printing paper and jig carefully in each round, the colors should register perfectly.

13 / Place your print on a flat surface and allow it to dry for several hours before handling it. Clean the acrylic printing plates and store them flat for another printing session. They can be used several times.

A stained-glass print is a multicolor print that uses a main key block. The black printed lines of the key block separate each area of color, just as in a stained-glass window. This printing style creates wonderfully bright art prints, and the colors are easily registered by a technique called trapping. To simplify registration of the different colors, I used acrylic sheets that are the same size as my printing paper. Each acrylic sheet will also act as the printing jig.

STAINED-GLASS PRINT: TOUCAN

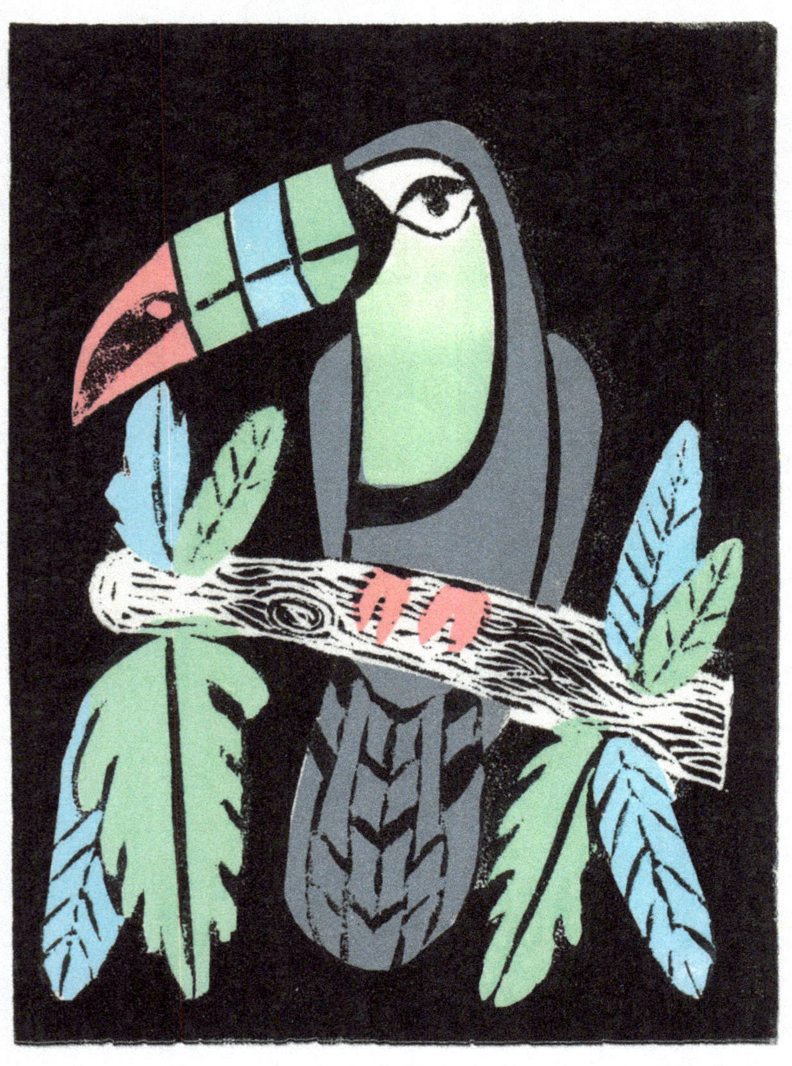

TOOLS AND MATERIALS

- drawing paper
- soft lead pencil
- tracing paper
- scratch foam sheet
- bone folder
- transparent acrylic ruler
- craft knife
- 3 adhesive-backed foam sheets
- pointed mark-making tool
- scissors
- 4 acrylic mounting sheets, all the same size
- double-sided tape
- water-soluble printing inks
- brayers
- inking platen
- palette knives
- baren or wooden spoon
- washi paper

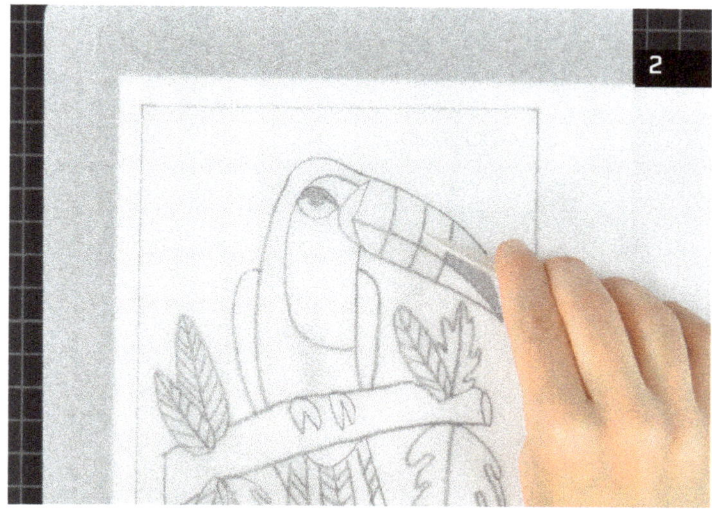

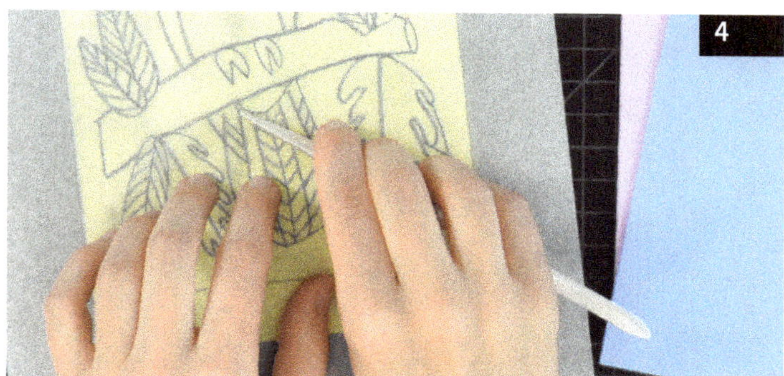

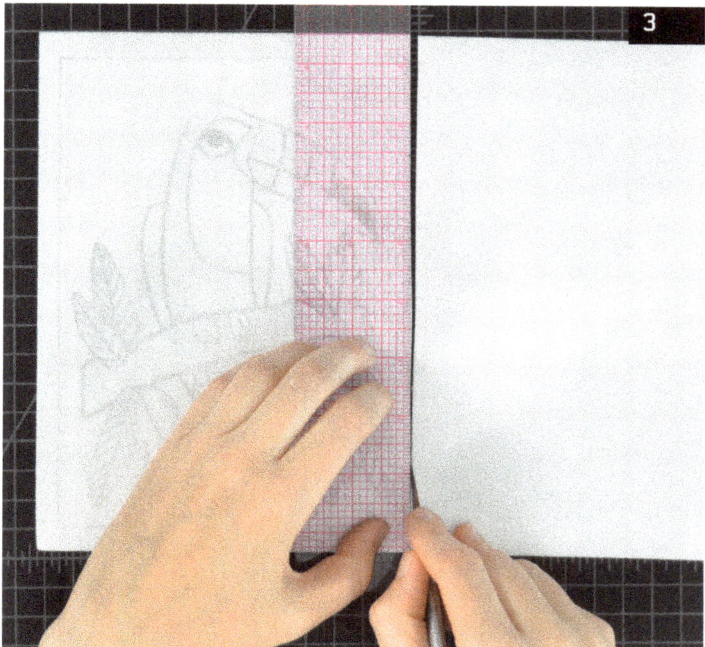

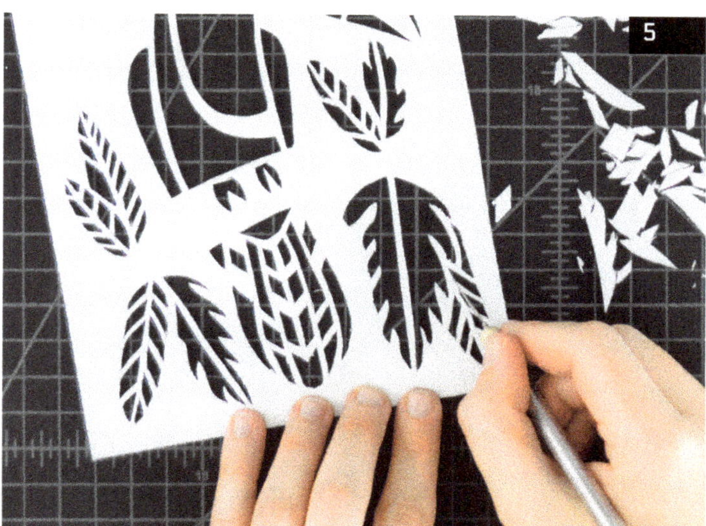

1 / Draw your design in pencil on paper. Keeping in mind that the image will print in reverse. Create a design, as with this toucan, that will allow for large sections of bright color. Place the drawing on your work surface. Cut a piece of tracing paper to the exact dimensions of the acrylic mounting sheets. Center the tracing paper over your drawing and trace it, using a soft lead pencil.

2 / Transfer the pencil drawing to the sheet of scratch foam, first. Place the scratch foam on your work surface. Place the transfer face down on top of it. Rub the back of the tracing paper with the bone folder to transfer the pencil lines. Take care not to gouge or scratch the foam too deeply with the bone folder. Any incised lines and marks will appear in your print.

3 / Once the transfer is complete, set the tracing paper aside. Use the ruler and a craft knife to cut around the image. The edge of this outline will print as the edge of your print, so take care to line up the ruler carefully and cut each edge as one continuous line.

4 / Repeat the transfer process from step 2 three more times on the three sheets of adhesive-backed craft foam. Set the sheets of craft foam aside.

5 / Prepare the plate for your key block. Place the sheet of scratch foam with the original transfer on your work surface. Use a craft knife to cut out the shapes, preserving the pencil lines. These will be the black outlines of the stained glass. All the lines must connect, one to another. For best results while cutting, start in one corner of the image and move methodically around the print, avoiding excessive contact with the pencil lines. Pencil lines rub off easily from scratch foam.

6 / Use a pointed tool to add any details to your image. I carved lines into the tree branch to create the look of bark. Experiment with wavy lines, cross-hatching, and more. Scratch foam is designed to hold these types of marks.

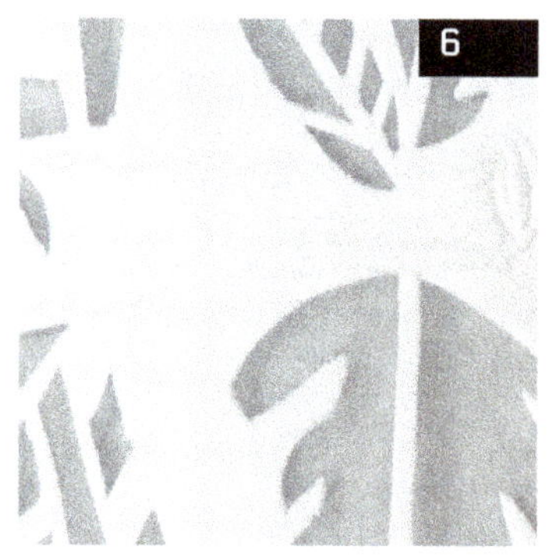

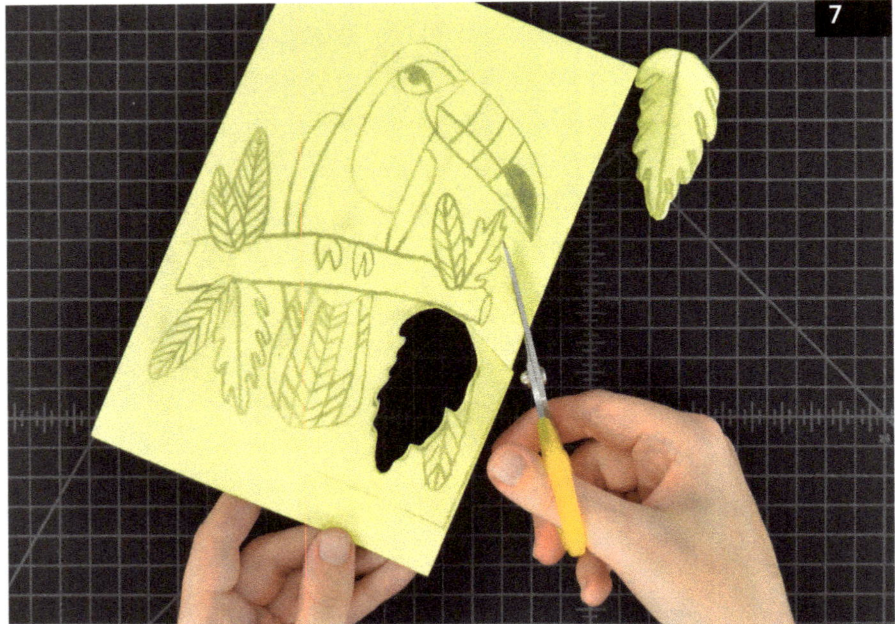

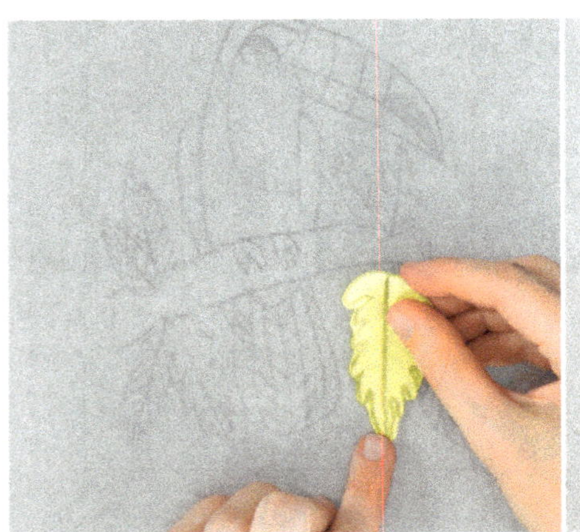

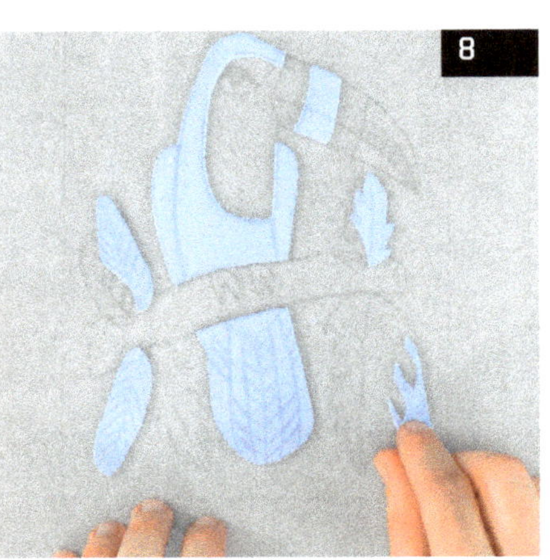

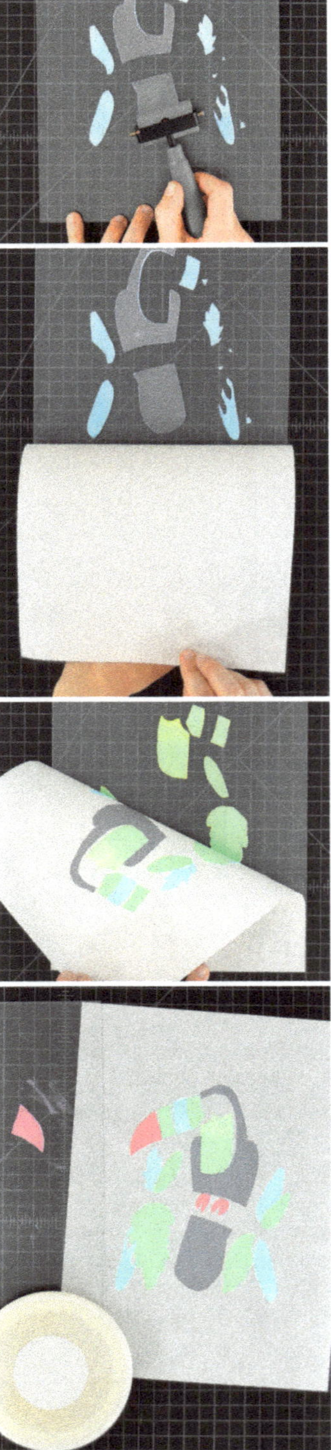

7 / Now move on to the craft foam sheets to prepare the colored-glass areas of your stained-glass print. Use scissors to cut out the large shapes just outside the transferred pencil lines. Continue cutting out all of the pieces that you plan to print in a single color.

8 / Place the tracing paper face down on your work surface. Place one of the acrylic sheets on top of the drawing, lining up the edges. Decide what color you want to print first and select all of the cut-out foam pieces that will print in that color. Peel the adhesive backing off the foam pieces. Using the drawing as a guide, adhere the foam pieces in the appropriate places on the acrylic sheet. Repeat with the other acrylic sheets, allowing for one or two colors per sheet.

9 / Now create your key block plate. Place the final acrylic sheet over the pencil drawing, lining up the edges. Place the cut-out sheet of scratch foam on top of the acrylic sheet, and line up the scratch-foam outlines with the lines of the drawing. Turn the scratch foam face down and place small pieces of double-sided tape on the back. Turn the scratch foam right-side up again. Line up one edge of the foam with one edge of the drawing, then carefully place the scratch foam down onto the plate. Make sure all the lines are perfectly aligned with the drawing. Press the scratch foam firmly into place.

NOTE

THE BENEFITS OF TRAPPING

Trapping allows for some overlap and leeway in printing. Your printing paper expands or contracts as ink is applied. These minute changes in paper size will affect even the most carefully planned registration. Trapping allows the printer to adjust to these small changes.

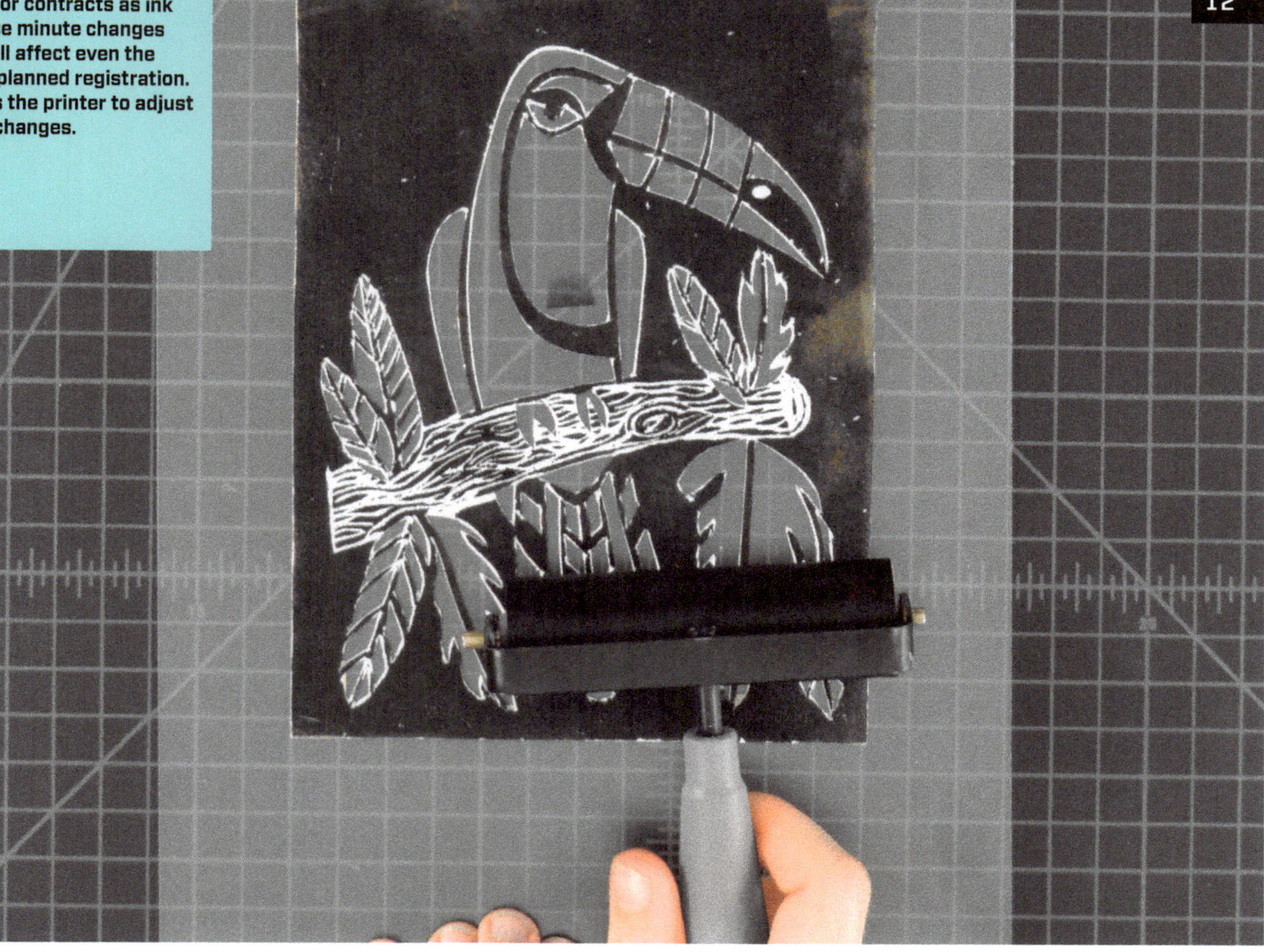

10 / Assemble your printing supplies. You will print all the colors except black first; save the black for last. Following the directions for inking on page 24, roll out a small amount of ink on the platen. Smaller brayers work well for prints with small pieces of foam. This first plate is printed with two colors. Roll out the two colors of ink with separate brayers on the same platen, then roll the ink onto the appropriate foam pieces with thin, even coats. Line up the edge of a sheet of printing paper with the edge of the acrylic sheet, and carefully roll the paper down onto the plate.

11 / Burnish the back of the paper with a baren to ensure a consistent transfer of ink to the paper. Repeat the inking and printing process for each of the color plates. You will begin to see the image taking shape as you print all your colors.

12 / Now you're ready to print the key block. Scratch foam is thinner than craft foam. Take your time and adjust your inking technique, as needed. You may find that you need less pressure with the brayer. If ink gets on the acrylic, wipe it away quickly. Repeat the printing process from steps 10 and 11. You may need additional pressure with the baren for the scratch foam. Peel back the paper and reveal your final print. It is amazing what can be achieved with foam!

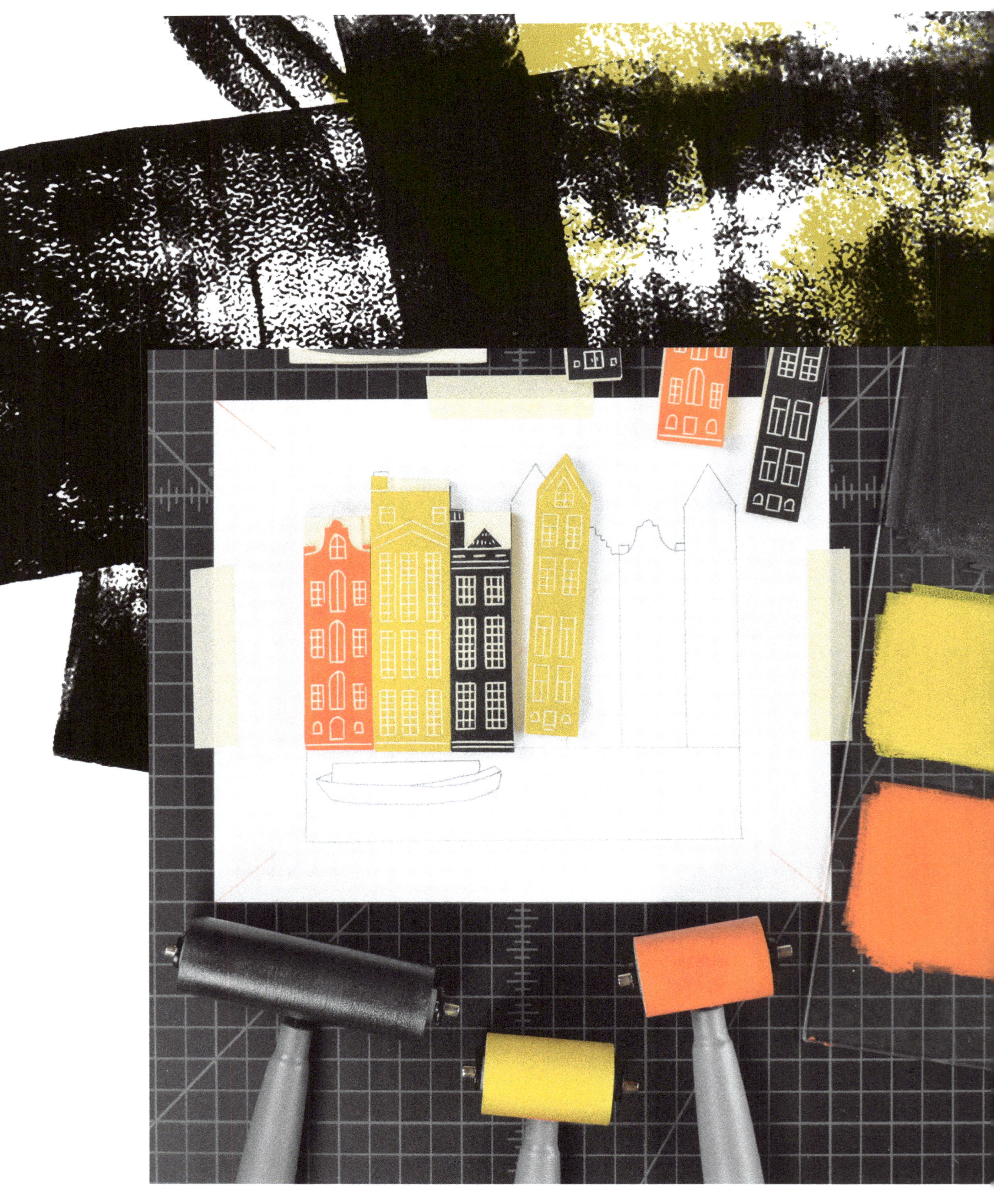

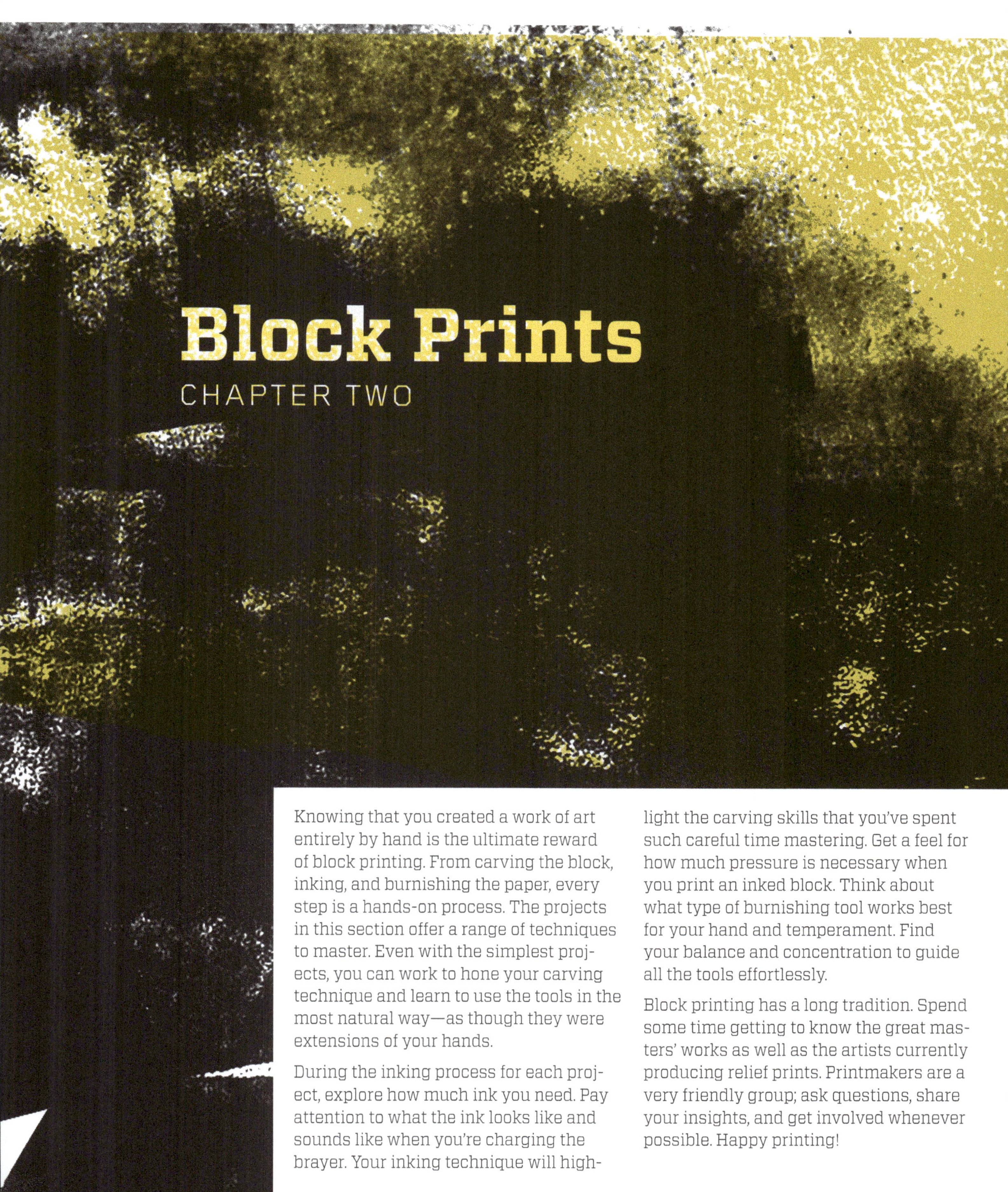

Block Prints

CHAPTER TWO

Knowing that you created a work of art entirely by hand is the ultimate reward of block printing. From carving the block, inking, and burnishing the paper, every step is a hands-on process. The projects in this section offer a range of techniques to master. Even with the simplest projects, you can work to hone your carving technique and learn to use the tools in the most natural way—as though they were extensions of your hands.

During the inking process for each project, explore how much ink you need. Pay attention to what the ink looks like and sounds like when you're charging the brayer. Your inking technique will highlight the carving skills that you've spent such careful time mastering. Get a feel for how much pressure is necessary when you print an inked block. Think about what type of burnishing tool works best for your hand and temperament. Find your balance and concentration to guide all the tools effortlessly.

Block printing has a long tradition. Spend some time getting to know the great masters' works as well as the artists currently producing relief prints. Printmakers are a very friendly group; ask questions, share your insights, and get involved whenever possible. Happy printing!

You can vary the look of a simple block by printing it with a single color. Or try a rainbow roll, a gradated inking technique for creating a multicolored print. This project also allows you to explore positive and negative space when you carve. Negative space is created by carving away the lines that you've drawn. Positive space is created by carving away everything except the lines, which is excellent practice for developing skill with the carving gouges.

ONE-COLOR BLOCK PRINT WITH A RAINBOW ROLL: COLOR VARIATION—RABBIT MOON

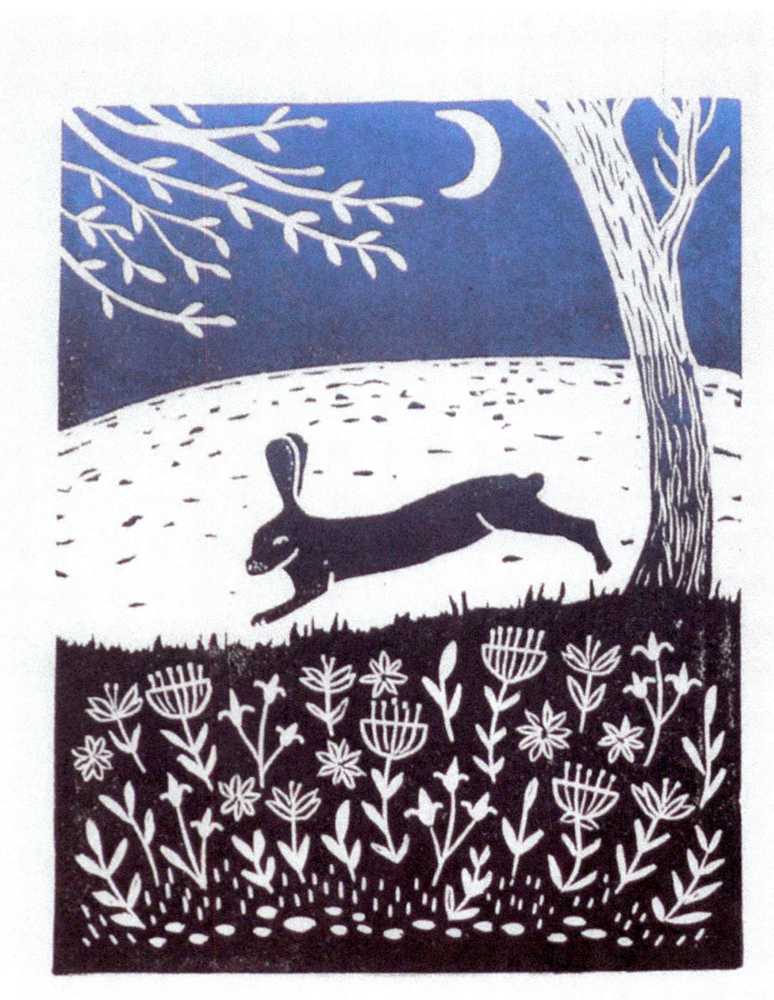

TOOLS AND MATERIALS

- soft lead pencil
- drawing paper
- light box (optional)
- tracing paper
- dense rubber carving block
- bone folder
- cutting mat
- craft knife
- transparent acrylic ruler
- gouges in various sizes
- soap, water, and sponge, or a baby wipe
- brush
- water-soluble printing inks
- brayers
- inking platen
- newsprint or scrap paper
- baren or wooden spoon (optional)
- masking tape
- printing paper

NOTE

If the orientation of the final image is important, remember that the image on your block will be printed in reverse. For this print, the rabbit will run to the left; the tracing is planned accordingly.

1 / Sketch your image on a piece of paper. Place the sketch on a light box or tape it to a bright window. Place a piece of tracing paper over the sketch. Trace the image in detail with a soft lead pencil. Be sure your lines are clean and clear on this copy. All marks will be transferred to the block, so erase any mistakes.

2 / Place the pencil image face down on the rubber block. Use a bone folder to transfer the pencil lines from the paper to the block. Keeping the sheet of paper in place with one hand, rub the back of the paper with the bone folder in the other. Work from the center outward. Lift a corner to check for a consistent transfer.

3 / Place the rubber block on a cutting mat. Using a craft knife and the transparent ruler, cut out the image from the block. Press down on the knife so that it cuts all the way through the rubber and carefully draw it toward yourself. For best results, make one smooth and continuous cut. In this image, the edge of the block will be part of the print, so take care to cut a smooth, even line. Set aside the cut-away sections of the block for later projects. Now you're ready to carve.

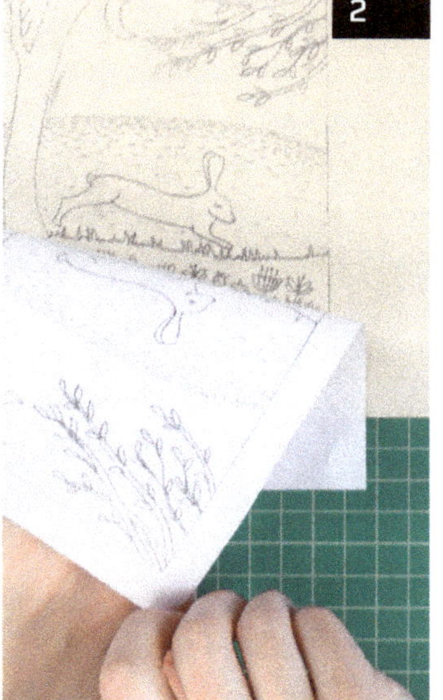

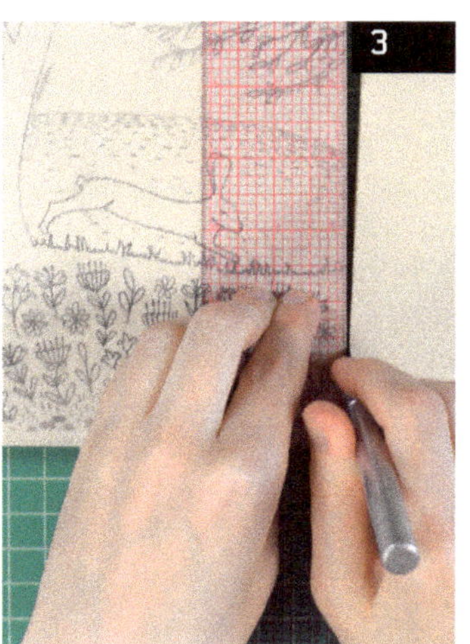

NOTE

Carving a curve or a circle is best completed by rotating the block as you carve. With your carving hand, insert the gouge at the starting place. With the other hand, rotate the block toward yourself while slowly and smoothly carving away from yourself along the curve.

4

4 / This image is roughly divided into three sections: dark top, light middle, and dark bottom. Start with the top sky section, which will largely be solid color. Remove the block material inside the pencil lines using a small V-shaped gouge.

5 / The middle section will have more light areas showing the paper color. Begin by carving just outside the lines with the small V-shaped gouge. Once completed, use a larger U-shaped blade to carve away the broader areas of block material. Complete the carving process for the final bottom section.

6 / When the image is fully carved, clean the pencil lines from the block surface with soap and water. If any additional scraps are still inside the carved lines, remove them with a bristle brush.

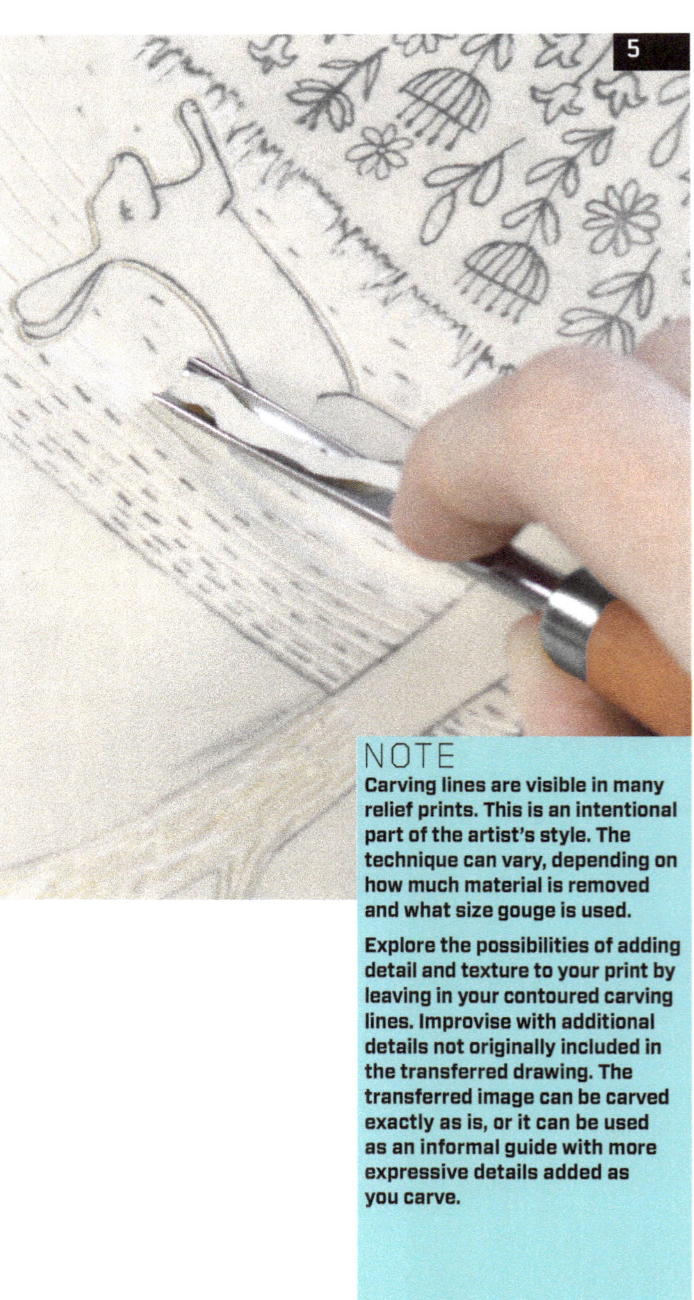

NOTE

Carving lines are visible in many relief prints. This is an intentional part of the artist's style. The technique can vary, depending on how much material is removed and what size gouge is used.

Explore the possibilities of adding detail and texture to your print by leaving in your contoured carving lines. Improvise with additional details not originally included in the transferred drawing. The transferred image can be carved exactly as is, or it can be used as an informal guide with more expressive details added as you carve.

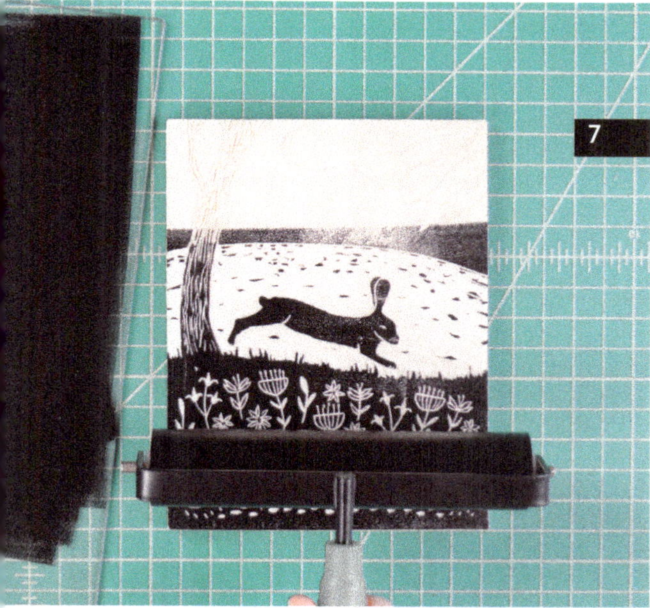

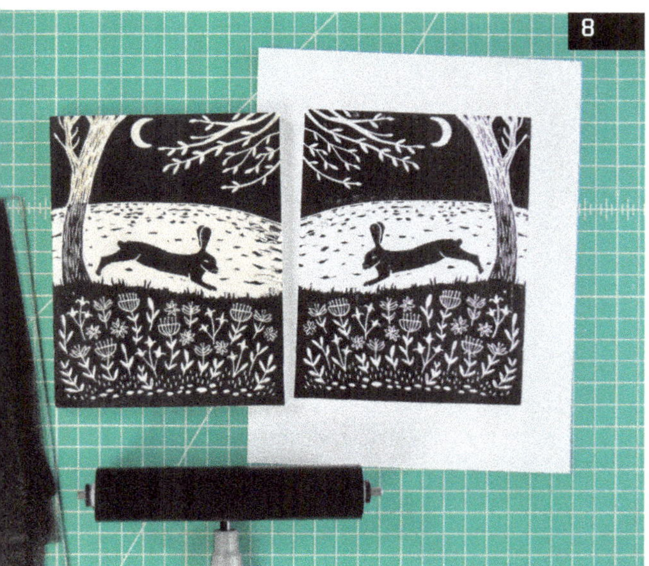

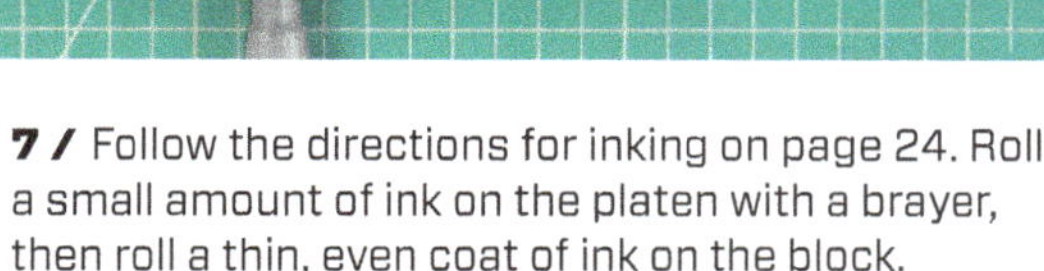

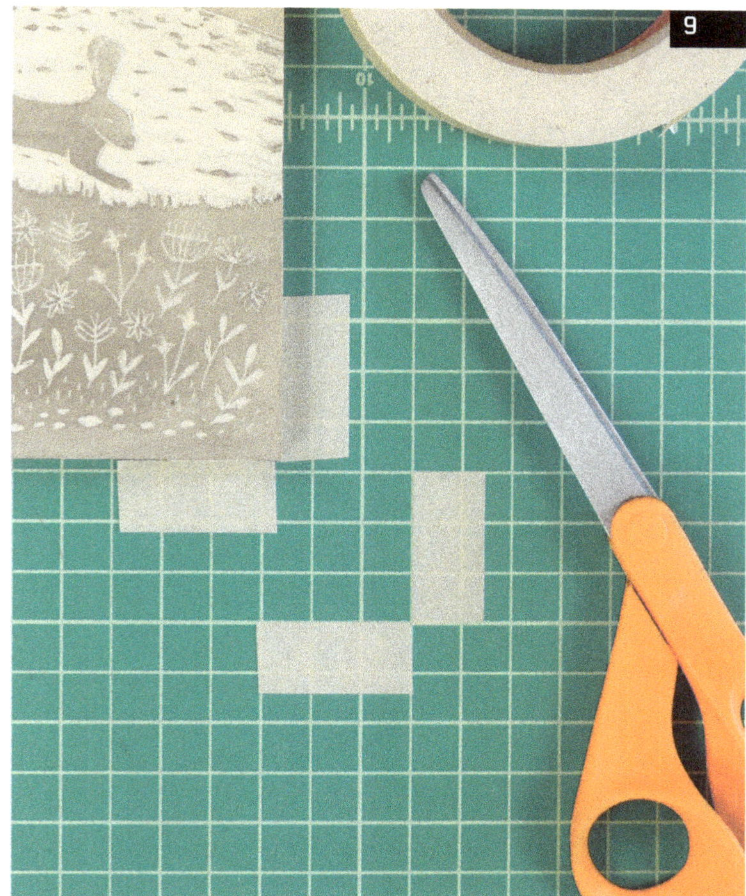

7 / Follow the directions for inking on page 24. Roll a small amount of ink on the platen with a brayer, then roll a thin, even coat of ink on the block.

8 / Carefully lay a piece of newsprint on the inked block, burnish the back of the paper with a baren or spoon, and pull off your test print. If there are changes necessary, refine the image by carving any areas that need fine tuning.

9 / Create a simple registration guide on your cutting mat, using the grid for placement. With masking tape, create a reverse L shape for the lower right corner of the block, and a second L shape for the corner of the printing paper. This simple registration will save time as you print multiple copies, and it will ensure that the print is centered properly on each.

10 / If you're happy with the test print, continue to roll your block with a single color and repeat the printing process. Display your finished prints thoughtfully once they have dried.

NOTE
The inking of a rainbow roll is directional so take care to re-ink in the same orientation.

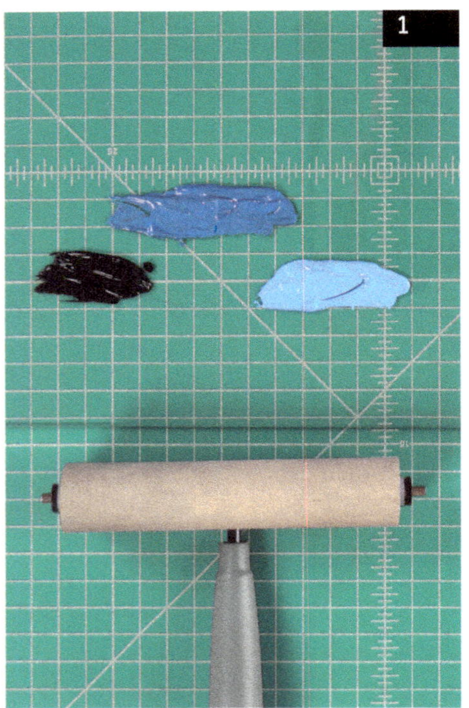

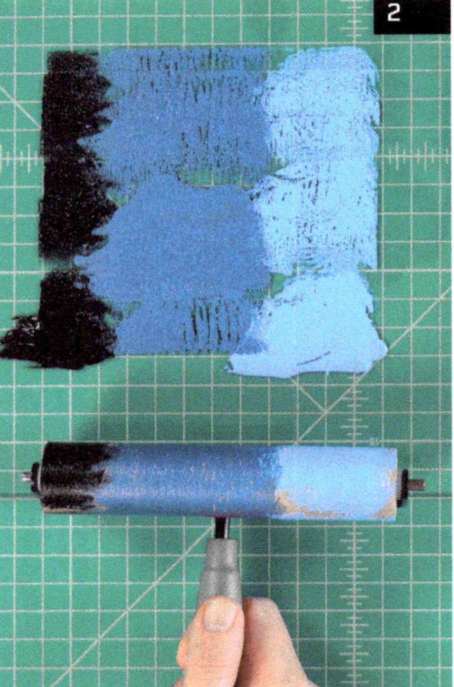

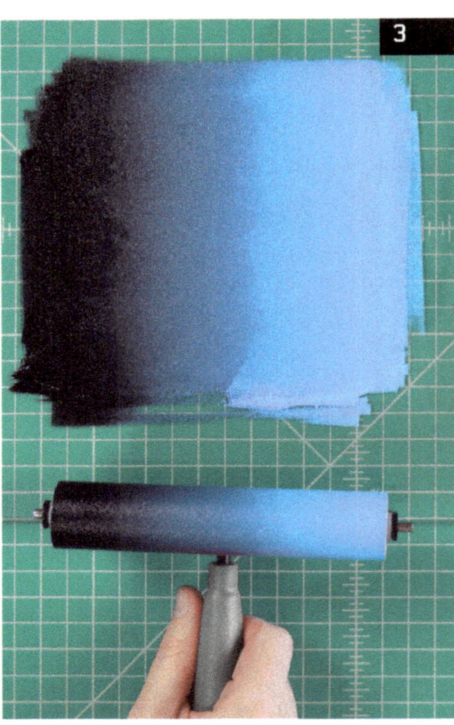

PRINTING A RAINBOW ROLL

To print a color gradation effectively, the brayer should be as wide as the block or slightly wider.

1 / Choose two or three ink colors. Using a palette knife, lay out the colors to match the width of the brayer, or a little wider. Place the colors slightly above or below each other so that the colors overlap slightly.

2 / Roll the brayer in a straight line back and forth to spread the colors on the platen.

3 / Lightly roll the brayer through the ink in a diagonal direction. This will blend the colors, creating an even gradient.

4 / Transfer the gradated ink on the brayer to the block in thin, even coats until the block is entirely covered.

5 / Set the inked block into position on the cutting mat, using the registration marks for placement.

6 / Align your printing paper with the registration marks. Carefully roll the paper down onto the inked surface. Burnish the back of the paper with a baren or spoon. Carefully pull back the print and allow it to dry. Enjoy your beautiful work!

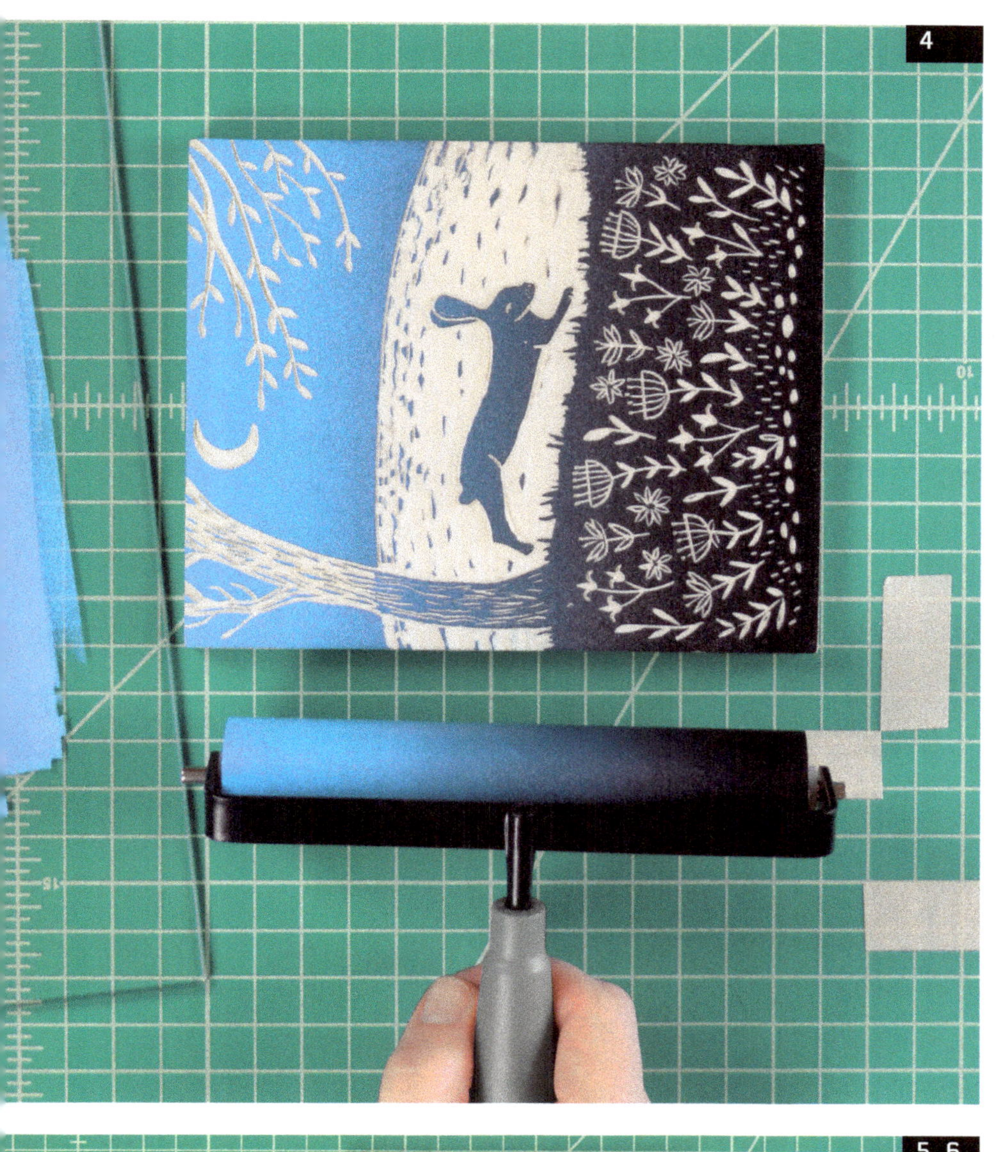
4

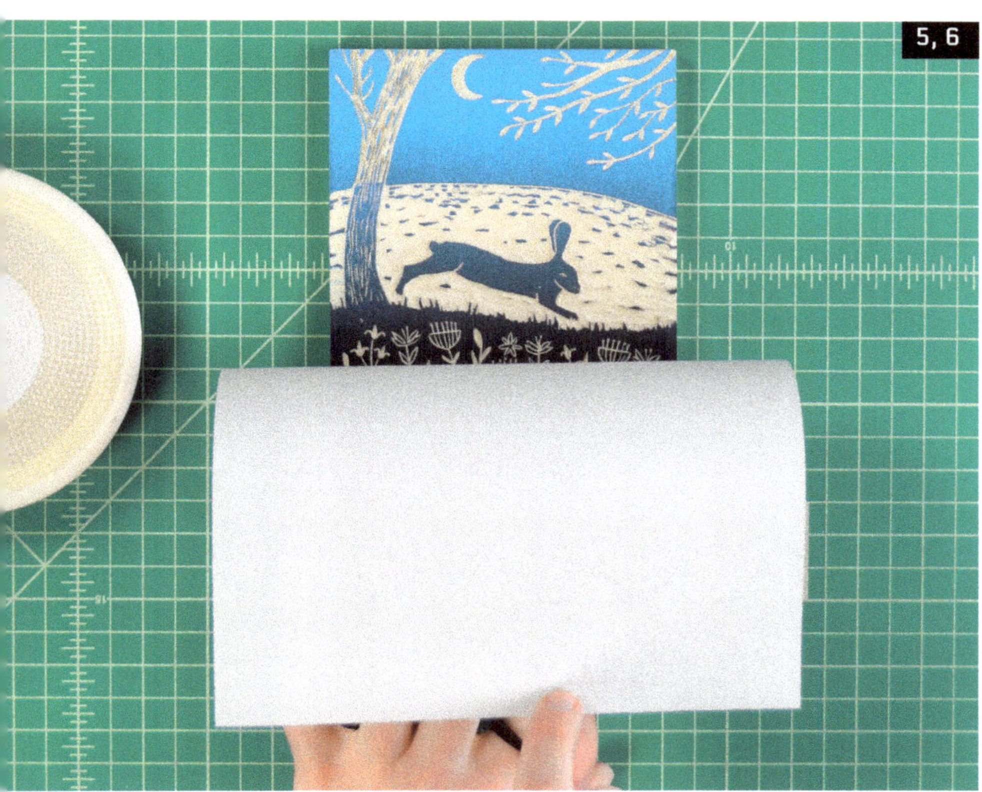
5, 6

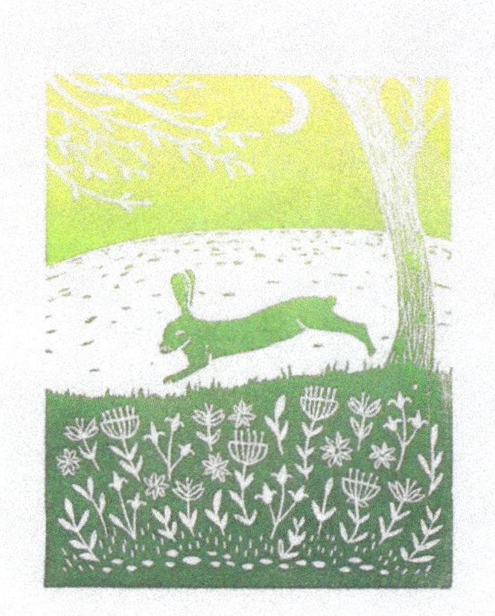

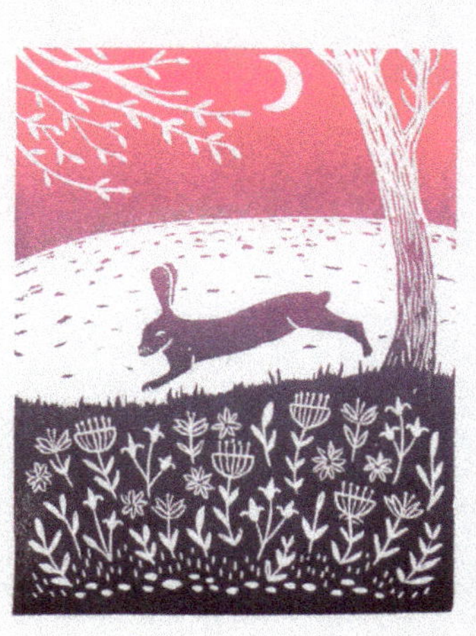

The picturesque neighborhoods, narrow streets, and charming architecture you enjoy on your travels can be the inspiration for simple, yet highly effective, prints when you get home. The great thing about this technique is that the image starts with a single, dense rubber block. In this Amsterdam scene, the sections are cut apart, inked separately, and then reassembled like puzzle pieces to create the finished art print. You can vary the mood and feeling of the print with your selection of colors. Romantic? Realistic? Imaginative? Choose colors that reflect your mood and style.

MULTICOLOR INTERLOCKING BLOCK PRINT: AMSTERDAM

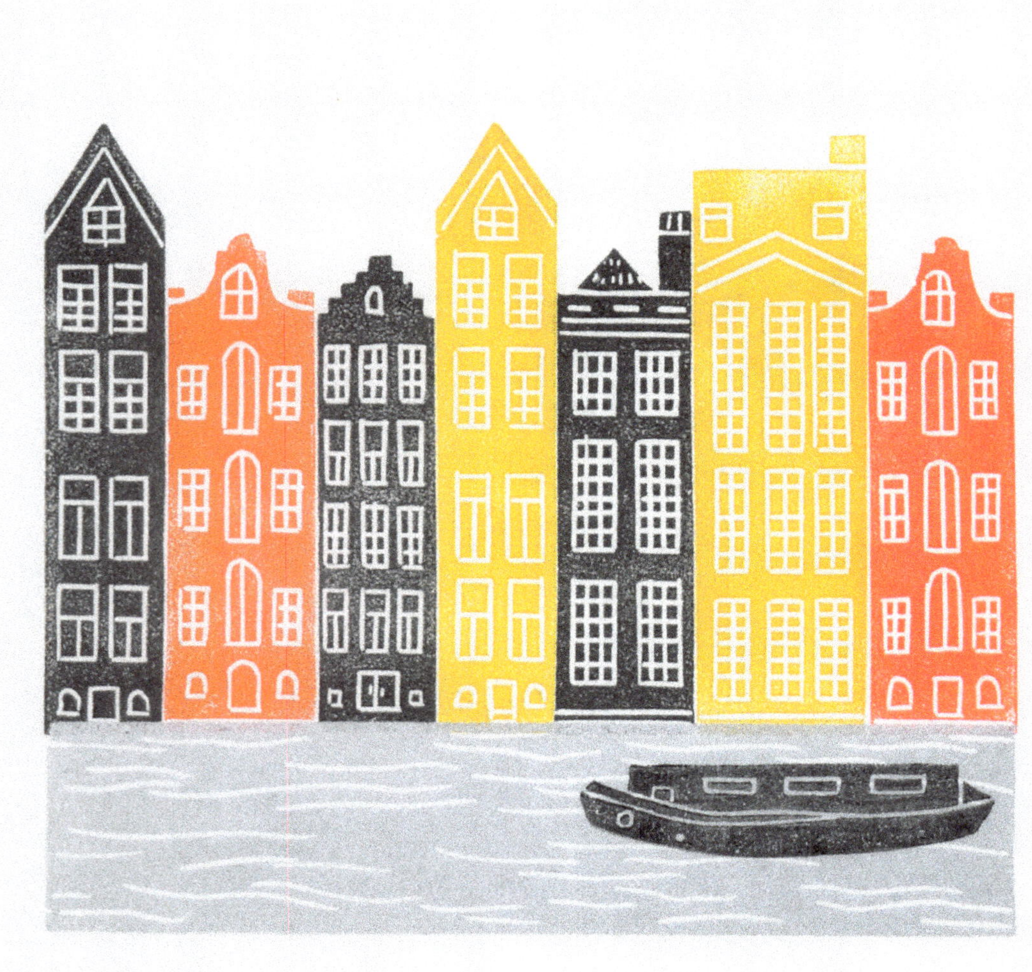

TOOLS AND MATERIALS

- soft lead pencil
- drawing paper
- light box (optional)
- tracing paper
- dense rubber carving block
- bone folder
- cutting mat
- craft knife
- transparent acrylic ruler
- gouges in various sizes
- mat board or card stock
- masking tape
- water-soluble printing inks
- brayers
- inking platens
- baren or wooden spoon (optional)
- printing paper

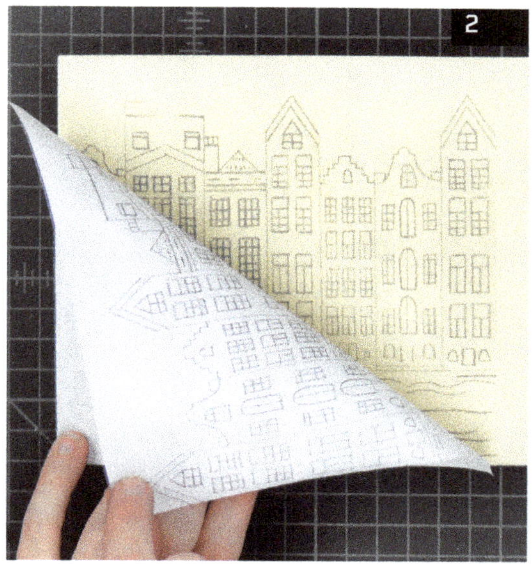

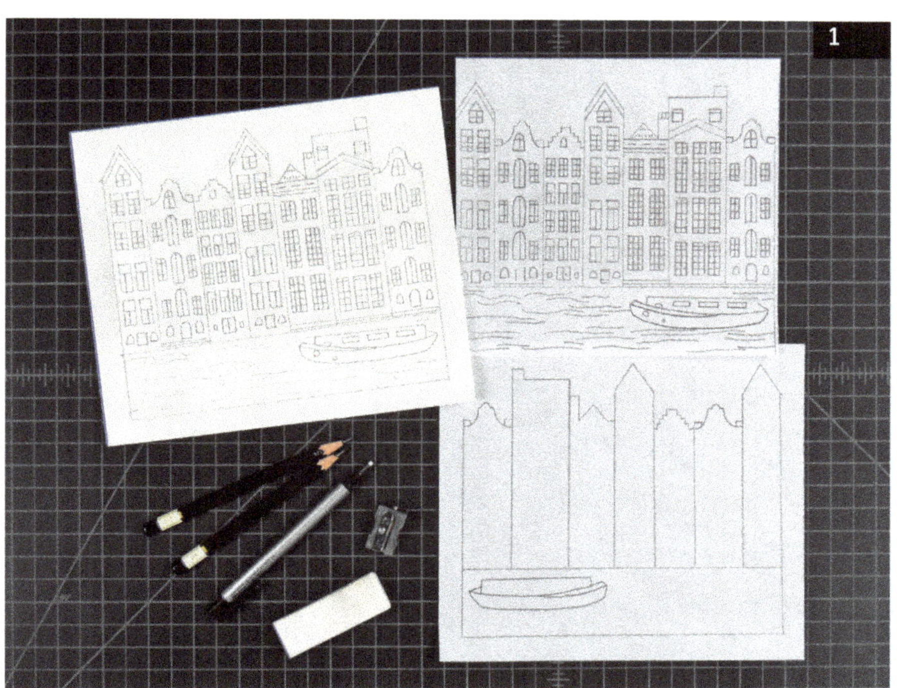

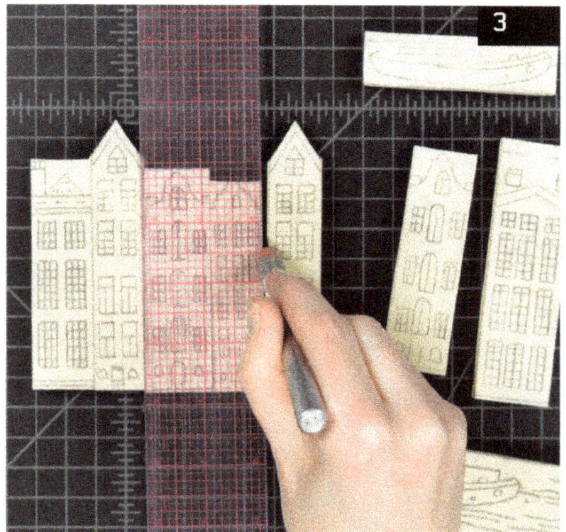

1 / Sketch your image on a piece of paper. Place the sketch on a light box, or tape it to a bright window. Place a piece of tracing paper over the sketch and trace it in detail with a soft lead pencil. Be sure your lines are clean and clear on this copy. All marks will be transferred to the block, so erase any mistakes. Turn the traced copy face down on your work surface and place another piece of tracing paper on top of it. This time, trace only the outlines of the large shapes in the design. Set the outline copy aside for later: It will be the guide for registering the colored sections of the print.

2 / Place your detailed pencil image face down on the rubber block. Use a bone folder to transfer the pencil lines from the paper to the block. Keeping the sheet of paper in place with one hand, rub the back of the paper with the bone folder in the other. Work from the center outward. Lift a corner to check for a consistent transfer.

3 / Place the rubber block on a cutting mat. Decide which colors to use on the different sections of your design. Using a craft knife and the transparent ruler, cut the block along the lines that divide the areas of color. Press down on the knife so that it cuts all the way through the rubber, and carefully draw it toward yourself. For best results, make one smooth and continuous cut for each line. Divide the sections. Now you're ready to carve.

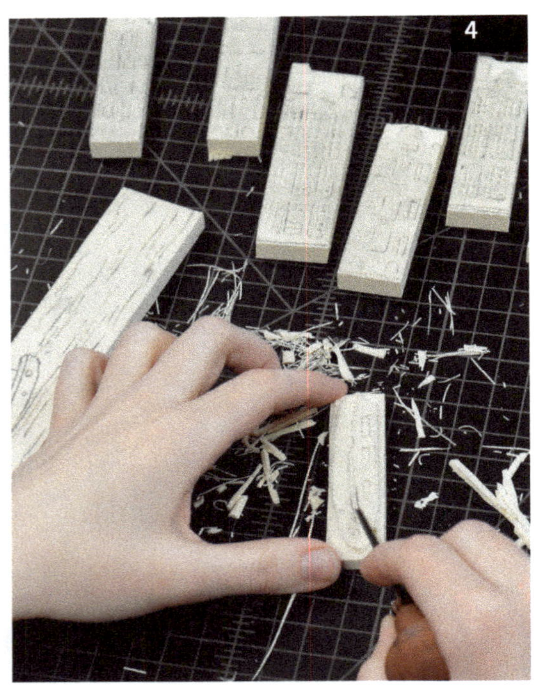

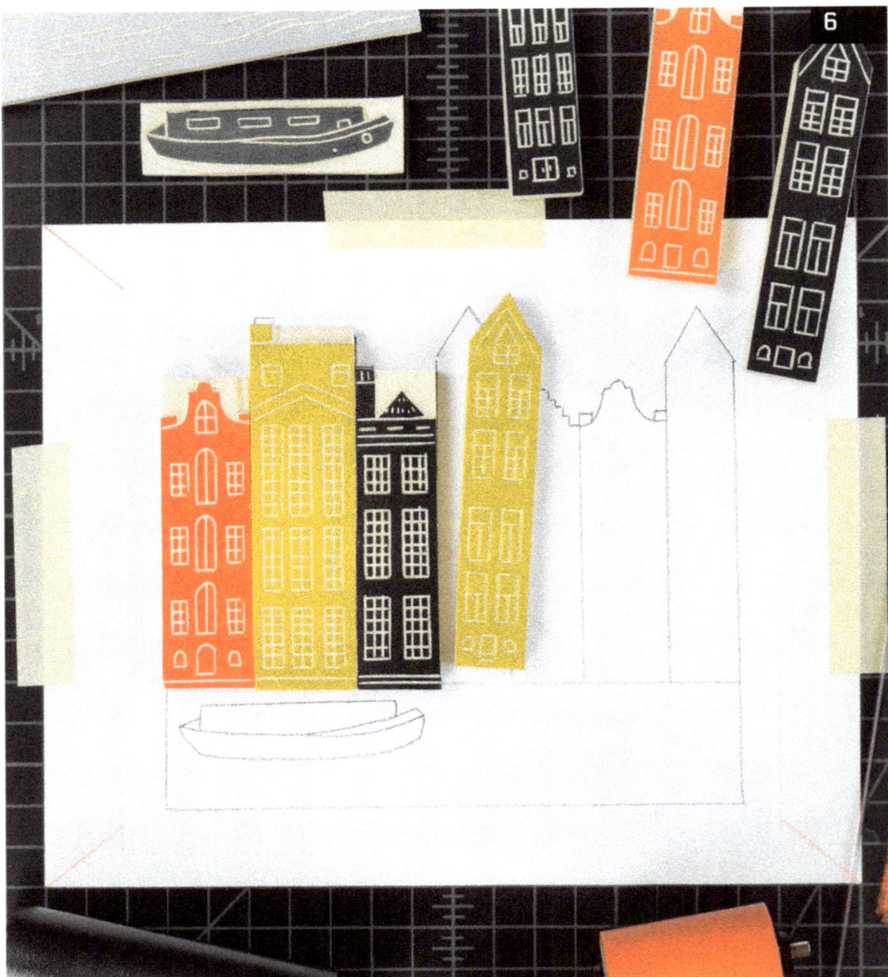

4 / Let your pencil lines be the guide for carving. Choose a narrow gouge that is close in width to your pencil marks for cutting the outlines. Choose a wider gouge for carving and removing the rubber material from broader areas around the pencil lines. Go slowly and let the tool do the work. Keep your fingers out of the way. Turn the block as you carve any curves.

5 / Decide on the size of your printing paper. Prepare a registration jig by cutting a sheet of mat board the same size as the printing paper. Tape the jig to your work surface. Take the outline drawing you created in step 1 and tape it to the center of the jig so that it matches the orientation of the carved sections of block. To eliminate potential white spaces between the sections, they will all be printed at the same time.

6 / Follow the directions for inking on page 24. Roll a small amount of ink on the platen with a brayer, then roll a thin, even coat of ink on the appropriate block. Place the inked blocks into position over the outlined drawing on the jig. You're ready to print.

7 / Line up the printing paper with the bottom edge and corners of the registration jig and hold it in place with one hand. Grasp the opposite edge of the paper at midpoint with your thumb and index finger. Hold the edge up so that no ink from the block is transferred prematurely. Once aligned, carefully lay the paper down in one fluid motion.

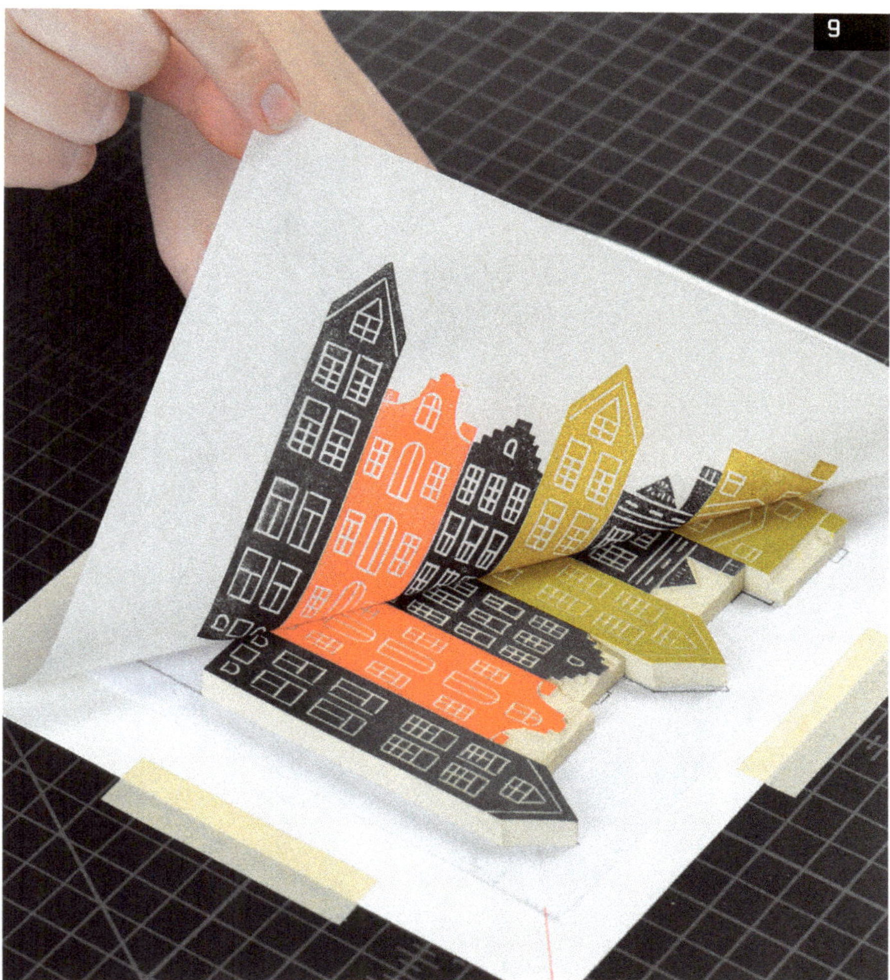

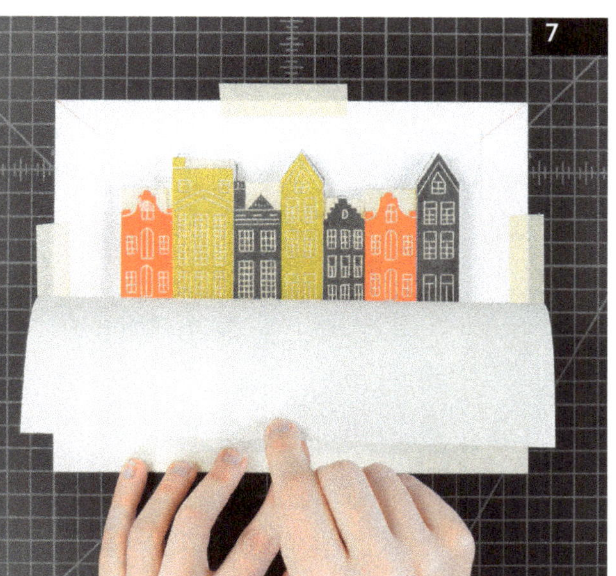

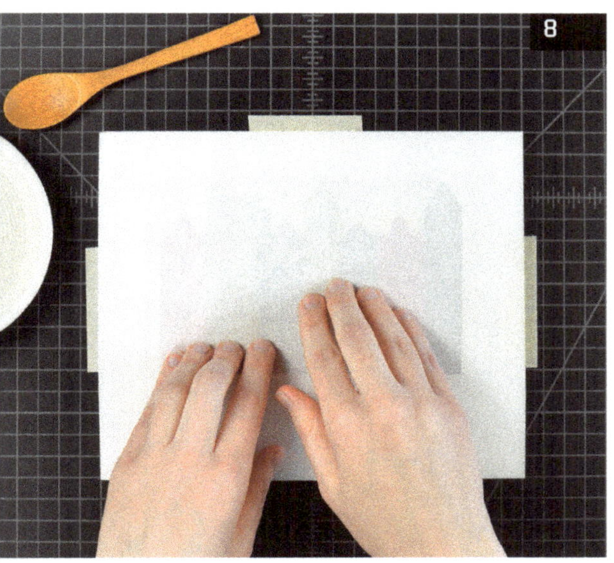

8 / Burnish the back of the printing paper to transfer the ink. Use a baren, the back of a wooden spoon, or your fingers to complete the transfer. Experience will teach you what works best, but be thorough and consistent as you burnish to ensure a smooth, even print.

9 / Slowly and carefully pull your print from the block, and allow it to dry. Save the jig for future printing sessions. Enjoy your print. Art prints make great gifts!

If you've already carved detailed blocks and are looking for printing variations, adding spot color is a great way to expand your technique. It's your creative choice whether to make the areas of color large or small, directly lined up with the image or offset. The transparency-sheet method of registration will be a valuable tool in your store of printmaking knowledge. With the help of the transparent sheet, you can create an accurate spot of color from your carved block as well as register multiple blocks for printing. Save the transparency sheet when you're done, and use it to print a new edition at a later time with the same accuracy.

SPOT-COLOR PRINT: FEATHERS

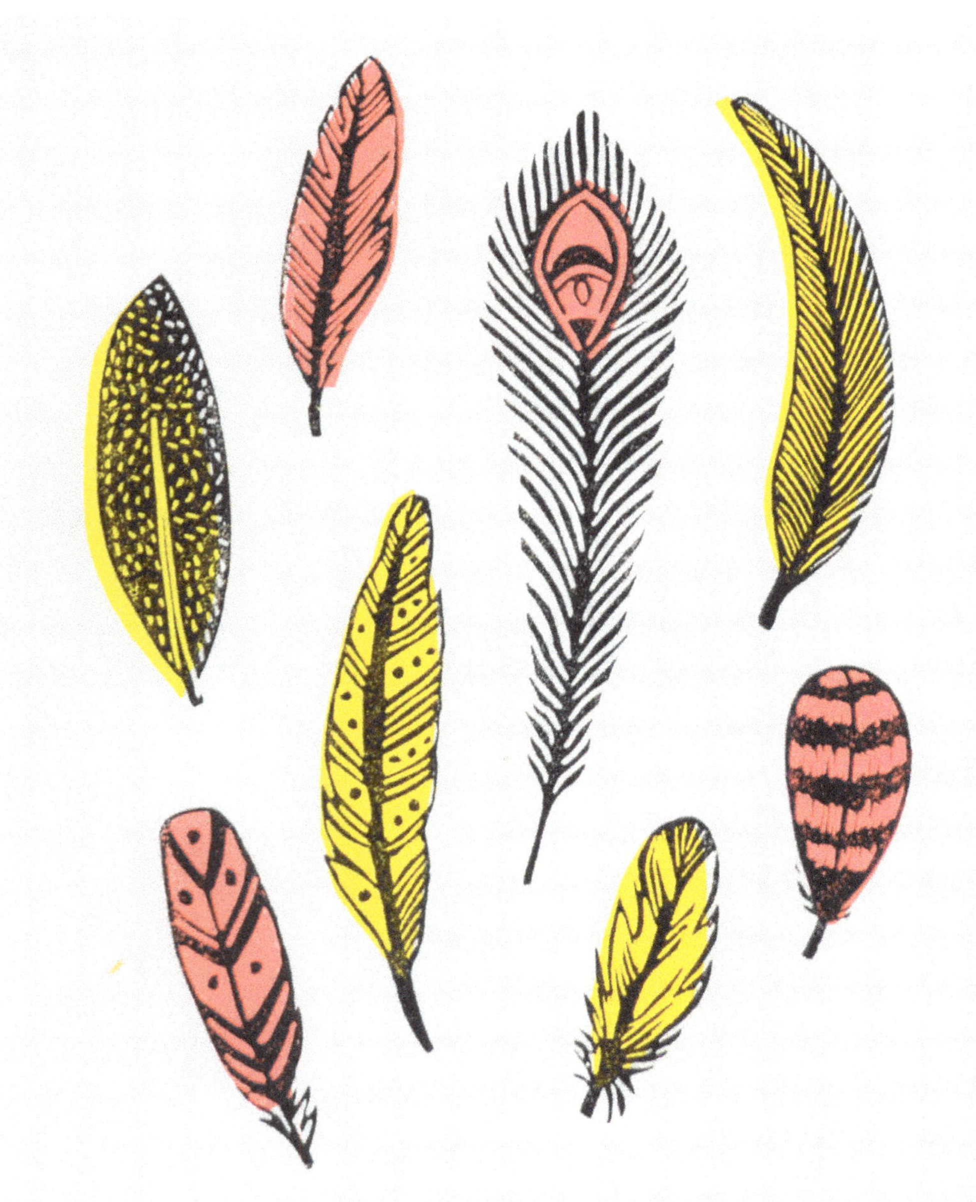

TOOLS AND MATERIALS

- drawing paper
- soft lead pencil
- 2 equal-size dense rubber carving blocks
- cutting mat
- bone folder
- craft knife
- gouges of various sizes
- mat board or card stock
- scissors
- masking tape
- acetate transparency sheet
- colored pencils
- water-soluble printing inks
- brayers
- inking platens
- baren or wooden spoon (optional)
- newsprint
- printing paper

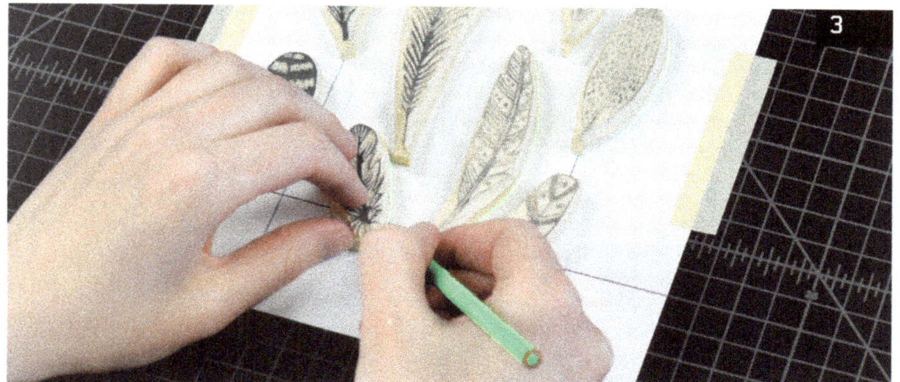

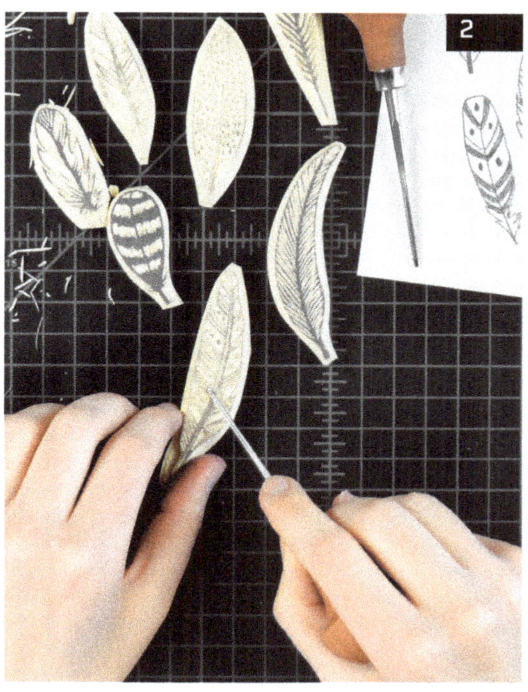

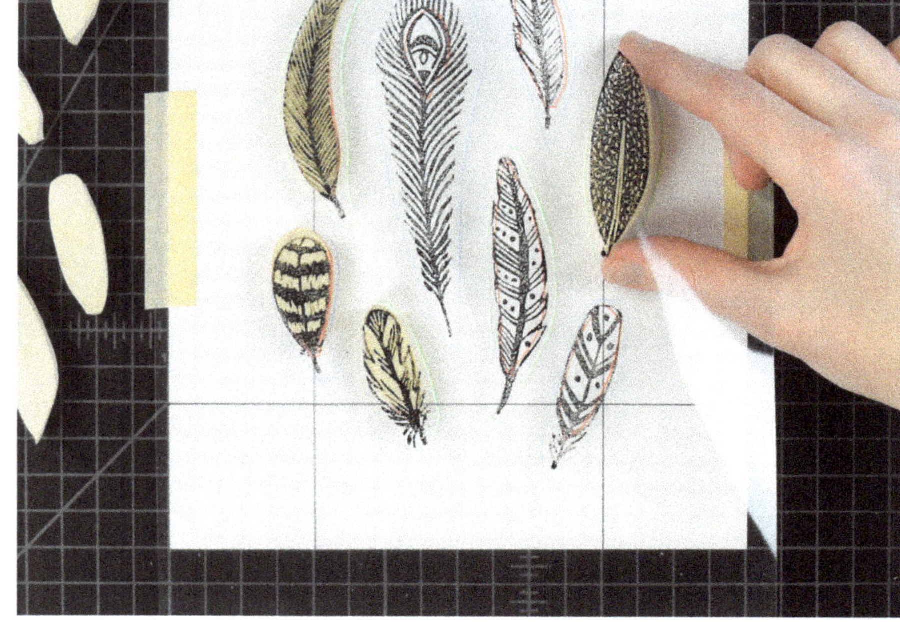

1 / Create your sketch on paper using a soft lead pencil. Place the drawing face down on one of the carving blocks. Transfer the image to the block by rubbing the back of the paper with a bone folder. Rub from the center toward the outside edges to achieve a clean, consistent transfer. Remove the drawing paper.

2 / Use a craft knife to cut the individual shapes from the rubber block. Leave a narrow border around each. Use the appropriate size gouges to carve the rubber away from the pencil lines. Go slowly, turning the block as you cut around curves.

3 / Cut a registration jig from mat board to the same size as your printing paper. Tape the jig to your work surface. Tape a transparency sheet below the bottom edge of the jig. Arrange your carved blocks on the jig. Use pencil lines to designate the border of the print. With a colored pencil, trace around the placement of the carved blocks. Remove the blocks for inking.

4 / Follow the directions for inking on page 24. Roll a small amount of ink on the platen with a brayer, and then roll a thin, even coat of ink on your carved blocks. Place the blocks back on the jig in their original positions within their penciled outlines. Slowly roll the transparency sheet onto the inked blocks. Apply light pressure with your fingers to transfer the ink onto the acetate.

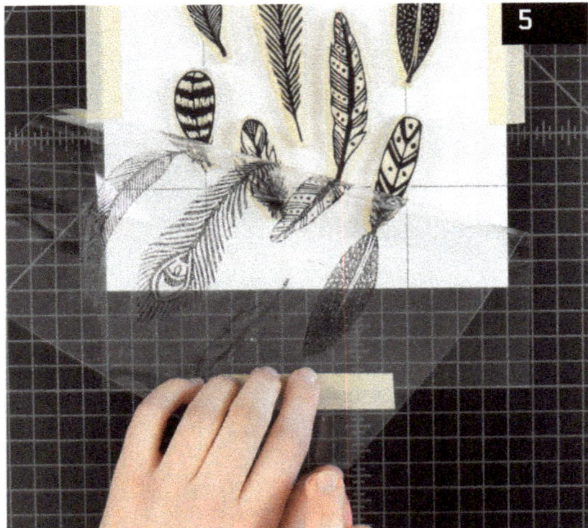

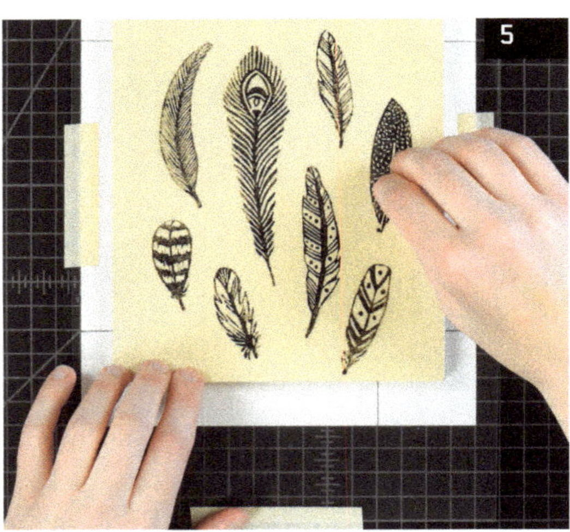

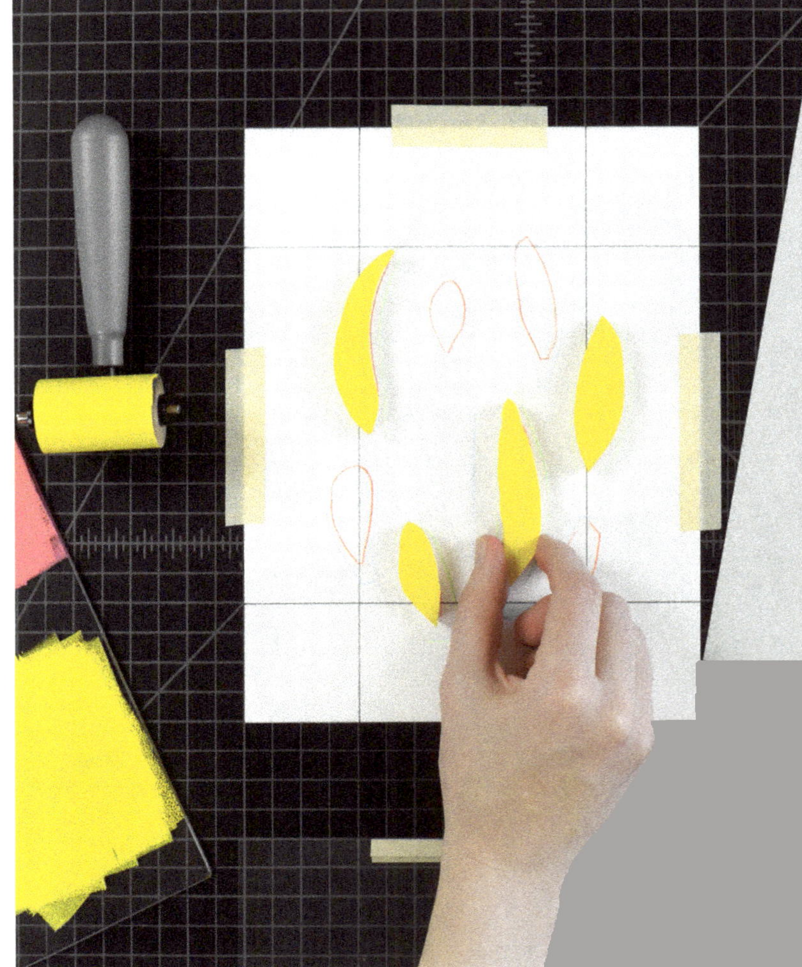

5 / Pull the transparency sheet off the carved blocks and remove the blocks from the jig. While the ink on the acetate is still wet, set the second, uncarved rubber block on the jig. Roll the transparency sheet down again, on top of the block. Rub the surface of the acetate with your fingers to transfer the inked design to the block. Pull the transparency sheet off the block and allow the ink on the block to dry.

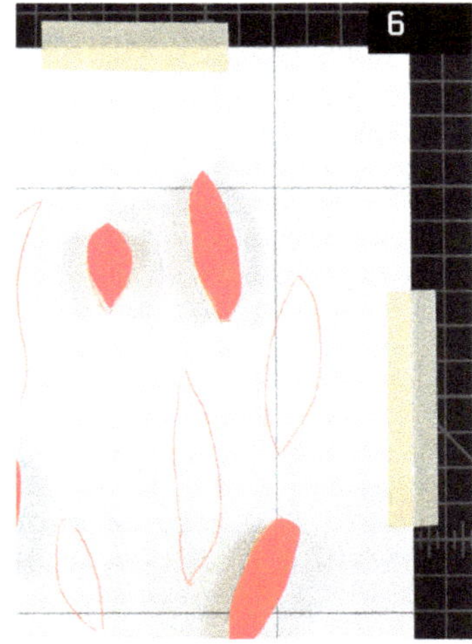

6 / Cut your color spots from the uncarved block with a craft knife, following the lines of the printed ink transfers. The color spots can be smaller than, the same size as, or larger than the corresponding shapes of your carved designs; it's up to you. Place the color spots on the jig, then roll up the transparency sheet to cover them. Use the transferred designs on the acetate to determine where you want the color spots to appear. Decide what color each should be. Then, using a different color pencil for each, outline the shapes of the color spots on the jig. You're ready to print.

7 / Using the inking and printing directions on page 24, roll a small amount of ink on the platen with a brayer. Roll the ink onto a spot-color block and position it on the jig, using the outlines that you created in step 6.

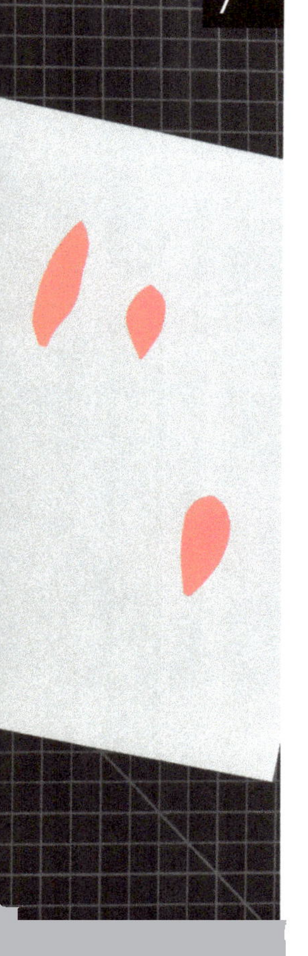

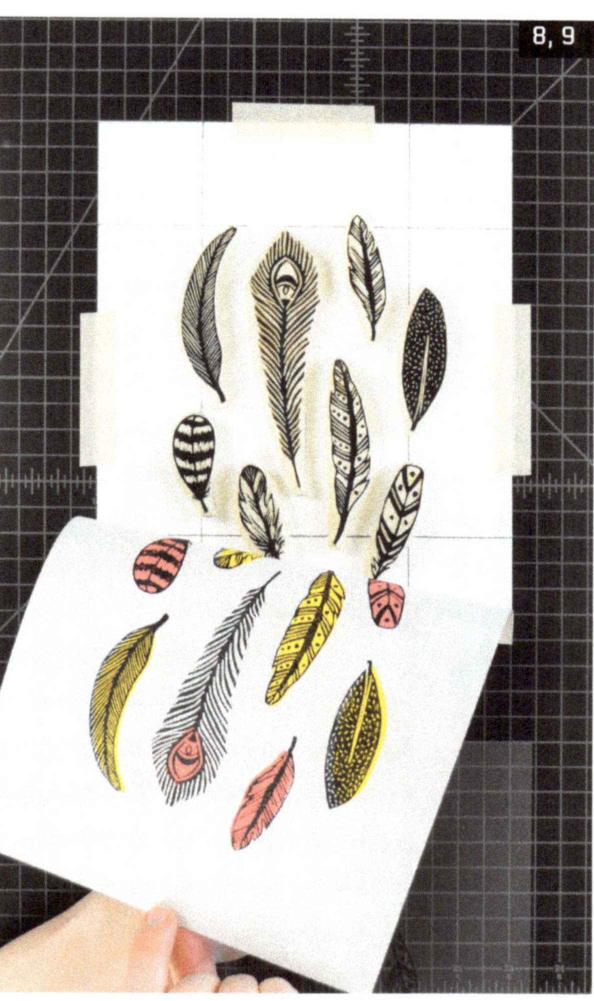

8 / Line up your printing paper with the bottom edge and corners of the jig, holding it in place with one hand and keeping it lifted with the other. Carefully lay the paper down in one fluid motion. Rub the back of the paper with your fingertips to transfer the ink from the spot-color blocks.

9 / Repeat, as necessary, until all the color spots have been printed. Set the color blocks aside and return to your original carved blocks.

10 / Ink the carved blocks and arrange them on the jig within the outlines. Repeat the printing process by carefully registering the printing paper on the jig and laying it down in one motion. Burnish the back of the paper with your fingers, the baren, or wooden spoon to transfer the ink. Carefully lift the printing paper and allow it to dry.

11 / You did it! Frame and display your new art print!

NOTE

If you have multiple brayers and inking platens, you can roll out all your colors at once and print them all together.

If you have only one brayer and platen, work with one color at a time, washing and drying the brayer and platen between printing each color.

VARIATIONS

Individual blocks can be used like stamps to create more than just art prints. Explore repeating patterns like this half-drop, or use them to print gift tags and wrapping paper. Be as exact or loose as you prefer. A ruler is a helpful guide when you eyeball the placement of each repeated block.

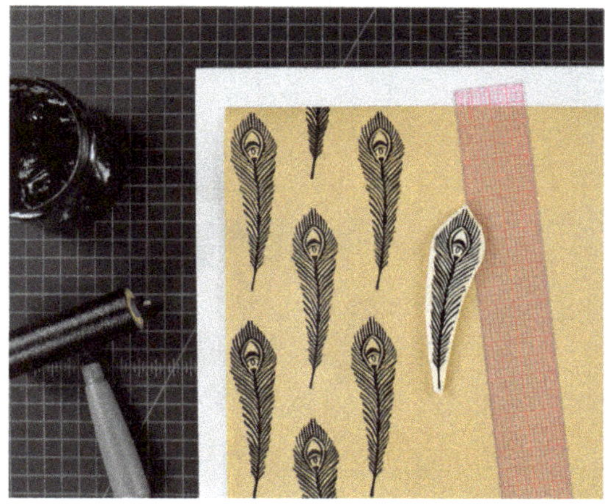

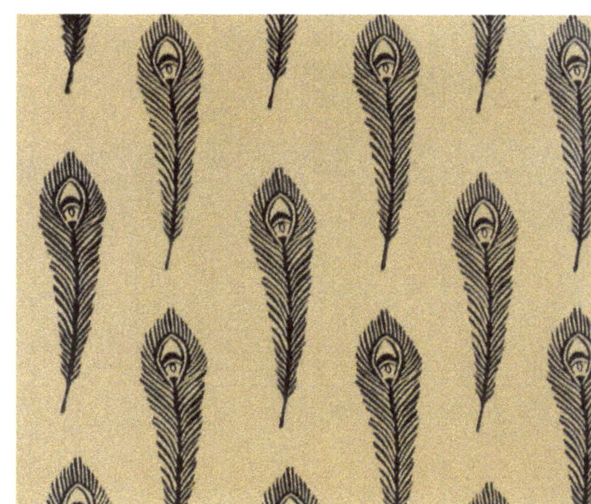

It's easy to create multicolored prints without complicated registration techniques. With a little planning in the early drawing stages of the design, creating a beautiful print is possible with just eyeballed registration. This type of simple print makes a great greeting card design or art print. The formula I often use with this type of simple registration is a single-color icon block in the center, combined with a second block to frame and complete the image.

TWO-COLOR PRINTING: UKULELE

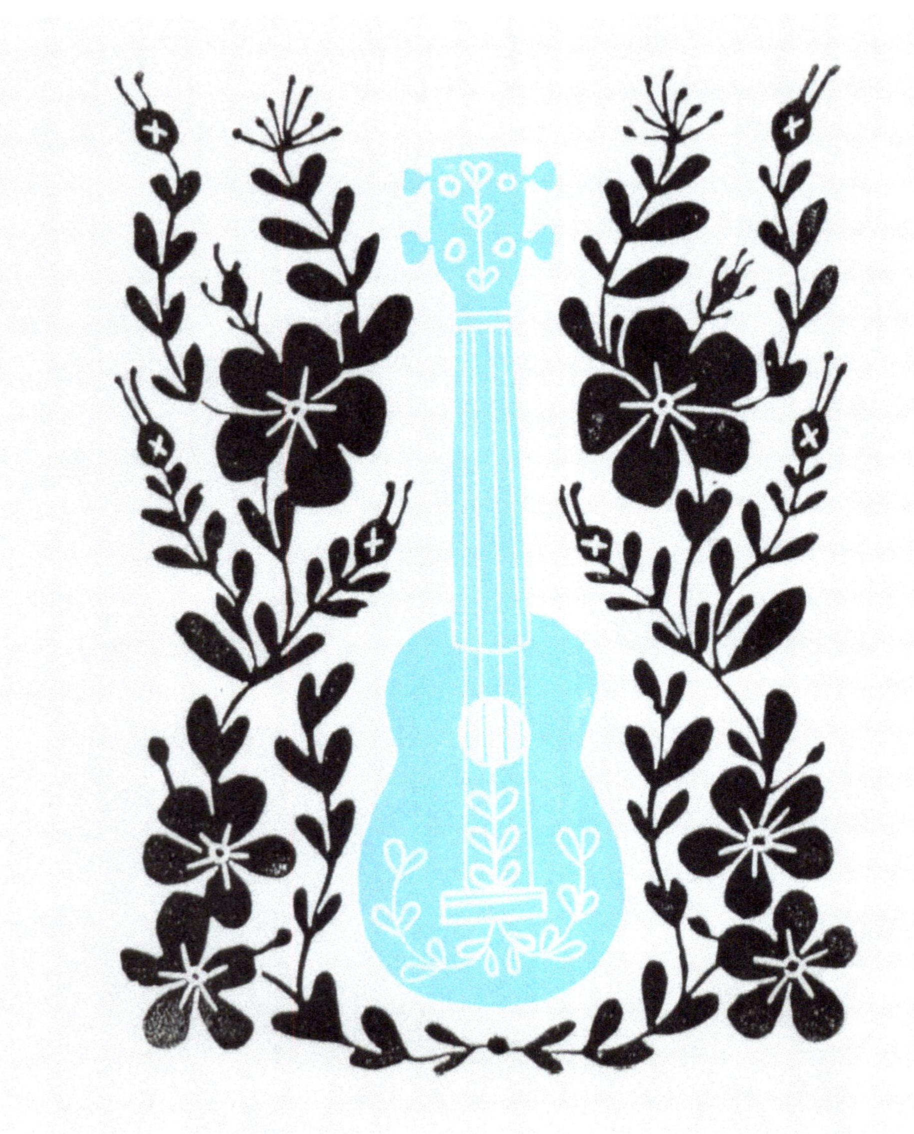

TOOLS AND MATERIALS

drawing paper
soft lead pencil
tracing paper
dense rubber carving block
bone folder
ruler
cutting mat
craft knife
gouges of various sizes
mat board or card stock
soap, water, and sponge
water-soluble printing inks
brayers
inking platen
palette knives
newsprint or scrap paper
masking tape
baren or wooden spoon
Japanese printing paper

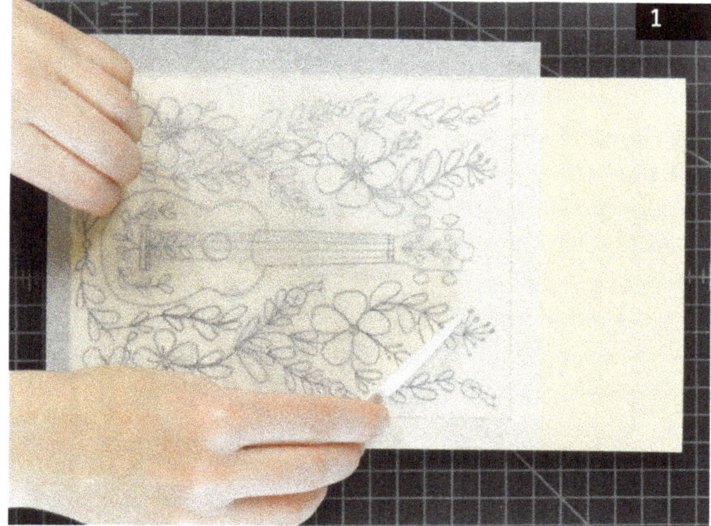

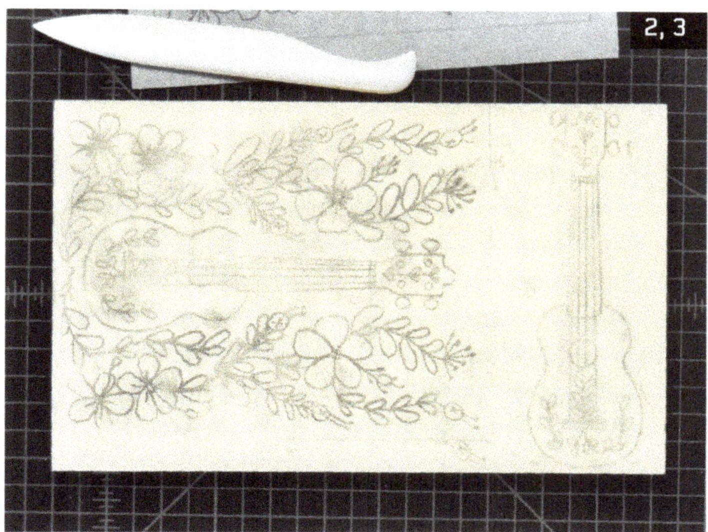

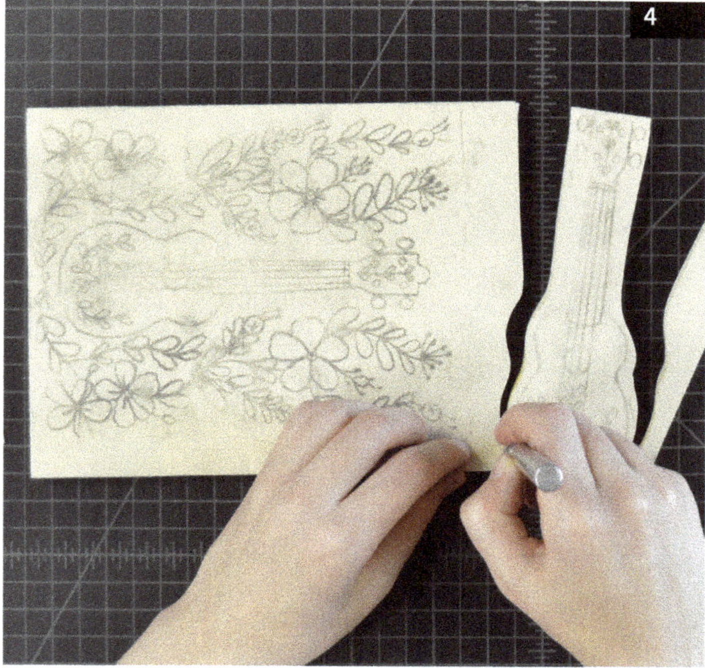

1 / Work out a design for your two-color print with a pencil and paper. Plan the different color areas so that they do not overlap when printed, and so that—once they've been carved—you'll be able to position the second color by eye after the first is printed. I like to work out a large, decorative background block with a smaller, simple element that can be used in other projects or as a stamp—like this ukulele.

2 / Once your image is complete, trace it onto tracing paper with a soft lead pencil. Place the traced drawing face down on your carving block. Rub the back of the paper with a bone folder to transfer the pencil to the block. Tracing paper allows you to see exactly where your image is and to use your block efficiently. Lift up one corner to check your transfer. If you're happy with it, remove the paper from the block.

3 / Transfer the main element of the print—the ukulele—to a separate printing block or to a separate area of the first block that can be trimmed off. The soft lead pencil will allow you to transfer the lines a couple of times without having to retrace your drawing.

4 / Once both images are transferred, use a ruler and craft knife to cut out the two main elements of the design border and ukulele. Insert the craft knife in the block so that you cut all the way through to the cutting mat underneath. Pull the craft knife toward yourself carefully, making clean cuts. Leave a small margin around the outline of the ukulele so that it can be placed accurately when you are ready to print.

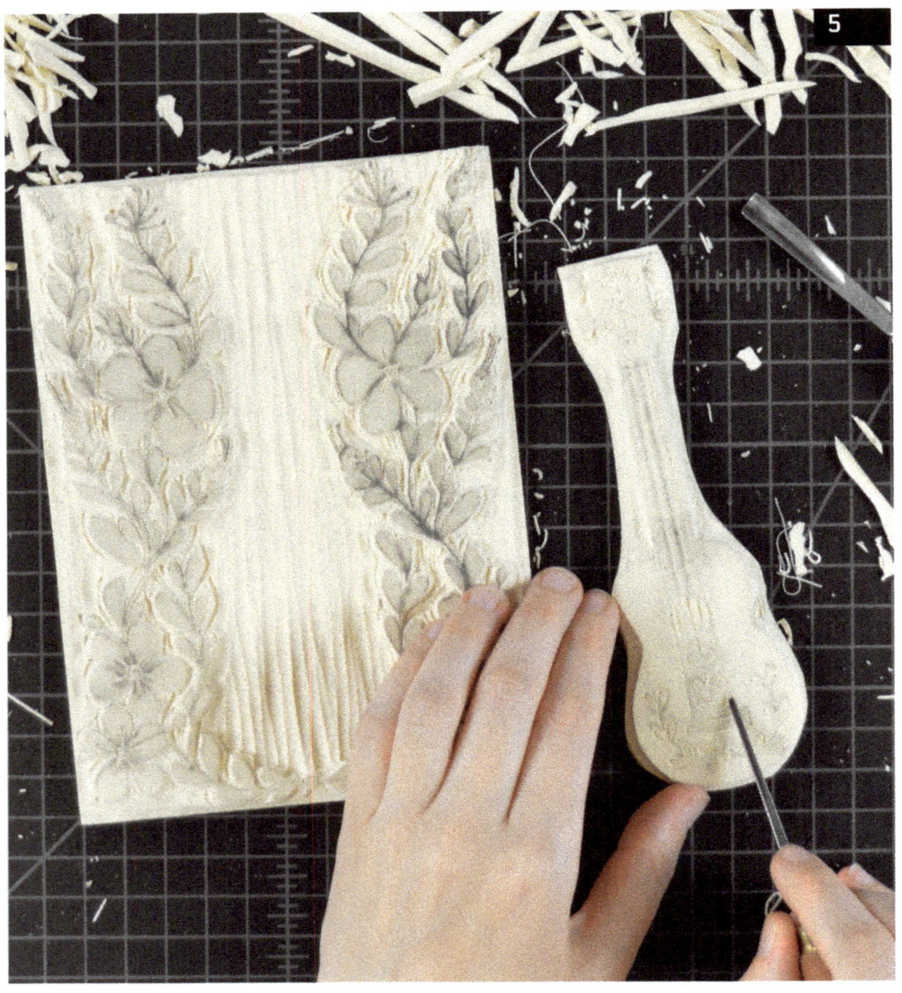

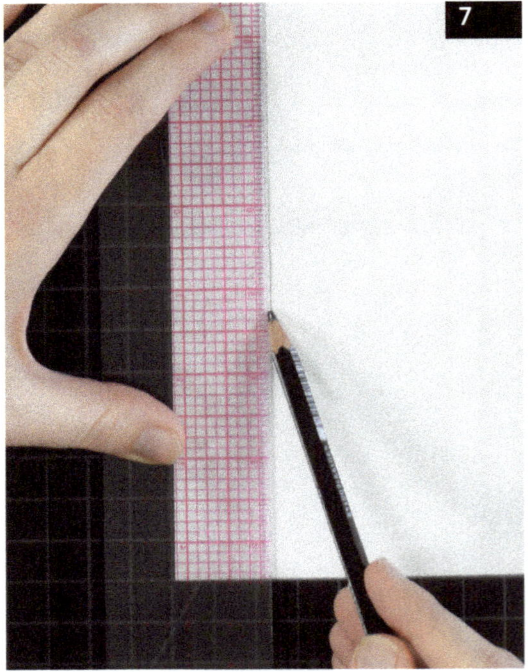

5 / With the blocks cut out, you are now ready to carve. Choose a larger V-shape gouge to outline the drawings. Use a wider U-shape gouge to remove the larger areas of material. Finish your blocks by carving details using the smallest veiner gouge. When complete, clean your block with soap and water. Allow it to dry.

6 / Prepare your printing area by assembling your blocks, inks, brayer, inking platen, palette knives, newsprint, mat board, and printing paper. It's helpful to have all of these supplies close at hand.

7 / Cut a printing jig the same size as your printing paper from the mat board. Draw margins on the jig at least 1" (2.5 cm) wide. Tape the jig in place on your work surface.

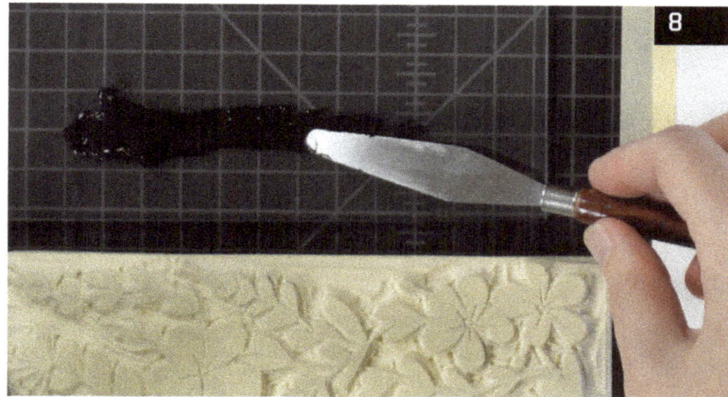

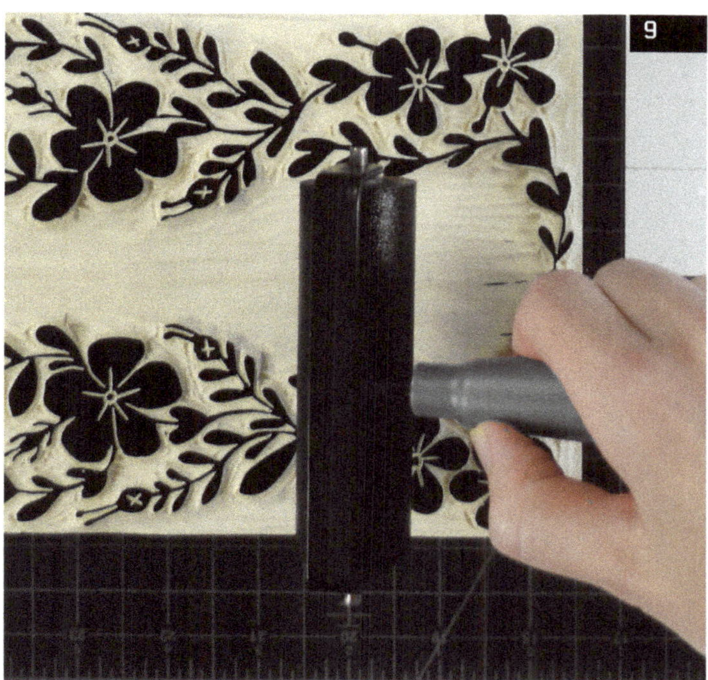

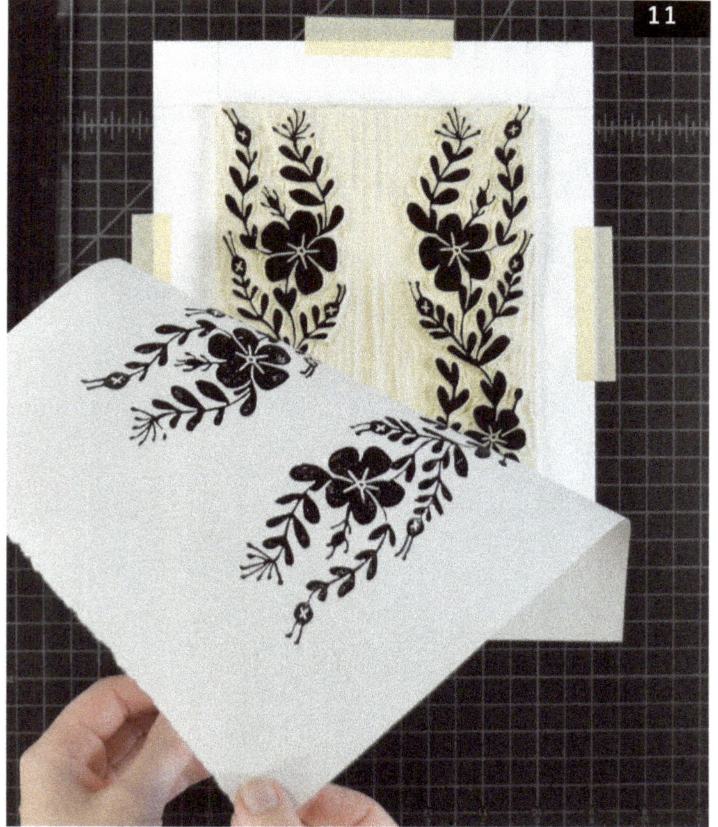

8 / Using a palette knife, spread a small amount of ink on the platen. Ink your brayer following the directions on page 24, then begin inking your block.

9 / Roll the block with thin, even coats of ink. Go back to the platen to pick up more ink, as needed. The ink should have a nice opaque look on the block but not be so thick that it fills in the carved lines. Test print your block using newsprint.

10 / When you're happy with your test print and have made any adjustments to the carving, re-ink your block and place it on the printing jig within the margin lines. Line up the printing paper along the bottom edge of the jig. Using one hand to stabilize the paper along the bottom edge, carefully roll the printmaking paper down onto the block in one continuous motion.

11 / Rub the back of the print using your fingers, a baren, or a wooden spoon. Japanese paper is thin enough that you will be able to see how the transfer is progressing. Peel back one corner of the print, checking for an even transfer. If you are happy with the look of the print, carefully peel the paper off the block and allow the print to dry.

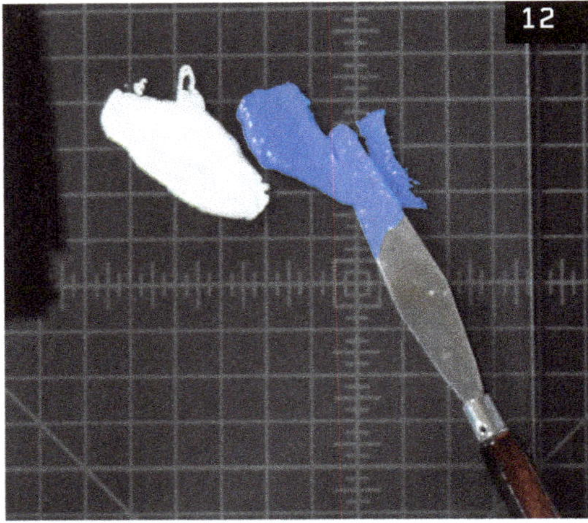

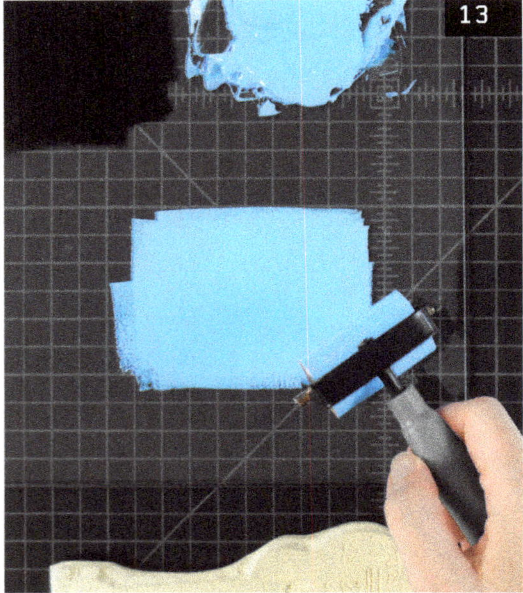

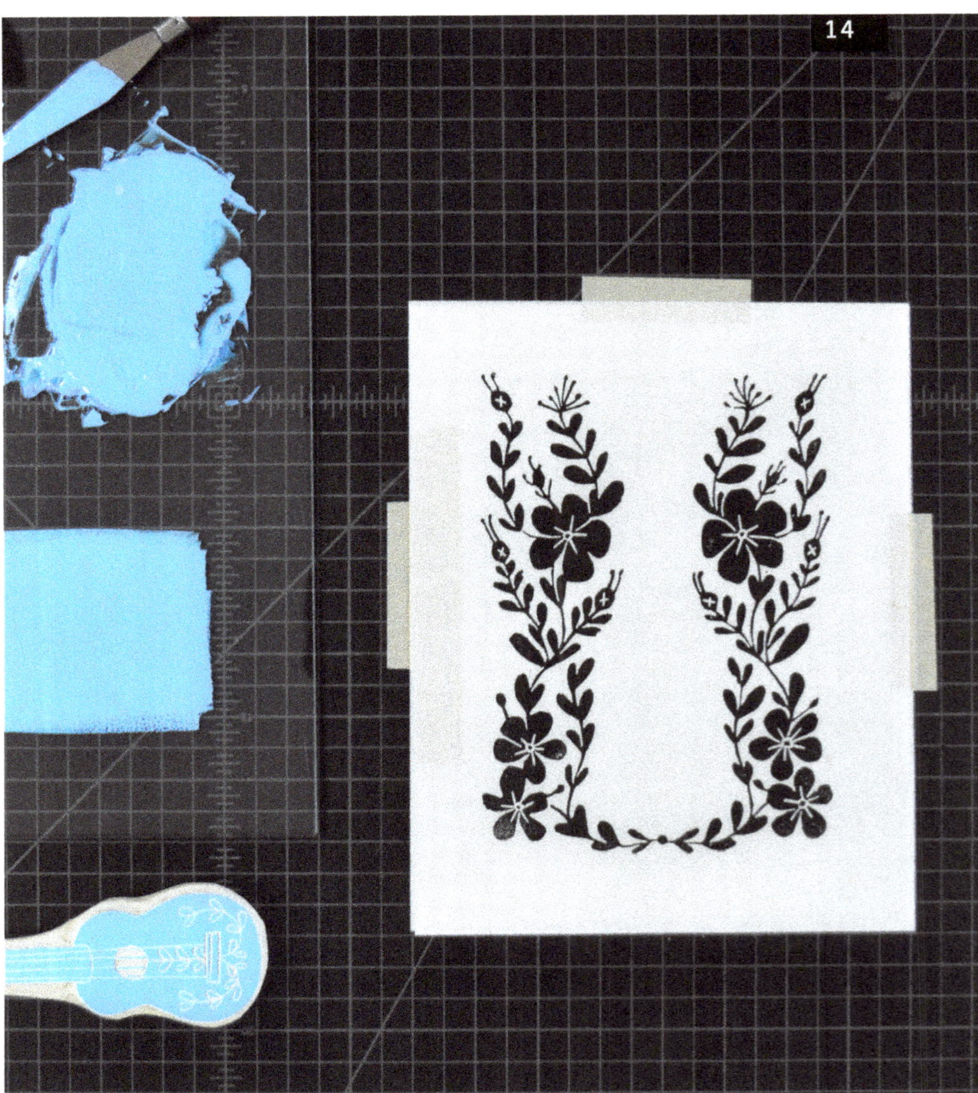

12 / You're ready to prepare for the second color. Wash and dry the platen and brayer. If, as shown here, you want to mix two ink colors for a new shade, place the two colors on the platen. Mix them with a palette knife, keeping the ink in a small area and leaving enough room to roll out your ink with the brayer.

13 / Roll the ink on the platen and your block with the brayer following the instructions on page 24.

14 / Place the dry print from step 11 on the jig, lining up the edges of the printing paper and jig. You will be printing the second color block, inked-side down.

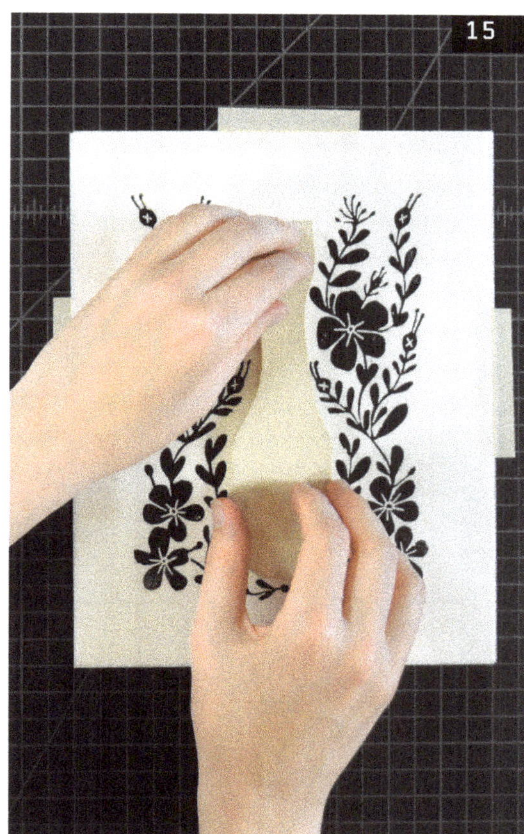

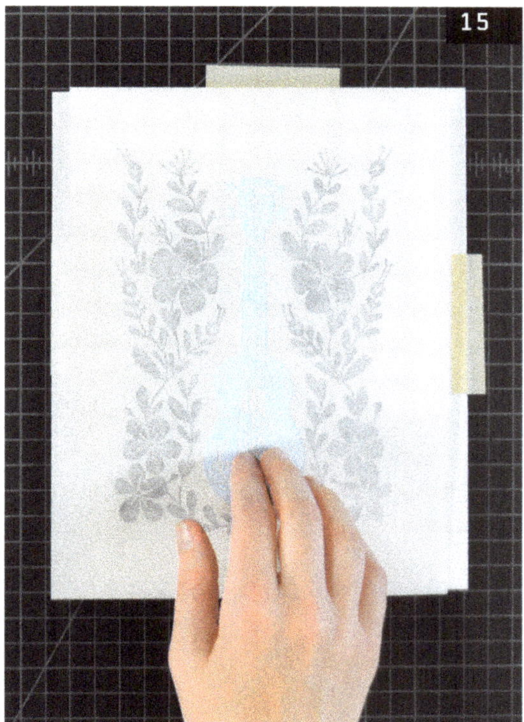

NOTE

The thickness of a dense rubber block can make registering the printing paper difficult if there isn't enough clearance in the margin. If the margin is less than 1 inch (2.5 cm), your printing paper can easily come in contact with the ink when you line it up along the edge of the jig.

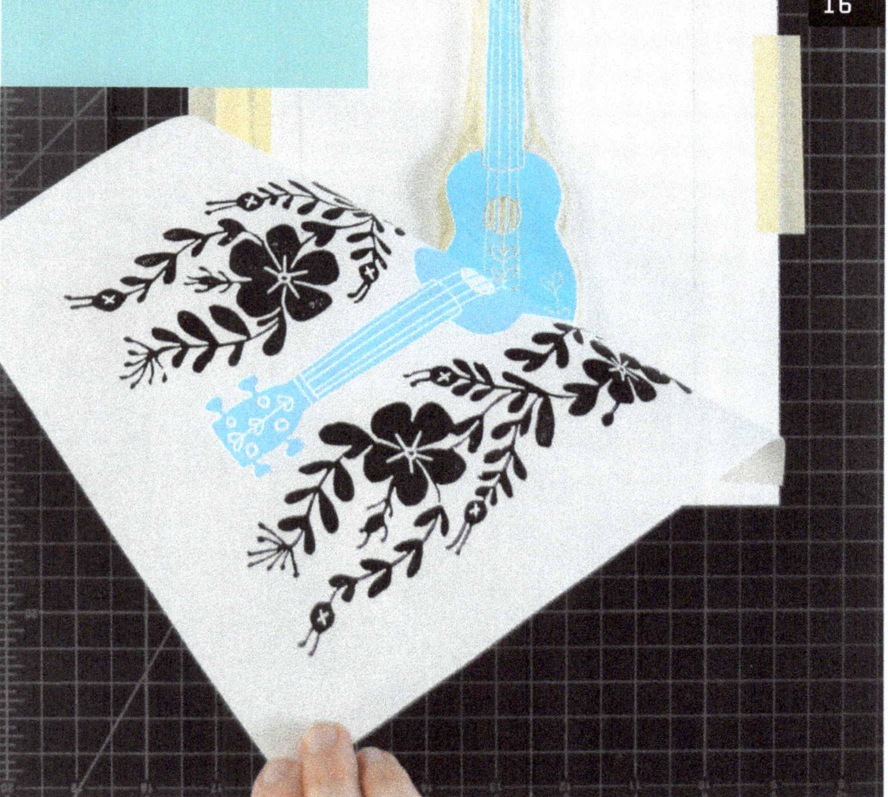

15 / Holding the inked block with two hands, carefully position it ink-side down on your paper lining it up by eye. For the best ink transfer, flip the block and paper over together and burnish the back of the paper. The easiest way to do this is to carefully slide the printing paper and block to the edge of your work surface, then support them from below with your hand and flip the two over together, without moving the print paper. Burnish the back of the paper with your fingers, a baren, or wooden spoon.

16 / Pull your print from the block and enjoy it. As you explore printmaking more, you'll discover this eyeballed, two-color registration method has many applications.

Hand-colored prints provide an interesting opportunity to blend printmaking with watercolor painting. This is a popular method of printmaking, one used often in children's book illustrations. This colorful print allows more spontaneity than a traditional linocut, and you do not have to worry about registration. Note: Use soy-based inks for this technique, as water-soluble inks will bleed if they come into contact with your watercolor paints.

HAND-COLORED LINOCUT: CORAL REEF

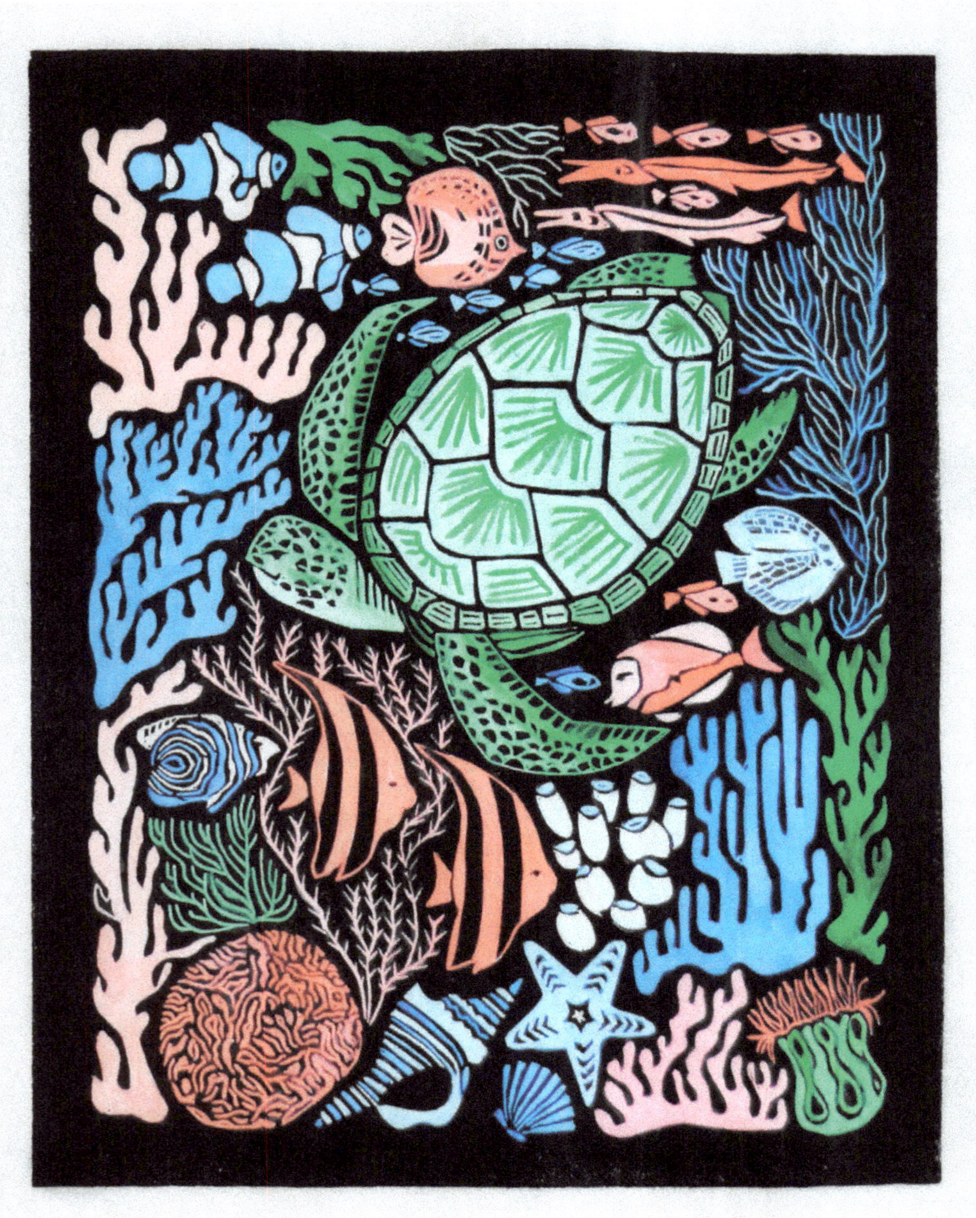

TOOLS AND MATERIALS

- drawing paper
- soft lead pencil
- battleship linoleum carving block
- cutting mat
- craft knife
- ruler
- india ink and brush
- white carbon transfer paper
- masking tape
- colored pencil
- gouges of various sizes
- mat board or card stock
- soy-based printing inks
- brayer
- inking platen
- newsprint or scrap paper
- Japanese printing paper
- baren or wooden spoon
- ategami paper (optional)
- watercolor paints
- small paint brushes

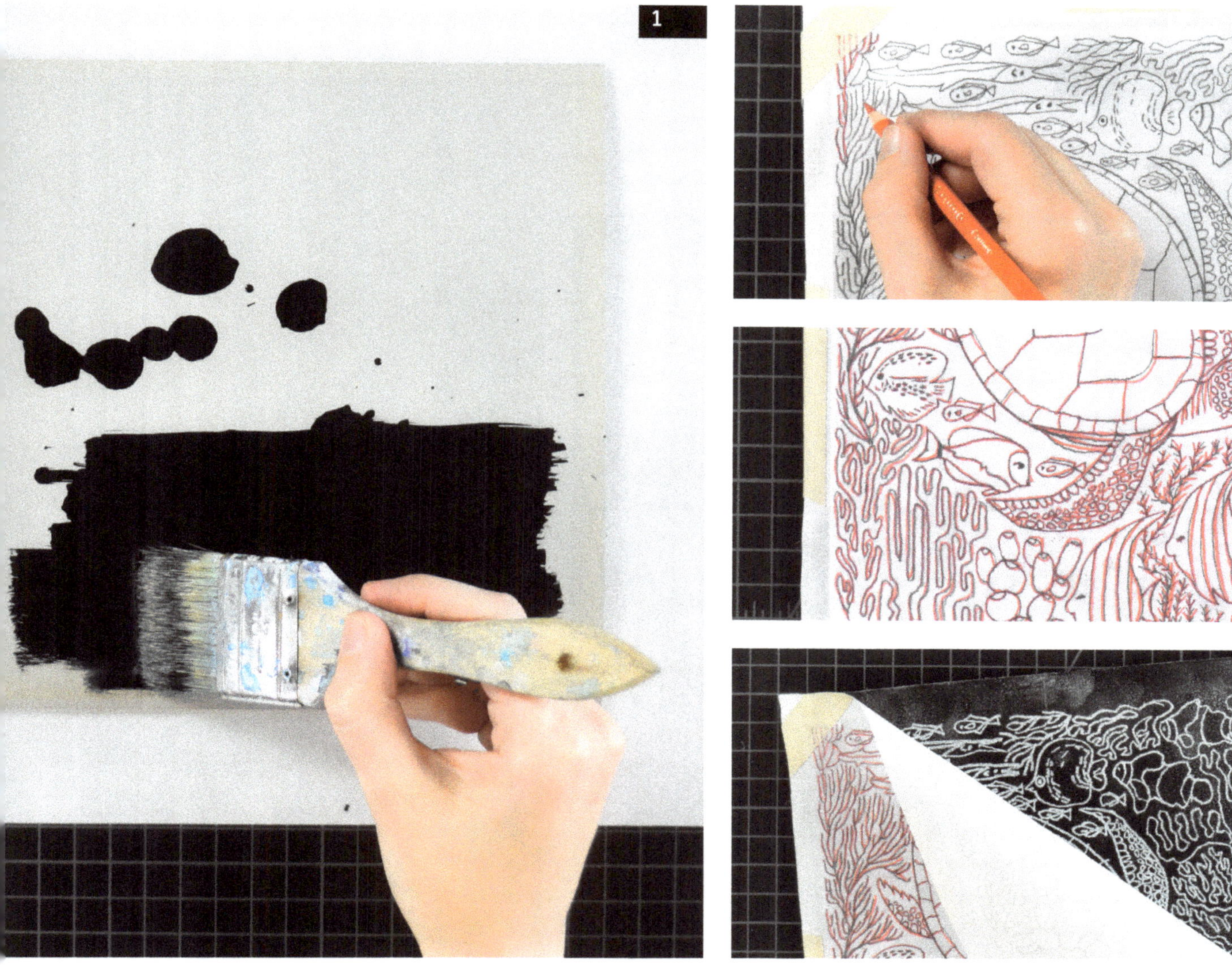

1 / Work out a detailed drawing for your image with a pencil and paper. Prepare a block of linoleum by cutting it to the size of your drawing using a craft knife and a ruler: Only one block is needed. Paint the carving surface of the block with the india ink and allow it to dry. When you carve the block, the removal of the painted areas will reveal a pale gray color. This will show an approximation of what the print will look like as your carving progresses.

2 / When the india ink on the block is dry, you're ready to transfer your image to the block. Use white carbon paper to transfer the image. Sandwich the carbon paper between your drawing and the block. Tape both the carbon paper and drawing into place.

3 / Redraw over your image using a colored pencil: The colored line will show which areas have been completed. Once finished, peel back one corner to check for a good transfer.

4 / If you're happy with the transfer, remove the carbon paper and drawing from your block.

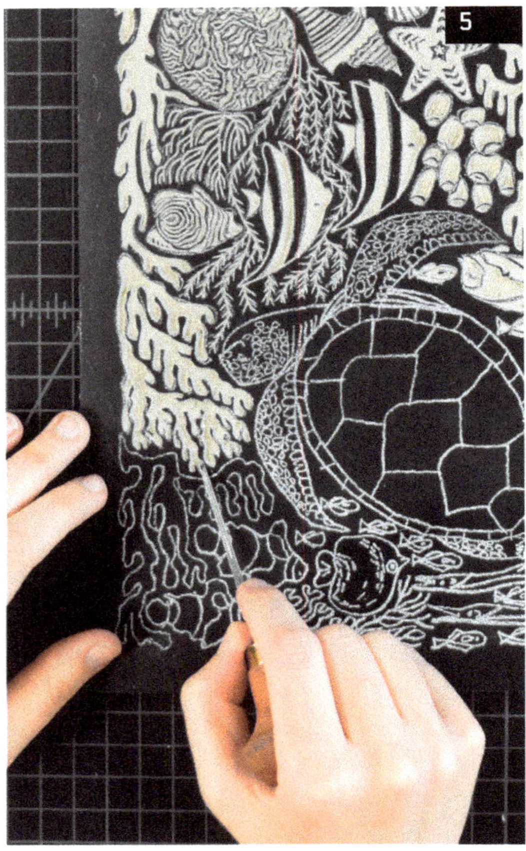

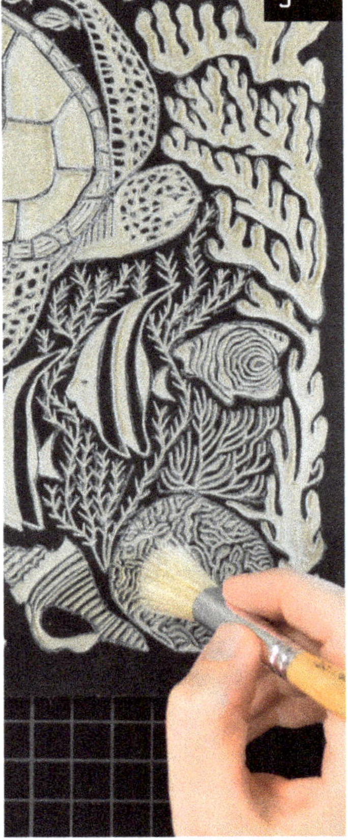

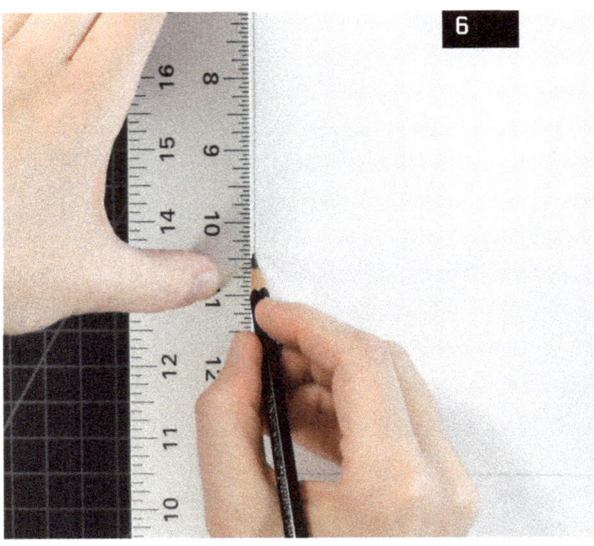

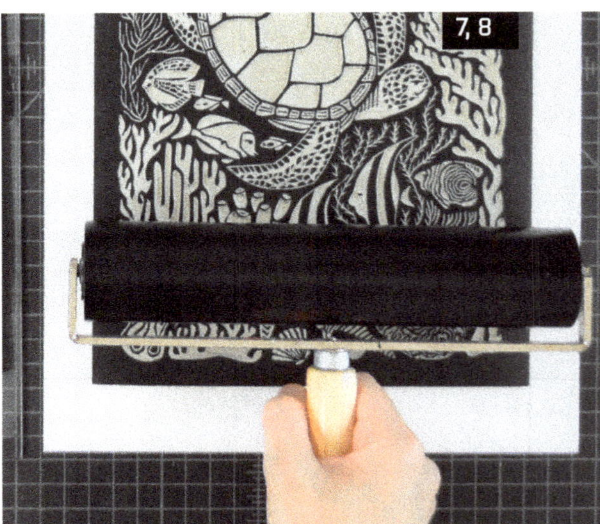

5 / You're ready to carve. Try different gouges, alternating their use to take away smaller and larger areas of linoleum, always remembering to carve away from yourself. To avoid smearing the carbon-transferred lines, it's best to carve inward from the edges of the block, rotating the block as you go. Avoid placing your hands on the transfer lines for too long. Once you finish carving, brush the block with a dry paintbrush, removing any remaining scraps of carved material.

6 / Prepare a simple registration jig from the mat board. Cut the jig to the same size as your printing paper to make registration easy. With a ruler and pencil, draw margins on the jig to indicate the placement of the block: This will ensure consistent prints. Tape the jig to your work surface.

7 / Prepare your printing area by assembling your block, inks, brayer, platen, newsprint, and printing paper within easy reach. Ink the block, following the directions on page 24. Roll a small amount of soy-based ink on the inking platen with the brayer. Roll the ink, thinly and evenly on the block.

NOTE

When working with soy-based inks, you will notice that you may need to do several test prints before you achieve a dark, rich color.

NOTE

If you are using a baren for burnishing, you might want to lay a piece of ategami paper in between the printing paper and the baren. Ategami is a slick paper similar to waxed paper, used in Japanese printmaking. It provides a smooth surface for working with the baren and protects the back of your printing paper.

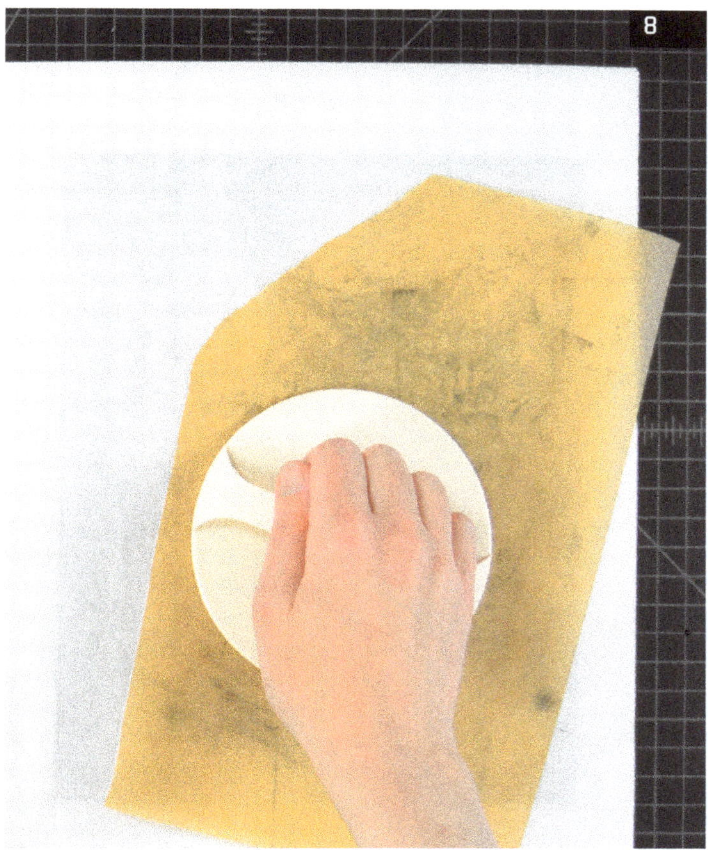

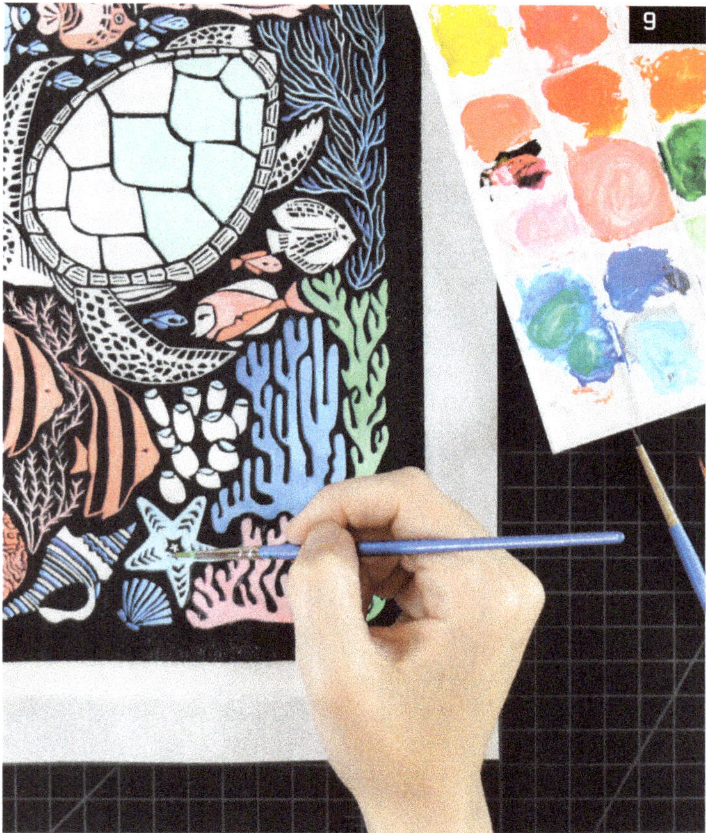

8 / Place the block on the jig and test print the block by laying a piece of newsprint on top of it and burnishing the back of the paper with a baren or wooden spoon. Check the test print and refine the image with your carving tools, if necessary. If your first prints are salt-and-pepper in appearance, continue test printing until the prints have a rich, even opacity. Set aside at least one of your test prints for step 9. Print your edition on the printing paper and set your prints aside to dry. Soy-based inks will need at least 24 hours to dry.

9 / Assemble the watercolor paints, brushes, and a cup of water. Try out your color palette and the strength of your watercolors on the test print that you set aside. Adjust the amount of water, as needed. Practice with the paints on the test print until you achieve the look you desire. When you are comfortable with the paints, you are ready to hand color your edition.

10 / Part of the charm of hand-colored prints is that no two are ever the same. Try painting them in a number of different color schemes and enjoy your one-of-a-kind linocut!

Chine-collé roughly translates as "glued tissue" in French. The *chine* refers to a fine tissue paper that was imported to Europe from China, India, and Japan. This technique is a popular method of adding color and texture to a print without having to carve additional blocks. Traditionally this technique is done with the help of a press, but the effect can be achieved by hand. The striking patterns of chiyogami paper are excellent for chine-collé. Alternatively, use a bright, mulberry washi paper or a patterned paper you create yourself.

LINOCUT WITH CHINE-COLLÉ: SAILBOAT

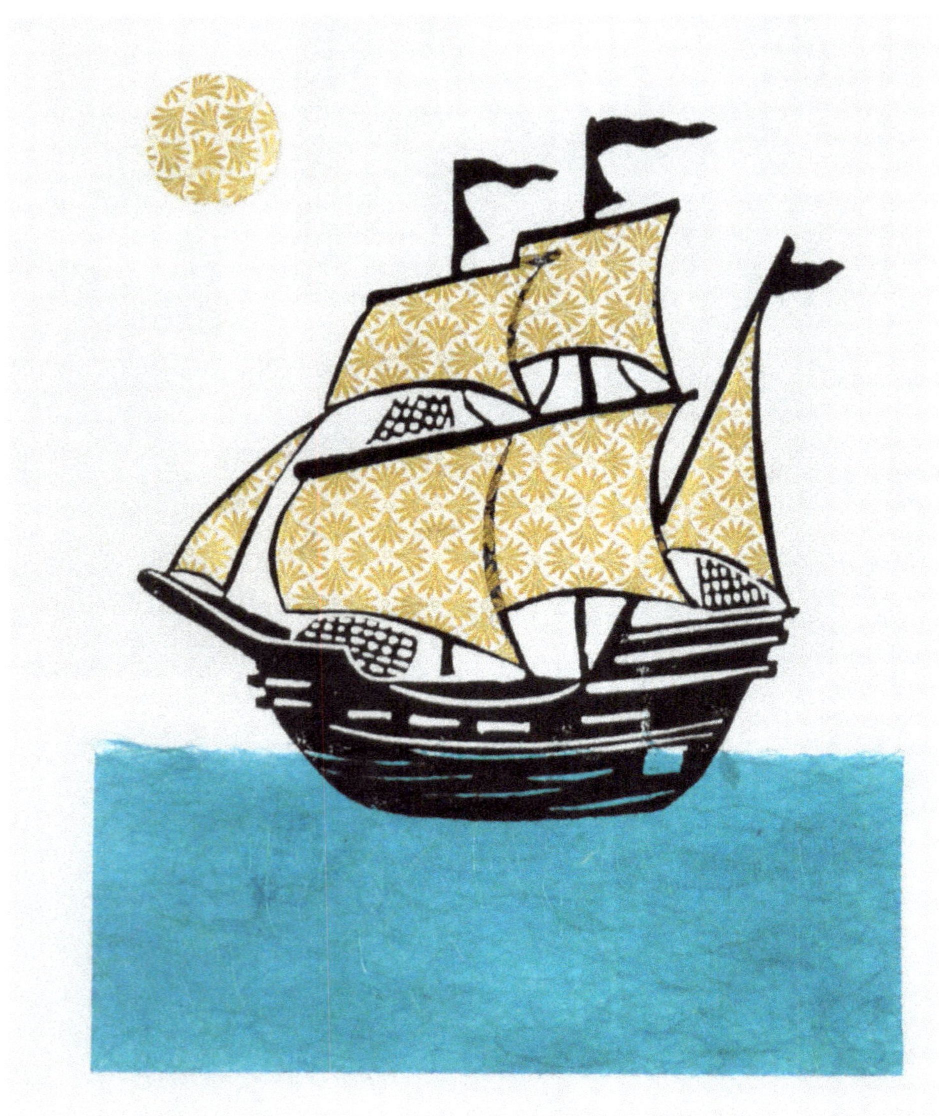

TOOLS AND MATERIALS

- soft lead pencil
- drawing paper
- light box (optional)
- tracing paper
- dense rubber carving block
- bone folder
- cutting mat
- craft knife
- transparent acrylic ruler
- carving gouges in various sizes
- mild soap, water, and sponge, or a baby wipe
- mat board or card stock
- masking tape
- water-soluble printing inks
- brayer
- inking platen
- palette knife
- Japanese printing paper
- washi paper for the water
- chiyogami paper for the sails
- nori paste or PVA glue
- brush for the paste
- newsprint or scrap paper
- baren or wooden spoon
- 1" (2.5 cm) round paper punch, or scissors

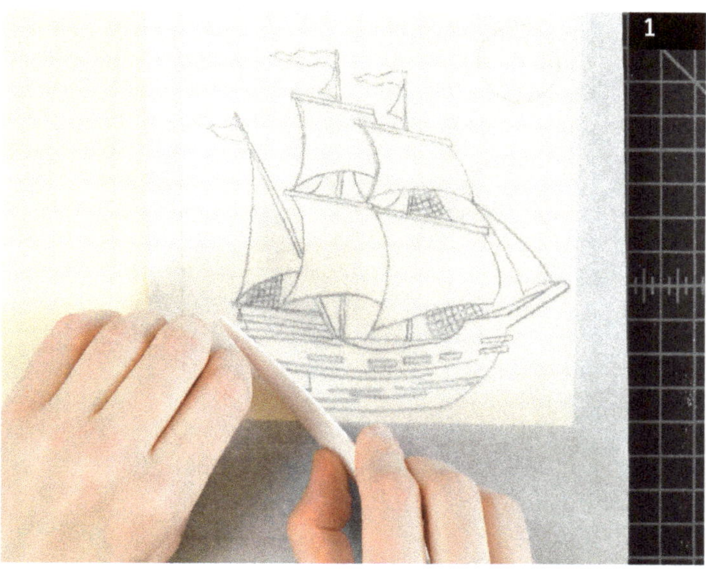

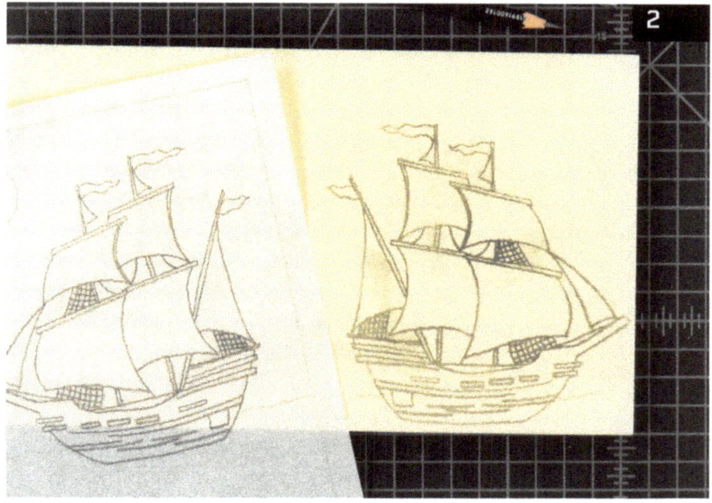

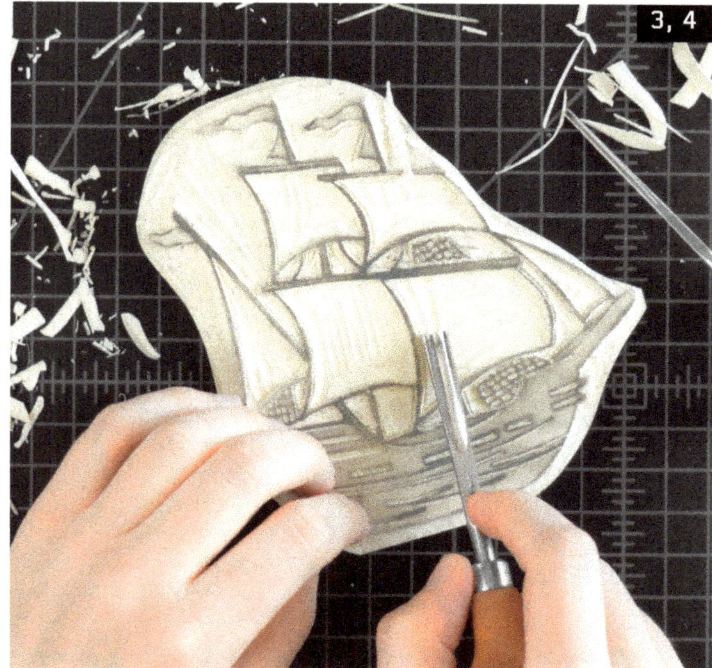

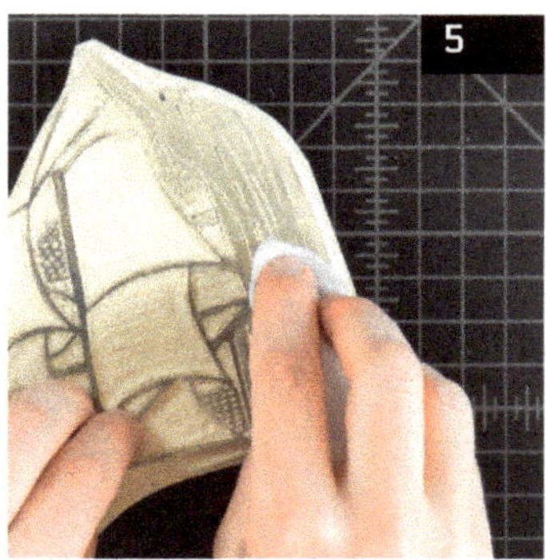

1 / Draw your design on a piece of paper. Place the sketch on a light box or tape it to a bright window. Place a piece of tracing paper over the sketch and trace it in detail with a soft lead pencil. Be sure your lines are clean and clear. All marks will be transferred to the block, so erase any mistakes.

2 / Place your pencil image face down on the rubber block. Use a bone folder to transfer the pencil lines from the paper to the block. Keeping the sheet of paper in place with one hand, rub the back of the paper with the bone folder in the other. Work from the center outward. Lift a corner to check for a consistent transfer.

3 / Place the rubber block on a cutting mat. Use a craft knife to cut out the image from the block. Press down on the knife so that it cuts all the way through the rubber, and carefully outline your image leaving a small margin. For best results, make one smooth and continuous cut. Set aside the cut-away sections of the block for later projects. Now you're ready to carve.

4 / Begin by carving along the outside of the lines with the small V-shaped gouge. Once completed, use a larger U-shaped blade to carve away the broader areas of block material outside the lines. Carve the details in the block using small V-shaped gouges.

5 / When the carving is complete, clean the pencil lines from the block using soap and water. Allow the block to dry, and brush away any carving scraps stuck in the recesses.

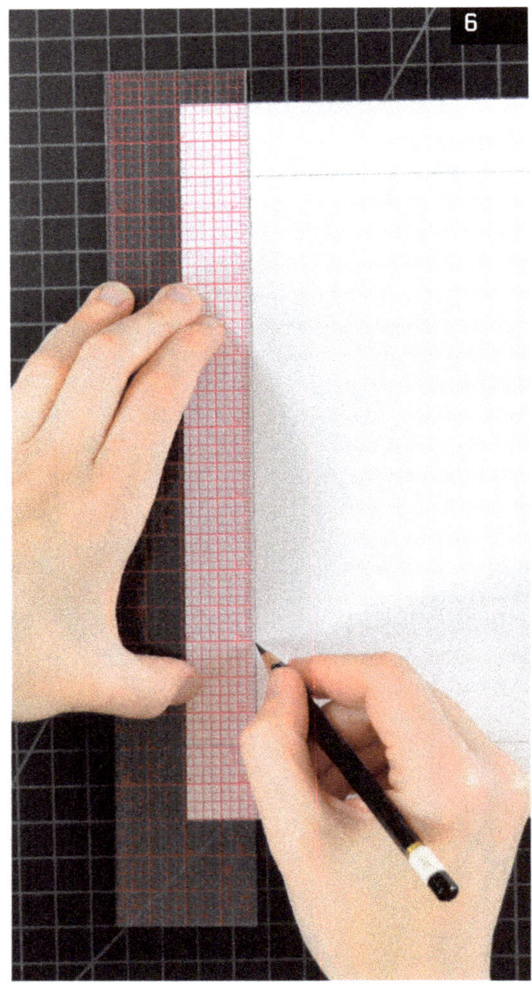

6 / Create a simple printing jig by cutting a sheet of mat board to the same size as your printing paper. Tape the jig to your work surface. With a ruler and pencil, draw margins on the jig for centering your design, the margins should be dark enough to show through the printing paper when you place it on top of the jig.

7 / Prepare your printing area with your printing jig, ink, brayer, inking platen, palette knife, and printing papers close at hand.

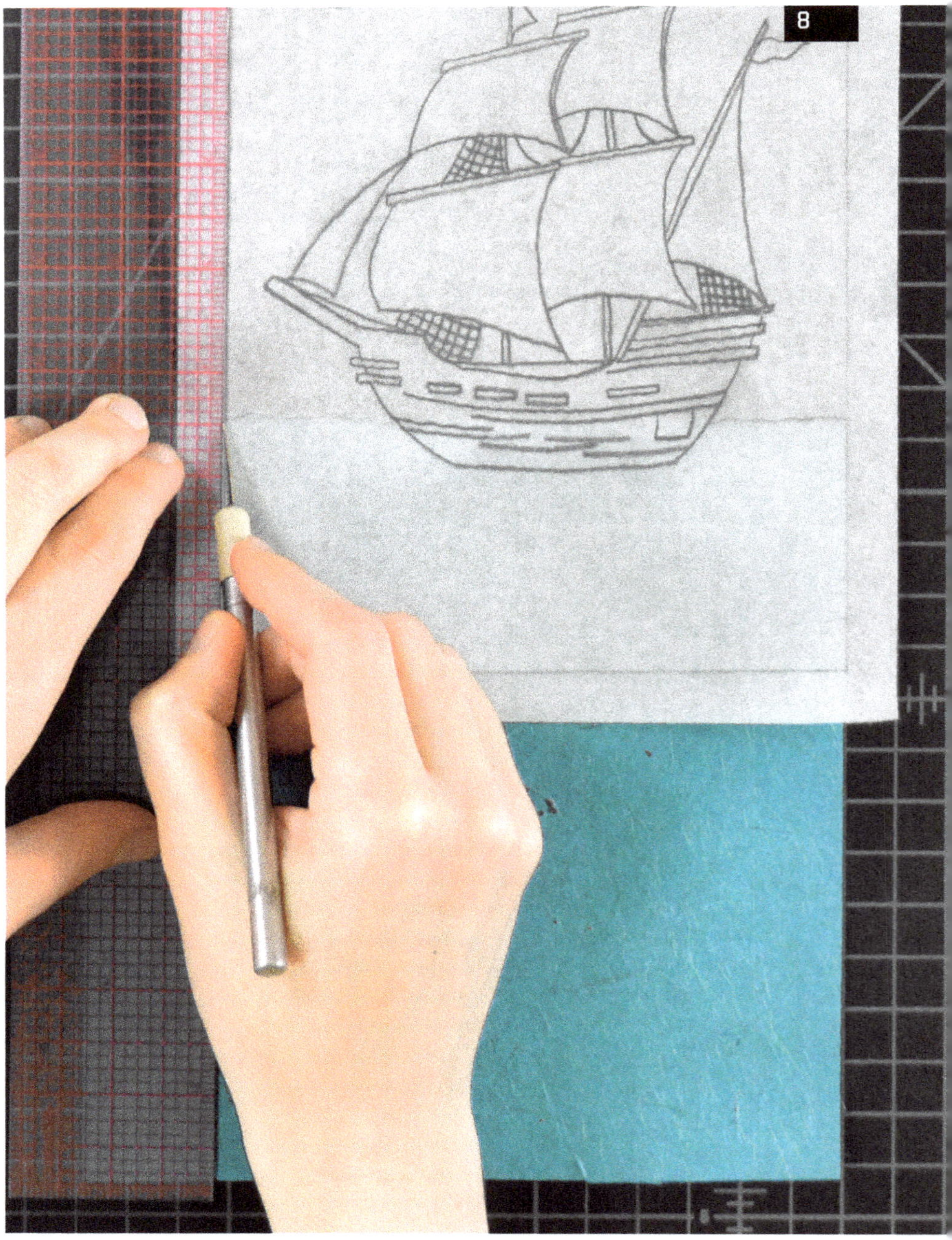

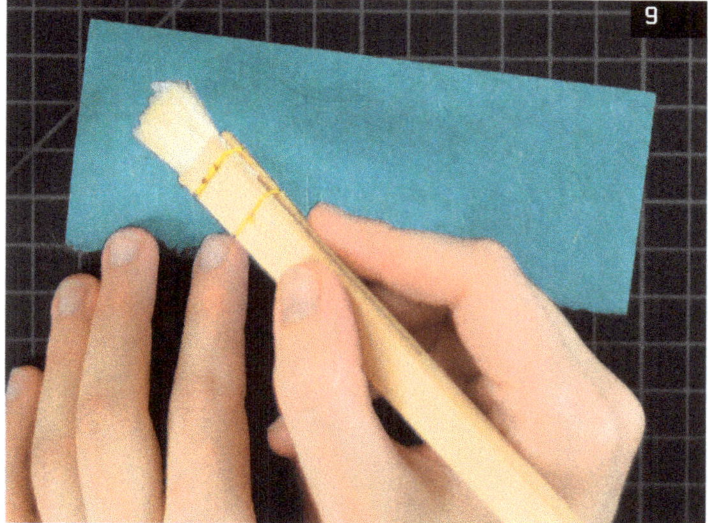

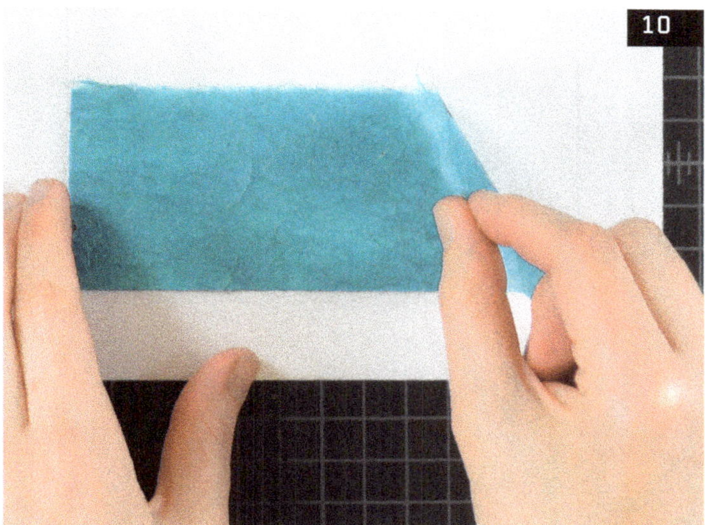

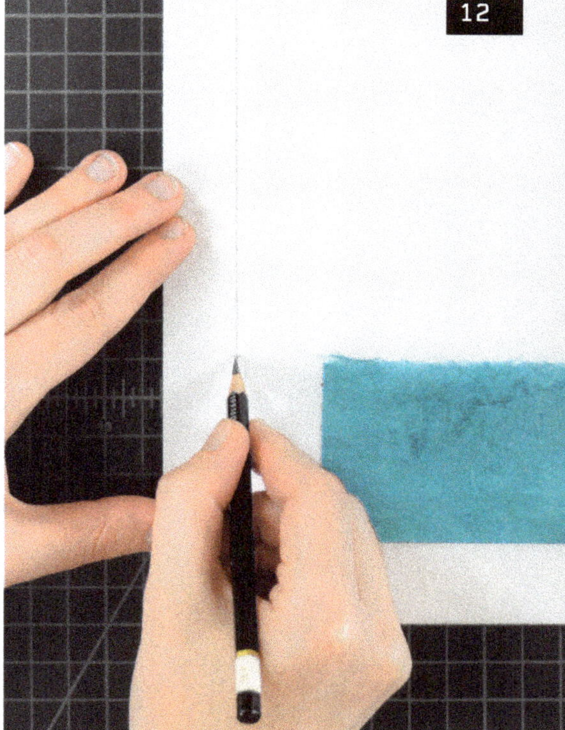

8 / Prepare the first piece of colored washi paper for creating the chine-collé "water." Place the tracing paper drawing on the cutting mat. Slip the blue washi paper under the tracing paper and position it to the correct water level. Use the craft knife and ruler to cut through both sheets of paper along the outside edge of your design.

9 / Brush paste onto the back of the trimmed piece of washi paper.

10 / Lay your printing paper on top of the jig. Because Japanese-style printmaking paper is slightly transparent, it will allow you to see the margin lines you have drawn on your jig. Starting at one edge, carefully paste the blue "water" onto the printing paper. Smooth the affixed washi paper with your fingers.

11 / Use a brayer with no ink to roll out any air bubbles in the pasted paper.

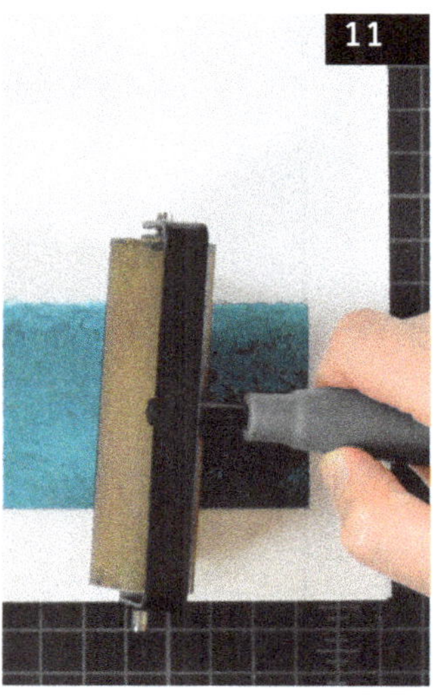

12 / Use a soft lead pencil to make a guideline on the jig for the correct placement of your inked block. It's important to know where the top of the water is because the boat should sit "in" the water. Set your printing paper aside until you're ready to print your block.

13 / Follow the directions for inking on page 24. Use a palette knife to dab a small amount of ink onto the platen. With a brayer, pick up a small amount of ink. Roll a thin, even coat of ink on the block. Carefully lay a piece of newsprint on the inked block, burnish the back of the paper with your fingers or a baren, and peel back your test print. If changes are necessary, rinse and dry the block, and refine the image with additional carving.

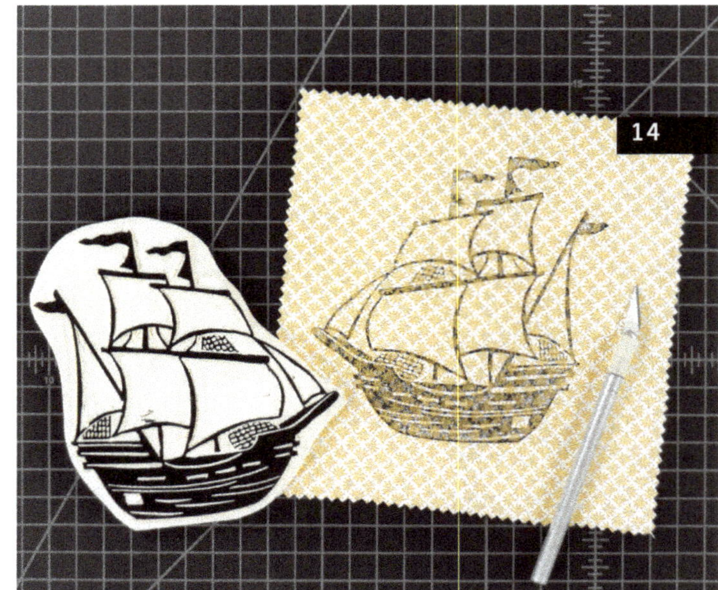

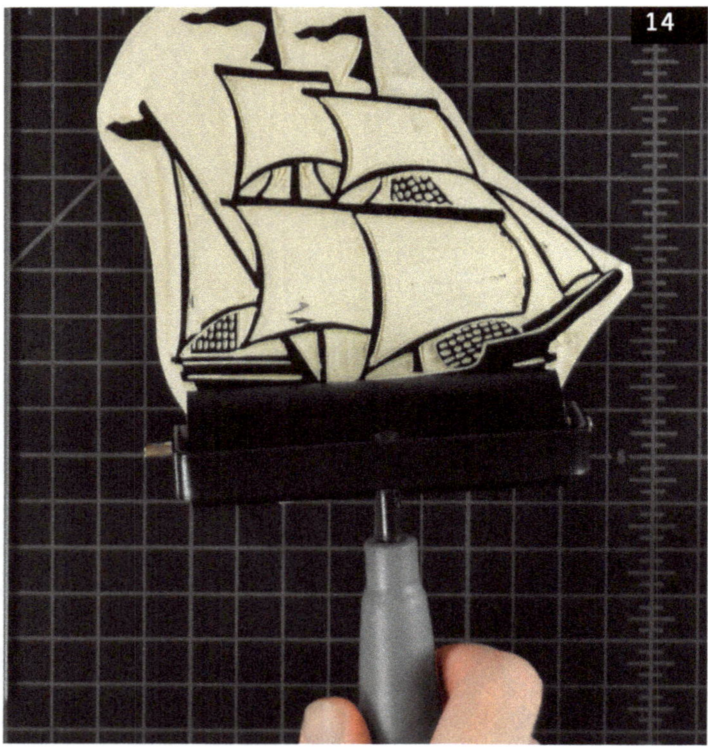

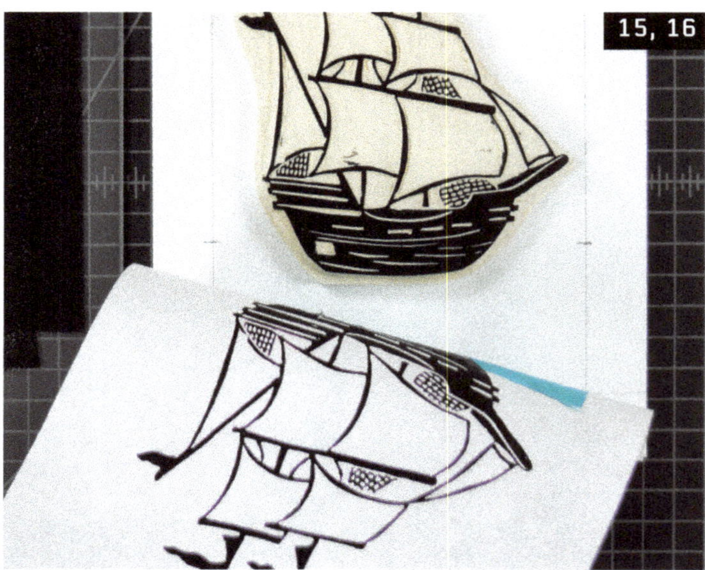

14 / Now you're ready to print your block onto a piece of chiyogami paper for the sails and sun. Ink the block as in step 13. Carefully lay the piece of chiyogami paper on top, decorative side down, and burnish the back with your fingers or baren. Pull the print off carefully and set it aside to dry.

15 / Repeat the inking process, this time for your final print. Place the inked block on the printing jig using your "water line" registration mark as a guide. Line up the printing paper using the bottom edge of the printing jig. Position the paper along one edge of the jig, then carefully roll it onto the inked block. Burnish the back of the paper.

16 / Peel up the paper at one corner to check for an even ink transfer. You are looking for a dark, even coverage of ink. If you have a spotty, salt-and-pepper look, continue burnishing. When the ink transfer looks good, starting at one corner, slowly peel the paper from the block. Set your print aside to dry.

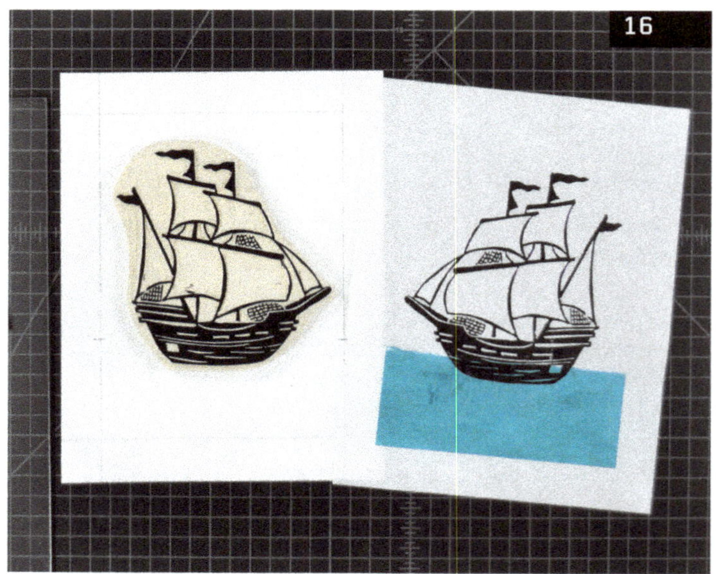

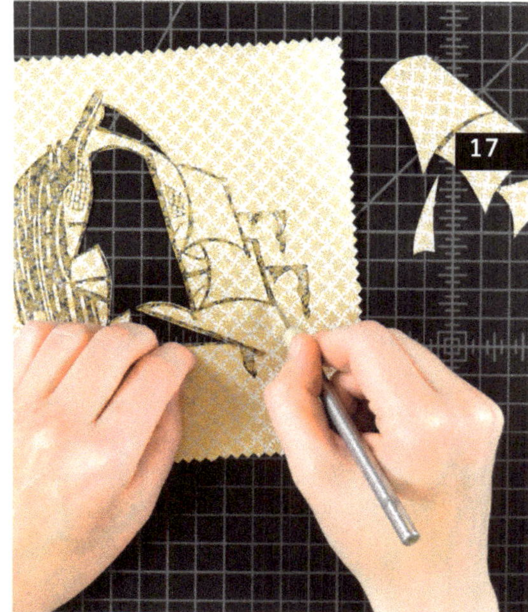

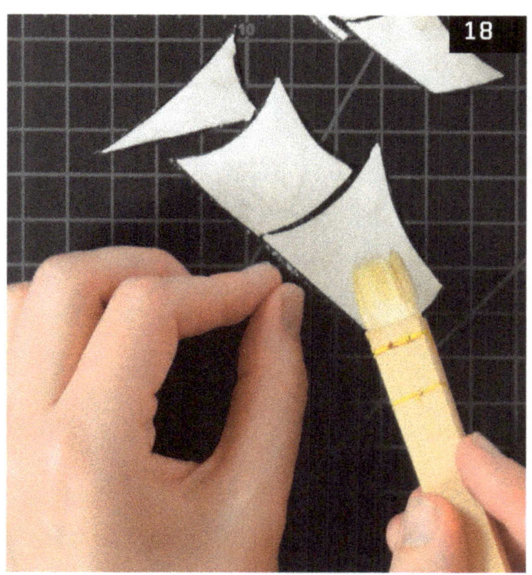

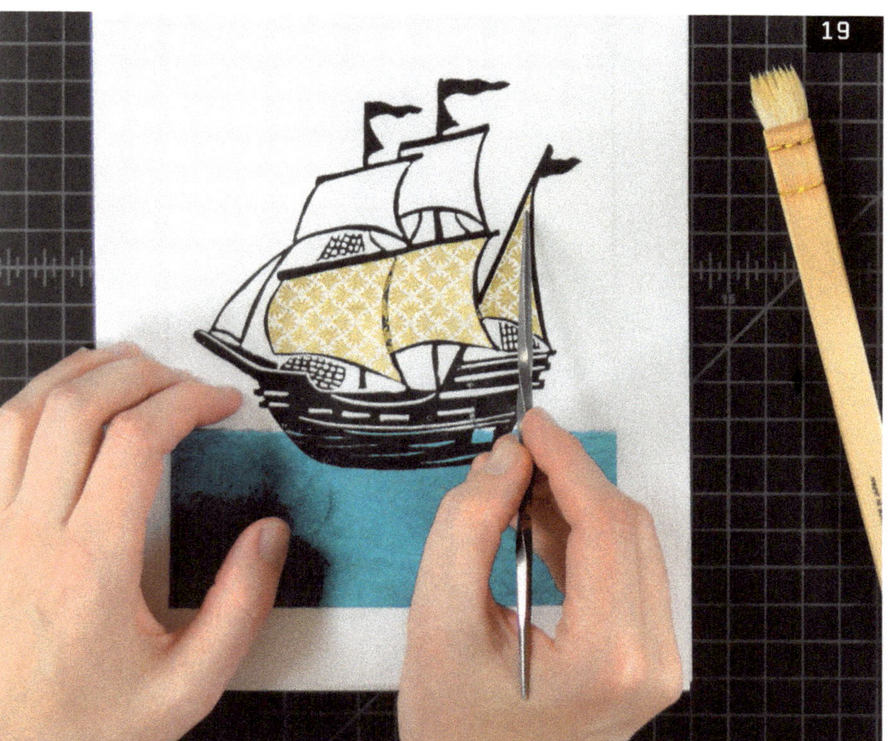

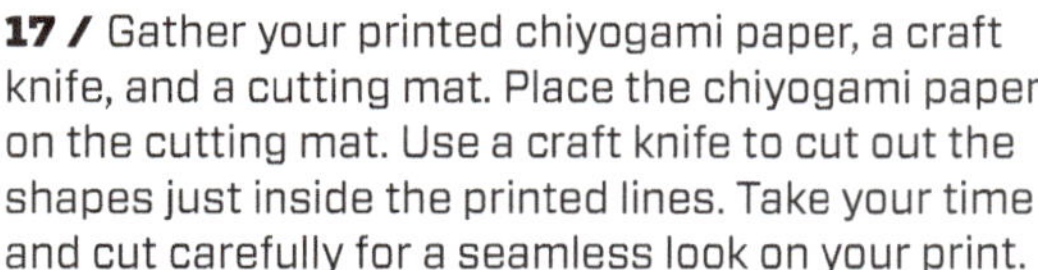

17 / Gather your printed chiyogami paper, a craft knife, and a cutting mat. Place the chiyogami paper on the cutting mat. Use a craft knife to cut out the shapes just inside the printed lines. Take your time and cut carefully for a seamless look on your print.

18 / Brush paste thinly onto the back of the chiyogami pieces. Too much paste will seep onto the print, so keep it light.

19 / Working now with your final print, carefully set the glued pieces into place. Use a small pointed tool or the end of a paintbrush to poke down the corners. Use your fingers to push out any air bubbles.

20 / Repeat the process for each of the chiyogami paper pieces.

21 / Use a hole punch or scissors to cut out the sun.

22 / Place the sun in place on your print paper and push out any air bubbles with your fingers. Allow your print to dry before displaying.

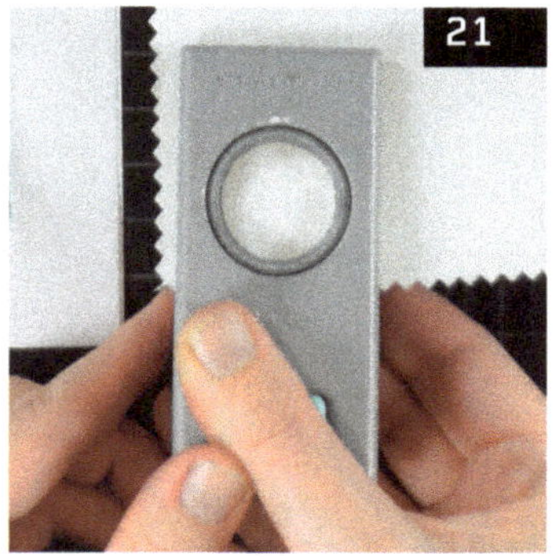

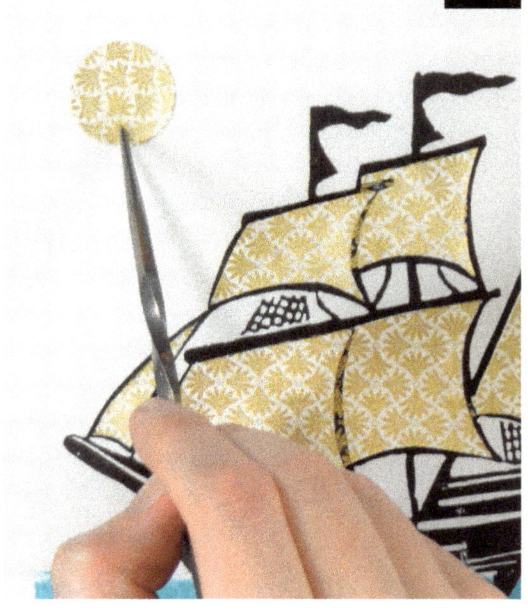

Ink modifiers allow you to experiment and play with layering colors and overlays. Plan your design with different colors for different blocks. By changing the amount of transparent ink modifier you use and the order in which you print the blocks, you can achieve a variety of results. This simple water scene with sea horses uses three colors and a transparent ink modifier to create a dimensional effect in the finished print.

TRANSPARENT INK PRINT: SEA HORSES

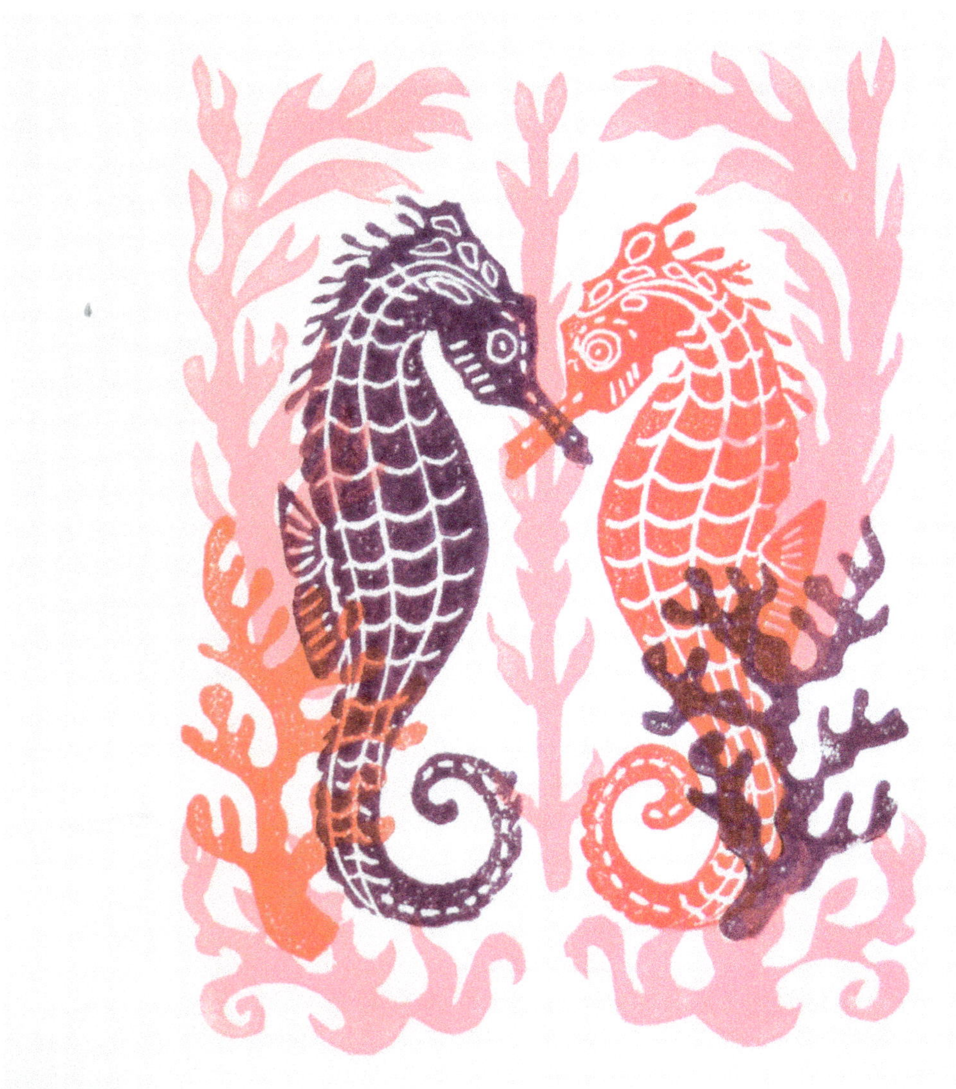

TOOLS AND MATERIALS

drawing paper

soft lead pencil

light box (optional)

tracing paper

dense rubber carving block

bone folder

cutting mat

craft knife

transparent acrylic ruler

carving gouges in various sizes

soap, water, and sponge, or a baby wipe

water-soluble printing inks

transparent ink modifier

brayers

inking platen

palette knives

newsprint

baren or wooden spoon (optional)

Japanese washi printing paper

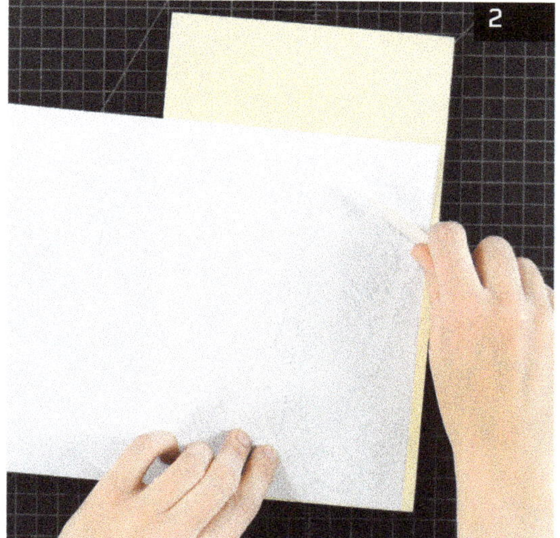

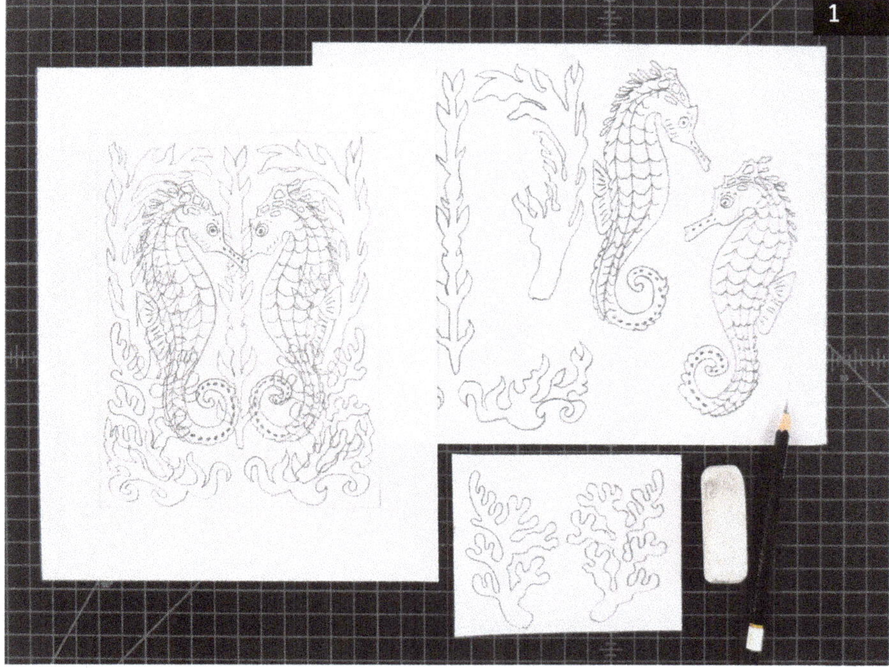

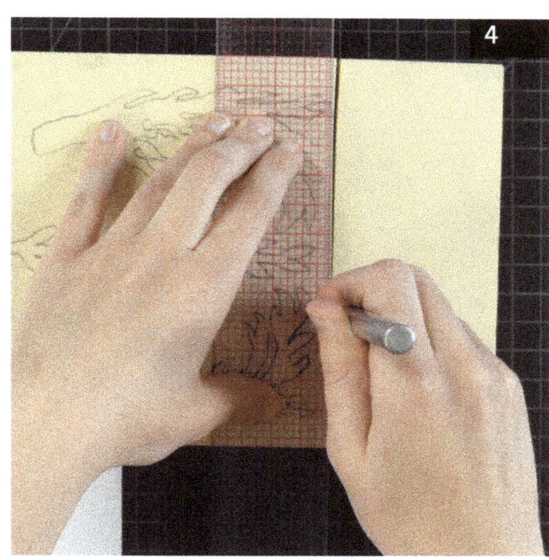

1 / Draw your design on a piece of paper. You will want to create a design with overlapping elements—a background, middle ground, and foreground—to be printed in different colors to achieve a dimensional effect. Place the sketch on a light box, or tape it to a bright window. Place a piece of tracing paper over the sketch, and trace it in detail with a soft lead pencil. Be sure your lines are clean and clear. All marks will be transferred to the block, so erase any mistakes.

2 / Place your pencil image face down on the rubber block. Use a bone folder to transfer the different sections of the design to the block separately. Start with the background portion of your design. Keeping the sheet of tracing paper in place with one hand, rub the back of the paper with the bone folder in the other. Lift a corner of the paper to check for a consistent transfer.

3 / Move the tracing paper to a clean section of block. Repeat the process, this time transferring the middle ground sections of your drawing. Then do the same for elements in the foreground of your drawing.

4 / Place the rubber block on a cutting mat. Using a craft knife and ruler, cut the block so that each element of the drawing has its own small block. Press down on the knife so that it cuts all the way through the rubber and carefully draw the knife toward yourself. For best results, make one smooth and continuous cut. Repeat this process until you have cut out all your pieces. Set aside the cut-away sections of the block for later projects. Now you're ready to carve.

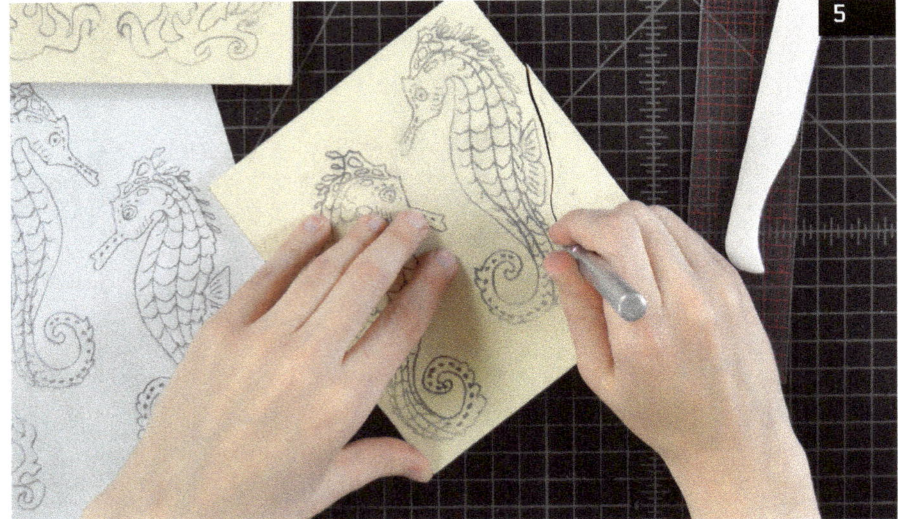

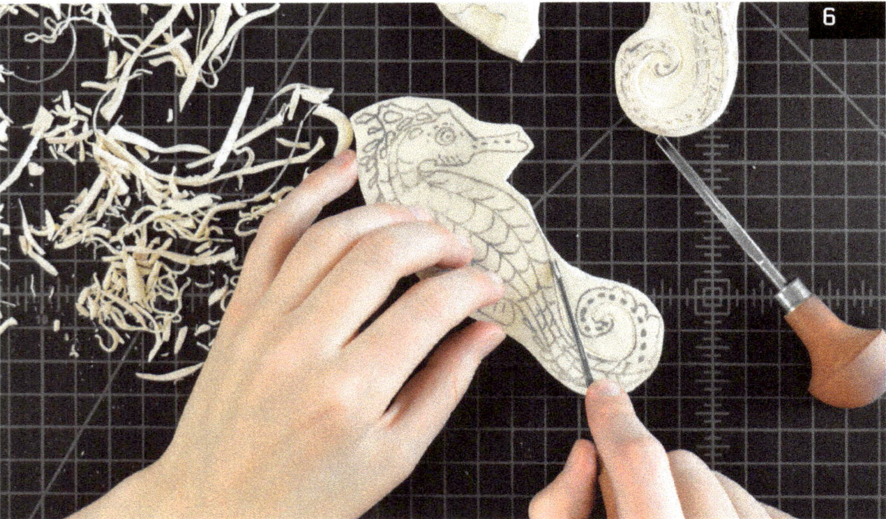

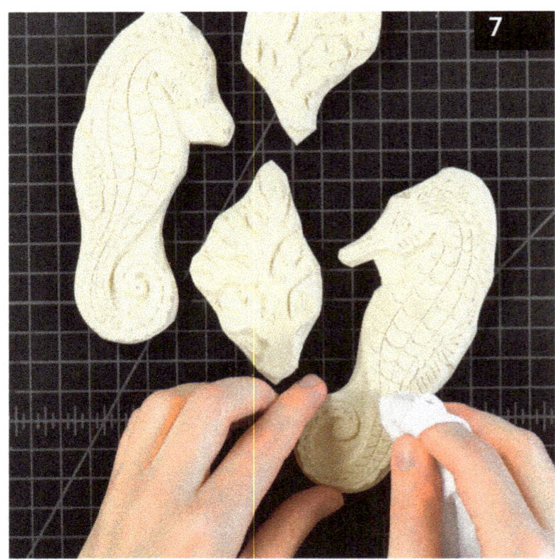

5 / Use the craft knife to cut away the large areas of the rubber block outside the lines of your drawing. Trim down each section, leaving a small border around the outer edge of the drawing. (If the border is too big, it will be difficult to judge the registration accurately when printing.) When your blocks are trimmed, you're ready to carve the details.

6 / Begin by carving along the outside of the lines with the small V-shaped gouge. Use a larger U-shaped blade to carve away the broader areas of block material outside the lines. Carve the fine details in each of your blocks using small V-shaped gouges.

7 / When the carving is complete, clean the pencil lines from the block using soap and water. Allow the block to dry, and brush away any carving scraps caught in the recesses.

8 / Make a printing jig using a sheet of mat board that is the same size as you printing paper. This will allow you to line up the printing paper with the edges of the jig each time you print. Tape the jig to your work surface. Draw the margins for your design on the jig with a pencil and ruler. Prepare your printing area with the printing jig, inks and modifier, brayers, inking platen, palette knives, and printing papers close at hand.

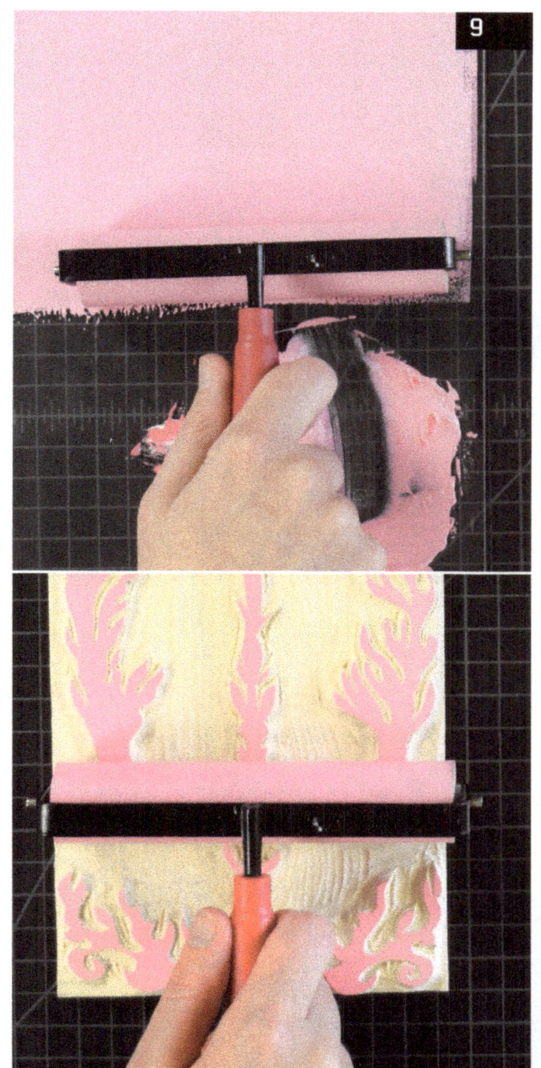

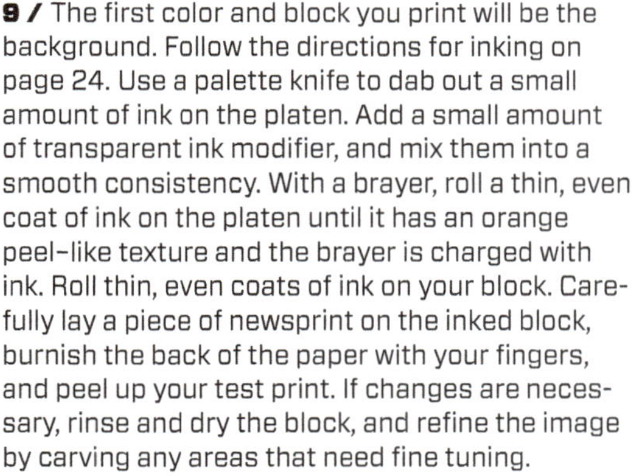

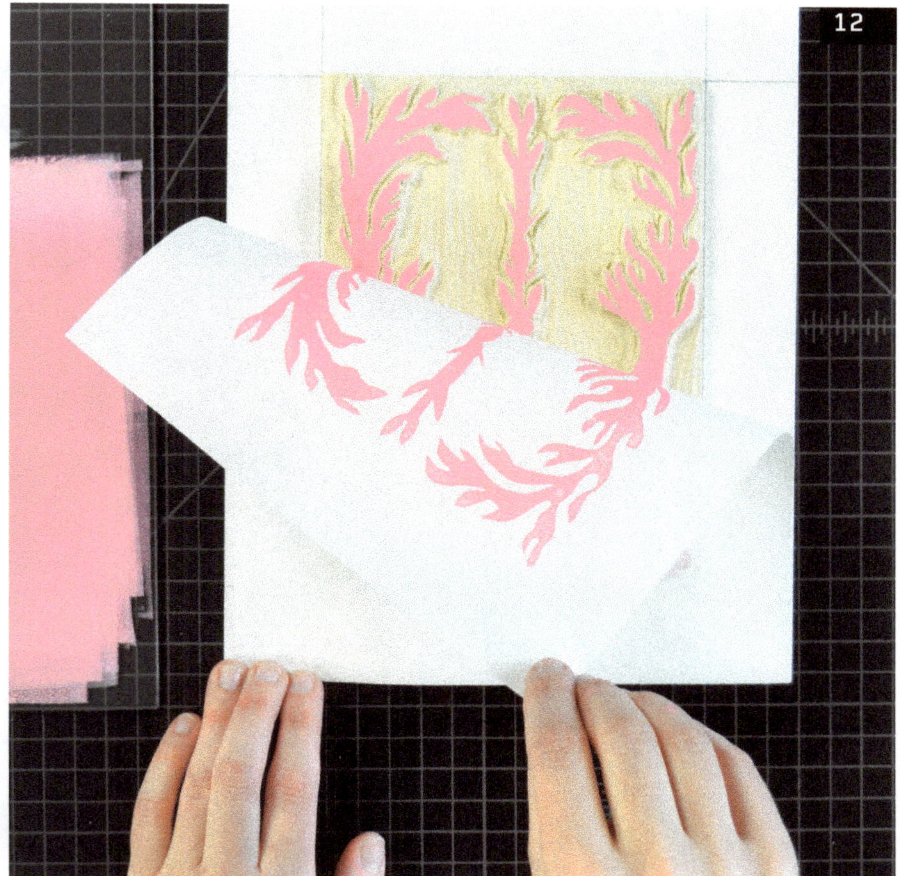

9 / The first color and block you print will be the background. Follow the directions for inking on page 24. Use a palette knife to dab out a small amount of ink on the platen. Add a small amount of transparent ink modifier, and mix them into a smooth consistency. With a brayer, roll a thin, even coat of ink on the platen until it has an orange peel–like texture and the brayer is charged with ink. Roll thin, even coats of ink on your block. Carefully lay a piece of newsprint on the inked block, burnish the back of the paper with your fingers, and peel up your test print. If changes are necessary, rinse and dry the block, and refine the image by carving any areas that need fine tuning.

10 / Repeat the ink-application process by rolling a thin layer of ink on your block with your brayer. Now you're ready to print the first color.

11 / Working quickly, position the inked background block on the jig, centering it between the margin lines. Line up the printing paper along the bottom edge of the jig. Holding it in place with one hand, carefully roll the paper down in one continuous motion onto the block. Burnish the back of the paper with your fingers or a baren. Because washi paper is slightly transparent, you will see the ink transfer to the paper. With practice, you will be able to notice when a good transfer has been achieved by the look of the ink through the back of the paper.

12 / Carefully lift one corner of the paper and check for an even ink transfer. If it looks good, pull up the paper slowly and carefully. Set it aside to dry.

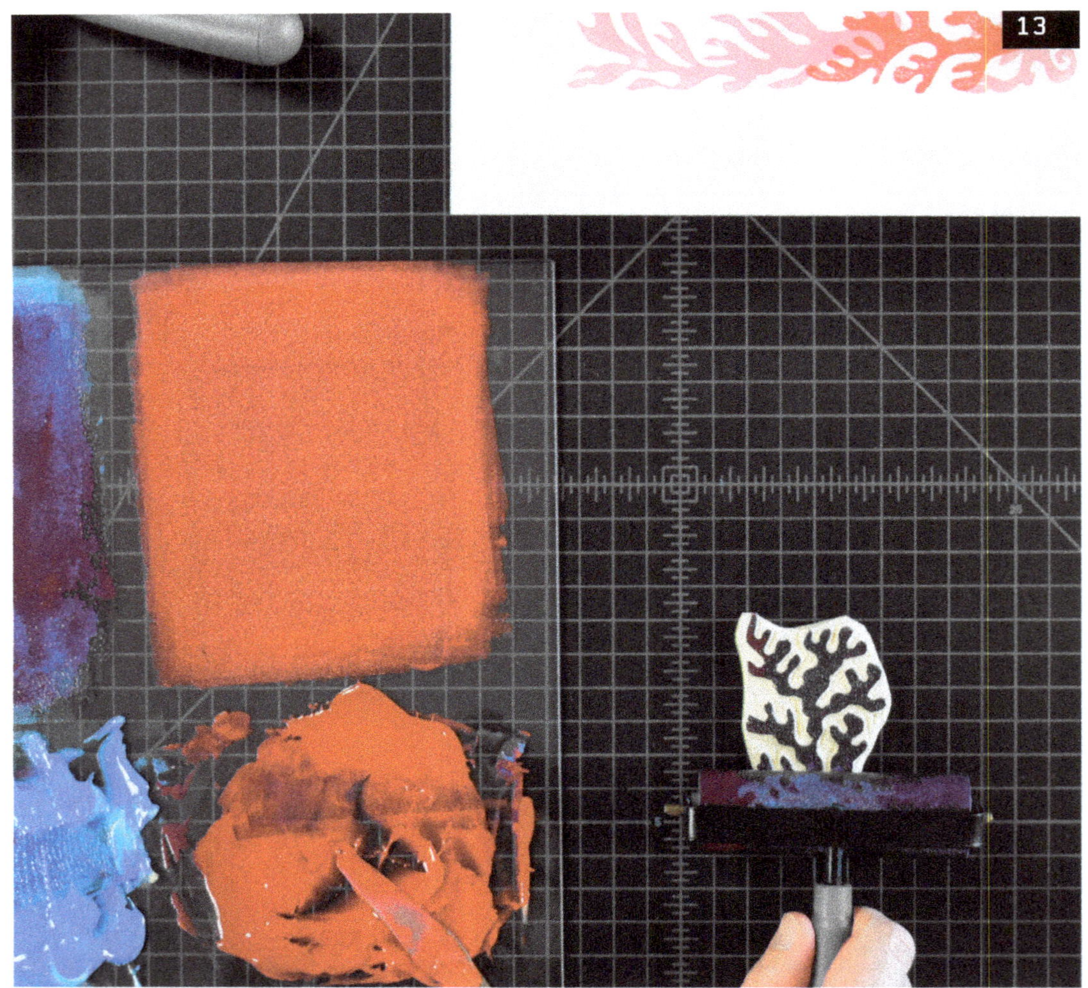

13 / Allow the first color to dry while you clean the platen. You will be printing the additional colors block-side down, eyeballing the registration as you print. Prepare the ink for the next block. Put a small amount of ink and a small amount of transparent ink modifier on the platen, and use a palette knife to mix the two. Roll the ink on the platen, with the brayer. If you are using a glass platen you will notice that the ink will roll out evenly, but you will be able to see through the ink and glass to the work surface below. If you cannot see through the ink, you may want to add more transparent modifier. You will not achieve any transparent effects in your print if the ink is too opaque.

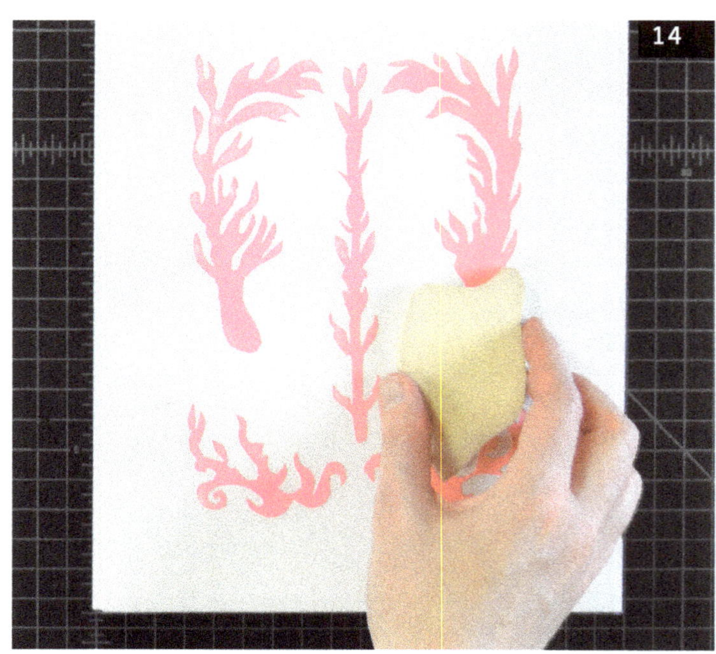

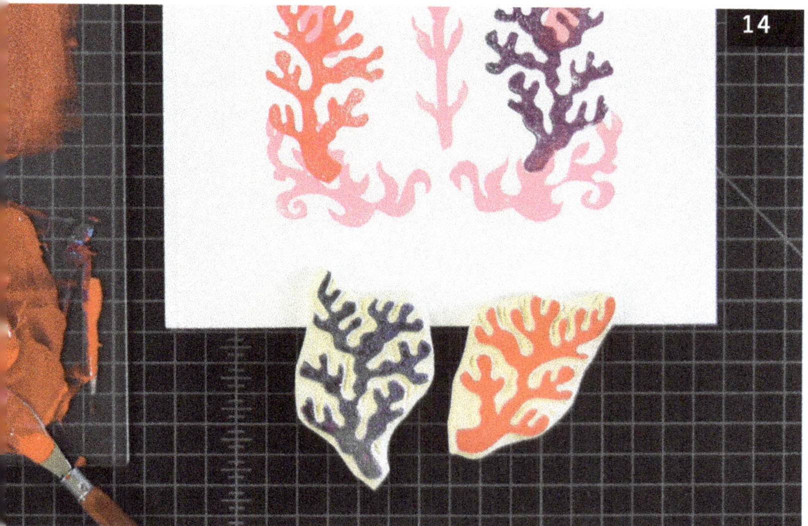

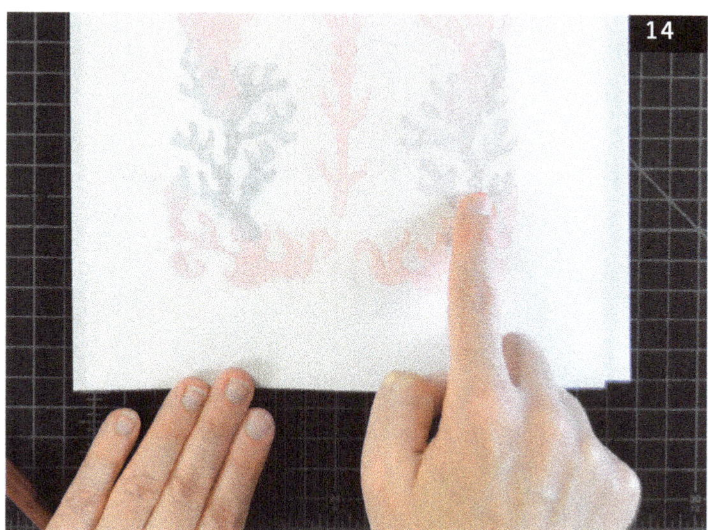

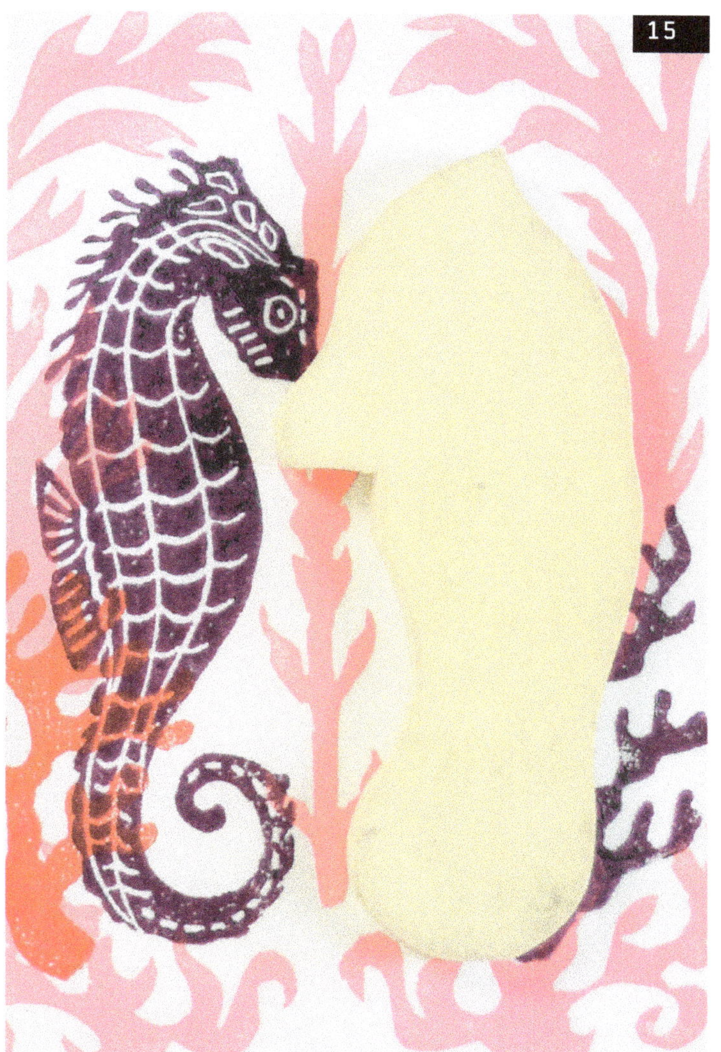

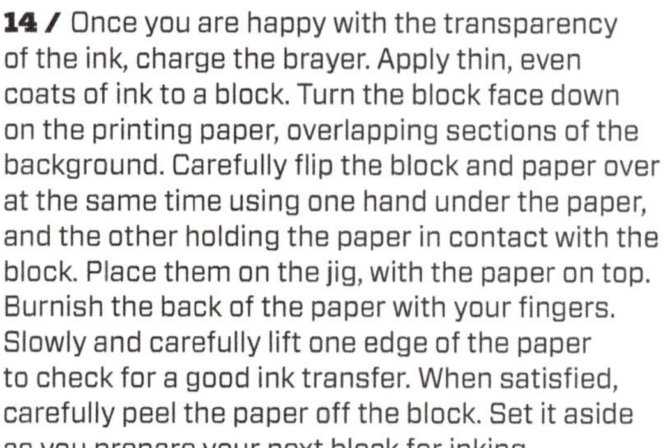

14 / Once you are happy with the transparency of the ink, charge the brayer. Apply thin, even coats of ink to a block. Turn the block face down on the printing paper, overlapping sections of the background. Carefully flip the block and paper over at the same time using one hand under the paper, and the other holding the paper in contact with the block. Place them on the jig, with the paper on top. Burnish the back of the paper with your fingers. Slowly and carefully lift one edge of the paper to check for a good ink transfer. When satisfied, carefully peel the paper off the block. Set it aside as you prepare your next block for inking.

15 / Repeat the printing process for each of the blocks. You can choose the order in which to print because you are using transparent ink modifier. The different order and combination of blocks will produce different results.

This project uses the key block technique, which opens up many possibilities for creative printmaking. With a few spot colors, a detailed black-and-white carving can turn into a much more impressive art print. The great thing about this technique is its flexibility: The key block can be presented as a single-color print, hand colored with watercolor, or printed with spot colors. Here, I've used two colors for the robin and the eggs, but there could be more—the flowers, leaves, and nest could each have its own block of color.

KEY BLOCK LINOCUT WITH SPOT COLORS: ROBIN'S NEST

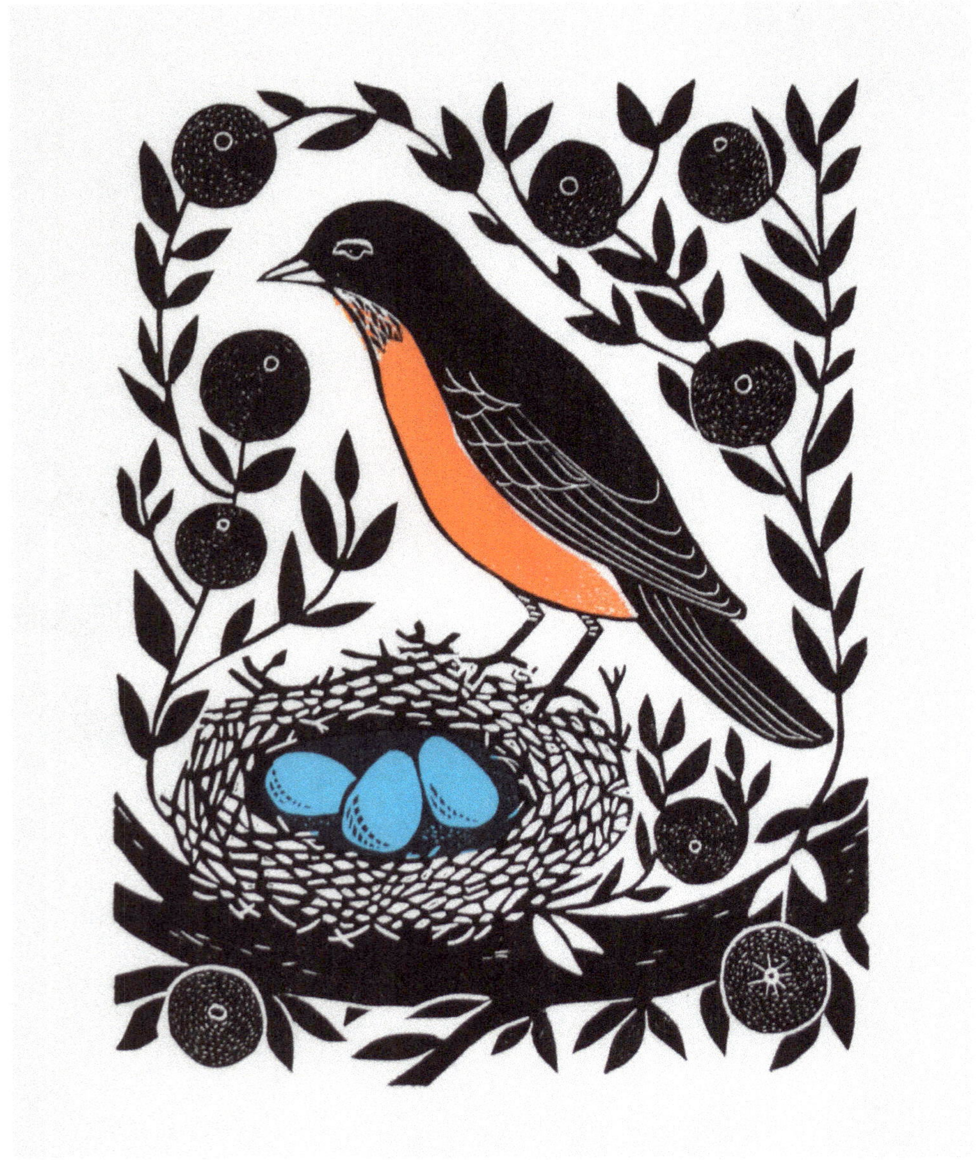

TOOLS AND MATERIALS

- 1 or more battleship linoleum carving blocks
- craft knife
- india ink and brush
- drawing paper
- soft lead pencil
- white carbon paper
- masking tape
- colored pencils
- gouges in various sizes
- mat board or card stock
- scissors
- soy-based printing inks
- brayers
- inking platens
- newsprint or scrap paper
- baren or wooden spoon
- acetate transparency sheet
- printing paper

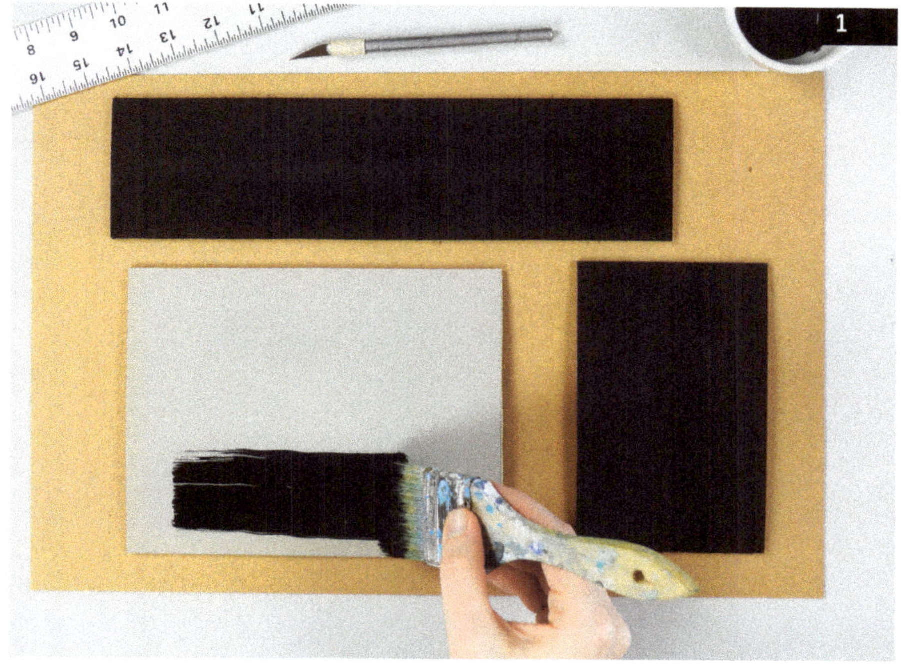

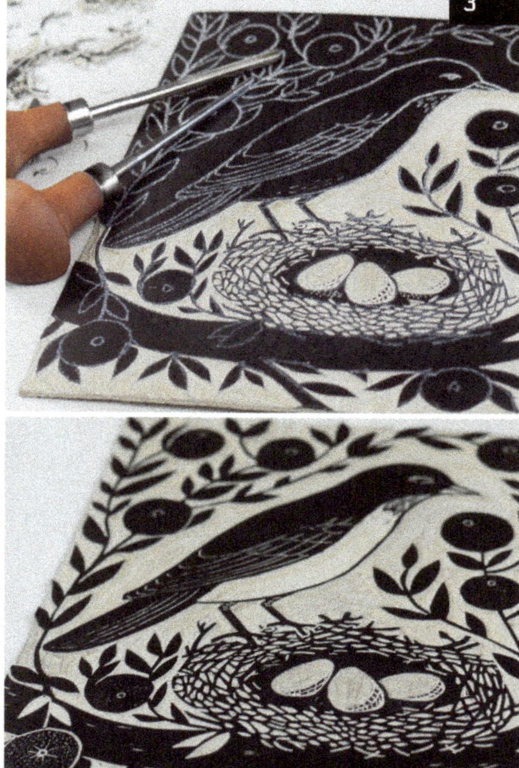

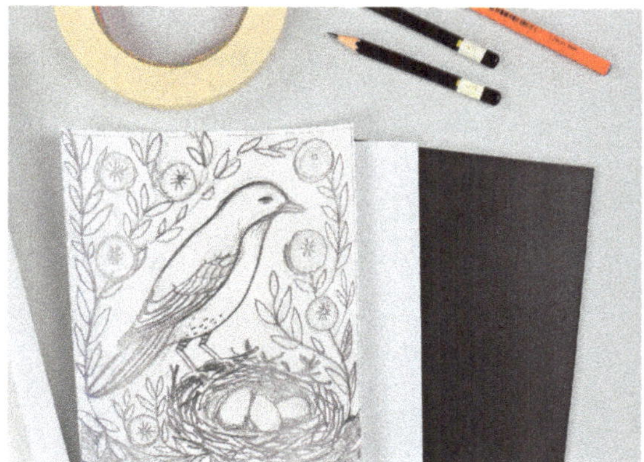

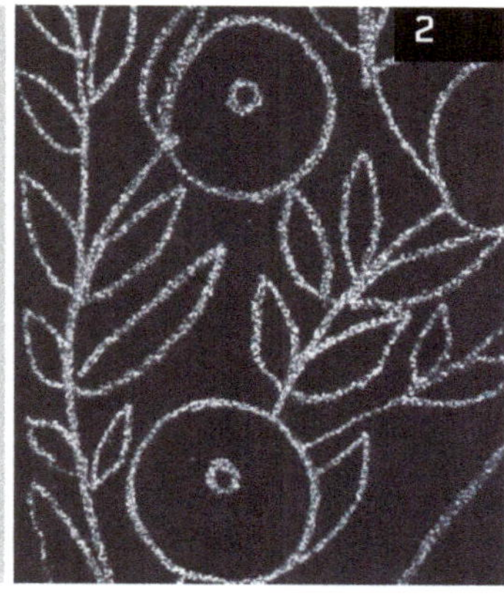

1 / Plan the size of your print and cut the linoleum block to size with a craft knife. In addition to the key block, you will need smaller pieces for your spot colors. Paint the surface of the blocks with the india ink and allow them to dry. When you carve the blocks, the removal of the painted areas will reveal a pale gray color and show what the print will look like as your carving progresses.

2 / Use the pencil and paper to draw your design for the key block. When the design is complete, use white carbon paper to transfer the image to the key block and to each of the spot-color blocks. Lay the carbon paper, ink-side down, on the key block and set the drawing on top. Tape the drawing in place. Redraw over the image using a colored pencil: The colored line will show which areas have been completed. Repeat the process, transferring the parts of the design that will be color spots onto the smaller linoleum block pieces.

3 / Begin carving your key block. Start with the outlines before removing larger sections of the background or empty space. Try different gouges, alternating their use to take away smaller and larger areas of linoleum.

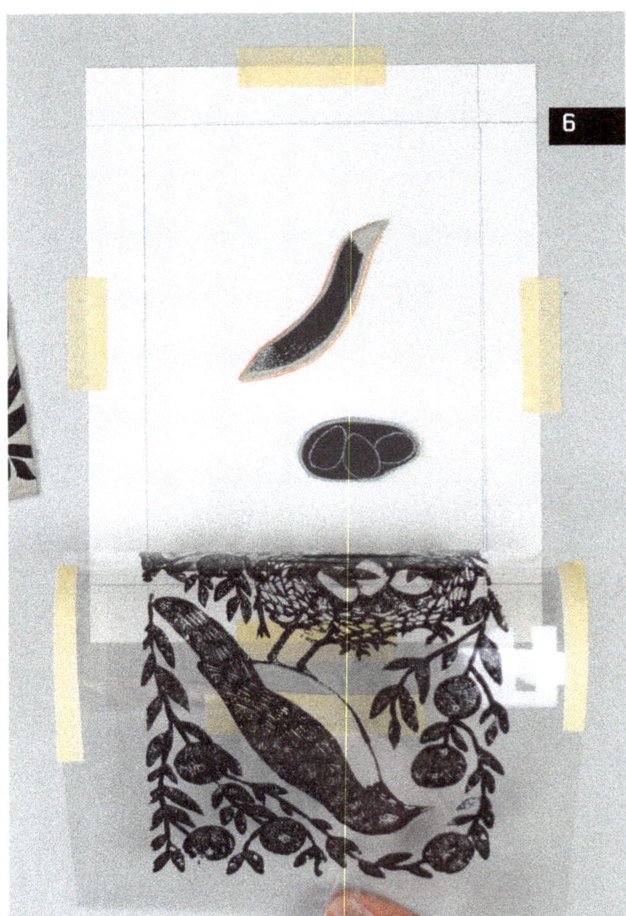

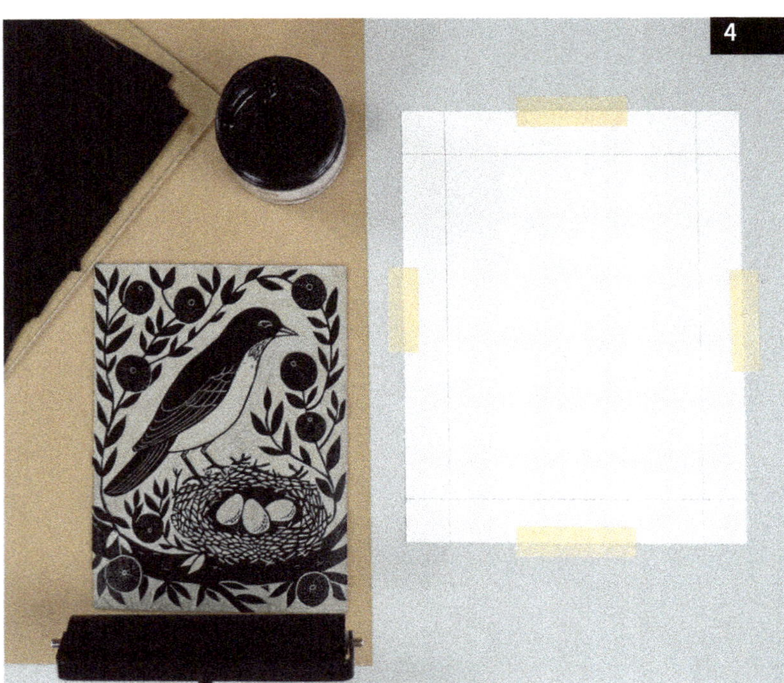

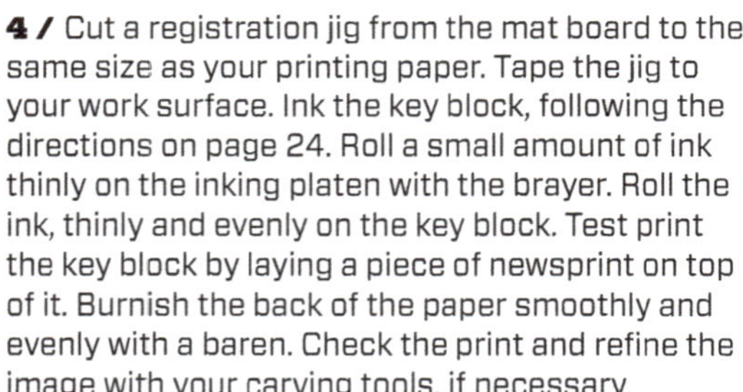

4 / Cut a registration jig from the mat board to the same size as your printing paper. Tape the jig to your work surface. Ink the key block, following the directions on page 24. Roll a small amount of ink thinly on the inking platen with the brayer. Roll the ink, thinly and evenly on the key block. Test print the key block by laying a piece of newsprint on top of it. Burnish the back of the paper smoothly and evenly with a baren. Check the print and refine the image with your carving tools, if necessary.

5 / Tape the acetate transparency sheet below the bottom edge of the jig. Center the inked key block on the jig and make an outline around it in colored pencil *while the ink is still wet.* Slowly roll the transparency sheet onto the inked block. Apply light pressure with your fingers to transfer the ink to the acetate. Roll the acetate back and allow the ink to dry. Set the key block aside.

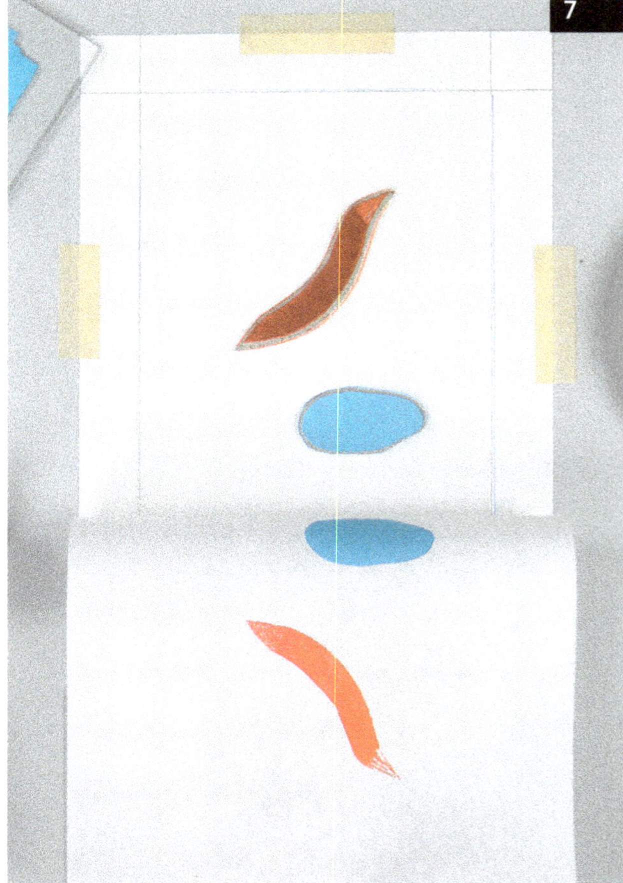

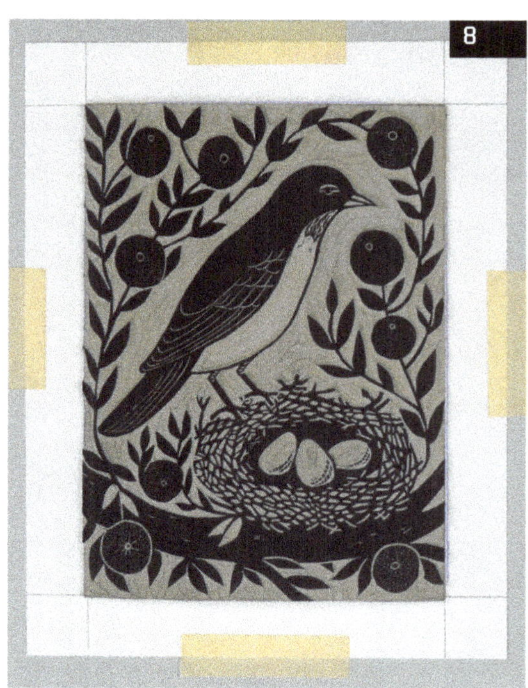

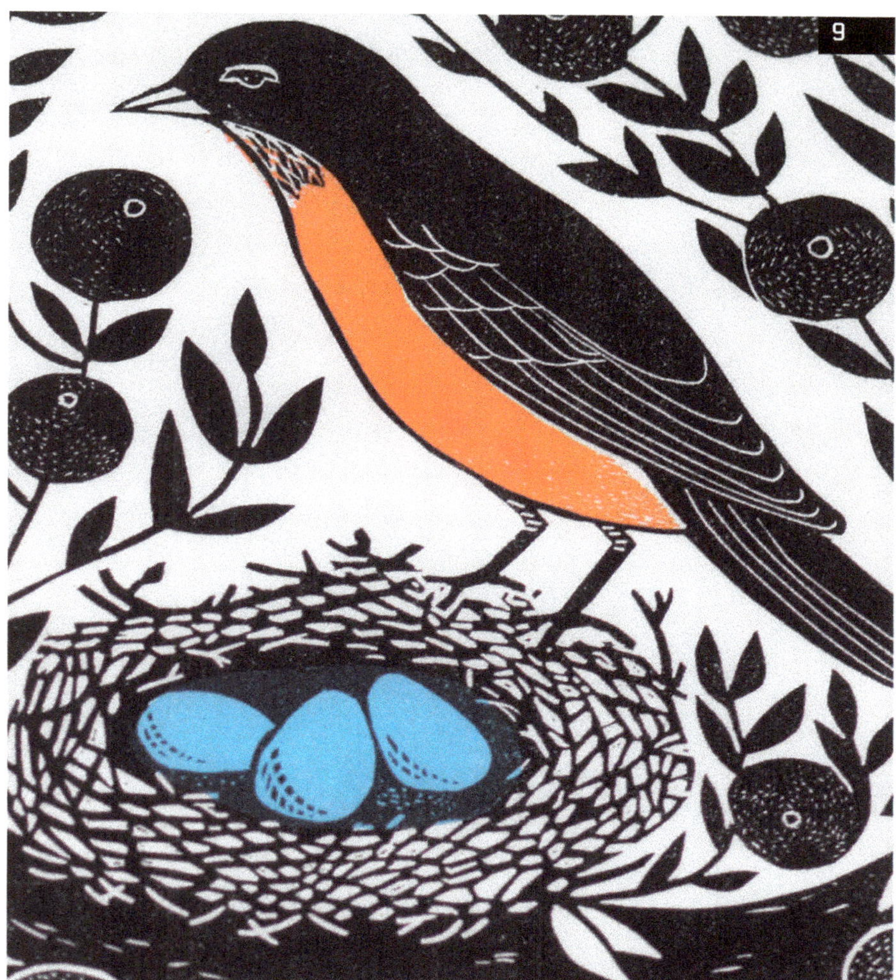

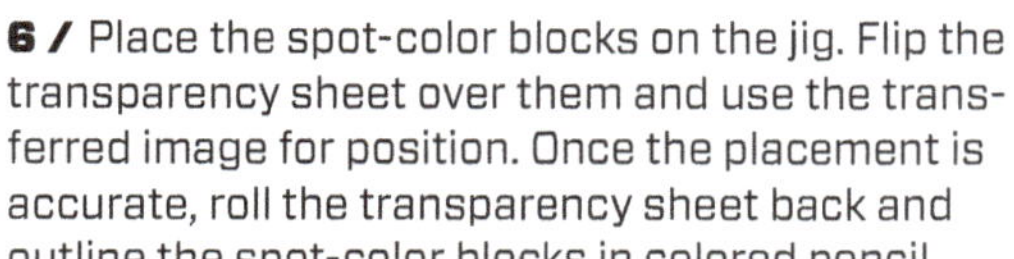

6 / Place the spot-color blocks on the jig. Flip the transparency sheet over them and use the transferred image for position. Once the placement is accurate, roll the transparency sheet back and outline the spot-color blocks in colored pencil.

7 / Ink the spot-color blocks. Place them inside their pencil outlines on the jig. Line up your printing paper with the bottom edge and corners of the jig, and hold it in place with one hand. Lay the paper on the blocks in one fluid motion. Burnish the back of the paper until the ink is fully transferred. Carefully lift the printing paper and allow the ink to dry. Set the color-spot blocks aside.

8 / Repeat the process in step 7 with your key block. Ink the block with thin, even coats. Take the time to line up the block accurately on the jig. Carefully align the printing paper as in step 7. Lay the paper down in one smooth motion. Burnish the back of it with a baren until the ink is fully transferred. Pull up your print!

9 / Enjoy the fruits of your labor!

Picasso developed the reduction printing method in tandem with master printer Hidalgo Arnéra. Reduction prints are created when the artist uses a single block to create a multicolored multilayered print. Removing only the areas of the image that will remain white, the entire block is inked and printed in the first color. Then the artist carves into the same block, removing only the areas they want to print in the next color. The process is repeated again and again, working from the lightest to the darkest colors until the image is complete. This style of printmaking requires careful planning, and the artist must print the entire edition at each stage of carving, because the carving on the block cannot be reversed.

REDUCTION LINOCUT: CAT

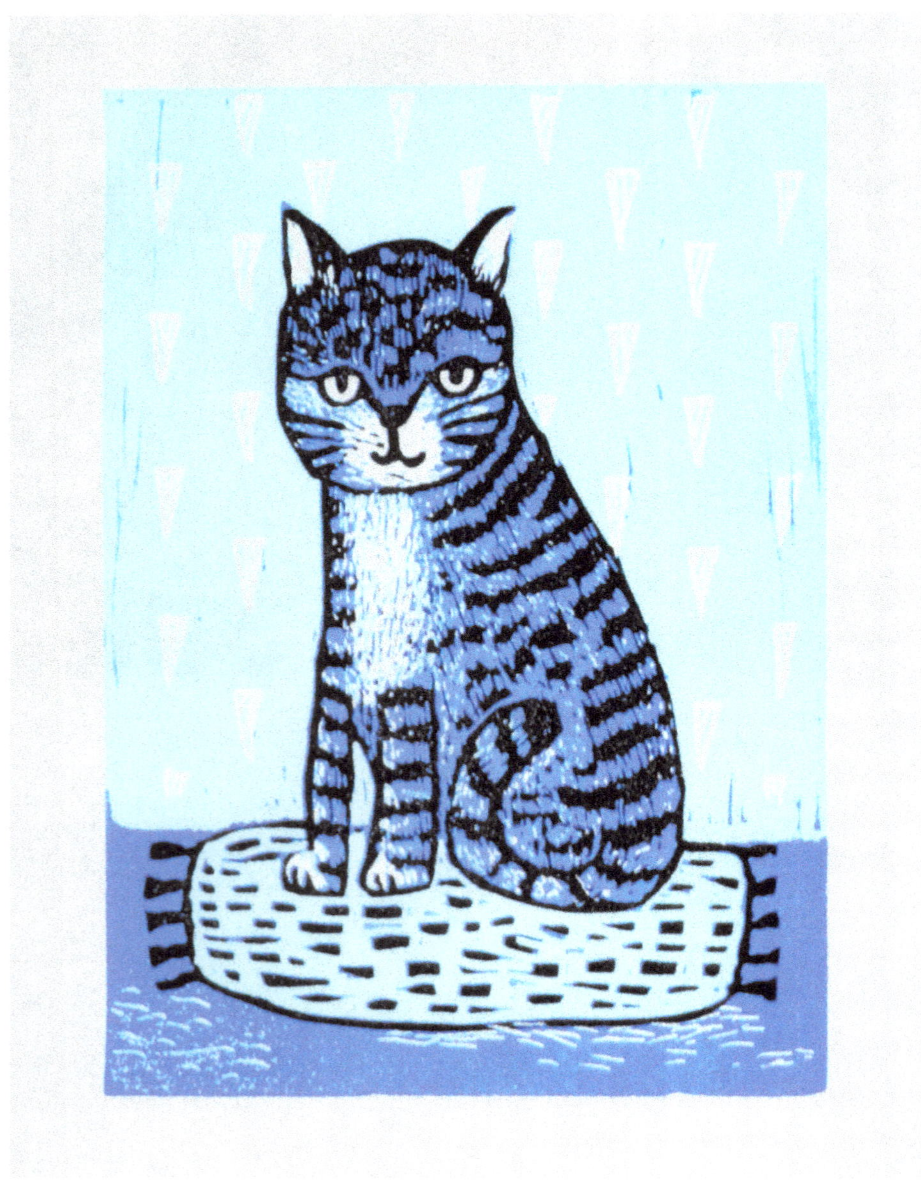

TOOLS AND MATERIALS

- tracing paper
- soft lead pencil
- colored pencils
- dense rubber block
- bone folder
- cutting mat
- gouges in various sizes
- mat board or card stock
- masking tape
- water-soluble printing inks
- brayer
- inking platen
- newsprint or scrap paper
- baren or wooden spoon
- Japanese printmaking paper

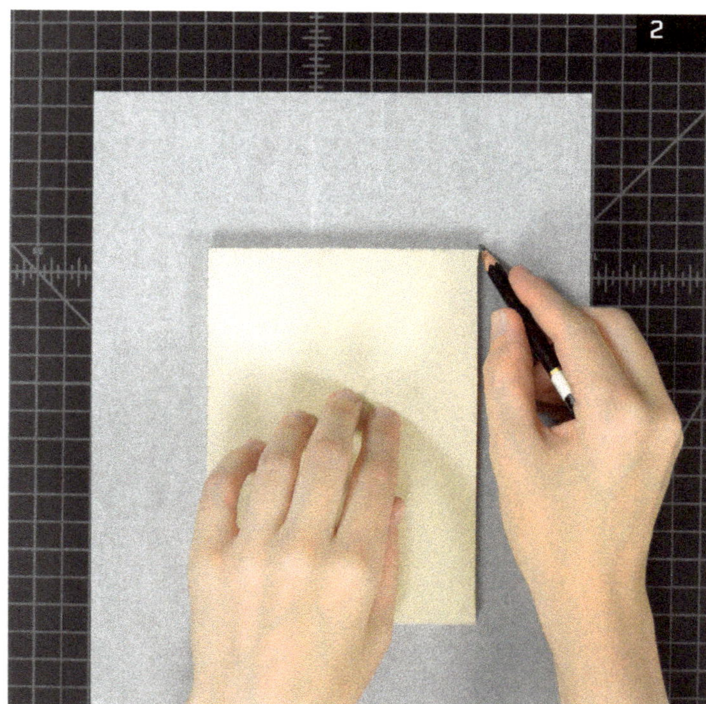

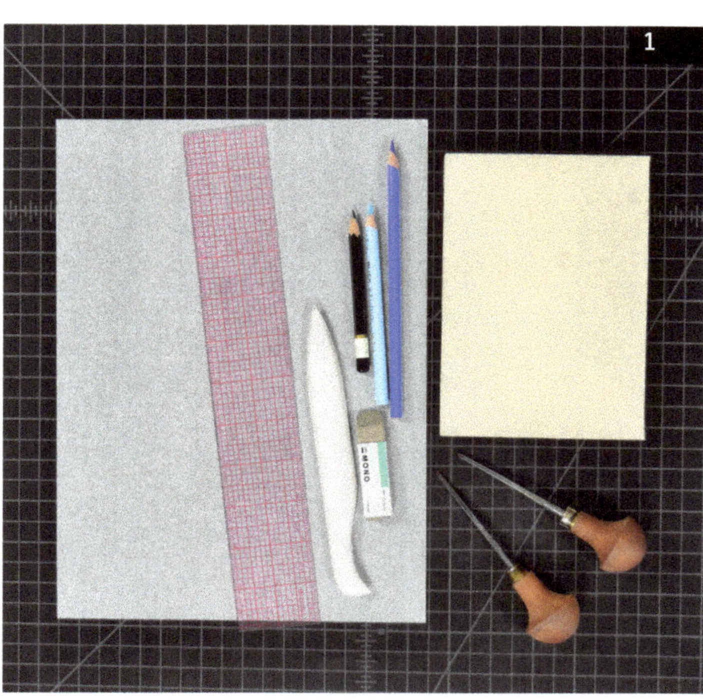

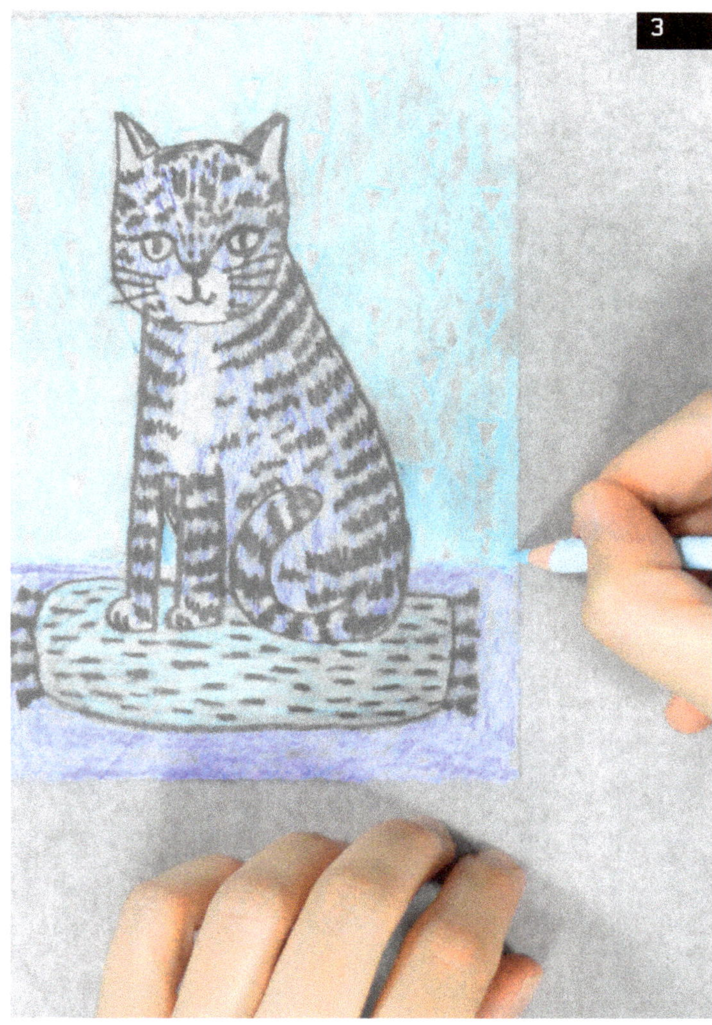

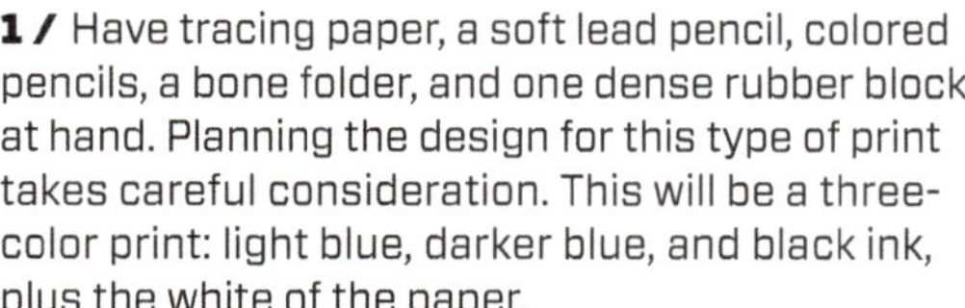

1 / Have tracing paper, a soft lead pencil, colored pencils, a bone folder, and one dense rubber block at hand. Planning the design for this type of print takes careful consideration. This will be a three-color print: light blue, darker blue, and black ink, plus the white of the paper.

2 / Place a piece of tracing paper on your work surface. Center the rubber block on the paper and trace around the edges with the pencil. Set the rubber block aside.

3 / Create your design inside the outline on the tracing paper. I use colored pencils when I design for reduction prints to help me visualize what I will be carving at each stage. I refer back to my initial drawing often during each round of carving.

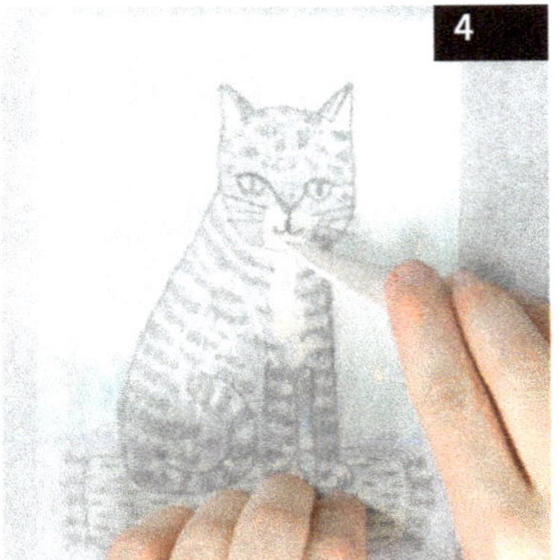
4

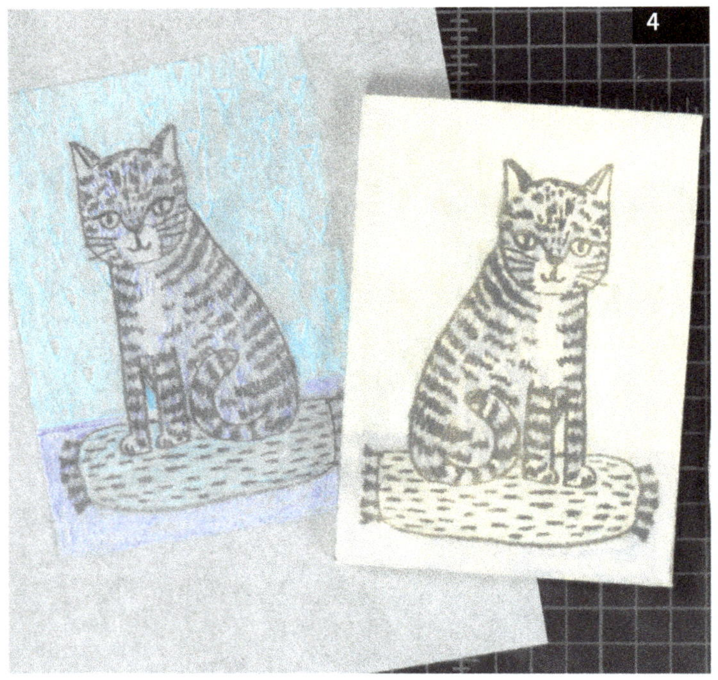
4

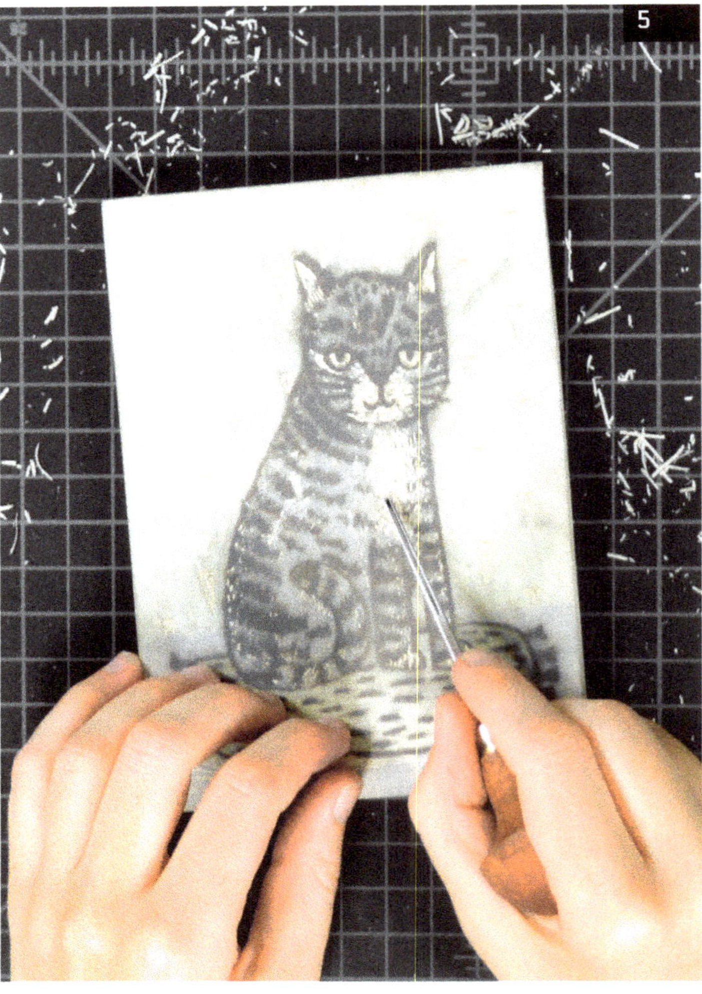
5

4 / When your design is complete, place the tracing paper face down on the rubber block, lining up the outline with the edges of the block. You will be able to see where you have drawn through the back of the tracing paper. Holding the paper in place with one hand, use the bone folder to transfer the design to the block. Work from the center outward with long, continuous sweeps and medium pressure. Lift a corner of the paper to check that you didn't miss any spots. When the transfer is complete, remove the tracing paper from the block.

5 / Begin carving using the appropriate V-shaped gouge. In this preliminary round of carving, you will be removing only the areas of the print that you want to remain white (or the color of the paper). In my cat illustration, the only areas I'll carve are the whites of the cat's eyes, some areas of the cat's face, bib, and the white detail of the wallpaper background.

6 / Prepare a printing jig by cutting a piece of mat board to the exact dimensions of your printing paper. Tape the jig to your work surface. Center the rubber block on the jig, and trace around it with a pencil. Remove the block for inking.

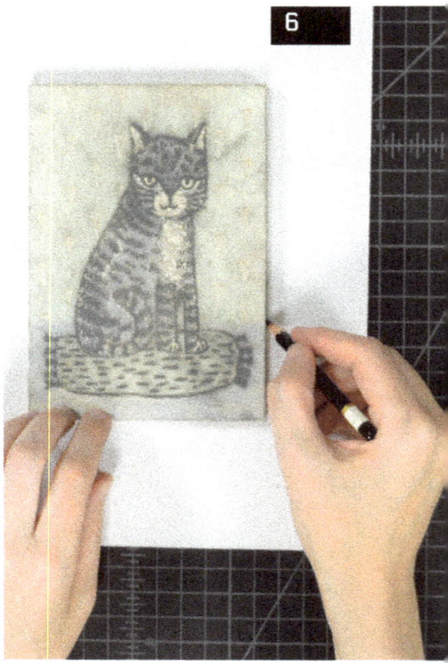
6

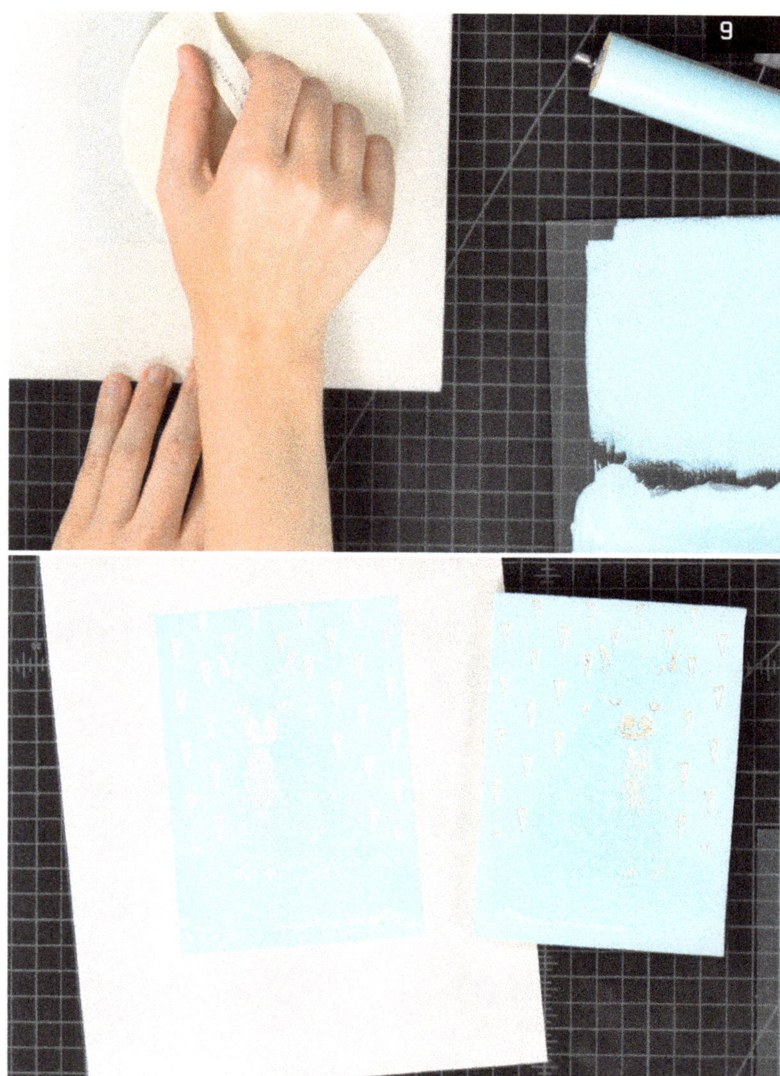

7 / Put a small amount of ink onto the platen. My lightest color is pale blue, so I start with that. Following the inking directions on page 24, charge up the brayer and carefully ink the block in thin, even coats. Carefully place the inked block on the jig within the penciled outline. You will want the placement of the block to be exact with each round of color. Test print the block several times on newsprint, and save the test prints for subsequent rounds of color.

8 / When you're happy with your test print, ink the block again and set it carefully inside the outline on the jig. Line up the edge of your printing paper with the edge of the jig. Use one hand to hold the paper in place and the other to carefully lay the paper down on top of the block.

9 / Burnish the back of the paper with a baren, wooden spoon, or your fingers. You will need to print the first round of all of your proofs and your entire edition of prints at this time. Set each print aside to dry thoroughly. Clean the block with soap and water, and allow it to dry.

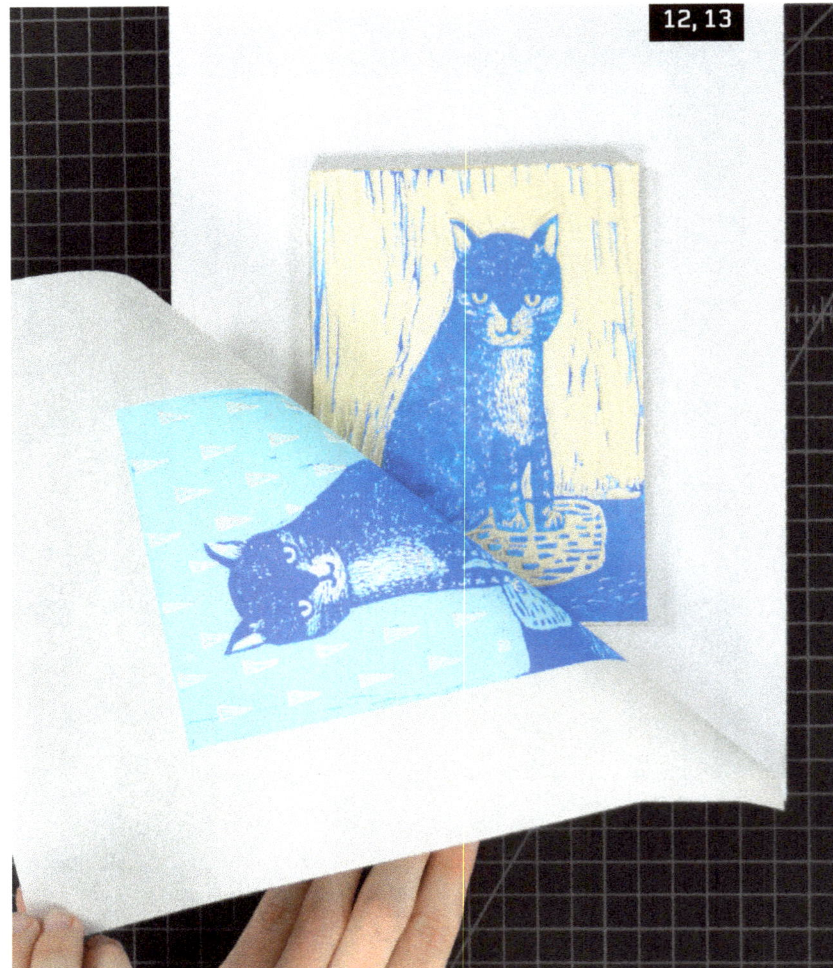

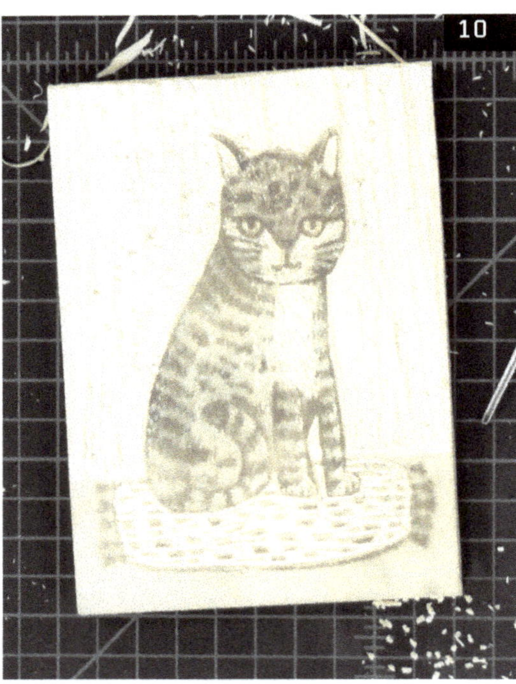

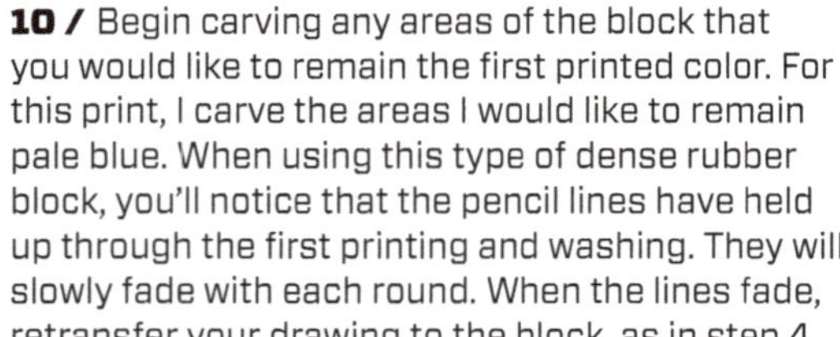

10 / Begin carving any areas of the block that you would like to remain the first printed color. For this print, I carve the areas I would like to remain pale blue. When using this type of dense rubber block, you'll notice that the pencil lines have held up through the first printing and washing. They will slowly fade with each round. When the lines fade, retransfer your drawing to the block, as in step 4.

11 / Prepare to print the second ink color—a darker blue in this print. Ink the block, as in step 7.

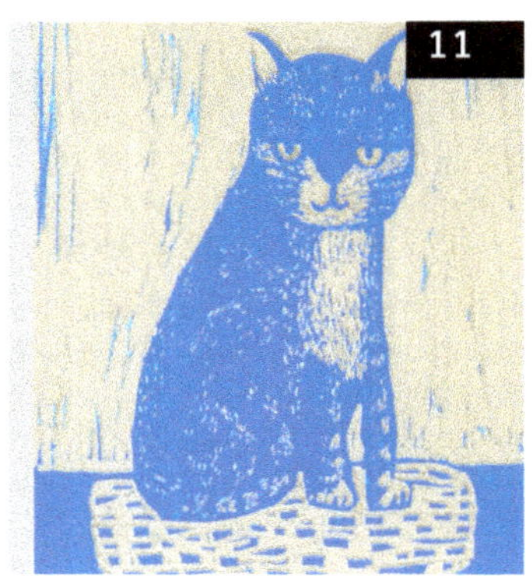

12 / Carefully place the inked block inside the outline on the printing jig. Test print the block using one of the test prints from the first round. This will give you a chance to check your registration and color choices. If your print does not line up properly, re-ink the block and test it again with one of the other test prints from the first round.

13 / When you're happy with your test, follow steps 8 and 9, printing the second round of color on your entire edition of prints. Again, clean the block with soap and water, and allow it to dry.

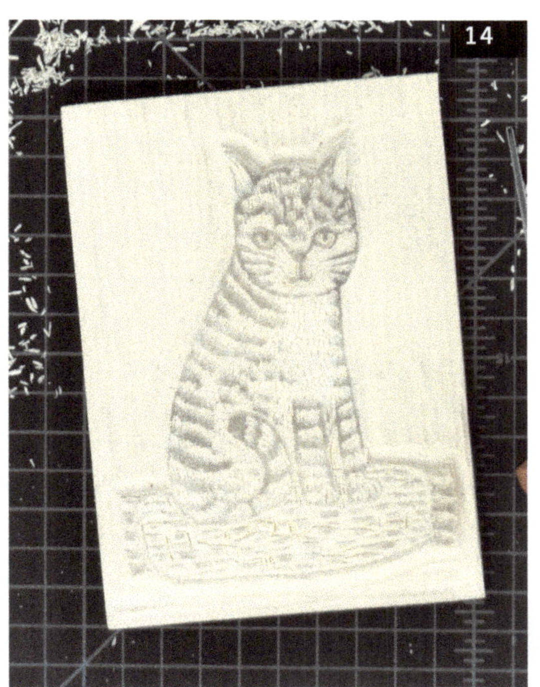

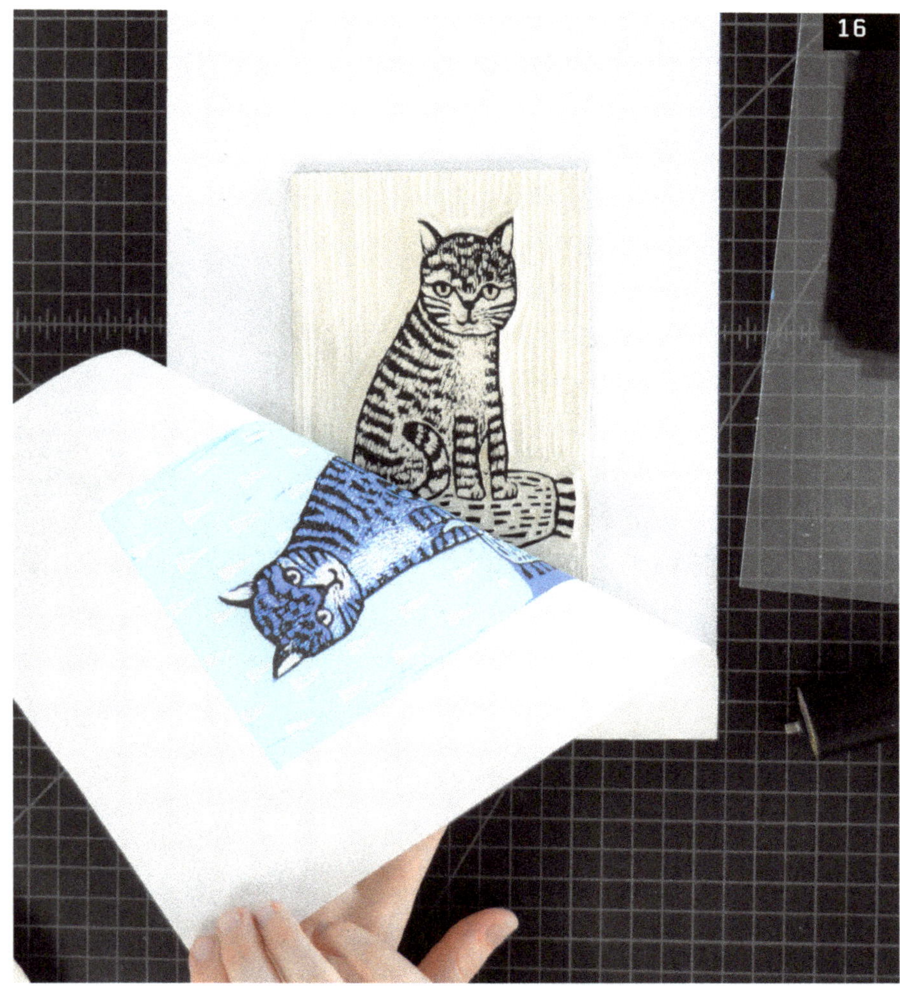

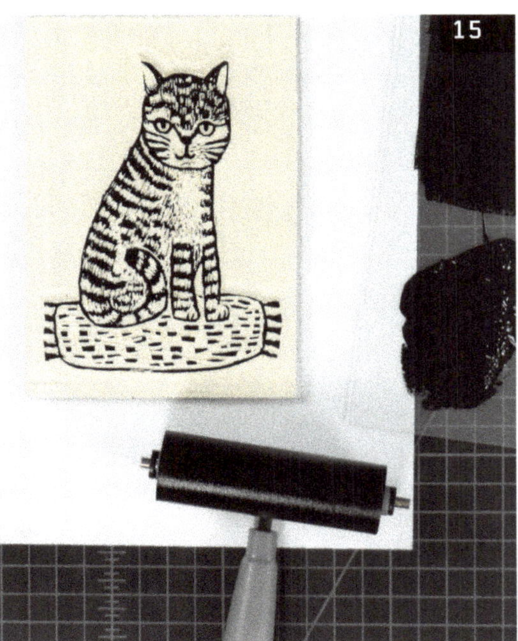

14 / Repeat the carving process for the areas where you want to retain the second color. In this print, I wanted the floor, part of the rug, and some of the cat's fur to remain bright blue. Check your block and reference your illustration to be sure you are happy with your new round of carving.

15 / The final round of the printing will be in black ink. Repeat steps 7 through 13.

16 / Pull the print off the block and pat yourself on the back. You've completed three rounds of color printing from a single block! Once you get the hang of it, you can design a block with up to a dozen different colors!

Everything for this print starts with the key block—the most detailed block, traditionally printed last in black ink. Multilayered prints can be achieved using several blocks of the same size; this allows for an easier registration process. Spot colors can be printed ahead of time using blocks of the same size that are transferred directly from your original illustration. This retro-inspired flower vase uses bright colors and shapes, which are reminiscent of the 1970s.

MULTIPLATE PRINT: RETRO FLOWER VASE

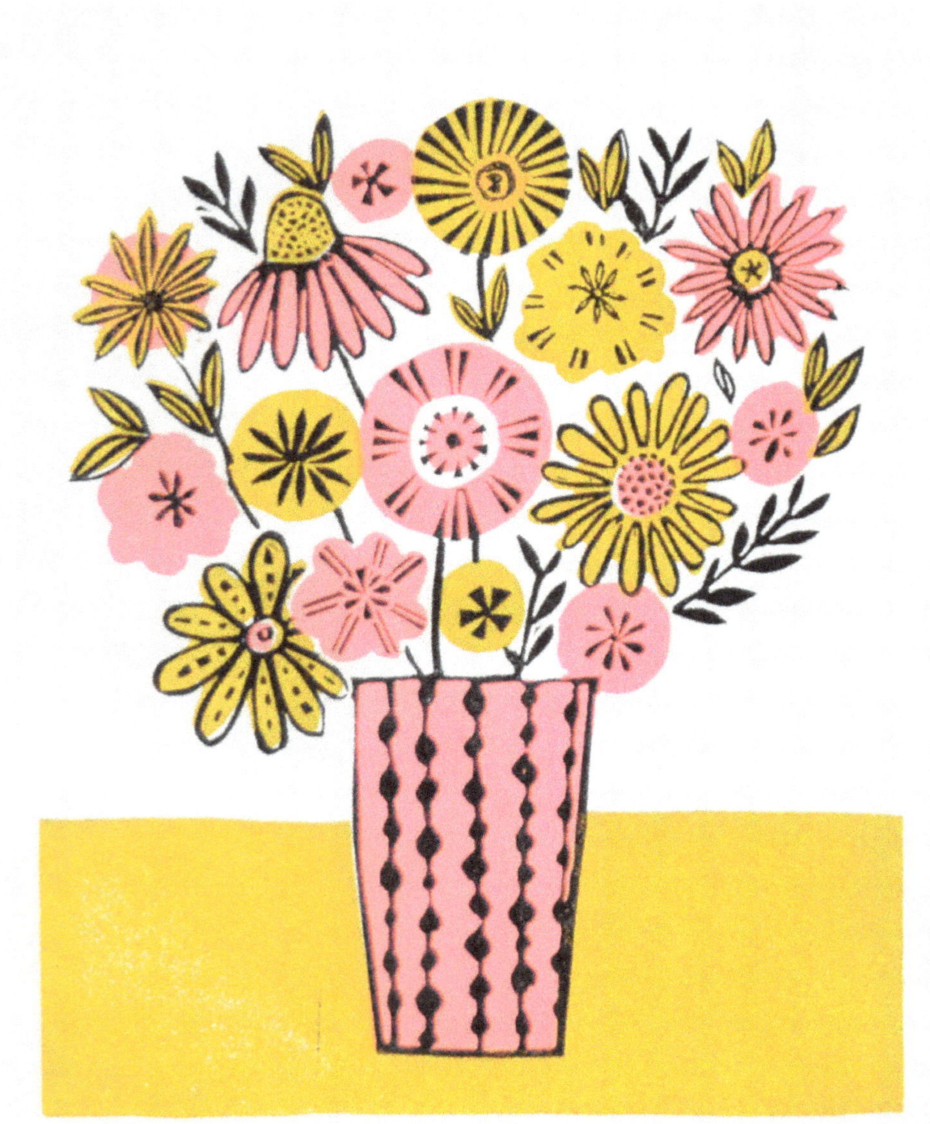

TOOLS AND MATERIALS

- soft lead pencil
- drawing paper
- light box (optional)
- tracing paper
- 3 dense rubber carving blocks
- cutting mat
- bone folder
- craft knife
- transparent acrylic ruler
- gouges in various sizes
- soap, water, and sponge, or a baby wipe
- mat board or card stock
- masking tape
- water-soluble printing inks
- brayer
- inking platen
- newsprint
- baren or wooden spoon
- Japanese washi printing paper

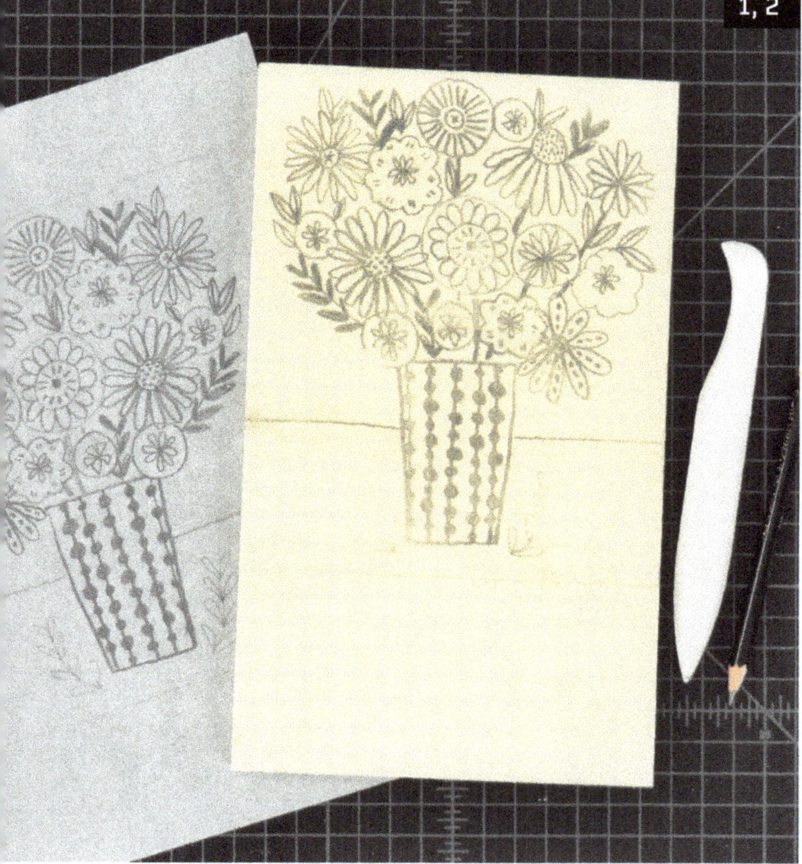

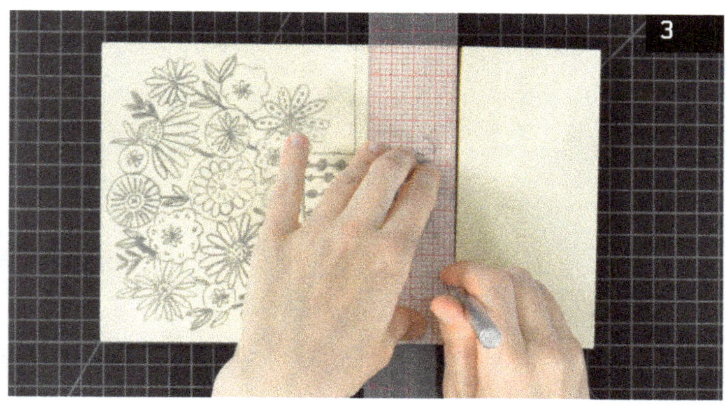

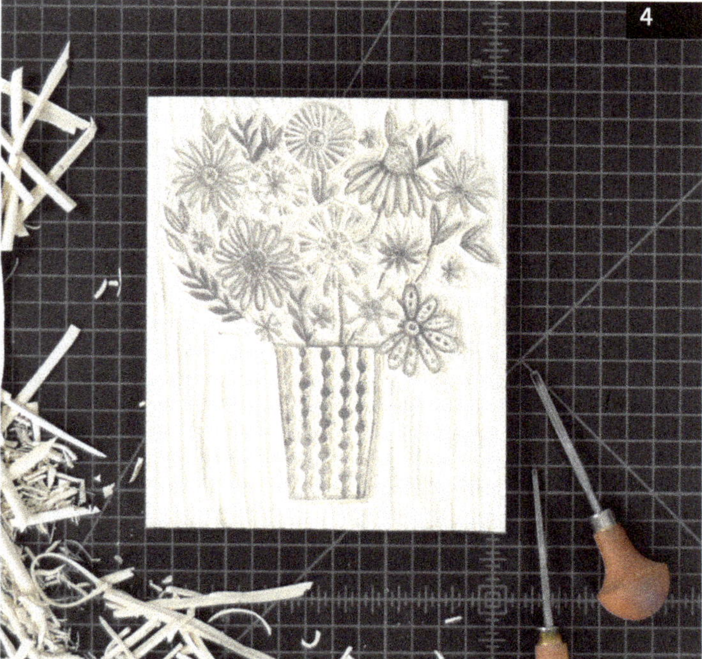

1 / Draw your design on a piece of paper. Make a border around the drawing. All of the blocks used for the print will be cut to the dimensions of the border. Place the drawing on a light box or tape it to a bright window. Place a piece of tracing paper over the sketch, and trace it in detail with a soft lead pencil. Be sure your lines are clean and clear. All marks will be transferred to the block, so erase any mistakes.

2 / Set the cutting mat on your work surface. Place the first block on the mat. Lay the tracing paper drawing face down on the rubber block. Use a bone folder to transfer the image to the block. Hold the paper in place with one hand, and smooth the bone folder over the back of the paper with long sweeping movements from the center out. Check to make sure the image as transferred. Repeat the process with the other two blocks.

3 / Use the ruler and craft knife to trim each block to the dimensions of the border that you drew in step 1. Make each cut with a single, smooth slice with the knife, cutting all the way through to the mat.

4 / Carve your key block first. Use a variety of U- and V-shaped gouges. Outline the drawing with a medium V-shaped gouge. Use a wider U-shaped gouge to remove large expanses of block.

Next, move on to the details, carving with a small V-shaped gouge. When the carving is complete, take a brush and remove any extra scraps from the recesses. Clean the block with soap and water.

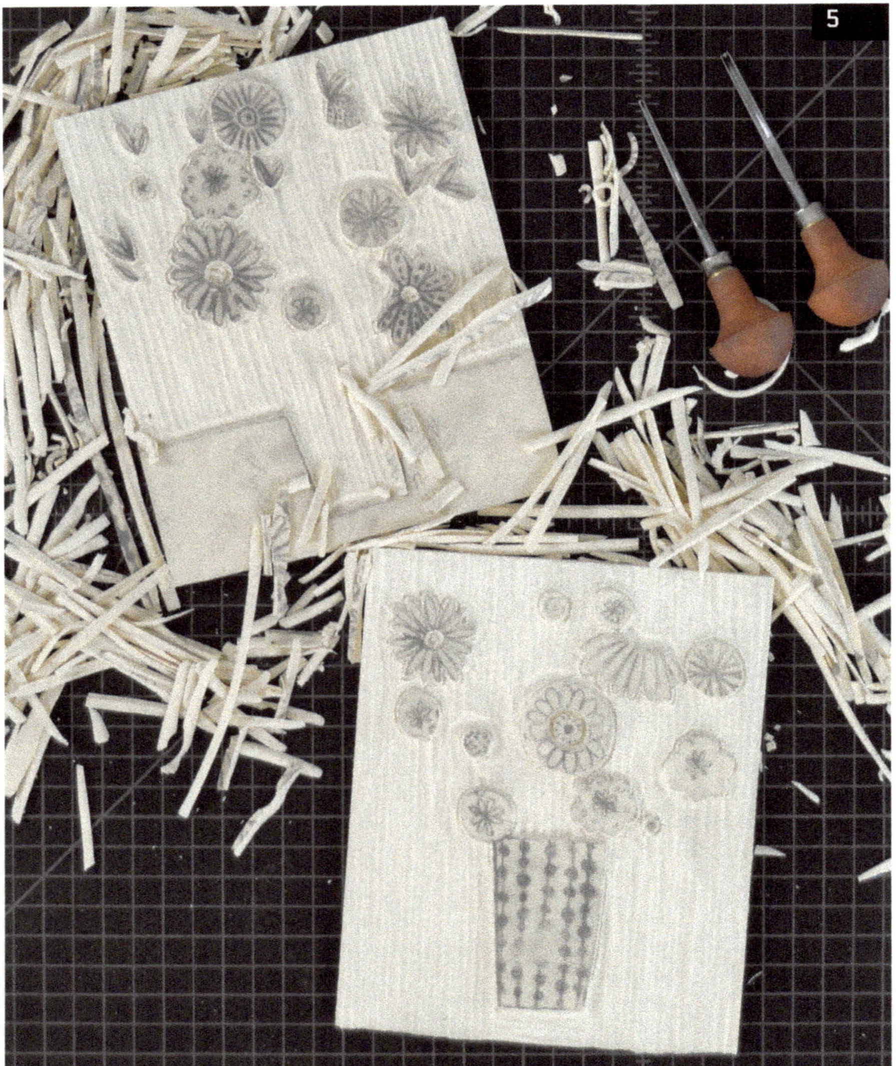

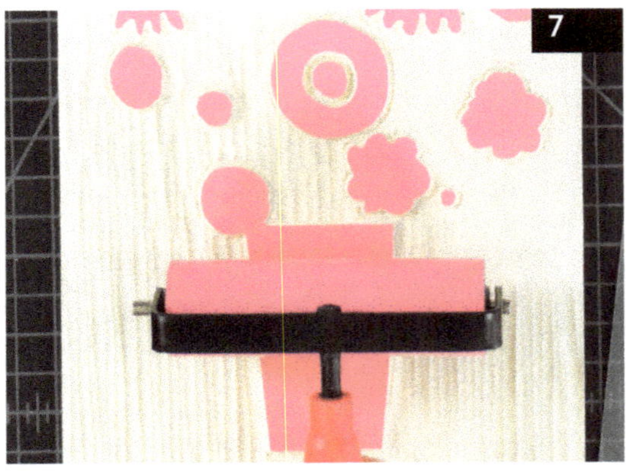

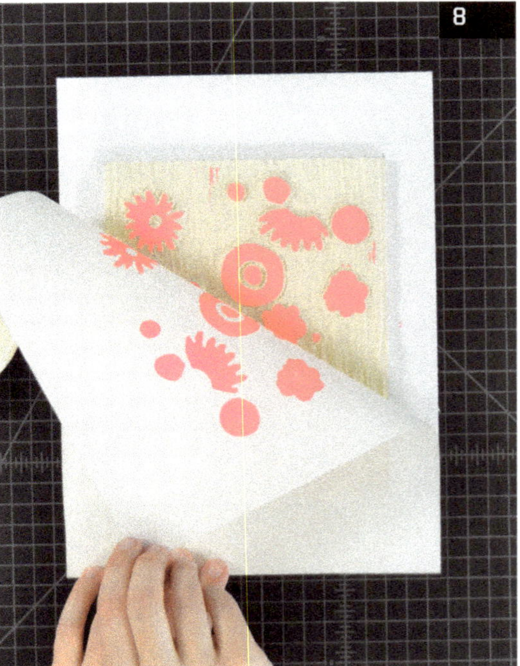

5 / With the key block complete, move on to the two blocks for spot color. In this case, pink and yellow. Decide which sections of the image you want in each color. Use the pencil transfer on the blocks to guide your carving. Carve away all the areas you don't wish to print. Check back on your original illustration, if necessary, to guide your way.

6 / Prepare a printing jig by cutting a piece of mat board to the dimensions of your printing paper. Tape the jig to your work surface. Center one of the blocks on the jig and trace the outline with a pencil. Remove the block and double-check to make sure the other two blocks fit accurately within the penciled outline.

7 / You will print the spot colors first. Decide which color to start with. Following the directions for inking on page 24, place a small amount of ink on the platen. Charge up the brayer and ink the block in thin, even coats.

8 / Carefully place the inked block inside the outline on the printing jig. Make a test print on newsprint, and set it aside. You will want to use the same test print for each color that you print. Then take a sheet of printmaking paper and line it up along the bottom edge of the jig. Keeping the paper in place with one hand, slowly roll the paper down on top of the inked block. Burnish the back of the paper with a baren, a wooden spoon, or your fingers. Lift the paper from the block: Your first color is printed. Continue printing the same color for the entire edition of prints. Set the prints aside to dry.

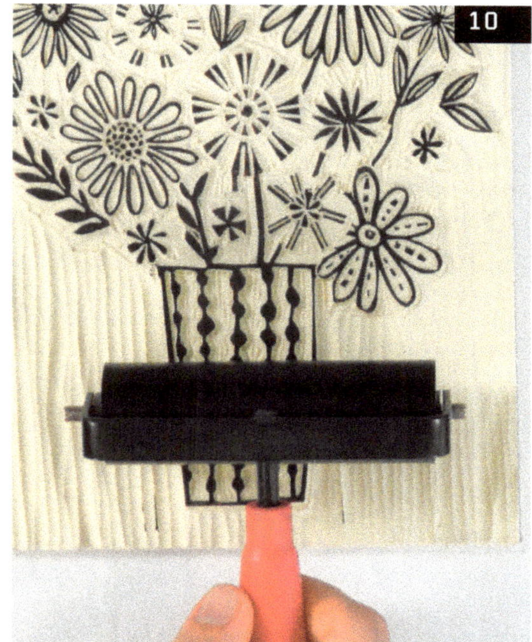

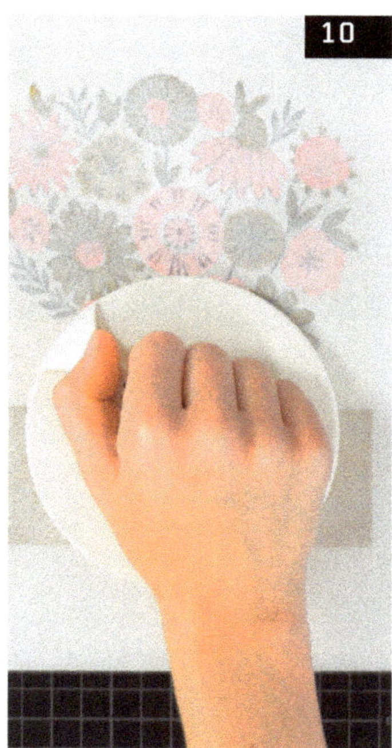

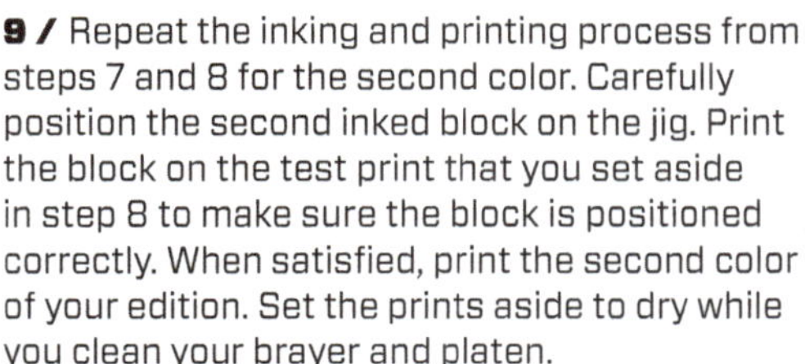

9 / Repeat the inking and printing process from steps 7 and 8 for the second color. Carefully position the second inked block on the jig. Print the block on the test print that you set aside in step 8 to make sure the block is positioned correctly. When satisfied, print the second color of your edition. Set the prints aside to dry while you clean your brayer and platen.

10 / Once the second color is dry, put a small amount of black ink on the platen. Roll out the ink and charge the brayer as before. Roll thin, even layers of ink onto the key block. Carefully position the inked key block within the outline on the jig. Test print the block on newsprint, then print the third color of your edition. Voilà—you've made a multiplate print.

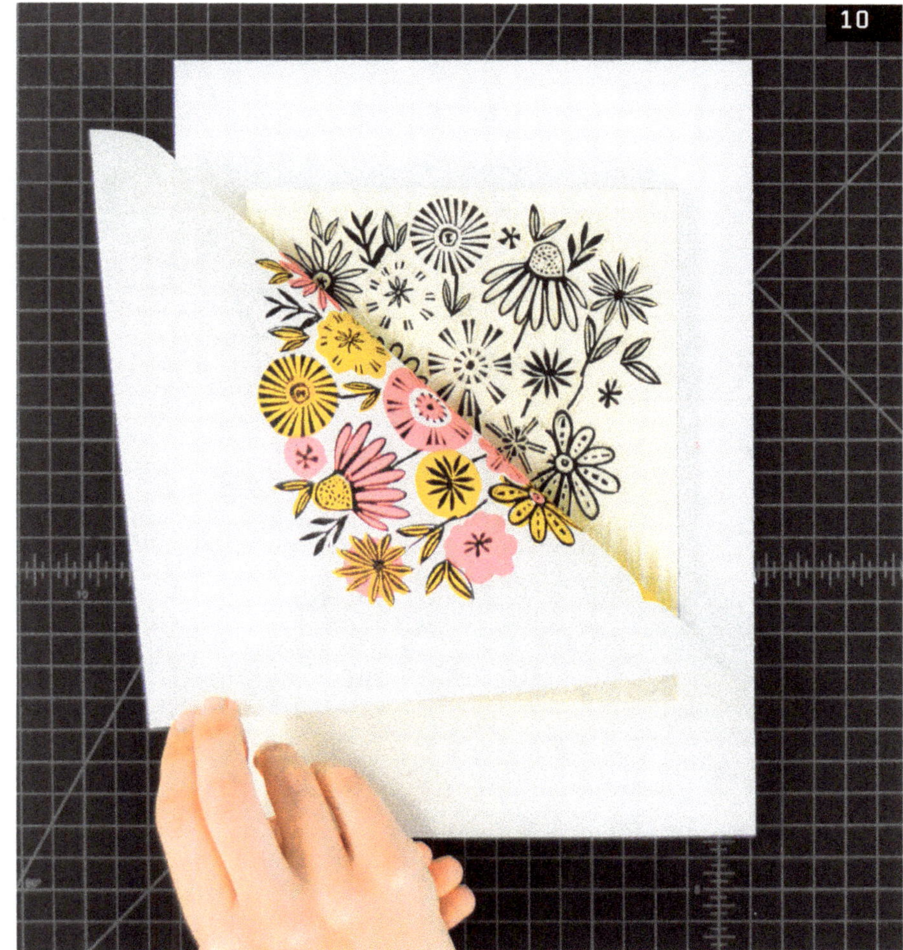

Printing in multiple colors can make your prints come alive. Using this simple jigsaw method of cutting up and arranging the spot-color blocks, you can create a four-color print using two blocks and only two rounds of printing. Dense rubber blocks are perfect for creating small prints using this jigsaw printing method.

TWO-PLATE PRINT: BIRD ON A BRANCH

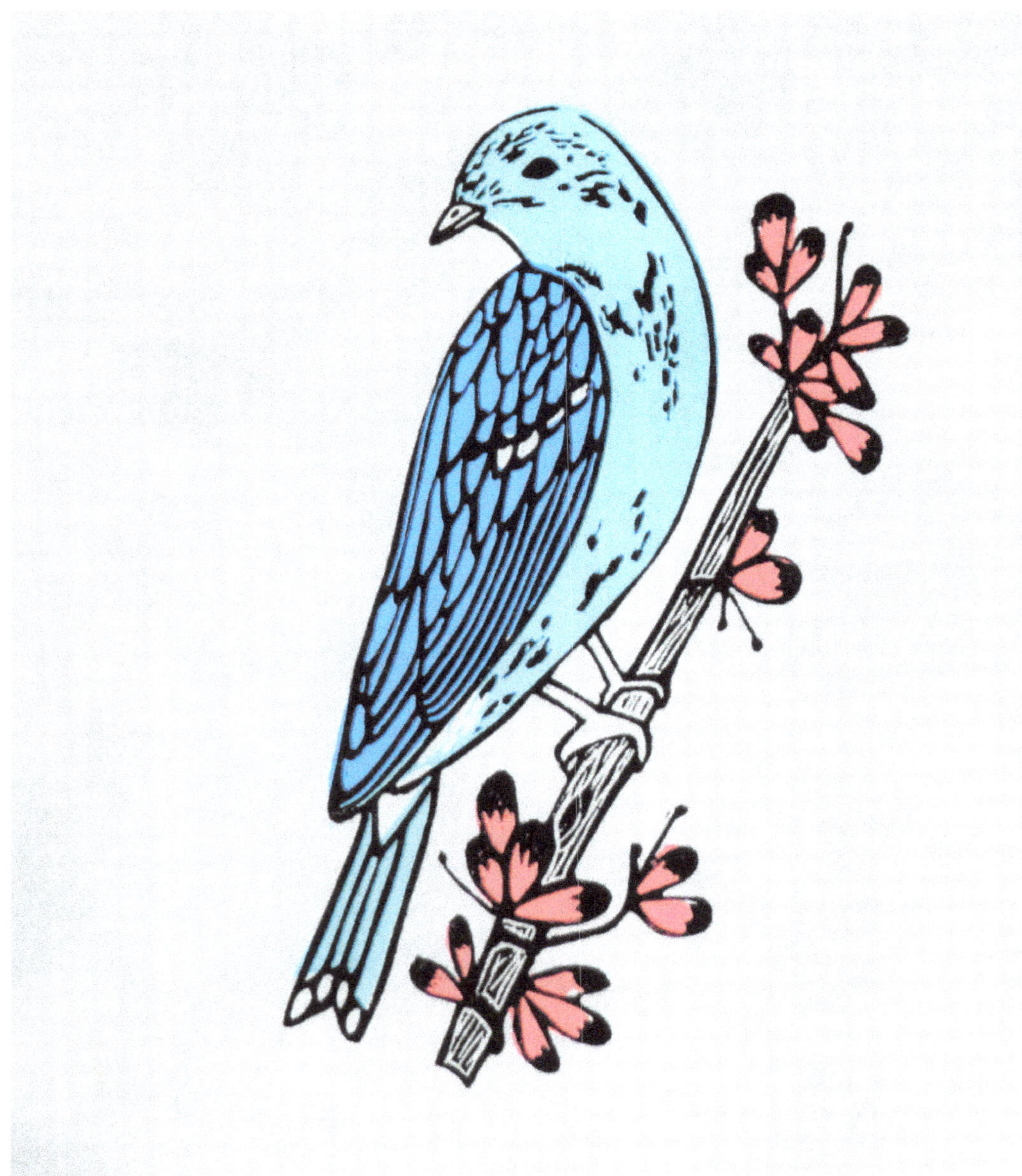

TOOLS AND MATERIALS

- soft lead pencil
- drawing paper
- light box (optional)
- tracing paper
- 2 dense rubber carving blocks
- bone folder
- cutting mat
- craft knife
- gouges in various sizes
- soap, water, and sponge, or a baby wipe
- ink
- brayers
- inking platens
- acetate transparency sheet
- mat board or card stock
- tape
- colored pencil
- newsprint
- baren or wooden spoon
- Japanese washi printing paper

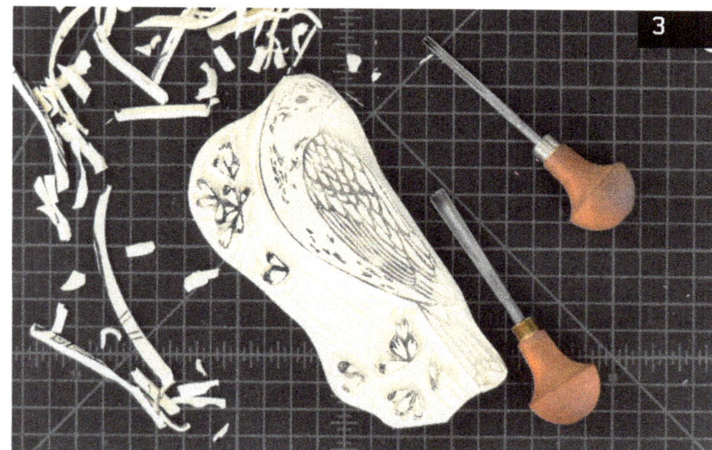

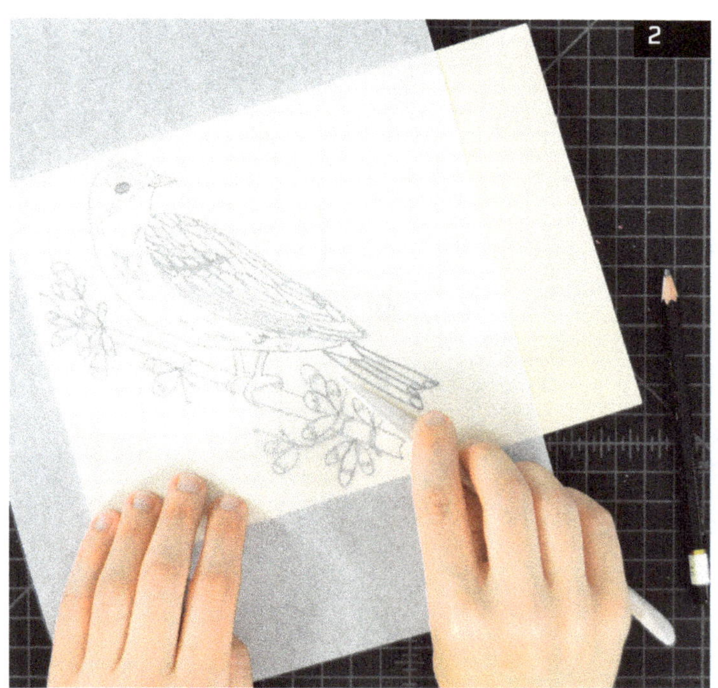

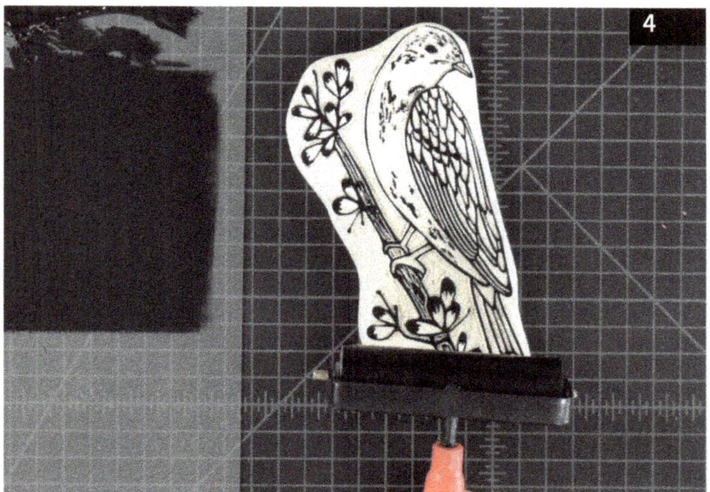

1 / This type of print relies on a key block. In a multicolor print, the detailed key block will be printed in black, tying all the spot-color areas together. Draw the design for your print—including the black and color areas—on paper with a soft lead pencil. Tape the drawing to a light box or a bright window. Trace over it with tracing paper and a pencil.

2 / Prepare you key block first. Turn the tracing-paper drawing face down on a dense rubber block. Holding the illustration in place with one hand, use a bone folder to transfer the image by rubbing the back of the paper from the center outward. Lift a corner and check your transfer. Remove the paper once complete.

3 / Place the block on a cutting mat and use a craft knife to cut around the outline of the transfer drawing, leaving a small, manageable border. Now you can begin carving your key block. Outline your design using a medium V-shaped gouge. Remove the large areas of background space with a U-shaped gouge. Carve the fine details of the drawing with a small V-shaped gouge. When complete, brush away any carving scraps left in the recesses. Clean the block with soap and water.

4 / Prepare to transfer the key block design to the second rubber block. Have the platen, black ink, brayer, and a transparent acetate sheet close at hand. Following the directions for inking on page 24, roll a small amount of black ink on the platen. Then ink your block with a few thin coats. You will need only a medium amount of ink, because it will be printing on the acetate sheet.

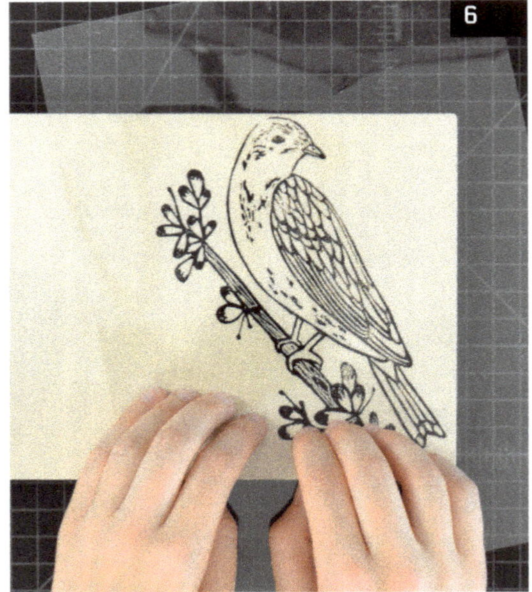

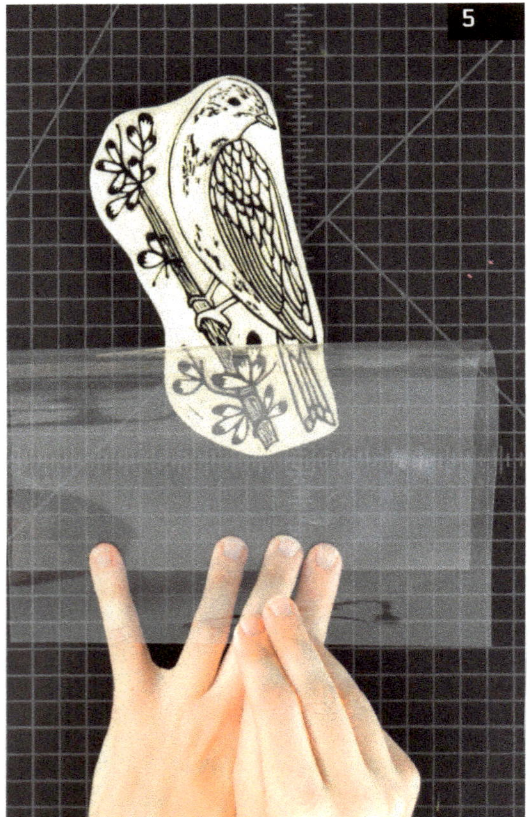

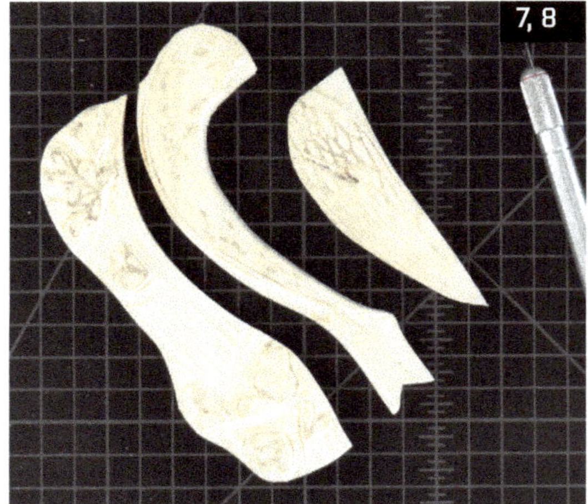

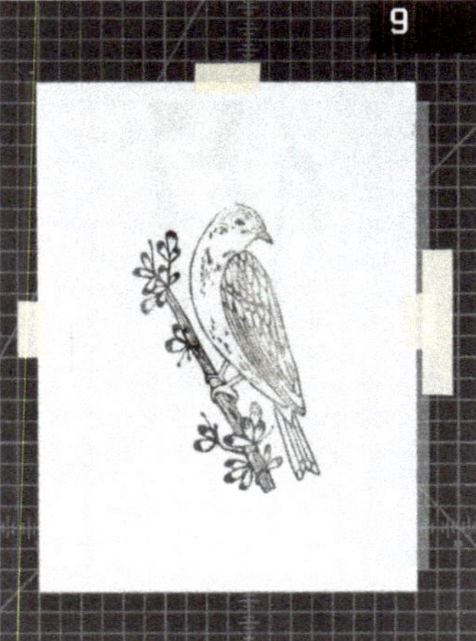

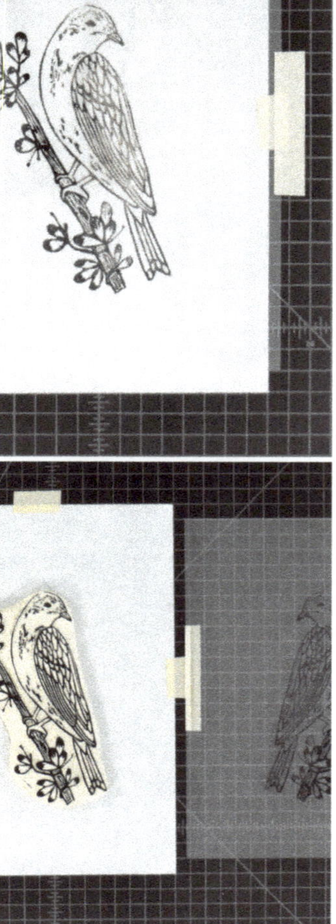

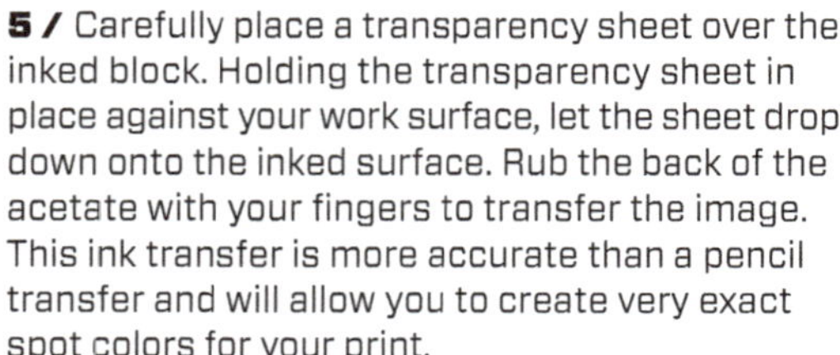

5 / Carefully place a transparency sheet over the inked block. Holding the transparency sheet in place against your work surface, let the sheet drop down onto the inked surface. Rub the back of the acetate with your fingers to transfer the image. This ink transfer is more accurate than a pencil transfer and will allow you to create very exact spot colors for your print.

6 / Set the second, uncarved, rubber block on your work surface. Lift the transparency sheet from the inked block and place it face down on the uncarved block. Rub the back of the acetate to transfer the ink. Lift the transparency sheet, set it aside carefully, and allow the ink on the uncarved block to dry. Save the transparency sheet and do not wash off the ink. You will use this same sheet to register the blocks during printing.

7 / Now you will carve your spot-color blocks. Use a craft knife to cut around the outline of the transferred design. Use gouges to carve away the blank areas of the background.

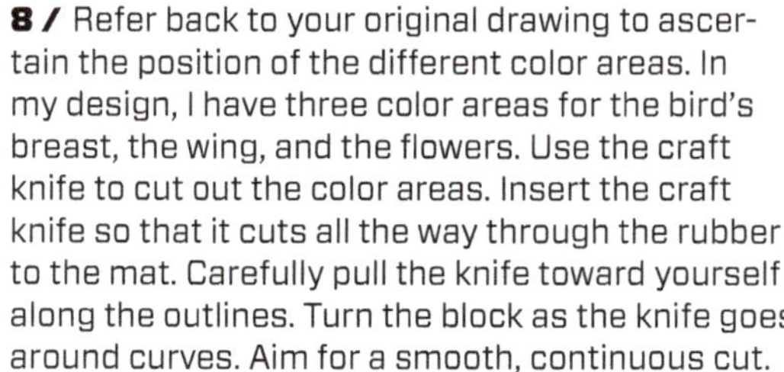

8 / Refer back to your original drawing to ascertain the position of the different color areas. In my design, I have three color areas for the bird's breast, the wing, and the flowers. Use the craft knife to cut out the color areas. Insert the craft knife so that it cuts all the way through the rubber to the mat. Carefully pull the knife toward yourself along the outlines. Turn the block as the knife goes around curves. Aim for a smooth, continuous cut.

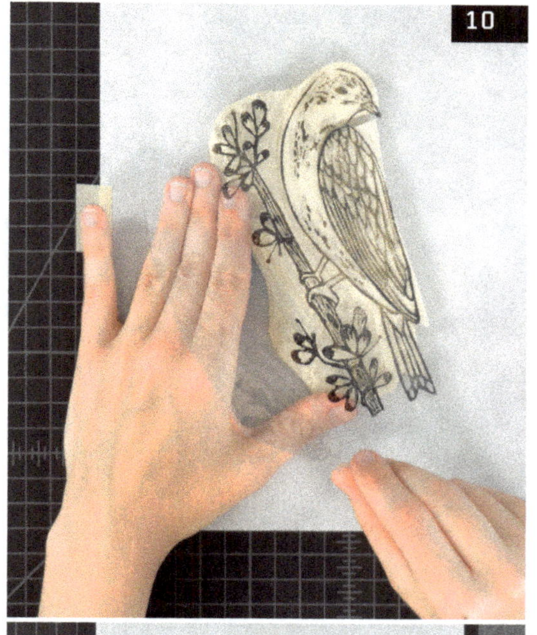

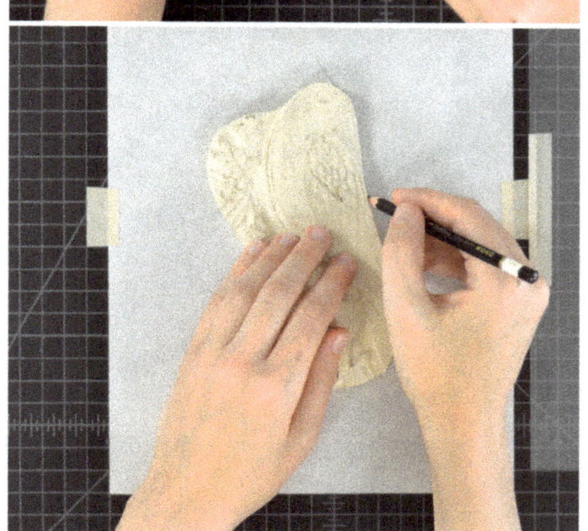

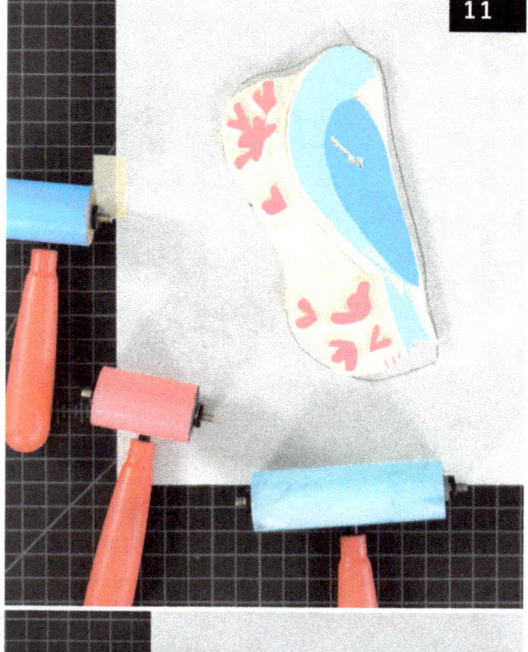

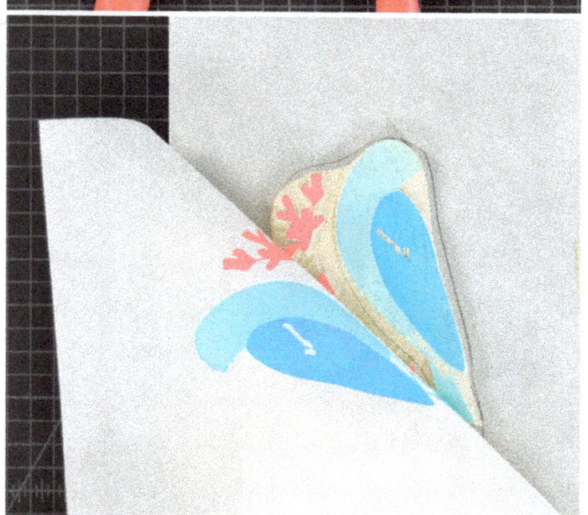

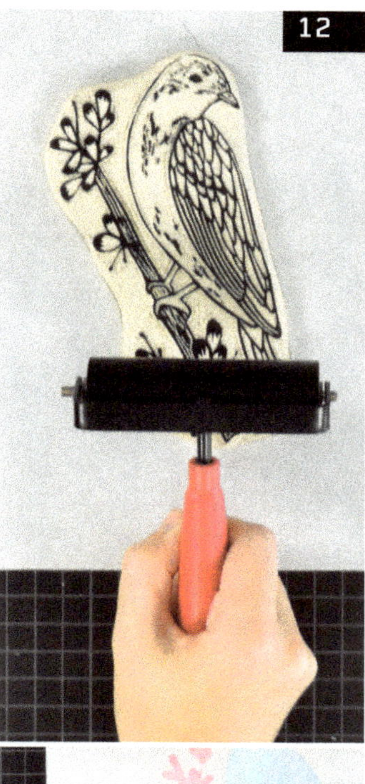

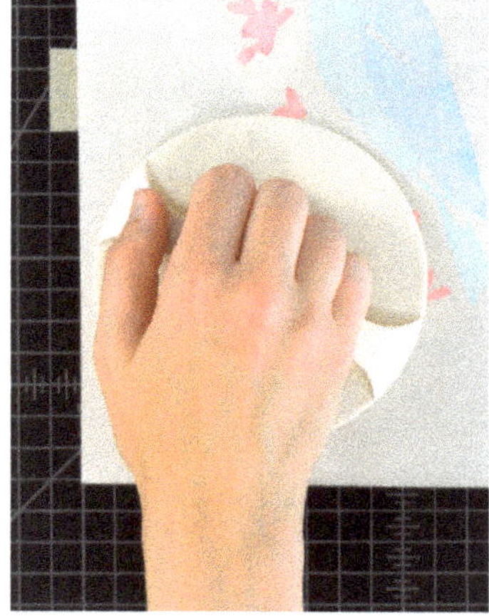

9 / Prepare a printing jig by cutting a piece of mat board to the same dimensions as your printing paper. Tape the jig to your work surface. Make sure the ink on the acetate sheet from step 5 is dry. Center the acetate on the jig, ink-side down, and tape it along one edge to create a hinge. Place your key block on the jig under the acetate sheet and line it up exactly with the printed image. Lift the acetate and trace around the block directly onto the jig with a pencil. Set the block aside.

10 / Reassemble the three spot-color blocks and place them on the jig, under the transparency sheet. Line up the blocks with the image on the transparency sheet. Lift the transparency sheet and use a colored pencil to trace the outline on the jig to differentiate it from the positioning of the key block. Remove the color-spot blocks from the jig.

11 / You're ready to print. Start with the spot colors. You'll print all of the colors together. Small brayers and individual platens are useful for this type of project. When the blocks have been inked individually, reassemble the three pieces on the jig within the colored-pencil outline. Try a test print on newsprint, then re-ink the blocks. Align a piece of printing paper along the edge of the jig. Carefully let it drop onto the inked blocks. Burnish the back with a baren. Lift the print and set it aside to dry. Re-ink and print the color areas for the complete edition. Allow the prints to dry.

12 / Prepare to print your key block with black ink. Roll out the black ink on the platen to charge the brayer. Roll thin, even coats of ink onto the key block. Place the inked block within the penciled outline on the printing jig lining. Test print on newsprint, then re-ink. Line up your printing paper with the edge of the jig, remembering to place it in the correct orientation for the print. Carefully roll the paper down onto the block. Rub the back of the paper with your fingers or a baren to transfer the ink. Carefully lift the paper to reveal your print!

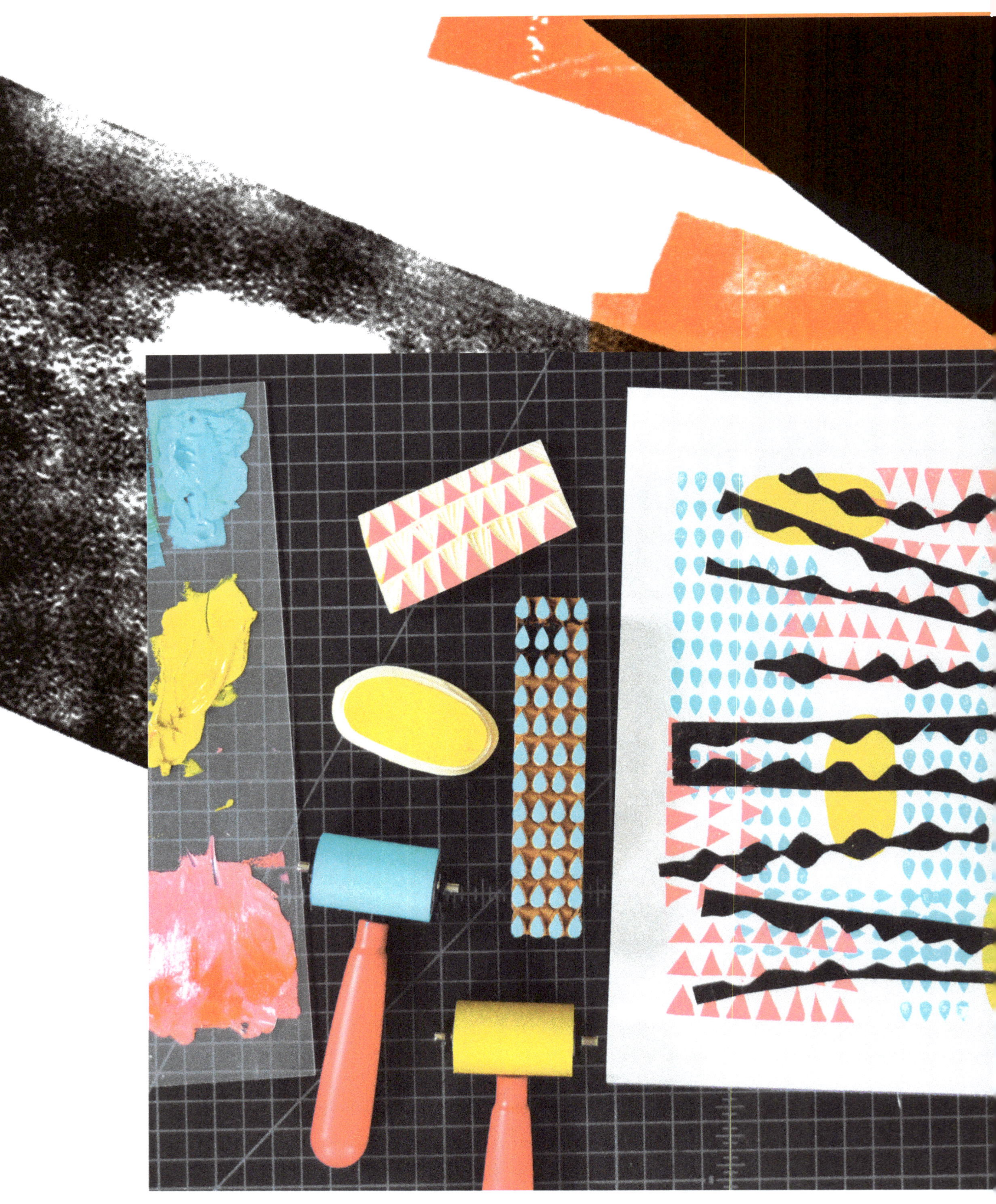

Stamps and Combined Techniques

CHAPTER THREE

Finding new ways to be creative can ignite an art series, revive your interest in printmaking, or offer a respite from other projects. Using premade stamps allows you the chance to dwell on things, such as placement, color, and multiple impressions, without having to make any major decisions about what the image will be. Happily, stamps are available in an enormous and interesting variety in art shops and craft-supply stores.

Getting your hands and mind active is crucial for maintaining a creative flow. Sometimes working with a set of stamps will lead to an inspiration for something completely original. The projects in this section can be mastered by the young and anyone new to printmaking. Experienced printers can adapt and expand the projects, or use them as a source of design ideas.

Repeat patterning has a long history in printmaking. Single-icon blocks, either precut or hand carved, can be used to create wrapping papers, wallpapers, and fabric designs for all kinds of fashion and home décor projects. The type of repeat you create, and the size of your block, will determine the look and feel of the overall pattern. Simple repeating patterns in bold colors can make excellent art prints. Once you've tried your hand at a few simple repeats, get creative with tossed, random, and multilayered repeats.

PRINTING IN REPEAT: OWL STAMPS

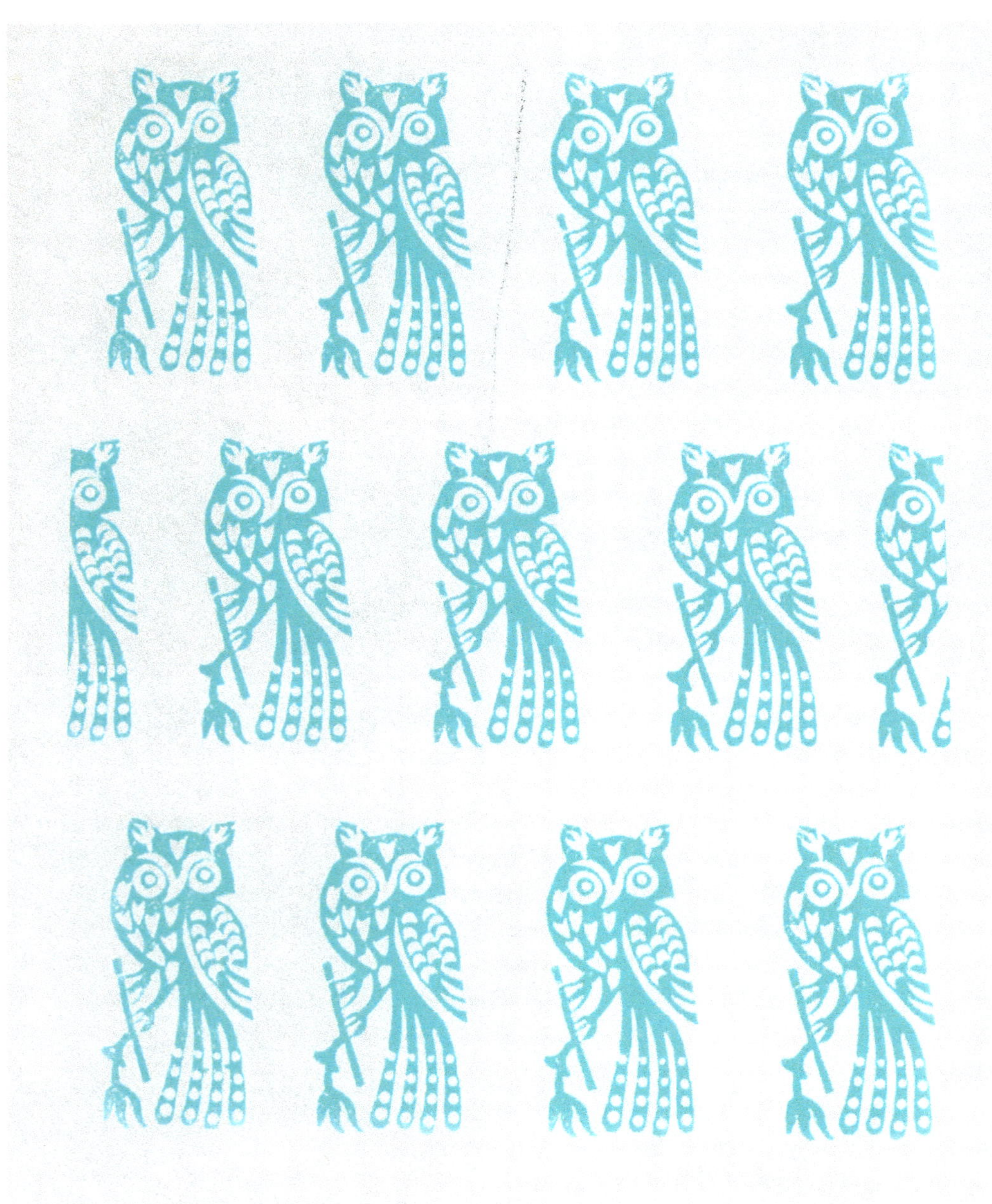

TOOLS AND MATERIALS

- water-soluble printing inks
- inking platen
- palette knife
- brayer
- precut stamps
- gridded cutting mat
- transparent acrylic ruler
- newsprint or scrap paper
- printing paper

NOTE

If you choose to print on fabric, look for block-printing ink suitable for fabric. Some inks may be used with both fabric and paper.

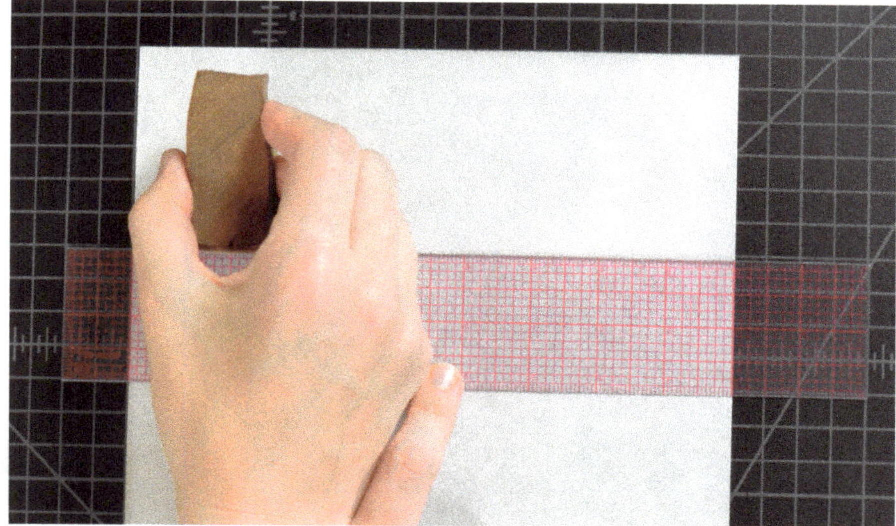

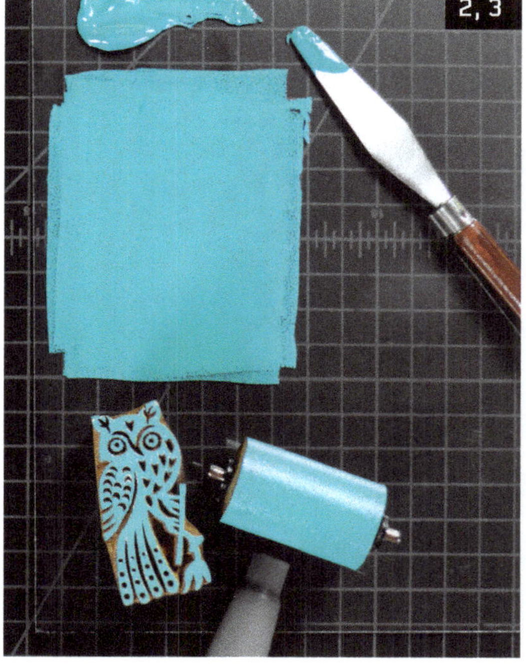

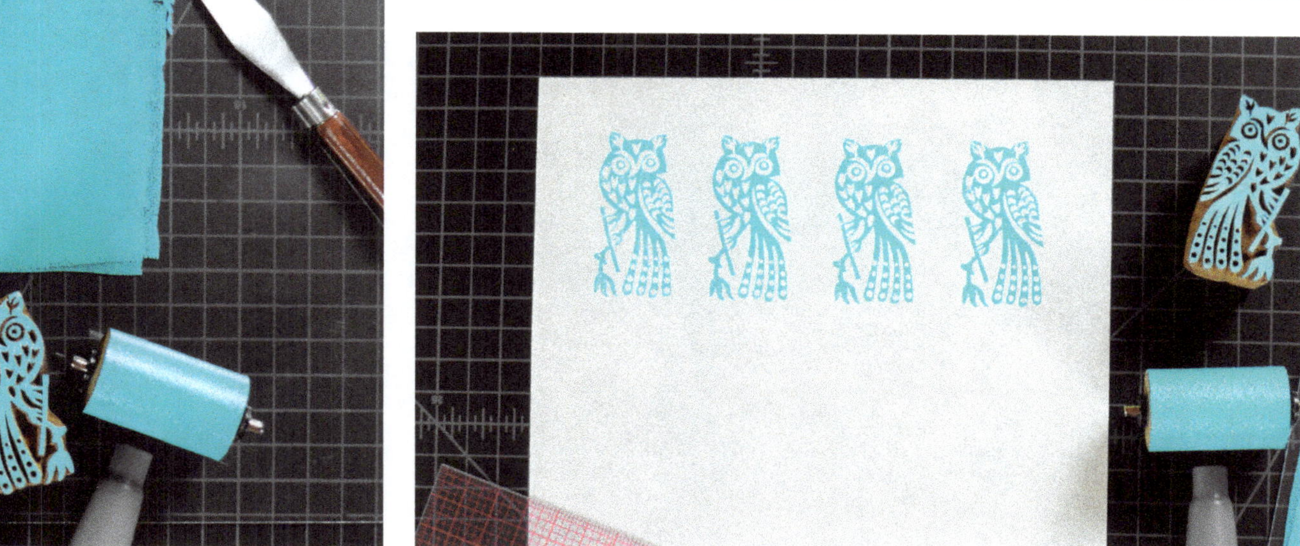

1 / Have your inks, inking platen, palette knife, brayer, and stamps close at hand. I recommend using a gridded cutting mat and a transparent ruler to check the spacing between repeats when you start. Once a few impressions are made, you can easily work by eye, if you prefer.

2 / Follow the directions for inking on page 24. Be sure to put only a small amount of ink on the platen and add more as you need it. Water-soluble ink dries quickly.

3 / Charge your brayer with thin, even applications of ink. Roll the ink onto the stamp several times for a thin-but-opaque application. Test print the stamp on newsprint after this first application of ink; the subsequent inking and printing of each impression will be much richer than the first impression.

Printing a Standard Repeat

The standard repeat is the simplest pattern to print. Each impression will be lined up vertically and horizontally like a grid. Before I start to print, I work out how many impressions I will be able to fit vertically and horizontally on the paper and how much space to leave between them.

Line up your paper on the gridded cutting mat. If you are right handed, start at the top left corner, so you won't accidently smear the ink each time you print. Place the ruler where you want the bottom edge of the stamp to fall. Press the inked stamp down on the paper, applying firm, even pressure. Carefully remove the stamp from the paper, you may need to hold down the paper with your other hand.

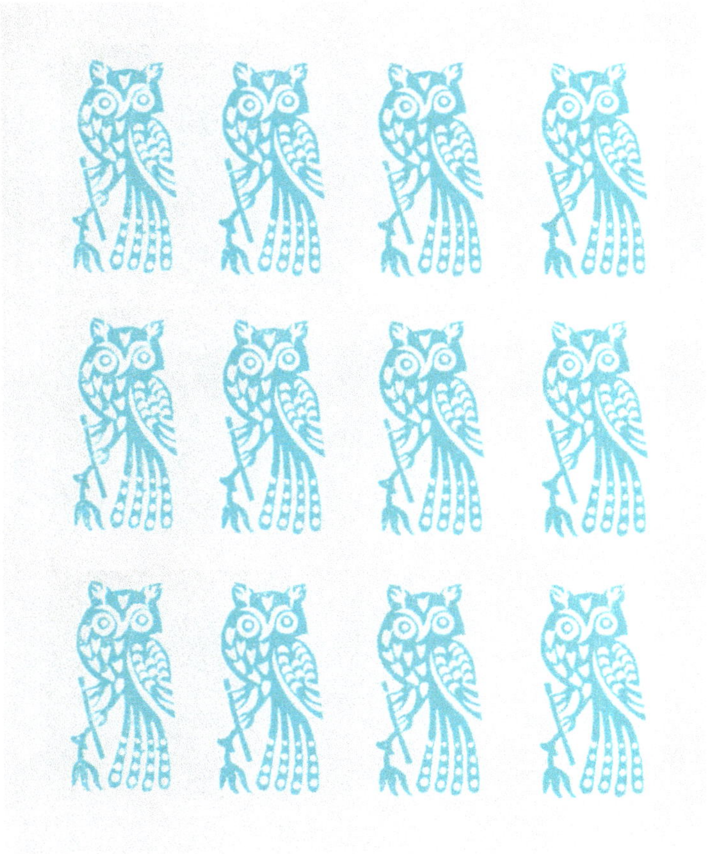

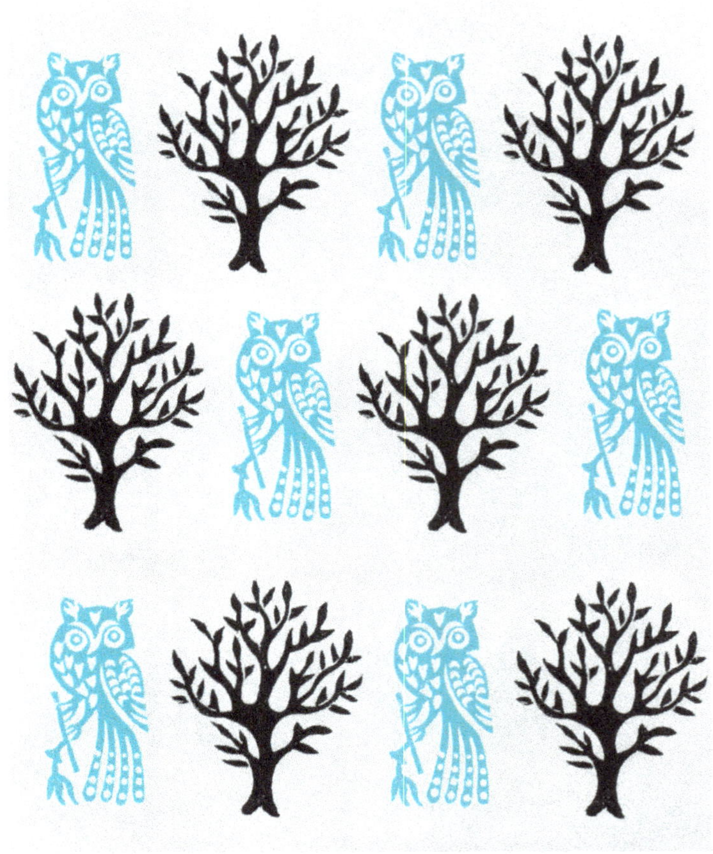

Repeat the inking and stamping process with each impression, using the ruler to measure the distance between the impressions. If the impressions begin to lose clarity, it might be because the stamp is overloaded with dried ink. You can remove the ink by washing and drying the stamp and waiting for it to dry, or by repeatedly stamping a scrap piece of paper until most of the ink is removed. Continue stamping in one direction using your ruler as a guide. When you have completed your row, move the ruler down to the next row. In a standard repeat, the second row will be directly below the first row.

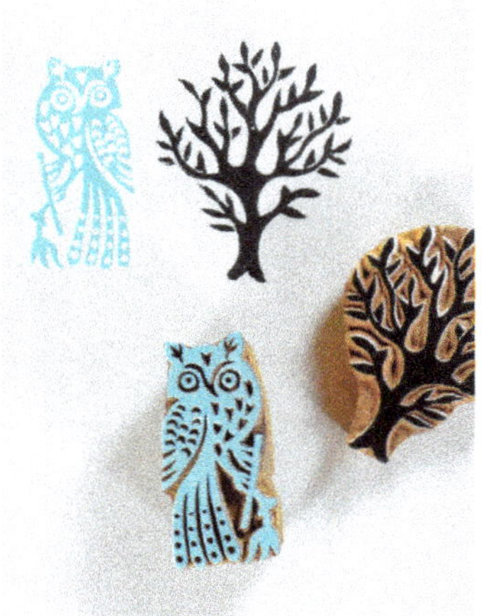

Alternating Two Stamps in a Standard Repeat

A simple way to make an interesting standard repeat is to use two stamps and alternating ink colors. Get an idea of how many impressions will fit on the printing paper by lining up the stamps before you ink them. Ink the stamp and prepare to print. Use the ruler to line up the first impression. Press down firmly, and carefully remove the stamp.

My second stamp is relatively close in size to the first. Ink the second stamp in another color. Aim for thin, even coats of ink on the stamp. Too little ink will make a salt-and-pepper impression, while too much ink may smear. Use the ruler to line up the second stamp. Place the stamp firmly on the paper, and press down evenly.

Alternate back and forth between the two stamps until you have completed your first row. When you are ready to move onto the next row, measure or eyeball the distance. Hold the stamp above the paper to get an idea where to place the second row.

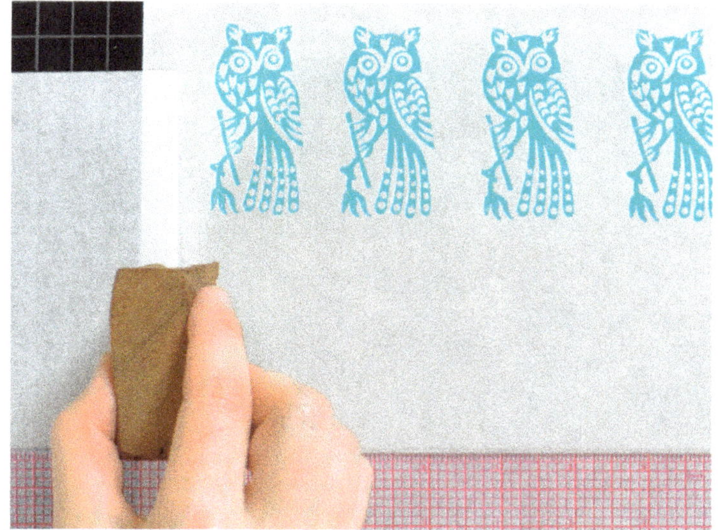

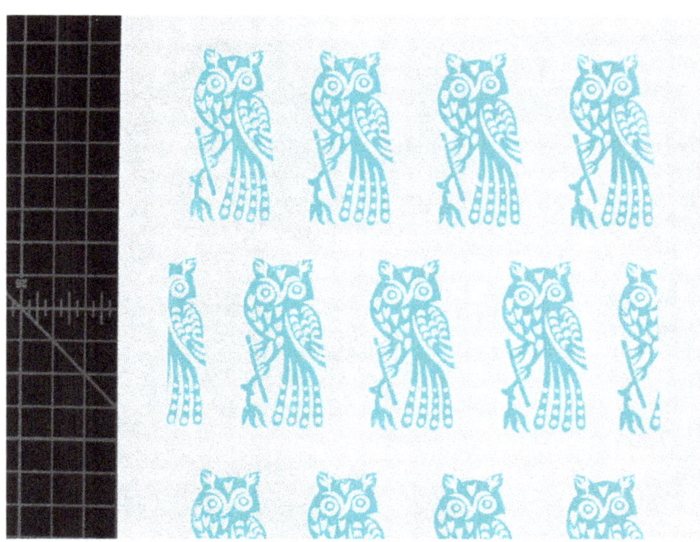

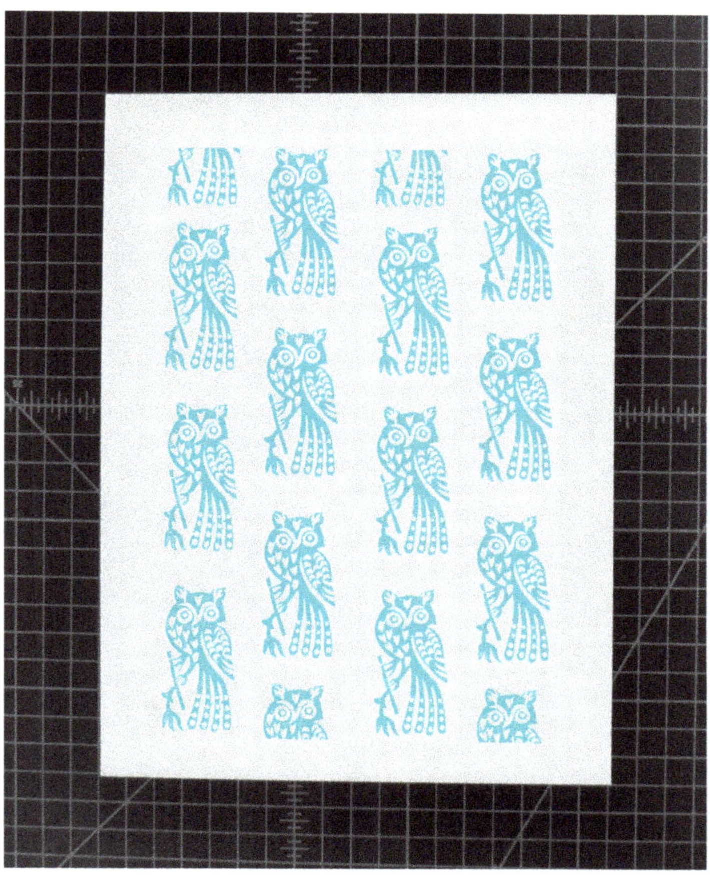

Printing a Half-Brick Repeat

A half-brick repeat is a repeat that looks like a brick wall. This type of repeat staggers the element in horizontal rows. Print the first row as in the standard repeat. Use a ruler to line up your first impressions in a horizontal row. Reapply ink to the stamp, as necessary.

When you are ready to print the second row, stagger the placement of the impressions to fall halfway between each of the stamps in the row above. When printing near the edge, place a piece of scrap paper on top of the printing paper and stamp over both. When you remove the scrap paper, you will have a clean border on the print.

When you have completed two rows, move on to your third row. The third row will line up directly below the first row. Each row will alternate in a staggered brick arrangement.

Printing a Half-Drop Repeat

A half-drop repeat is a simple repeating print where the elements are staggered in vertical rows. This style of repeat works exceptionally well for vertical stamps and also for creating vertical stripes in a pattern.

Ink the stamp and prepare to print using your ruler as a placement guide. For this pattern, I will print a vertical row first and work down the page. When I have completed this row, I will move to the second row placing my stamp halfway between two established impressions. If you wish to create a clean border, use a piece of scrap paper, as described in the half-brick repeat instructions.

Add personality to a precut stamp by creating your own complementary spot-color stamp. Precut stamps come in a variety of materials and in almost any imagery you can imagine. For this design, I am using a wooden, Indian textile stamp of a tree. These types of blocks can be found at antique shops and flea markets. I bought this one directly from a seller in India via etsy.com. I created spot-color stamps of foliage; these can be printed in colors from beautiful spring greens to autumnal reds and oranges.

PREMADE STAMP WITH CARVED STAMP: TREES

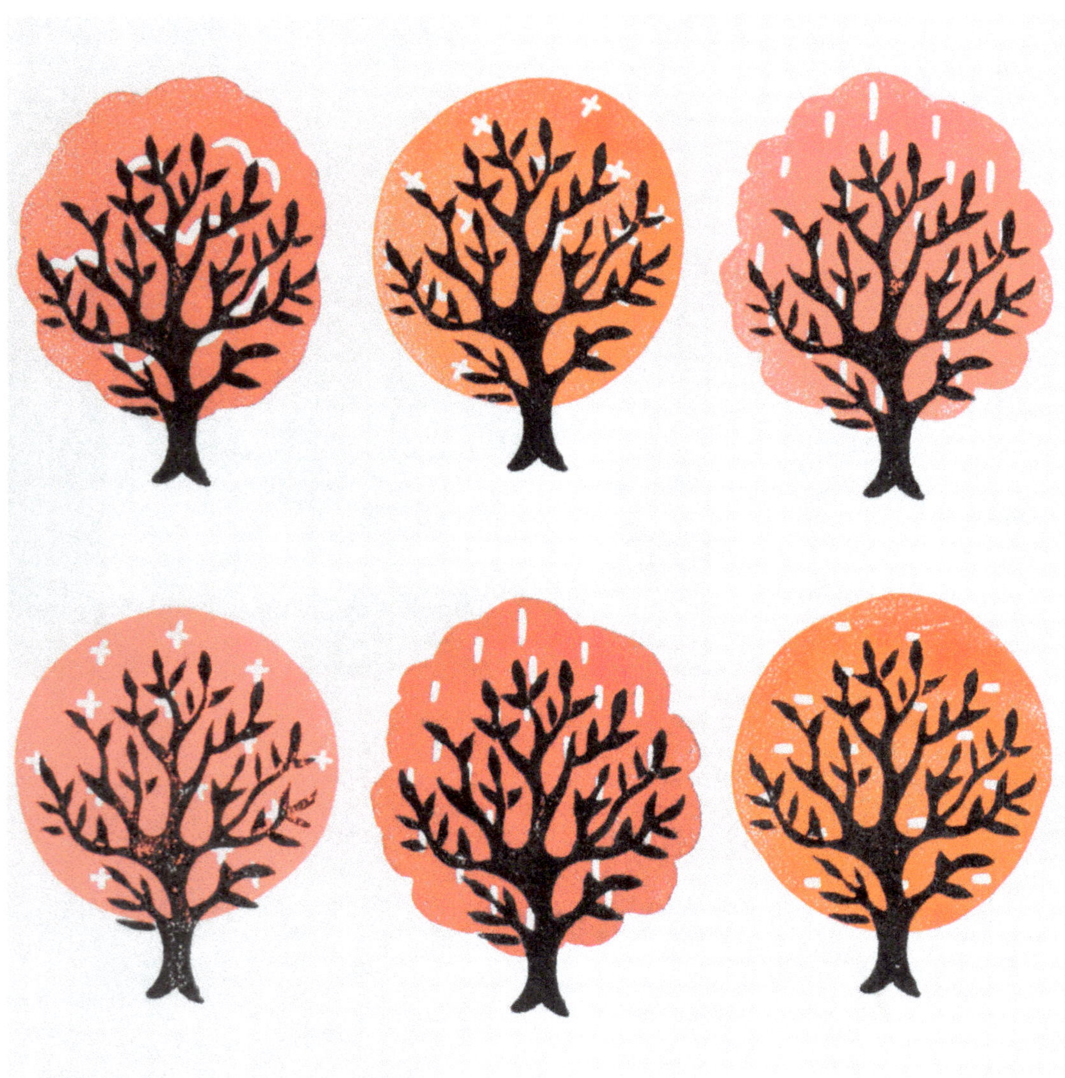

TOOLS AND MATERIALS

premade stamp

tracing paper

soft lead pencil

dense rubber block

bone folder

cutting mat

craft knife

gouges in various sizes

soap, water, and sponge, or baby wipe

water-soluble printing inks

brayers

inking platen

palette knife

newsprint or scrap paper

printing paper

baren

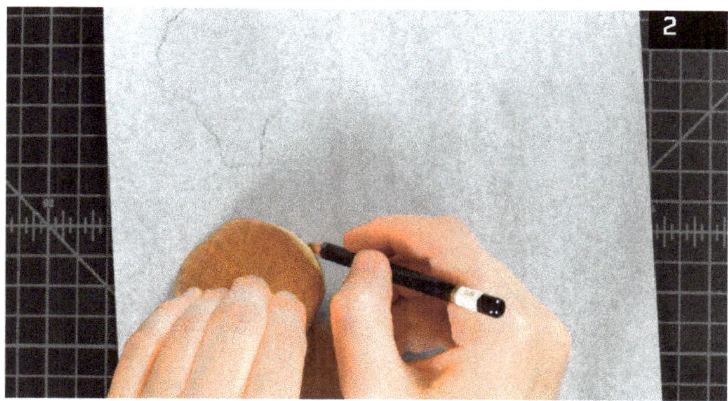

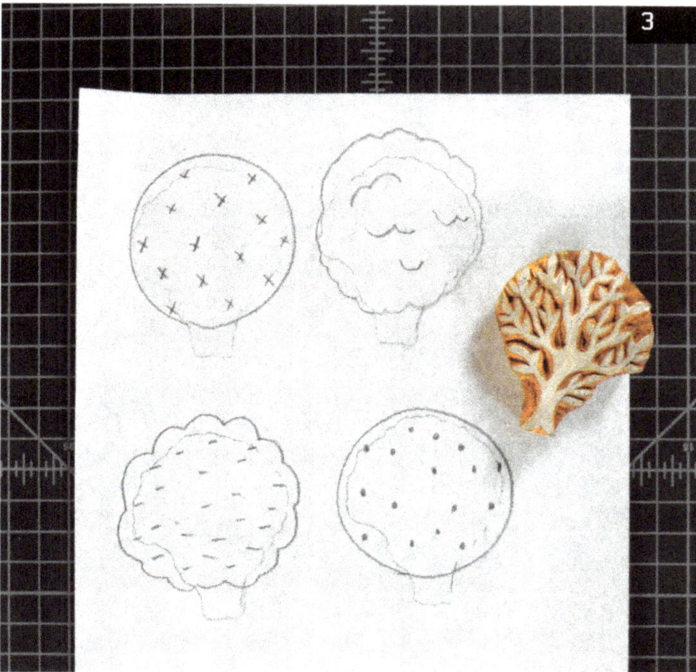

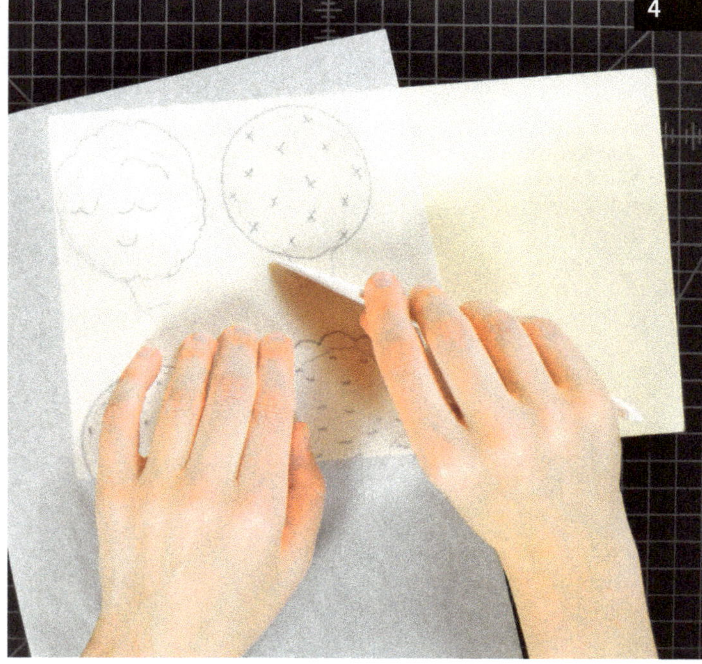

1 / Assemble the precut stamp, tracing paper, soft lead pencil, dense rubber carving block, bone folder, and gouges to begin.

2 / Place the precut stamp on a sheet of tracing paper. Use the soft lead pencil to trace the outline.

3 / Move the stamp on the paper and trace around it as many times as you need for the number of spot-color stamps you intend to carve. I've traced this stamp four times and added my penciled foliage designs.

4 / Place the tracing paper face down on the rubber block. You will be able to see your outlines through the back of the paper. Line up your drawings on the block, making sure there's room for a small border around each. Use a bone folder to transfer the pencil lines to the block. Work from the center outward, holding the paper in place with one hand and moving the bone folder in long sweeps with medium pressure. Lift a corner of the paper to check for a consistent transfer. When you're happy with the transfer, remove the tracing paper from the block.

5 / Place the rubber block on a cutting mat. Use a craft knife to cut out the shapes from the block. Cut outside of your pencil lines leaving a small margin.

NOTE

If you are cutting in a circle, turn the block as you go around.

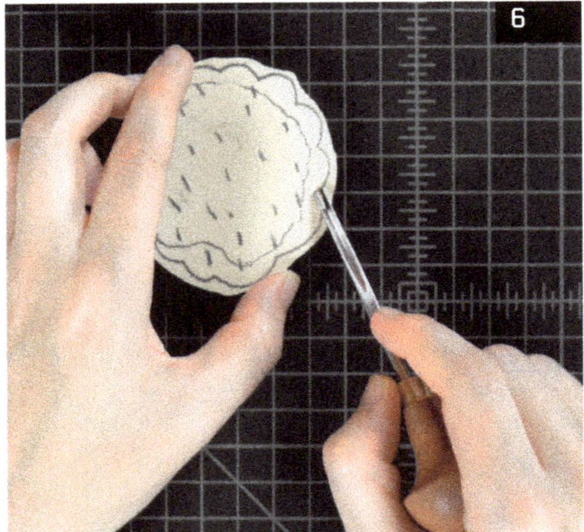

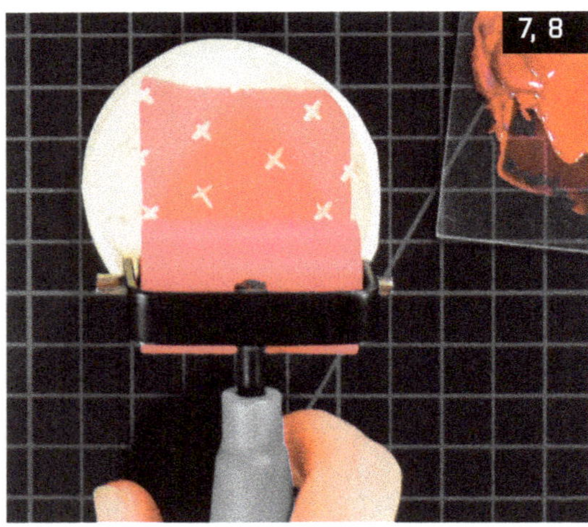

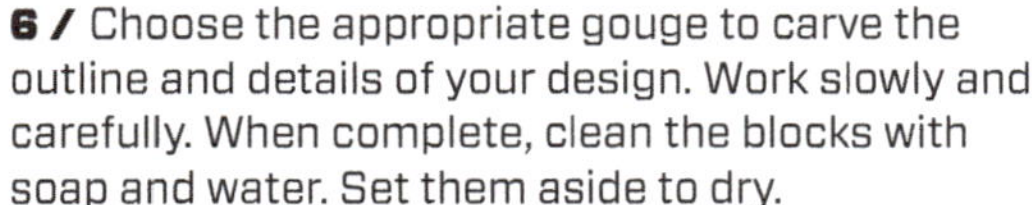

6 / Choose the appropriate gouge to carve the outline and details of your design. Work slowly and carefully. When complete, clean the blocks with soap and water. Set them aside to dry.

7 / Have the inks, brayers, inking platen, and printing paper close by. Choose a brayer that is about the same width as your design.

8 / Follow the directions for inking on page 24. Place ink on your inking platen with a palette knife or squeeze it out of a tube. Roll out the ink on the platen with the brayer, then roll thin layers of ink onto your block.

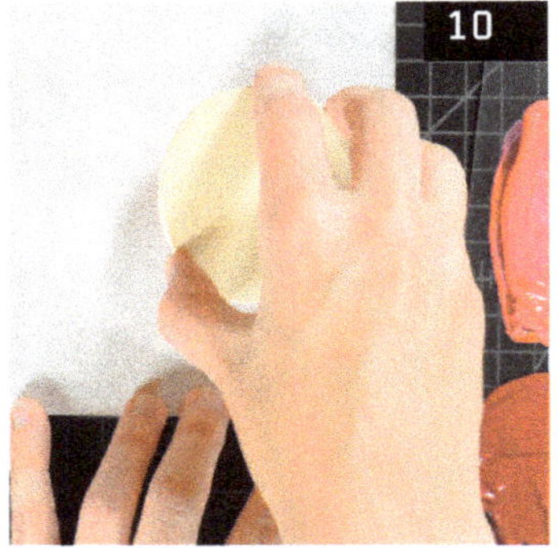

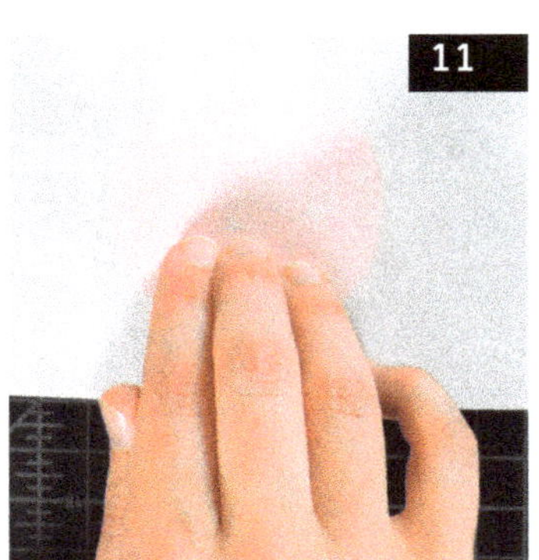

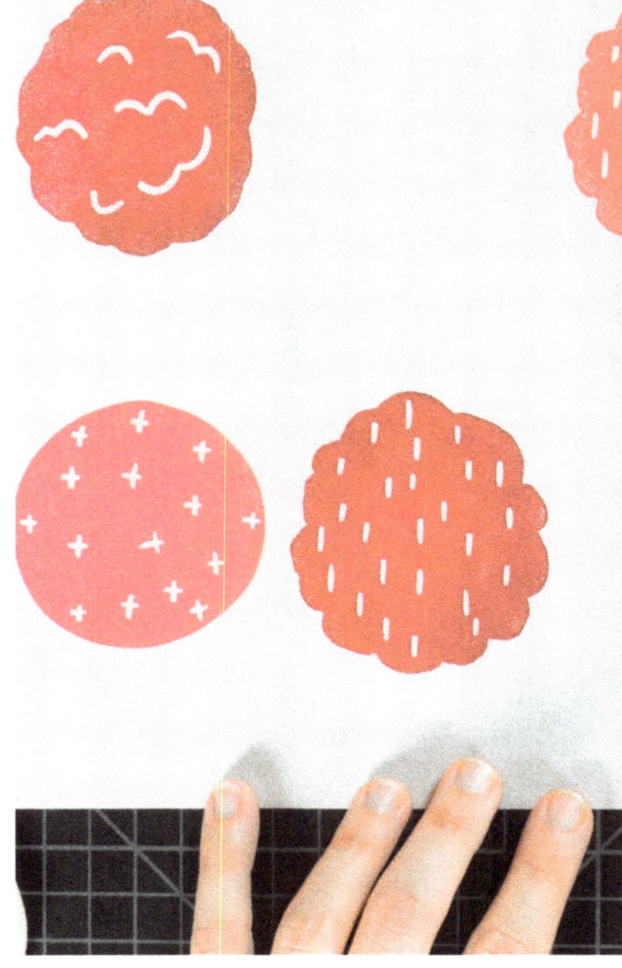

9 / Test print your block by laying a piece of newsprint on top of it. Rub the back of the paper with your fingers. Peel back the paper and look at your print. When you're happy with it, you're ready for your printing paper.

10 / Place the paper on your work surface, holding it in place with one hand. Ink your block and place it ink-side down on the paper.

11 / Flip the paper and block over. Carefully slide the paper and block to the edge of your work surface. Then, supporting from underneath with one hand while holding the block in place with the other, flip the two over together. Place them on your work surface. Rub the back of the paper with your fingers or a baren.

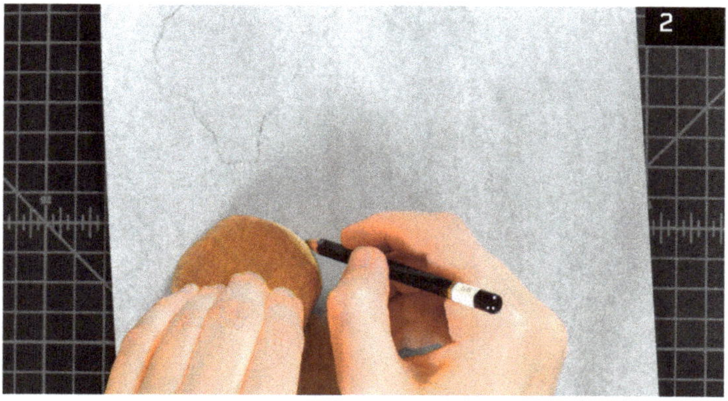

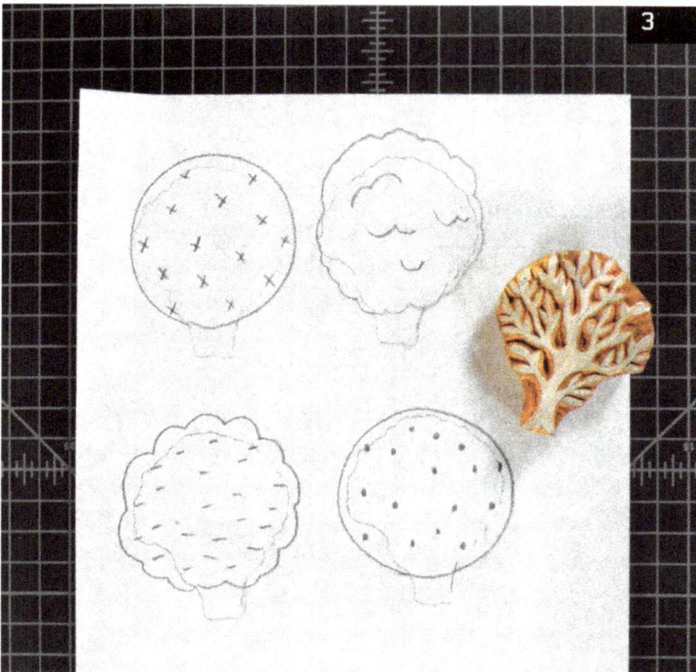

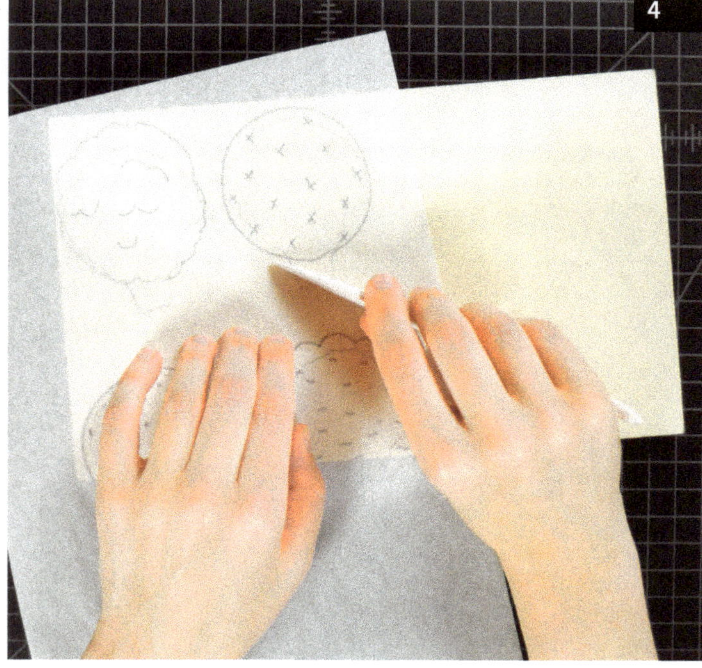

1 / Assemble the precut stamp, tracing paper, soft lead pencil, dense rubber carving block, bone folder, and gouges to begin.

2 / Place the precut stamp on a sheet of tracing paper. Use the soft lead pencil to trace the outline.

3 / Move the stamp on the paper and trace around it as many times as you need for the number of spot-color stamps you intend to carve. I've traced this stamp four times and added my penciled foliage designs.

4 / Place the tracing paper face down on the rubber block. You will be able to see your outlines through the back of the paper. Line up your drawings on the block, making sure there's room for a small border around each. Use a bone folder to transfer the pencil lines to the block. Work from the center outward, holding the paper in place with one hand and moving the bone folder in long sweeps with medium pressure. Lift a corner of the paper to check for a consistent transfer. When you're happy with the transfer, remove the tracing paper from the block.

5 / Place the rubber block on a cutting mat. Use a craft knife to cut out the shapes from the block. Cut outside of your pencil lines leaving a small margin.

NOTE

If you are cutting in a circle, turn the block as you go around.

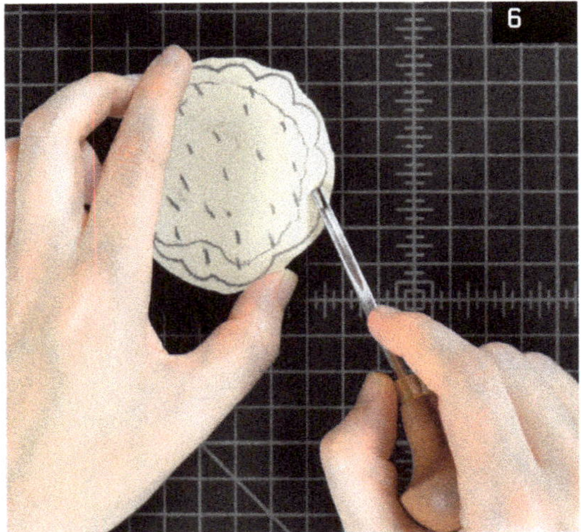

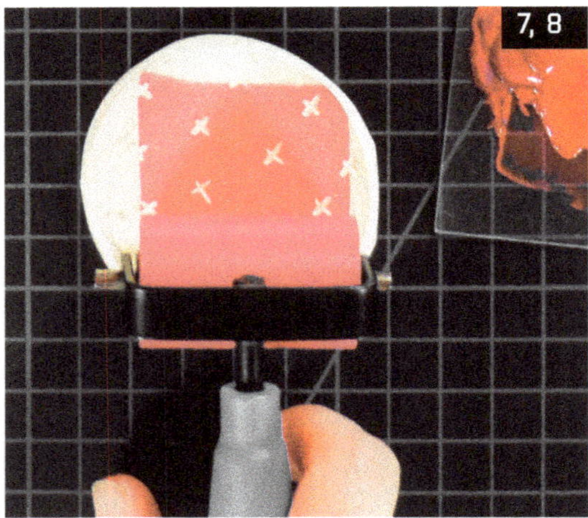

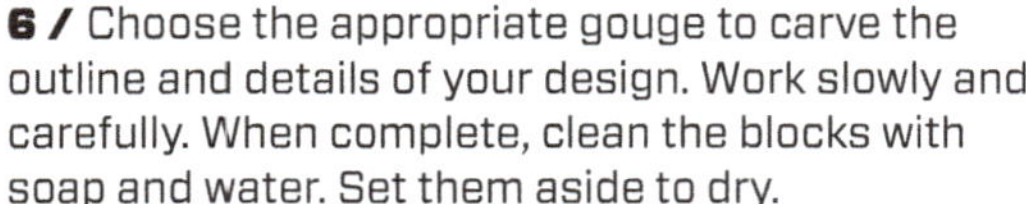

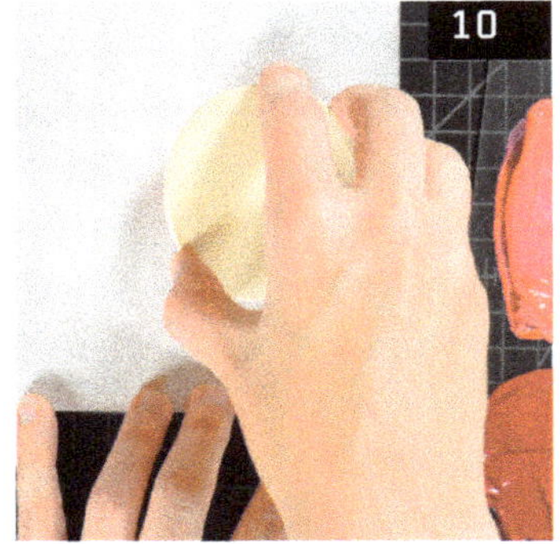

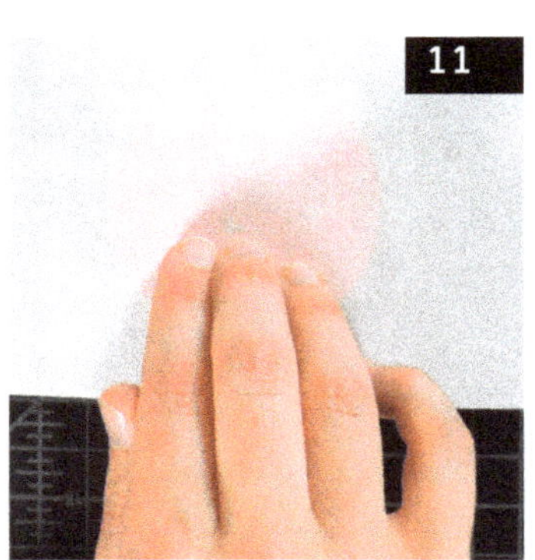

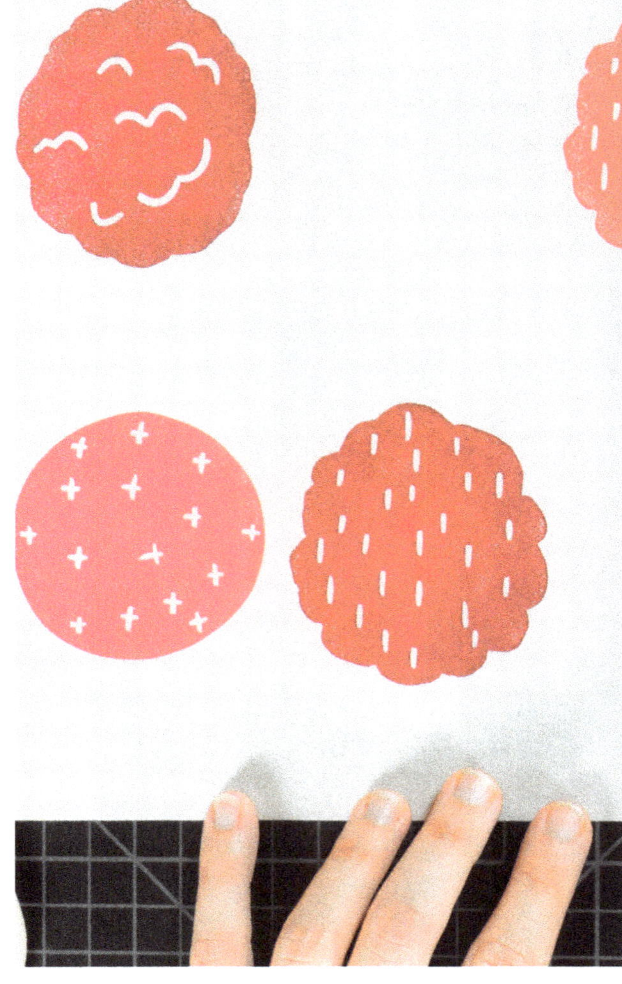

6 / Choose the appropriate gouge to carve the outline and details of your design. Work slowly and carefully. When complete, clean the blocks with soap and water. Set them aside to dry.

7 / Have the inks, brayers, inking platen, and printing paper close by. Choose a brayer that is about the same width as your design.

8 / Follow the directions for inking on page 24. Place ink on your inking platen with a palette knife or squeeze it out of a tube. Roll out the ink on the platen with the brayer, then roll thin layers of ink onto your block.

9 / Test print your block by laying a piece of newsprint on top of it. Rub the back of the paper with your fingers. Peel back the paper and look at your print. When you're happy with it, you're ready for your printing paper.

10 / Place the paper on your work surface, holding it in place with one hand. Ink your block and place it ink-side down on the paper.

11 / Flip the paper and block over. Carefully slide the paper and block to the edge of your work surface. Then, supporting from underneath with one hand while holding the block in place with the other, flip the two over together. Place them on your work surface. Rub the back of the paper with your fingers or a baren.

NOTE

Save your spot color for other printing sessions. This type of spot-color block will transfer easily to textile printing. You could also reverse the order of printing to print your spot color on top of the precut stamp.

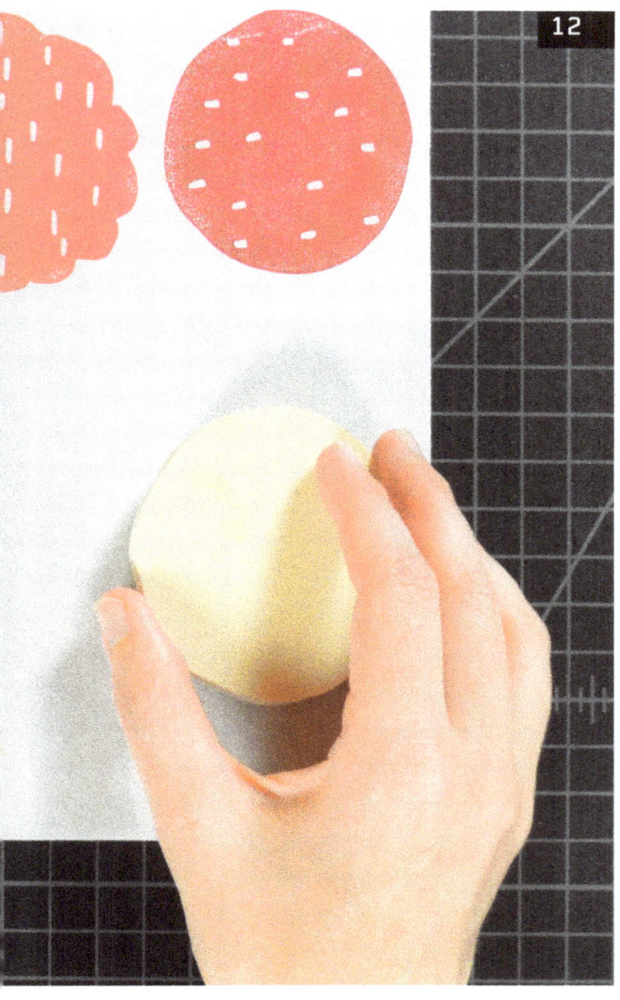

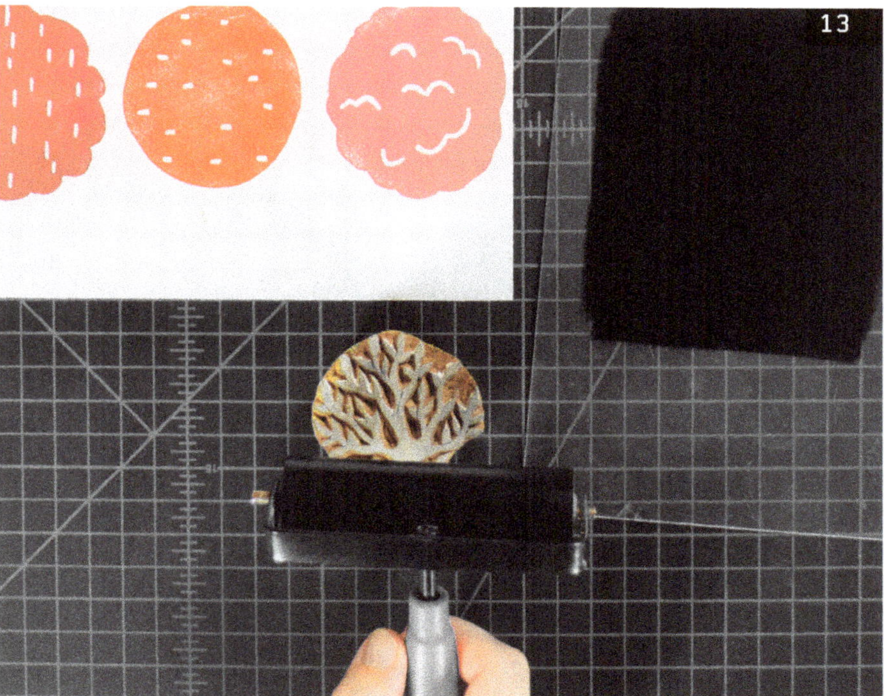

12 / Repeat steps 10 and 11 for all of the spot colors on your printing paper. Set the print aside to dry. Clean your inking platen, brayers, and blocks with soap and water.

13 / You're ready to print with the precut stamp. Follow steps 7 and 8 to ink the stamp.

14 / Place the print on your work surface and hold it in place with one hand. Holding the inked stamp in your other hand, eyeball its placement, then place it down in one smooth movement. Press firmly on the back of the stamp, then carefully lift it.

15 / Repeat the stamping process for all the colors. Enjoy your print!

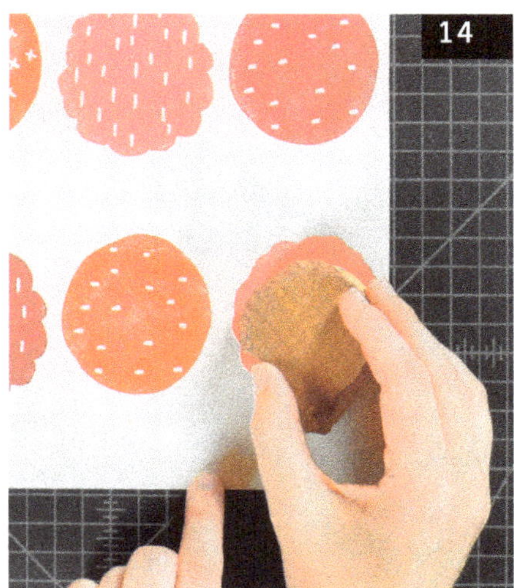

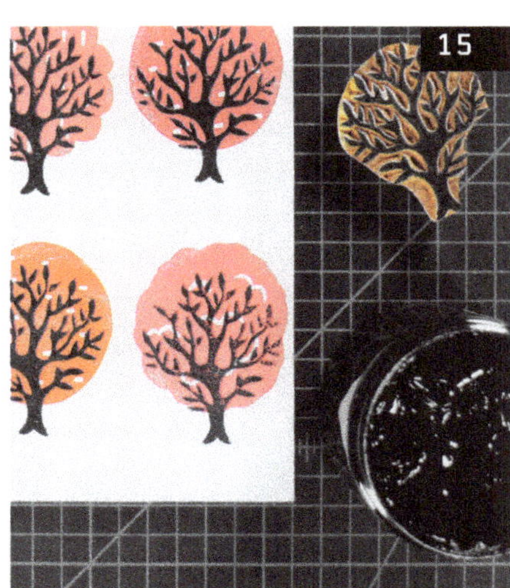

Experimentation with materials is the key to expression and creativity. Combining printing techniques is a great way to try new things and push your boundaries. In this abstract monoprint, I used all of the printing materials in this book—foam sheets, dense rubber blocks, and precut stamps. A monoprint is one that can be made only once, because of the unique, random arrangement of the printing materials. There is no right or wrong to this technique: Follow my steps, or create your own.

COMBINING FOAM, STAMPS, AND CARVED BLOCKS: ABSTRACT

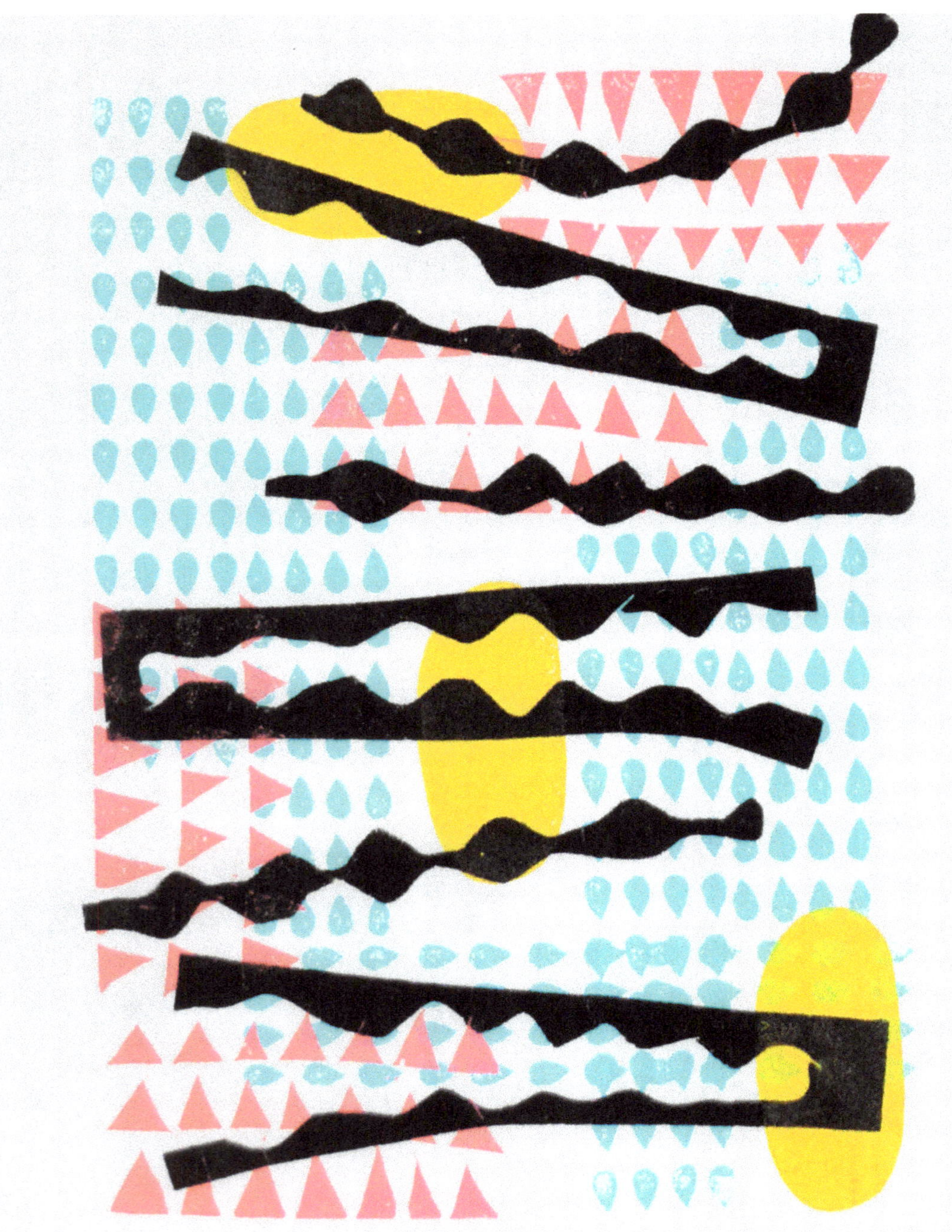

TOOLS AND MATERIALS

- scissors
- adhesive-backed foam sheet
- acrylic mounting sheet
- small pieces of dense rubber block
- precut wooden stamp
- palette knife
- inking platen
- water-soluble printing inks
- brayers
- baren or wooden spoon
- Japanese-style printmaking paper

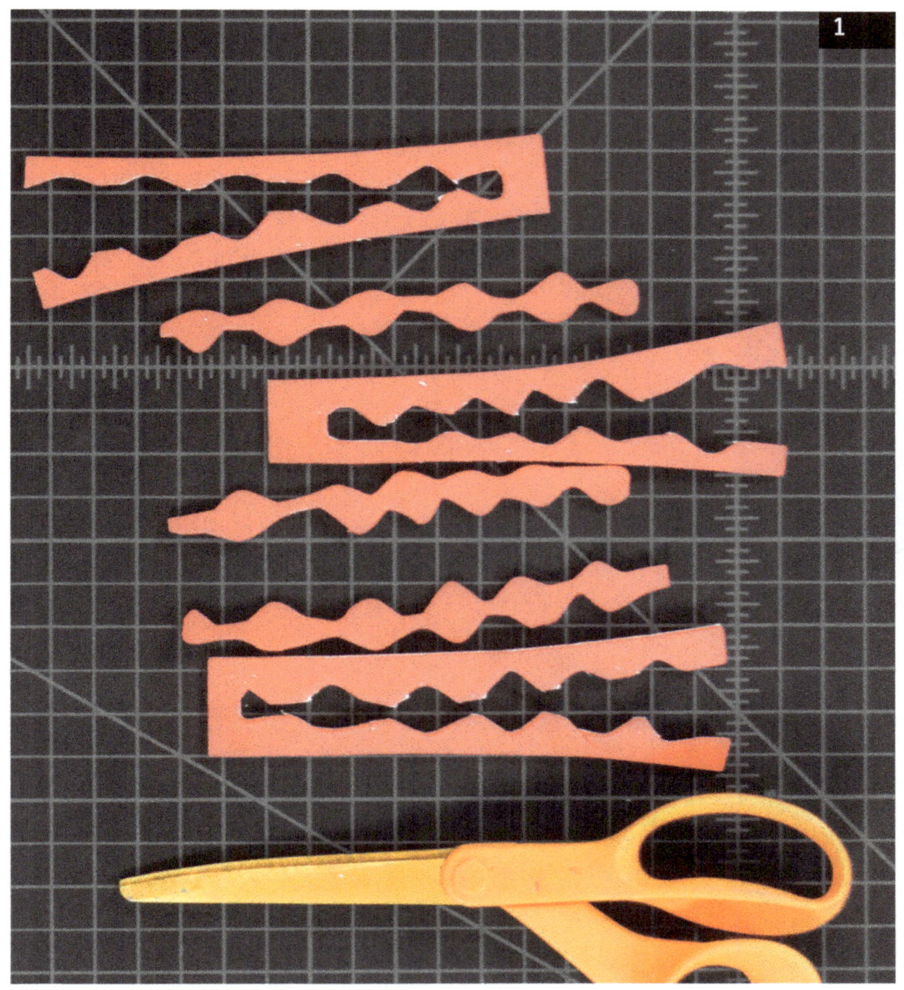

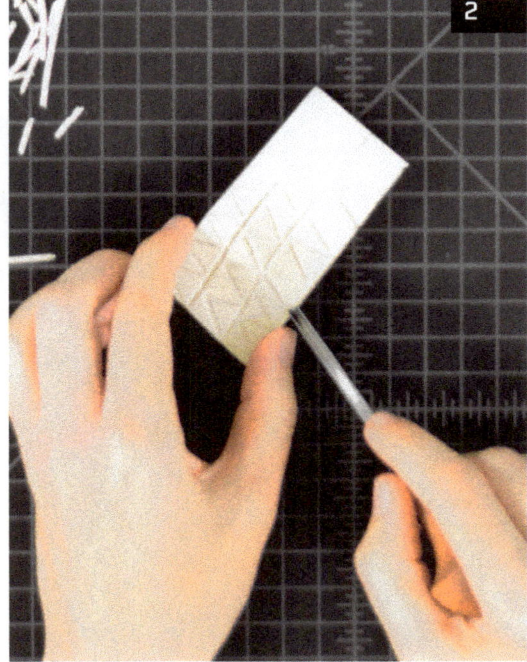

1 / Use scissors to cut the foam sheet into shapes. Cut as many or as few as you choose. Peel off the adhesive backing, arrange the shapes on the acrylic sheet, and adhere them.

2 / Decide how you'd like to carve the blocks. I started at the edge and created a few rows of triangles on one block. Then I carved a solid, oblong shape into the second.

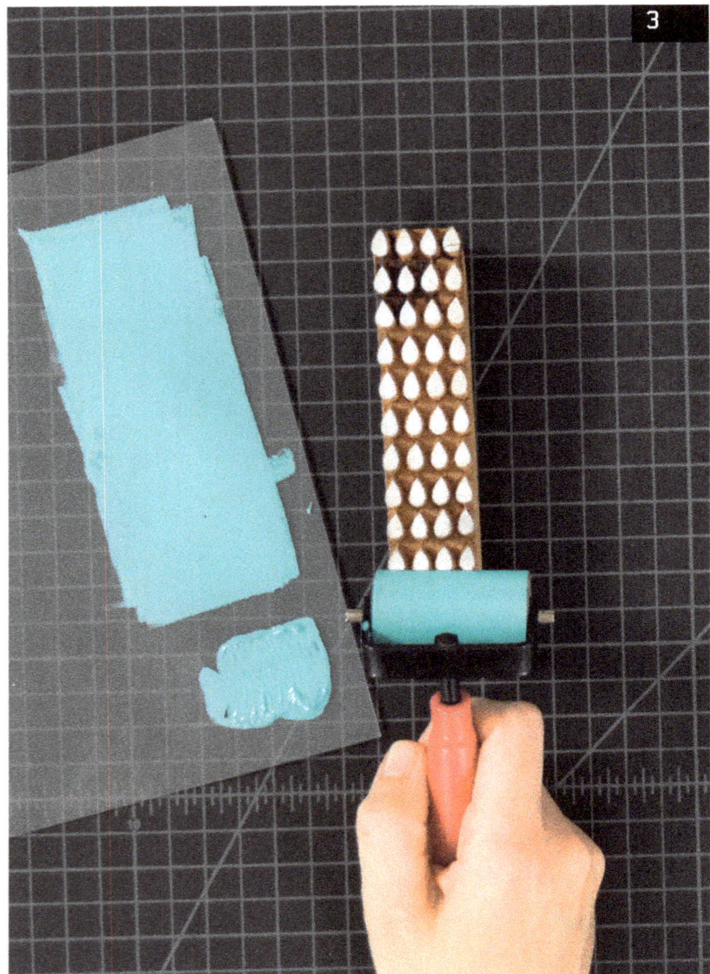

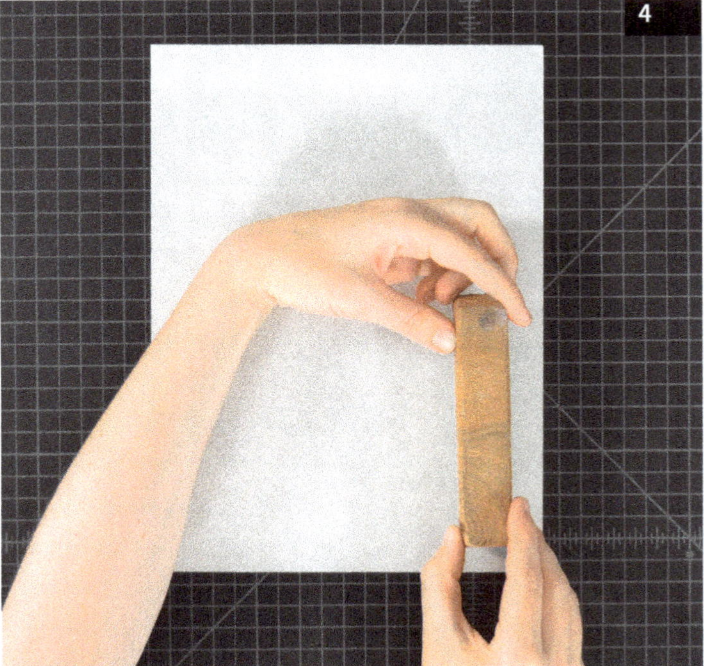

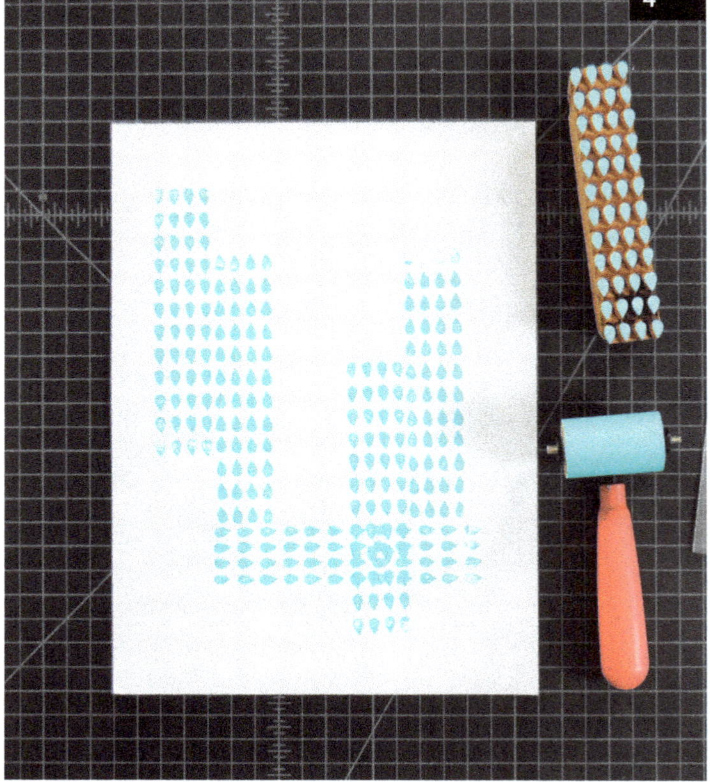

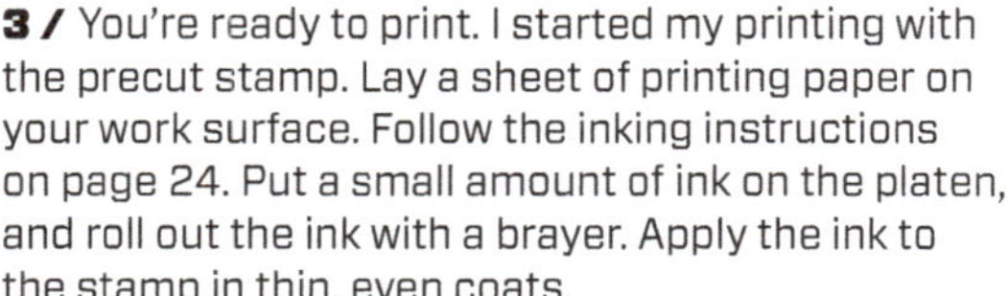

3 / You're ready to print. I started my printing with the precut stamp. Lay a sheet of printing paper on your work surface. Follow the inking instructions on page 24. Put a small amount of ink on the platen, and roll out the ink with a brayer. Apply the ink to the stamp in thin, even coats.

4 / Place the inked stamp face down on the paper, applying even pressure. Lift the stamp, re-ink, and print again. Move the stamp around and experiment with its orientation. Print the stamp again with full ink. Try out a ghost print, a second impression made without re-inking.

NOTE

Using stamps and blocks of different materials will require adjusting your printing and inking methods for each.

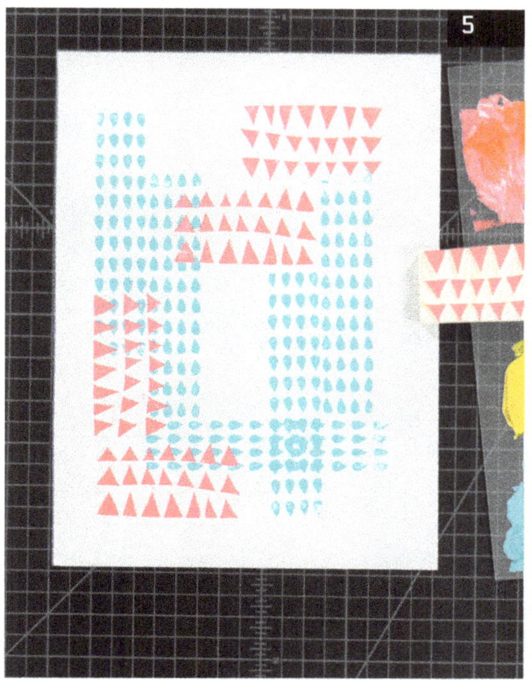

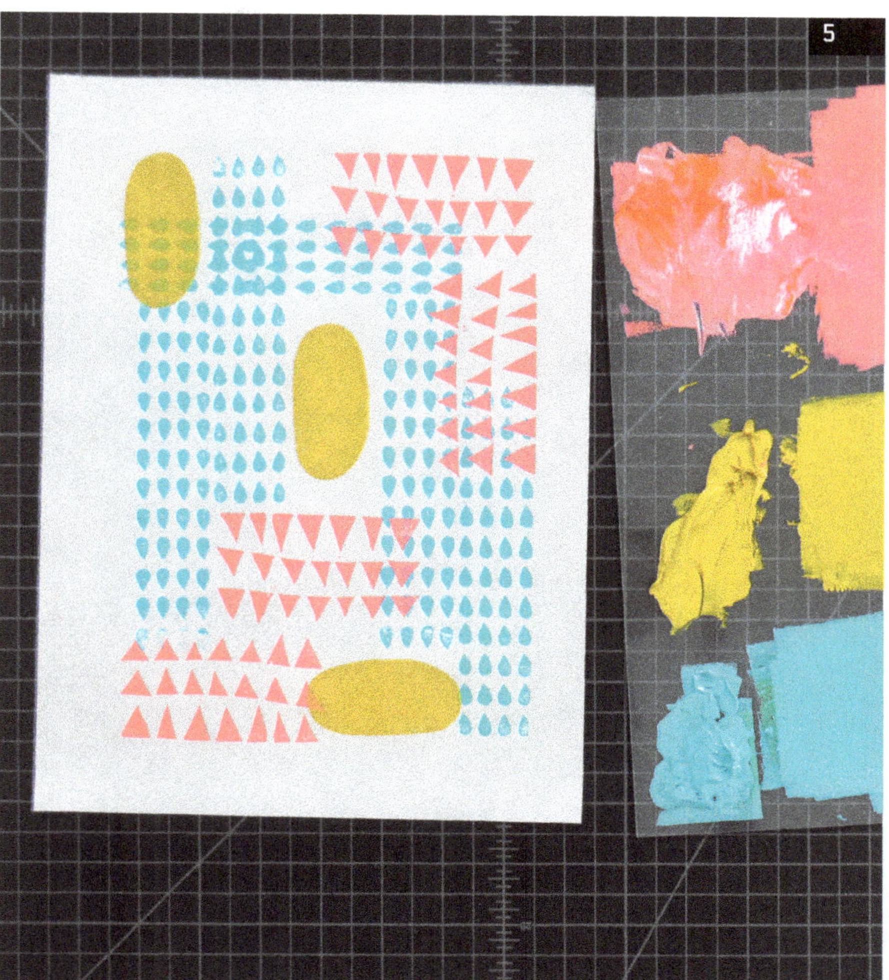

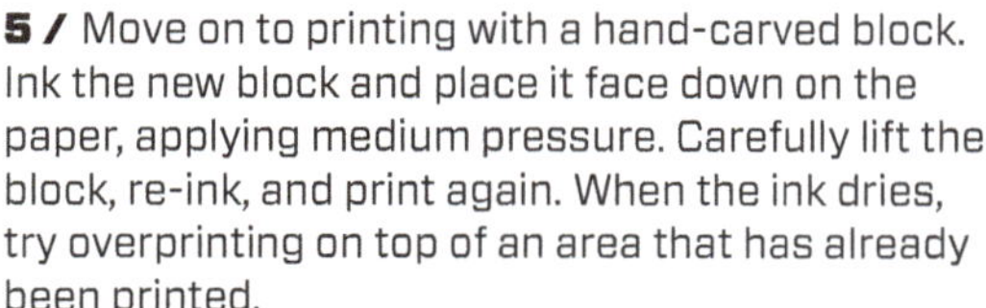

5 / Move on to printing with a hand-carved block. Ink the new block and place it face down on the paper, applying medium pressure. Carefully lift the block, re-ink, and print again. When the ink dries, try overprinting on top of an area that has already been printed.

6 / Now print with the foam pieces—this time printing with the paper on top. Set the print aside. Ink a foam piece and lay it face up on your work surface. Carefully lay the print on top of the inked block. Burnish the back of the paper with a baren. Lift the paper and decide where to print next. Continue to experiment and explore creative block-printing abstracts!

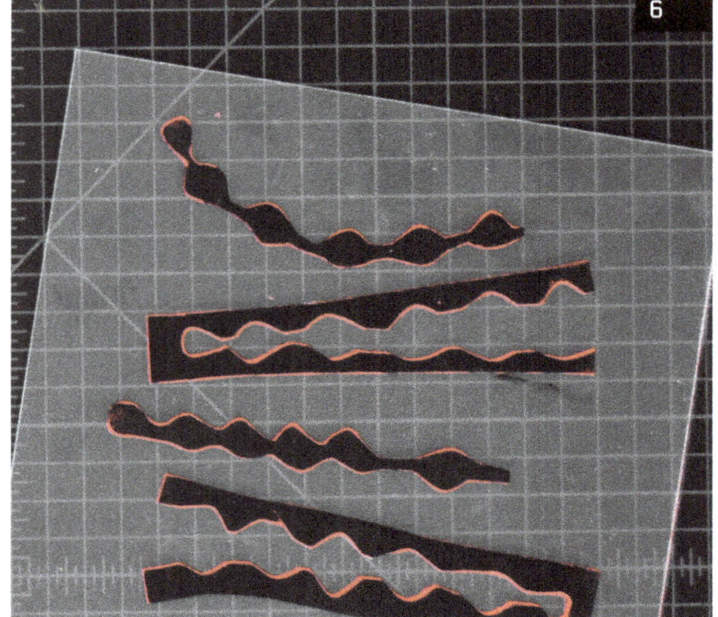

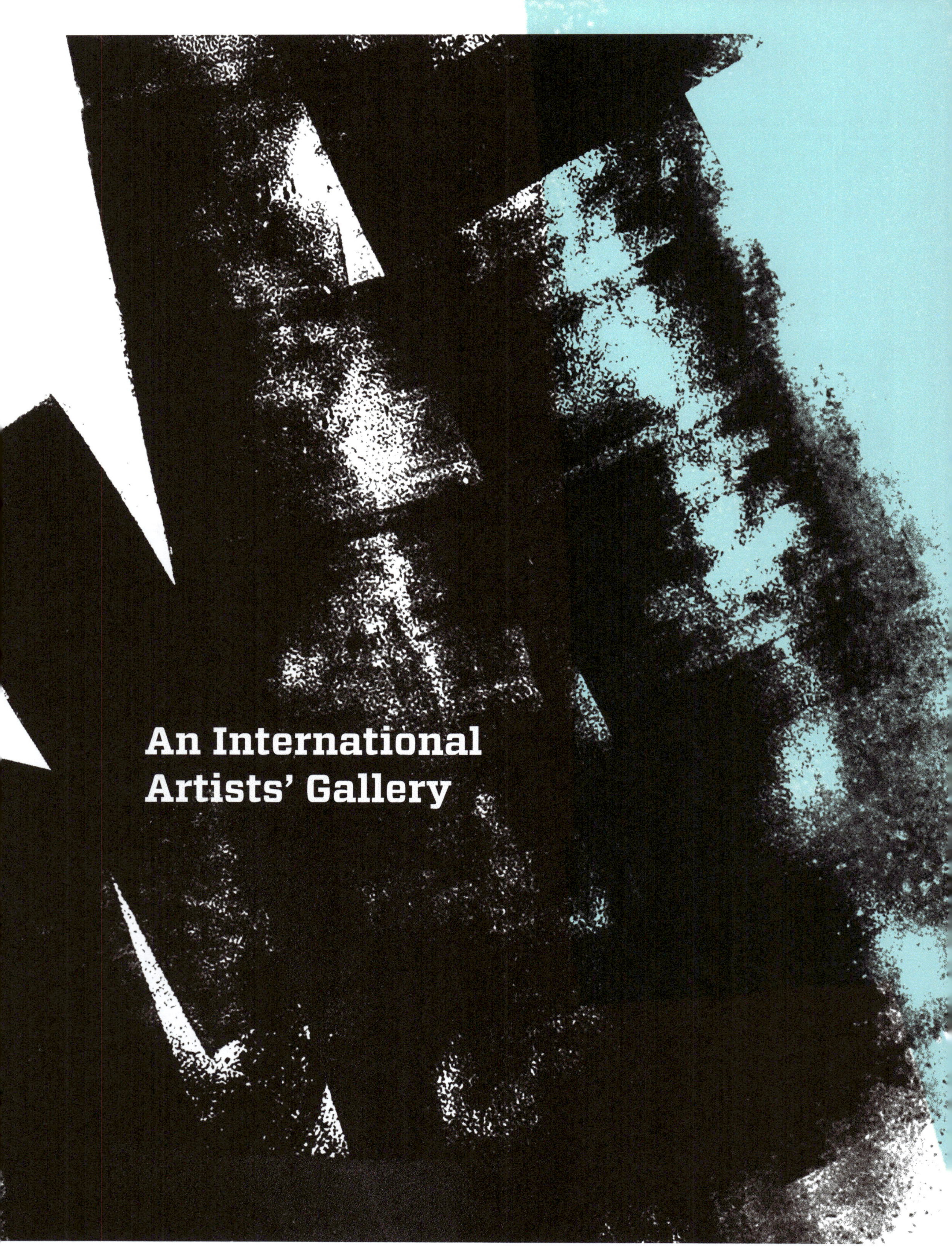
An International
Artists' Gallery

An important aspect of creating your own artistic work is taking the time to appreciate other artists' creations. As a fellow printer, when I approach a new piece by someone else, I automatically start with the technical details, then work my way toward a more interpretive evaluation. It's a good way to train your eye and understand what makes a good print work. Think about how the use of color, line, texture, and shape work with the theme. What are you drawn to in the print? Is there something that stands out in the composition? Is there balance? Movement? Is there a story line that quickly gets your imagination and feelings engaged? Once you start looking, you can quickly become immersed!

The artists featured in this gallery are some of my favorites from the wonderful community of relief printmakers actively working today. In addition, in museums and collections throughout the world, there are countless historic masterworks for you to discover. Seek out artists who share your visual language as well as those who offer something completely different. As you'll soon find out, printmakers are a friendly group, eager to build new connections and share their contributions to this wonderfully rich art medium.

Many thanks to the artists featured here for sharing their work. I hope readers will enjoy learning about their unique printmaking journeys and viewing this selection of their works.

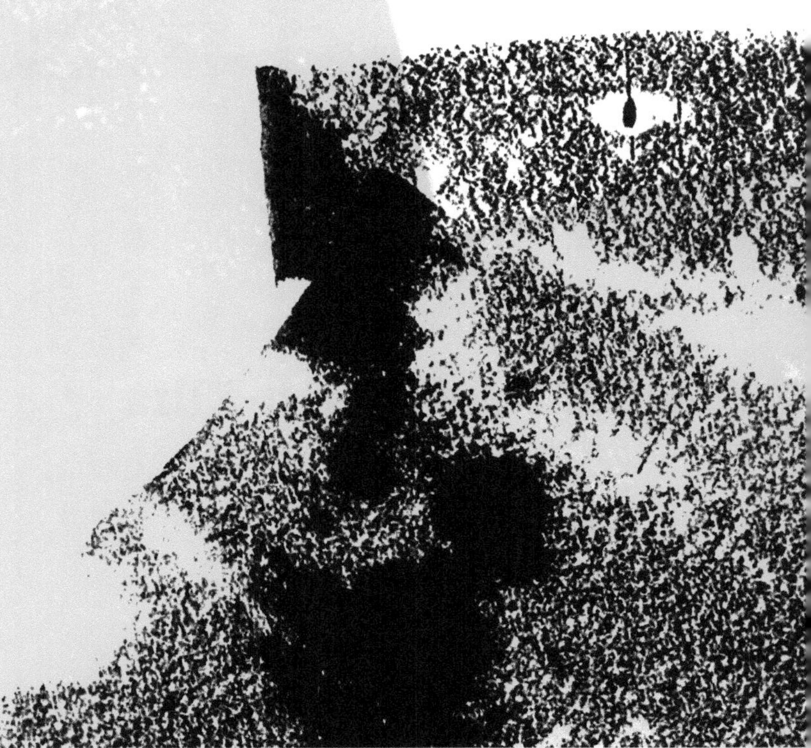

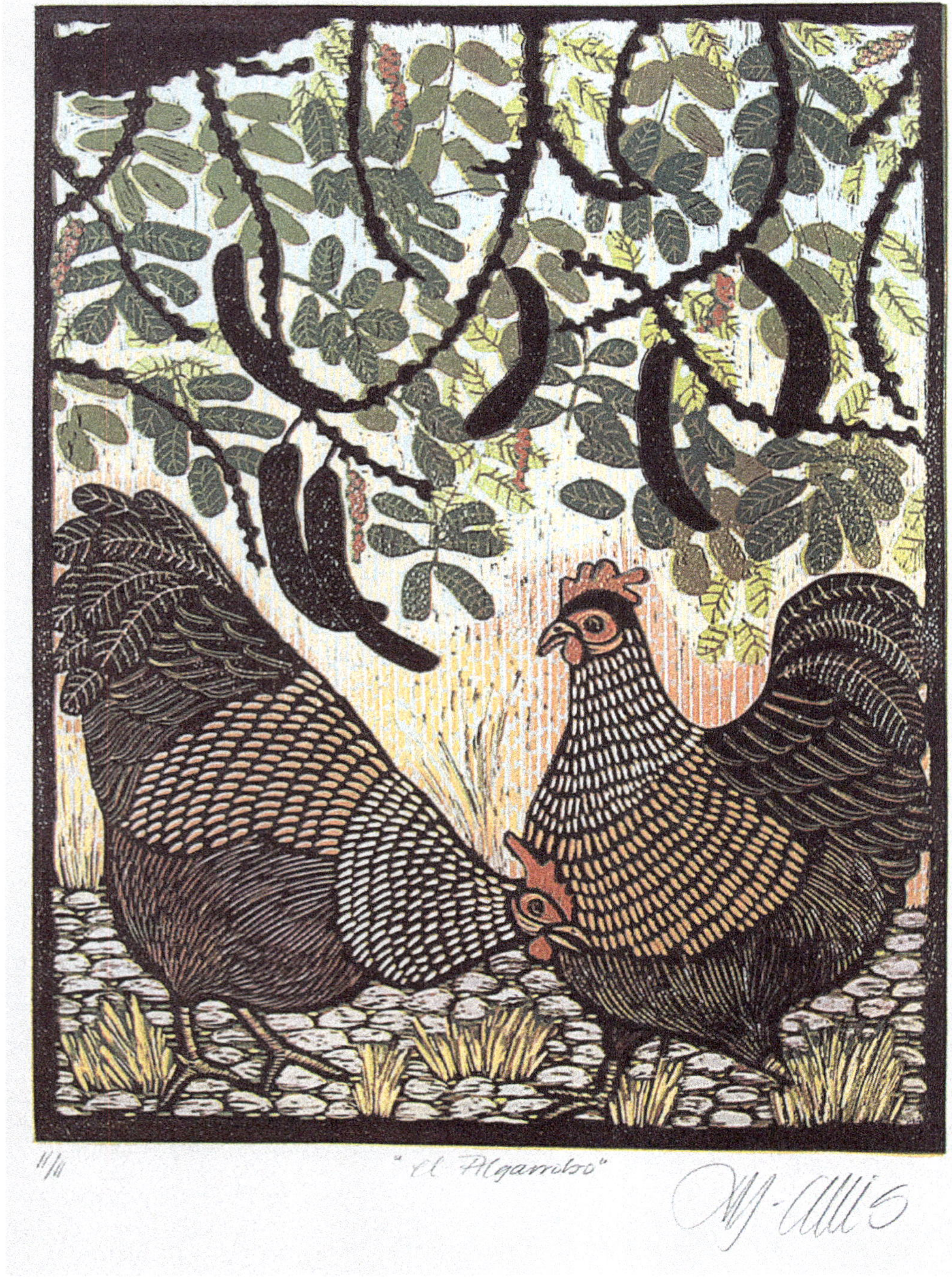

1

1
El Algarrobo
EIGHT-COLOR LINO REDUCTION PRINT

2
On the Beach
SIX-COLOR LINO REDUCTION PRINT

3
Mid Day Sun
PRINTED FROM THREE DIFFERENT LINOPLATES PLUS WOOD PLATE FOR BASE COLOR

Mariann Johansen-Ellis

DENMARK

SITE	**mariannjohansen-ellis.com**
SHOPS	**etsy.com/shop/mariannjohansenellis**
	etsy.com/shop/linocutheaven
	etsy.com/shop/cushioncushion

Everything about printmaker Mariann Johansen-Ellis prompts a story. She was born in Denmark, raised in Sweden, married a Welshman while living in Spain, and taught herself printmaking when they moved to Brunei and, later, Singapore. Now they're back in Denmark, where Mariann has opened a gallery on the island of Møn, an artists' haven and a favorite place from her childhood where she spent summers with her grandparents.

"My work originally started as stories that I told to my little sister," she says. "They introduced humor into my printmaking. My sister is much younger than me and it was such fun making her laugh. We share a childish sense of humor, and we both love animals and delight in little detailed things. Animals to a large extent replace humans in my work, which is always figurative, though I rarely 'look' at my subjects. I prefer to go in search of their souls in my own way. I'm more interested in the personality I invest them with.

"I rarely do a lot of presketching for my prints, but draw straight onto the lino, correcting and redrawing right on the block. I strongly believe it makes for a 'fresher' line, and I hate tracing. This approach does mean that I make a lot of lino blocks that don't work, but I don't mind that at all. Every artist has to find her own optimal approach to being creative. My solution was to find industrial linoleum—good, old-fashioned lino flooring—to work with. This is so much less expensive than art lino that my 'wasted' blocks are not a problem.

"I see the cutting of the linoleum as the purest part of the process. You are, as a matter of fact, sculpting your image, and you should never forget that. The cut is the image, and it has to have your full attention at all times. Over the years, I've taught many students, and I've told all of them over and over again, 'Feel the image. If the tree branch is round, then cut it that way.' Once you start realizing that, you simply make better linocuts. Don't for a minute think, though, that I don't forget, too, sometimes . . . hence the lino flooring!

"Reduction prints have become something of a specialty of mine. They have a great deal of personality, but they're very demanding. Some prints are great friends and others are downright ornery. I find that if I can turn my head off and not overthink things, the process goes much better. There's no better feeling than pulling up the first finished reduction print to find out what it looks like. The first moment of seeing every single block printed gives me a thrill. The fact that I can make a living from being a printmaker is icing on my personal cake."

2

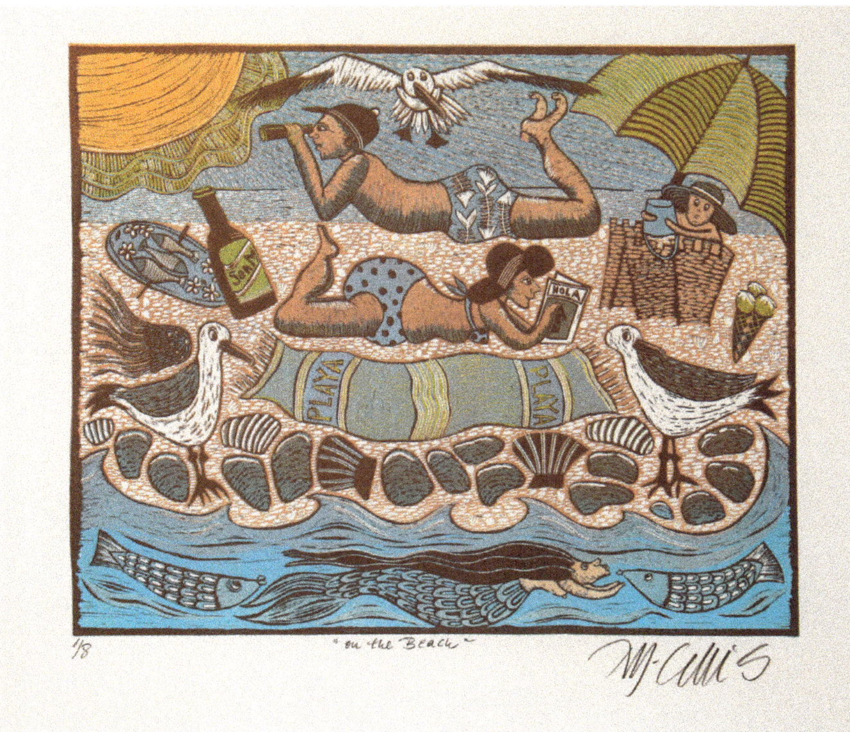

3

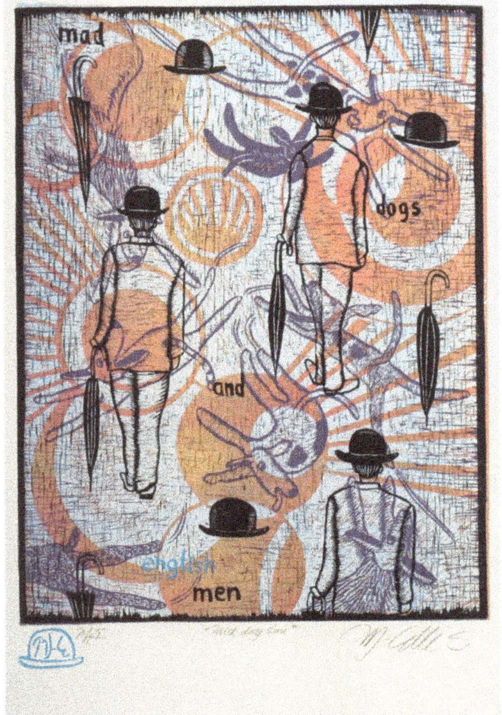

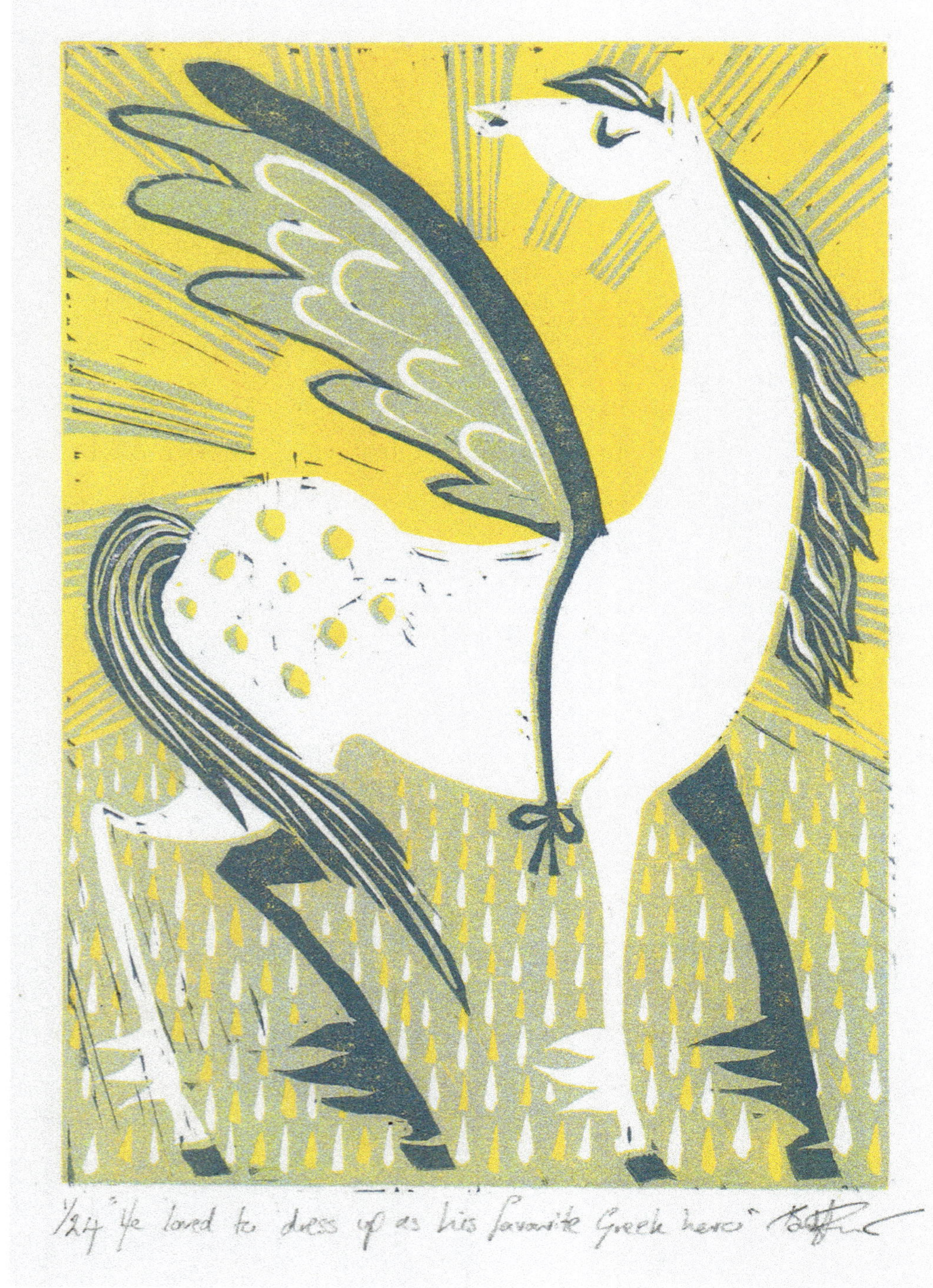

1

Bridget Farmer

AUSTRALIA

1
Greek Hero
LINOCUT

2
Forest Fox
LINOCUT

3
New Holland Honeyeater
LINOCUT

SITE	mariannjohansen-ellis.com
SHOPS	etsy.com/shop/mariannjohansenellis
	etsy.com/shop/linocutheaven
	etsy.com/shop/cushioncushion

Everything about printmaker Mariann Johansen-Ellis prompts a story. She was born in Denmark, raised in Sweden, married a Welshman while living in Spain, and taught herself printmaking when they moved to Brunei and, later, Singapore. Now they're back in Denmark, where Mariann has opened a gallery on the island of Møn, an artists' haven and a favorite place from her childhood where she spent summers with her grandparents.

"My work originally started as stories that I told to my little sister," she says. "They introduced humor into my printmaking. My sister is much younger than me and it was such fun making her laugh. We share a childish sense of humor, and we both love animals and delight in little detailed things. Animals to a large extent replace humans in my work, which is always figurative, though I rarely 'look' at my subjects. I prefer to go in search of their souls in my own way. I'm more interested in the personality I invest them with.

"I rarely do a lot of presketching for my prints, but draw straight onto the lino, correcting and redrawing right on the block. I strongly believe it makes for a 'fresher' line, and I hate tracing. This approach does mean that I make a lot of lino blocks that don't work, but I don't mind that at all. Every artist has to find her own optimal approach to being creative. My solution was to find industrial linoleum—good, old-fashioned lino flooring—to work with. This is so much less expensive than art lino that my 'wasted' blocks are not a problem.

"I see the cutting of the linoleum as the purest part of the process. You are, as a matter of fact, sculpting your image, and you should never forget that. The cut is the image, and it has to have your full attention at all times. Over the years, I've taught many students, and I've told all of them over and over again, 'Feel the image. If the tree branch is round, then cut it that way.' Once you start realizing that, you simply make better linocuts. Don't for a minute think, though, that I don't forget, too, sometimes . . . hence the lino flooring!

"Reduction prints have become something of a specialty of mine. They have a great deal of personality, but they're very demanding. Some prints are great friends and others are downright ornery. I find that if I can turn my head off and not overthink things, the process goes much better. There's no better feeling than pulling up the first finished reduction print to find out what it looks like. The first moment of seeing every single block printed gives me a thrill. The fact that I can make a living from being a printmaker is icing on my personal cake."

2

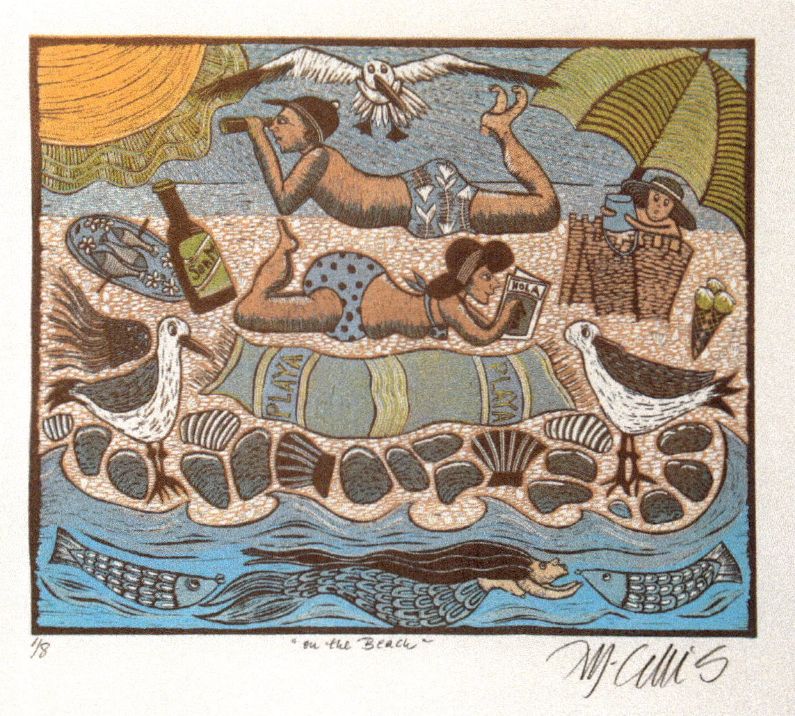

3

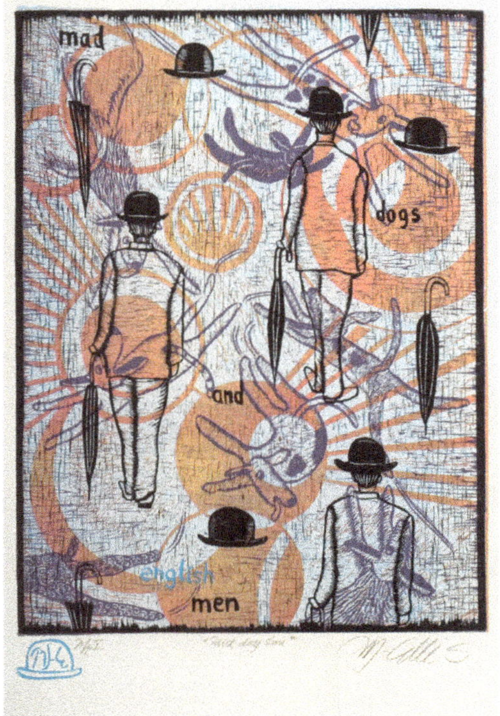

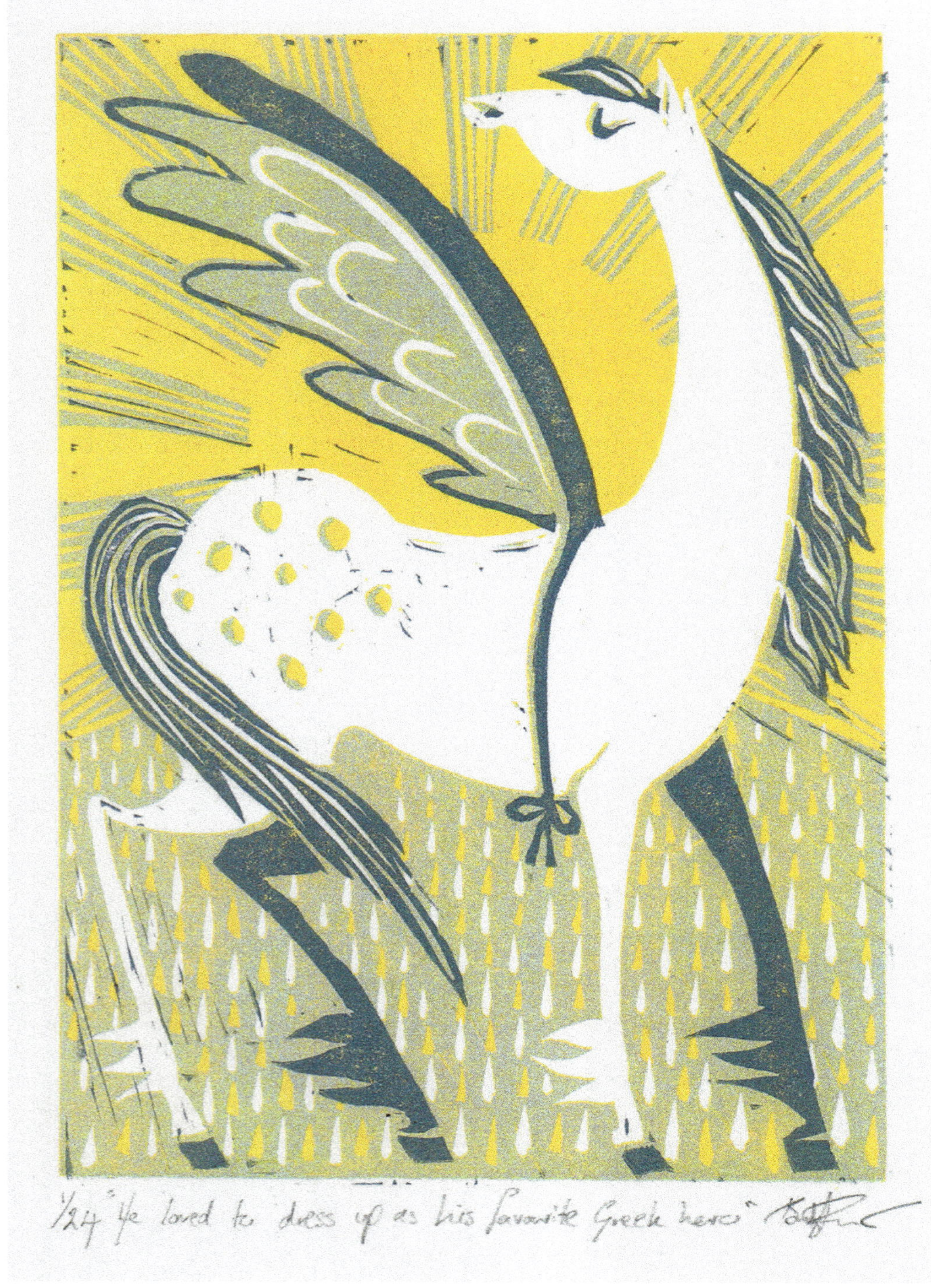

1

1
Greek Hero
LINOCUT

2
Forest Fox
LINOCUT

3
New Holland Honeyeater
LINOCUT

Bridget Farmer
AUSTRALIA

SITE	**bridgetfarmerprintmaker.com**
SHOP	**etsy.com/shop/bridgetfarmerartist**

Originally from Belfast, Northern Ireland, but now living in Victoria, Australia, printmaker Bridget Farmer shares her story of how she found her way to relief printmaking, what inspires her work, and the current projects she is balancing alongside a growing family.

"I did a lot of monoprinting in my art college days, but it wasn't until I arrived in Australia in 2006 and signed up for a weekend printmaking course that I really got into the medium. From there, I did a master of fine arts at Royal Melbourne Institute of Technology, and the following year, I was granted a scholarship at the Australian Print Workshop. In the past, I've mainly concentrated on intaglio printmaking, but in the last two years I've moved more into relief printmaking. This is partly because I had a baby, and lino printing is a more immediate way of working and easier to stop and start.

"Much of my work during my pregnancy incorporated animals curled inside circular shapes. I had not noticed I was doing this until someone pointed it out to me. I think inspiration often comes from deep inside you and you're not always aware of it. The animals I used were all native to the UK—foxes, hares, crows—and, perhaps, I was thinking of my own childhood and how different my son's will be now that we are living in Australia.

"My current project also keeps my son in mind. I am making a children's book of Australian birds. When I arrived in Australia, I felt like a child seeing all these new birds for the first time, and now that we live in the country, we are surrounded by even more. Cockatoos, kookaburras, gang-gangs, currawongs, and fairy wrens—all so Australian.

"I don't think I'm a natural relief printmaker. I lean more toward monotone, linear work. Each time I start a new linoprint, I procrastinate because I'm scared of the blank lino and making that first cut. Then, if there are multiple layers, I get very confused trying to work out what to cut next. But it is good exercise for my brain and I enjoy that. With each new work, I feel a little bit more confident.

"My aforementioned bird book is going to take a year or so to finish. I think it'll be an ongoing project, and even if I finish and get the book published, I'll want to continue with a new set of birds. I like making a body of work with a book in mind. I know every new parent suddenly feels qualified to write a children's book, but I guess children are a great source of inspiration."

2

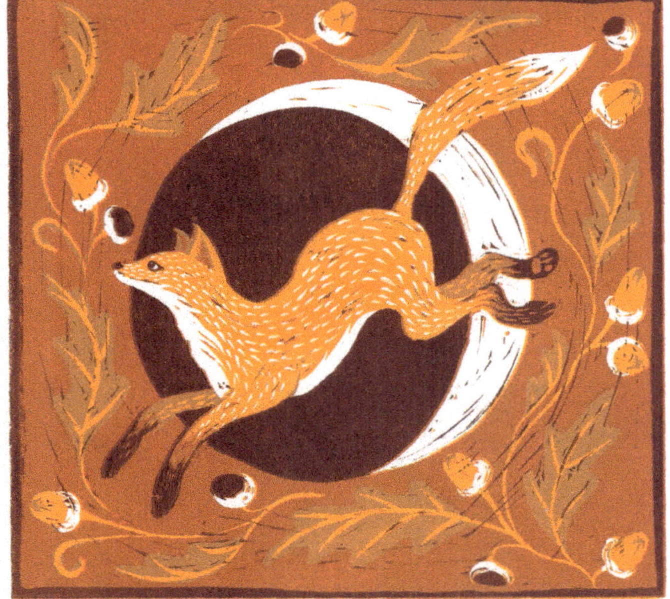

3

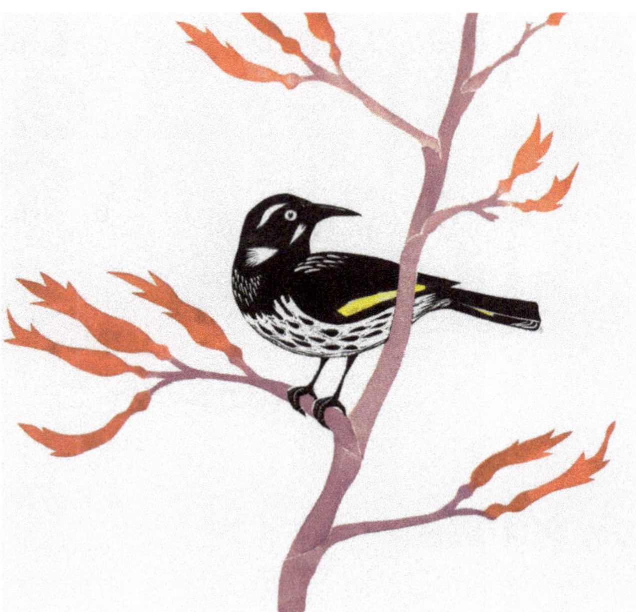

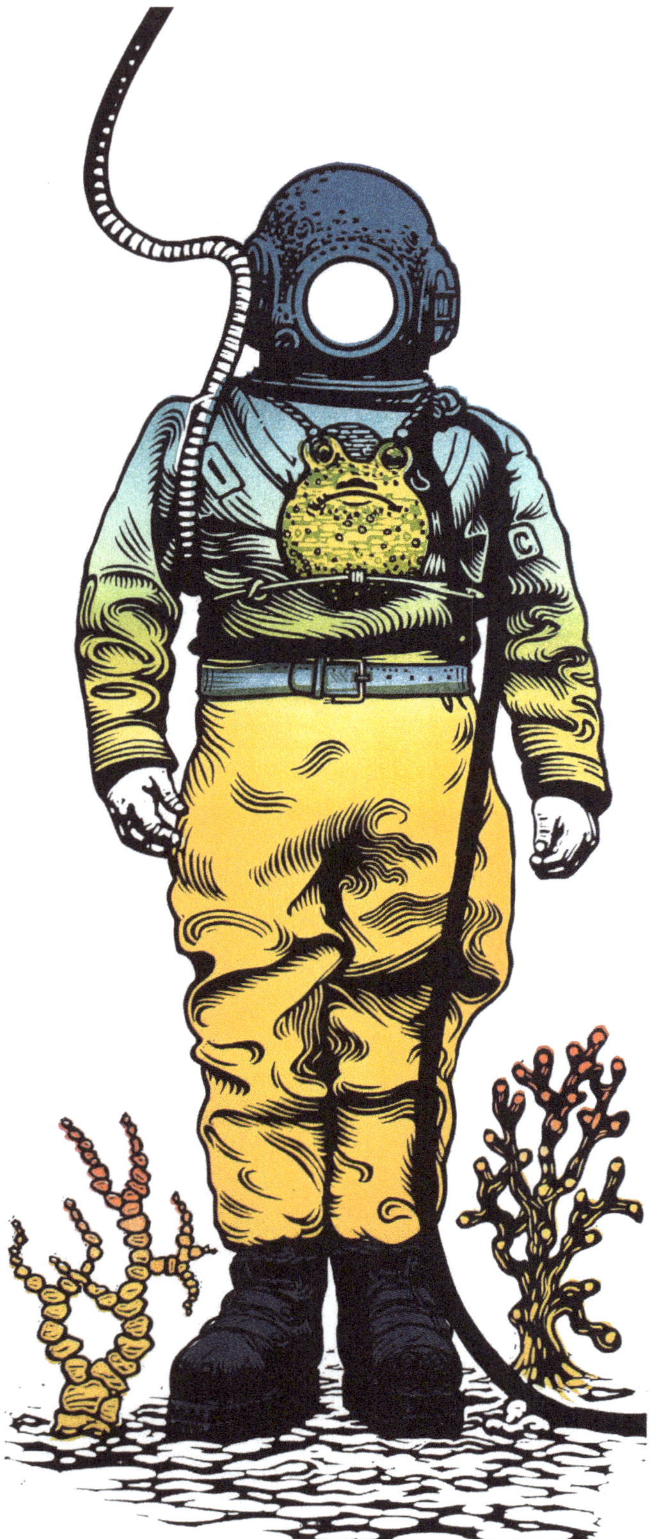

1

1
Deep Sea Diver
LINOCUT

2
Yoyo
LINOCUT AND
SCREEN PRINT

3
Cactus Cowboy
LINOCUT

Nick Morley
UNITED KINGDOM

SITES	**linocutboy.com**
	helloprintstudio.com
BLOG	**linocutboy.com/blog**
SHOP	**linocutboy.com/shop**

Nick Morley is an exciting printmaker creating book-cover imagery with linocuts and fine-art prints. He also runs a very active studio out of Margate, England, teaching printmaking.

"After taking a degree in fine art at Sheffield Hallam University, I did a semester at Emily Carr Institute of Art and Design in Vancouver, where I did loads of etching. I didn't get into linocut until a few years later when I was doing a residency at Intaglio Printmaker in London. I wanted a strong graphic look and thought I'd try linocut. I taught myself with advice from colleagues, and I discovered you can do a lot of things with it. Since then, I have spent more than ten years developing my knowledge by talking to other printmakers and experimenting in the studio.

"I'm inspired by interesting and beautiful imagery, old photographs, prints, illustration, and anything funny or strange that makes me laugh or feel a bit sick. I tend to work in series. In the past, I have done series on the World Beard and Moustache Championships, wrestlers, and extinct animals. Right now, I'm working on a series of cowboy prints, including a linocut of a pair of Mexican skeleton cowboys inspired by José Guadalupe Posada and the Day of the Dead tradition.

"As I carve the lino block, each mark I make becomes a huge decision, and the weight and movement of each line is carefully considered. I try to balance this slowing down with being more spontaneous in the preparation of the drawing. The final print has to have life and energy. This is achieved through a fluidity of line and boldness of mark.

"I think relief printing—linocut in particular—is the most democratic medium. It's easy to learn and doesn't take a lot of equipment, but it has the potential to be very sophisticated in the right hands. Pulling the first print is always exciting and nerve wracking. Sometimes you hate the result, sometimes you love it. Usually the first thing I see are my mistakes. The printing process always adds something though—it pulls the image together, unifies it. And prints are very sensual things, the way they feel and look, but also the smell of the ink.

"I set up Hello Print Studio in Margate in 2013 and I'm still developing it. I offer workshops and studio hire, and the facilities are available for the members of Resort Studios to use. At the moment, I am on the look-out for letterpress type. This is something I have been getting into recently. I am also writing a linocut handbook so I am looking forward to that being published. Last, but not least, I am looking forward to fatherhood and introducing my firstborn son to linocutting."

2

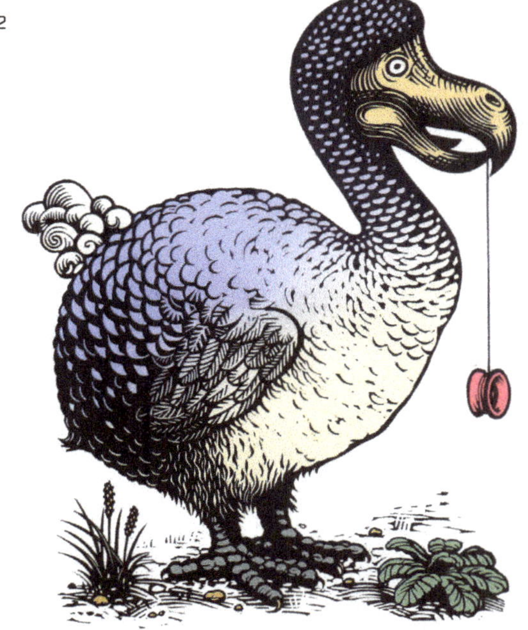

3

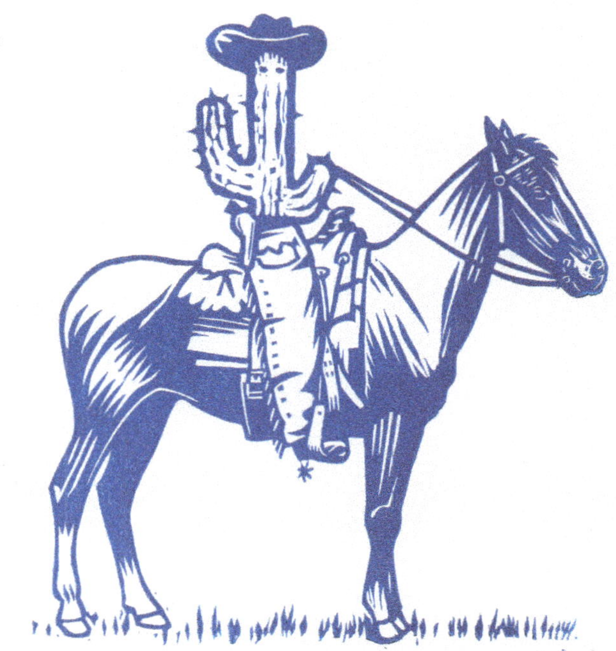

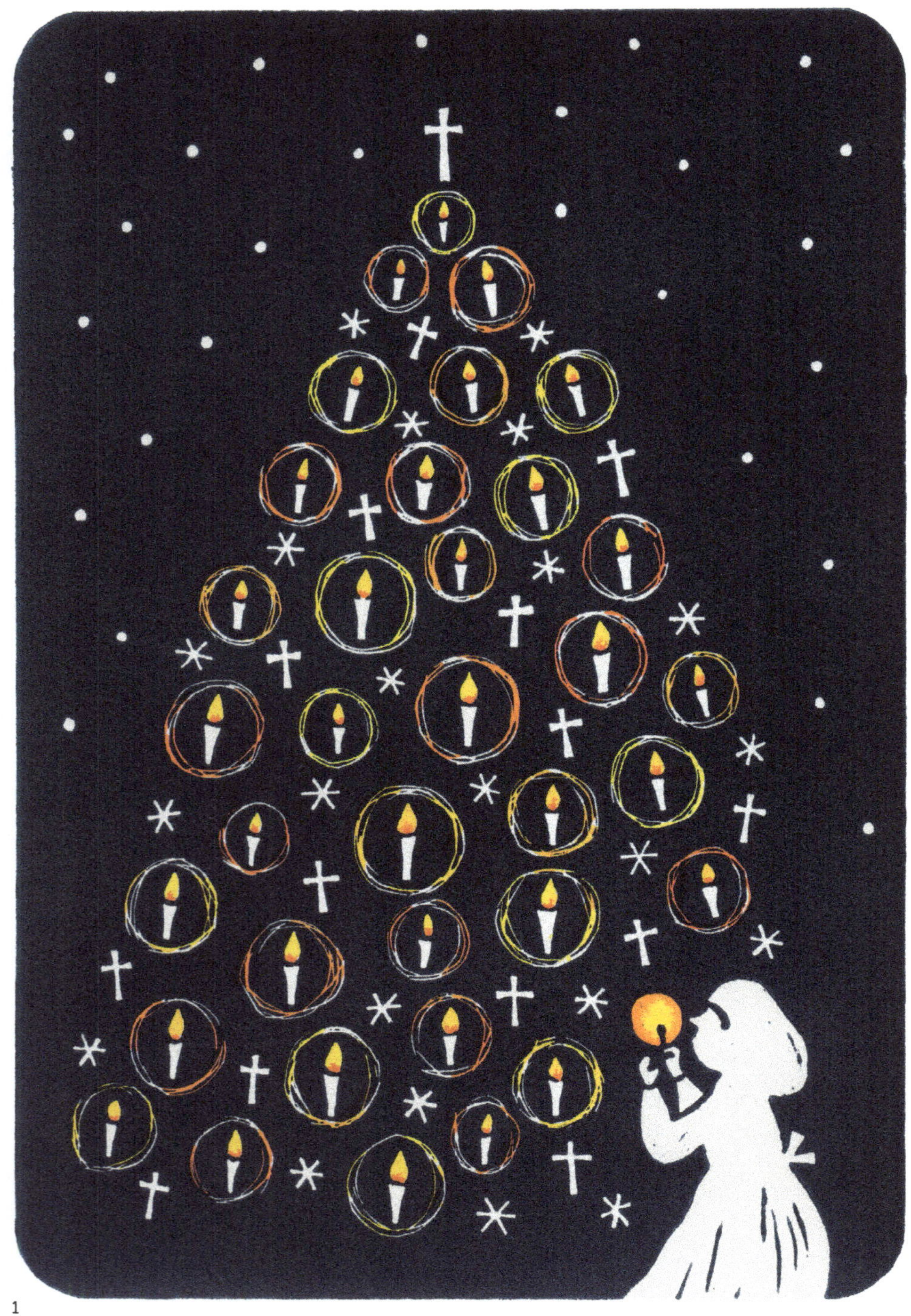

1

1
The Little Match Girl
LINOCUT

2
Little Red Riding Hood
LINOCUT

3
The Elves and the Shoemaker
LINOCUT

Hitomi Murakami
JAPAN

SITE	pikotan.com
INSTAGRAM	@murakami_hitomi
BLOG	pikotan.com/sblo.jp

The print works of artist Hitomi Murakami are startlingly refreshing: A palette cleanser. A breath of fresh air. Her pared-down aesthetic perfectly embodies the style of her native Japan. She studied printmaking in Italy at a studio in Florence, and she now lives and works in Tokyo.

With a specialty in illustrative storytelling, Murakami has published a number of children's books featuring her linocuts, including *Grimm's Fairy Tales.* Through her fabulous use of positive and negative space to create contrasts, and a very limited color palette, she is able to create an illustration that draws the viewer into a tale, while keeping only the most essential elements in the composition.

It is clear from viewing more of her work that nature and the environment are very important as a subject matter. A recently published children's story illustrated by Murakami explores renewable energy resources through the character of a dormouse.

Murakami also devotes time to teaching relief printmaking. By combining foam pieces, rubber stamps, and kid-friendly materials, she brings her passion for printmaking to young students as well as adults.

2

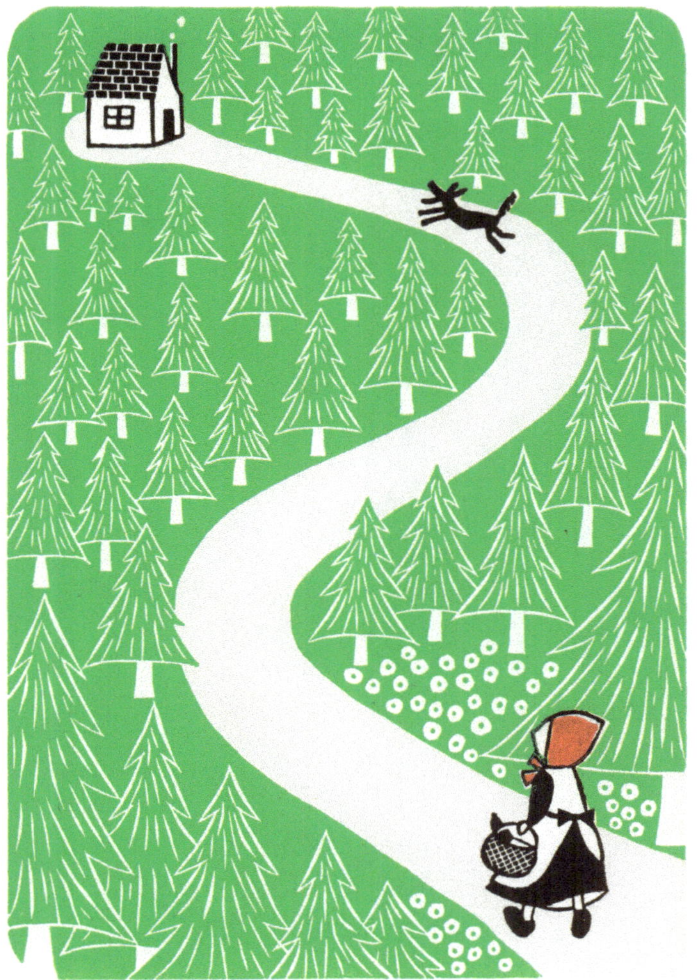

3

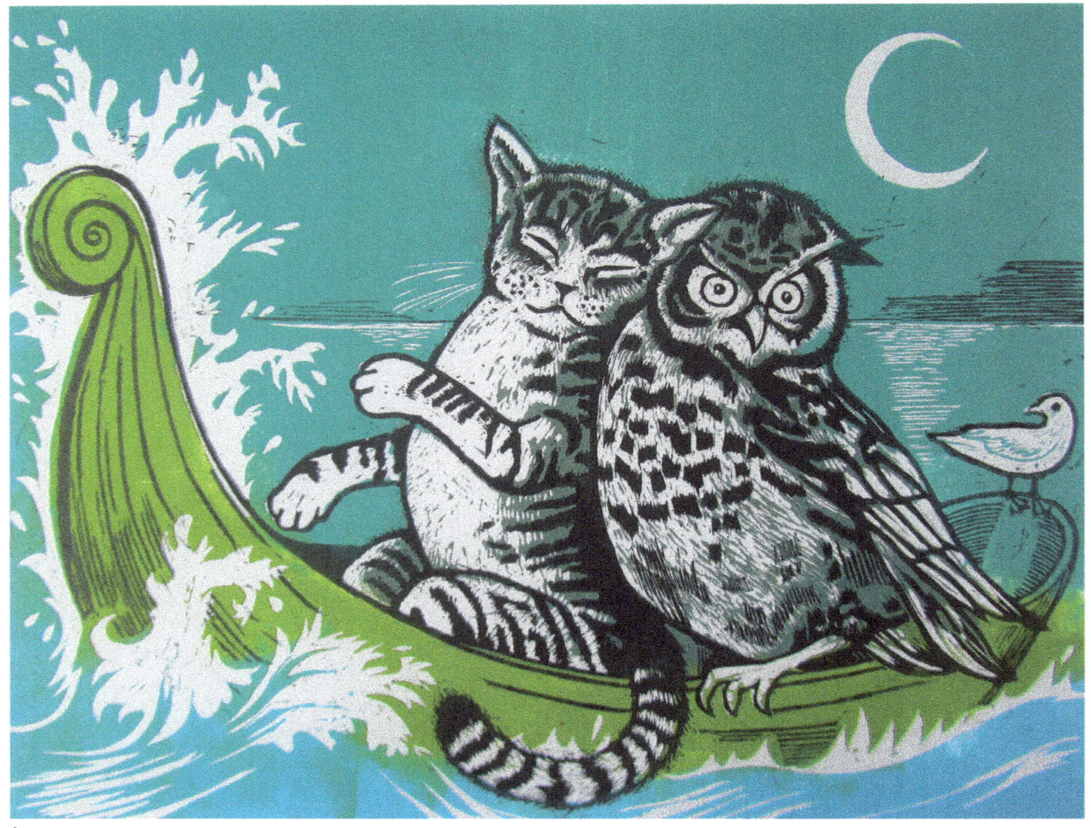

1

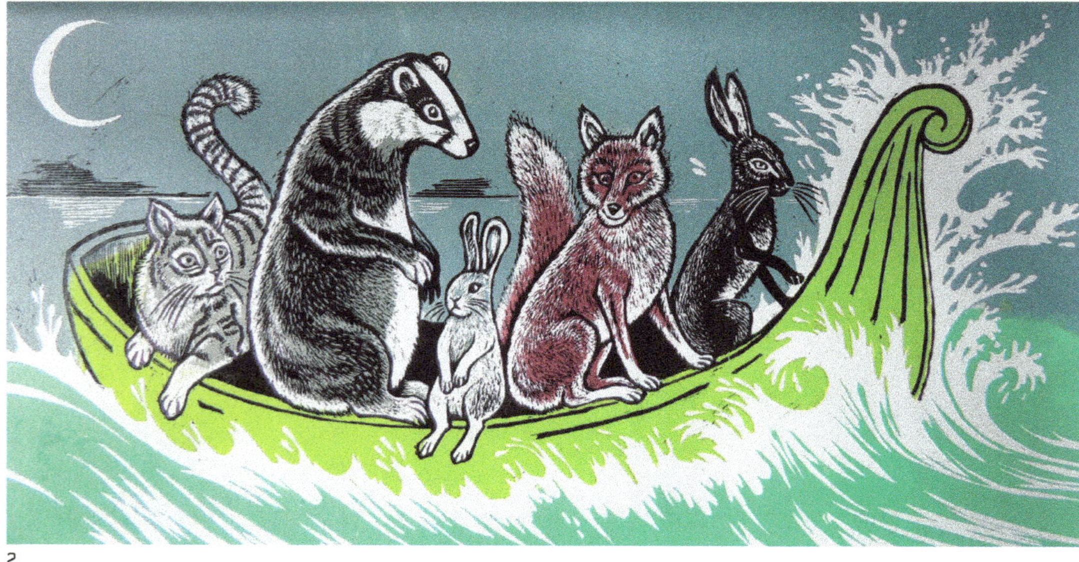

2

1
A Year and a Day
LINOCUT

2
An Unlikely Journey
LINOCUT

3
The Strawberry Thief
LINOCUT

4
The Witch Hare
LINOCUT

Teresa Winchester

UNITED KINGDOM

SITE	**teresawinchester.co.uk**
SHOP	**teresawinchester.co.uk/cards.html**

Teresa Winchester's linocut prints are steeped in an English tradition of animal folktales, nostalgic countrysides, and masterfully rendered imagery.

"I was born at Eastbourne in Sussex and, after flirtations with London and Surrey, I'm back in Sussex, where I feel very much at home. I studied printmaking at Goldsmiths in London, and initially loved lithography, but it's the more rugged nature of lino prints that came to suit my work in recent years.

"As the eldest child in the family, I had a fair bit of time on my own and I would spend hours reading, and then drawing images inspired by the tales I'd read. Apart from the world of wonder tales, the countryside also inspires me. The woods, meadows, and hills I walk through are full of textures, colors, and patterns. I love to look at plants and animals and also people! I draw people endlessly and return from trips to faraway beautiful places, such as India and Africa, with sketchbooks full of faces and my head full of ideas.

"So my prints are full of stories. A few of the stories you will recognize, such as 'The Red Shoes' and 'The Gingerbread House,' but most of my prints contain a narrative that I would like viewers to discover for themselves. Ideas slip into my head all the time, quite often when I'm just falling asleep, which perhaps explains why they're often described as being dreamlike!

"I use Japanese woodcutting tools. The lino I use is also from Japan: a vinyl version of our familiar old lino and much easier to cut. I generally work with two blocks. The first block lays down the color, and I use a number of colors. Sometimes I merge the colors with a large roller. Other times I use a different roller for each color, which feels almost feels like painting with rollers. The second block brings together the design and lays down most of the drawing in a much darker tone. I avoid using black and prefer to use something like a combination of ultramarine and violet, which I feel is more vibrant.

"The magical moment for me is when I peel back the paper from the first print. It's often a surprise, and I love that bit of uncertainty. The challenge is fascinating, and the process reminds me of a chess game where you have to project the results! The way I print demands accuracy to register the prints successfully. Inevitably, there are variations in the prints. The registration is not the same, and the colors vary. This means that every print is different, even though it is part of an edition, and every print is an original piece of artwork."

3

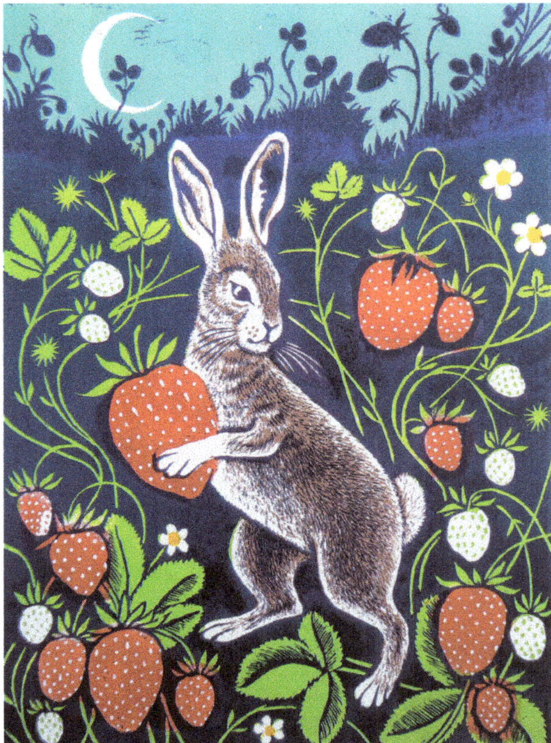

4

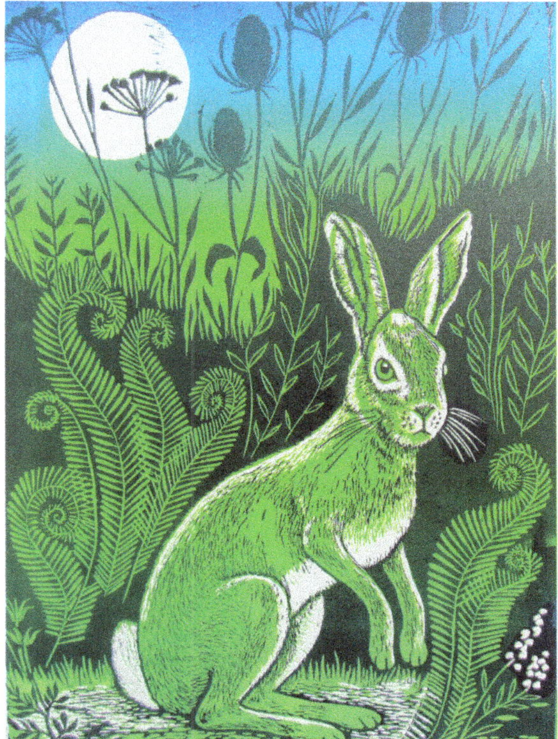

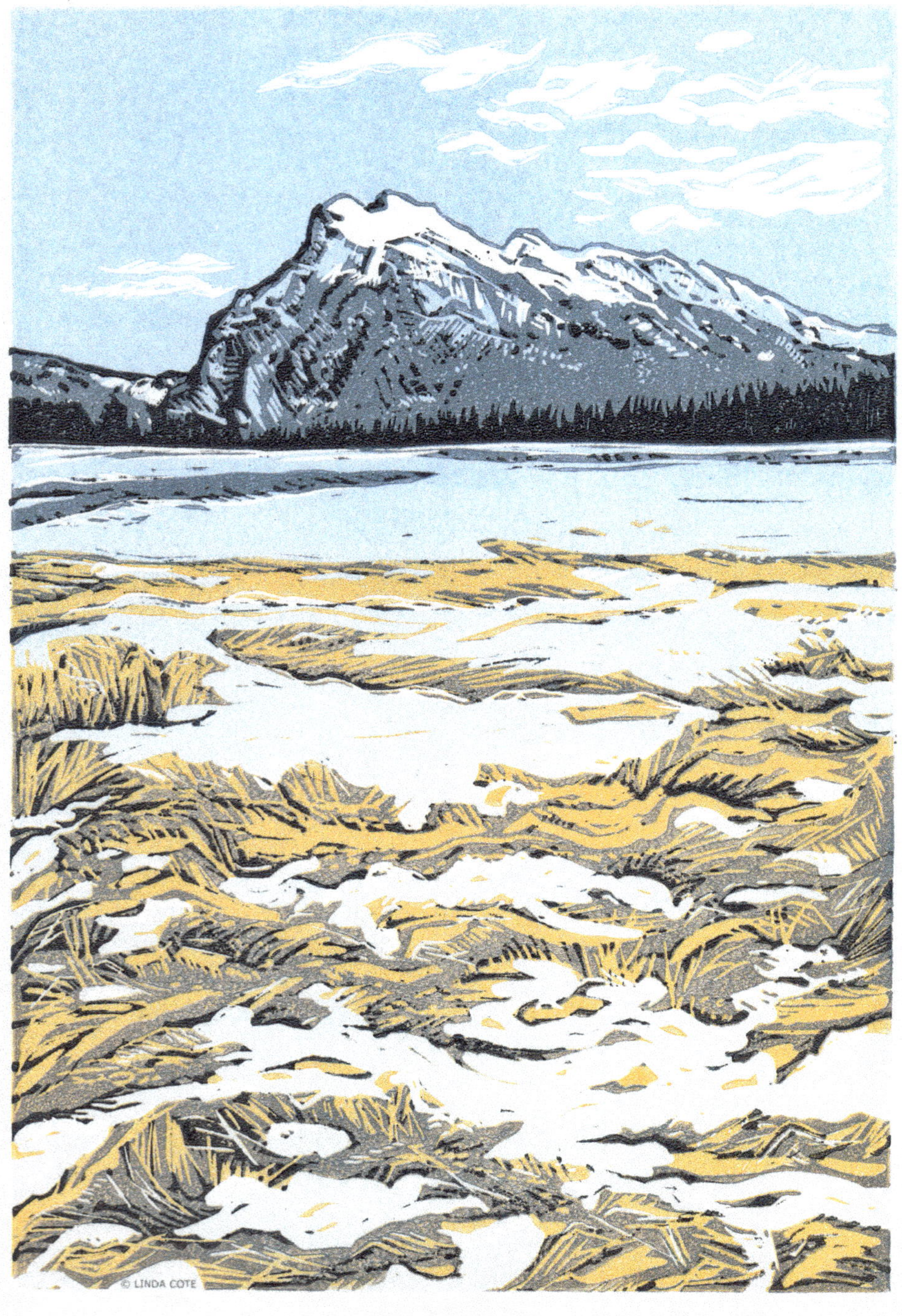

1

1
Mount Rundle Spring
FOUR-COLOR LINOCUT REDUCTION PRINT

2
Magpie Morning
ONE-COLOR LINOCUT PRINT

3
Blue Jay's Perch
THREE-COLOR LINOCUT REDUCTION PRINT

Linda Cote
CANADA

SITE	lindacote.ca
BLOG	lindacote.ca/#!blog/c1cfw
SHOP	lindacote.ca/#!store/c21kz

Linda Cote lives and works in Canmore, Alberta, a small town perfectly located where the prairie foothills meet the Canadian Rockies.

"While my art journey has been long and winding—exploring many mediums including drawing, painting, watercolor, collage, and wood carving—when I picked up my carving tools and applied them to my first relief print, I somehow knew I was home.

"As a printmaker, I am largely self taught, though I've had many wonderful mentors and have attended numerous workshops. I've always adored books with traditional woodcut, lino print, and etching illustrations, and I have found artists such as Sir John Tenniel, Betsy Bowen, George Walker, and Albrecht Durer all inspire me greatly.

"My art expresses texture and depth with a few lines or colors, thus reducing the subject to its essence. Although I explore a variety of themes with my art, my favorite subjects are birds and the lovely mountains and foothills around my home in Canmore. All of my artwork is printed by hand without a press, and I make a small number of prints from one original. (I like to call them "multiple originals.") My limited-edition print runs are typically thirty prints or fewer, and all are numbered and hand-signed.

"Printmaking encompasses an abundance of creative approaches, and it excites me that I can explore it for years to come. One of the biggest challenges of printmaking is that people don't always understand why an original hand-pulled print is priced higher than a mechanically produced art reproduction. Educating buyers about our process is key for printmakers. I am passionate about giving my buyers and followers an inside look at how I create my art through my blog, YouTube, and at open studio events. I feel that when people see the hands-on nature of the process, they can better appreciate the unique aspects of printmaking.

"I love pushing myself to explore more complex designs and creating with multilayered reduction linocuts. I have created several multiple-color prints and love the challenge of building up the ink colors. I have also had the good fortune of finding an antique Chandler proof press earlier this year with a collection of wood and metal type. I am inspired by the idea of using letterpress and linocuts together, and will be exploring this in the near future. Wherever printmaking takes me, I know I will continue to find inspiration with this amazing and rewarding art practice."

2

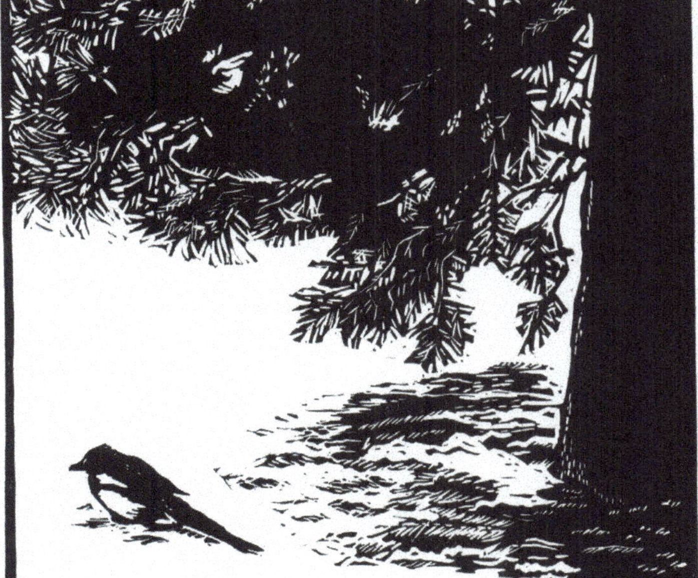

3

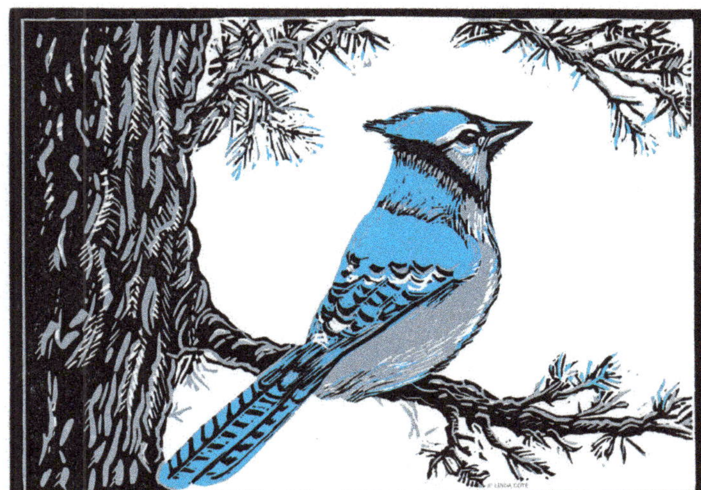

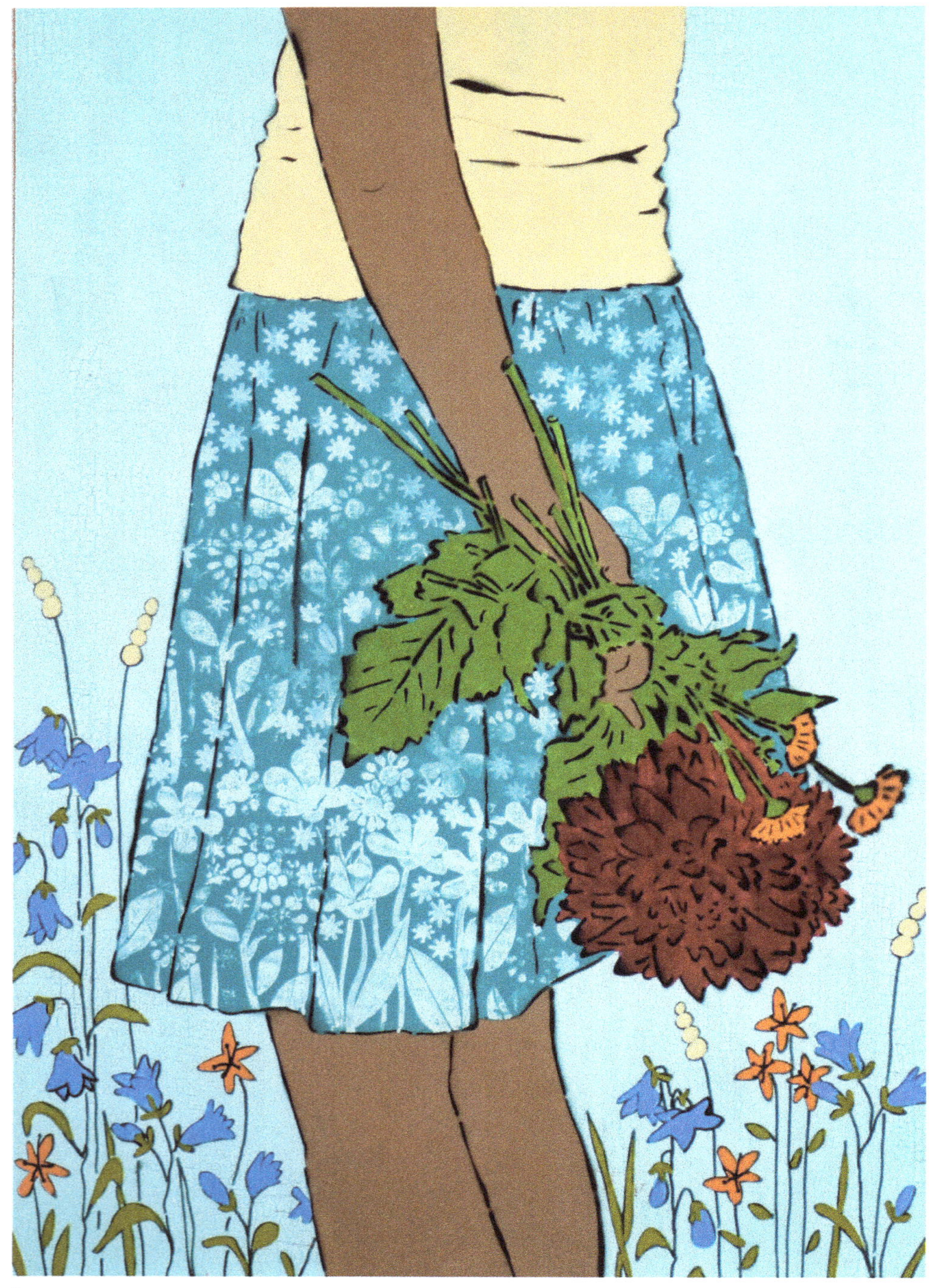

1

1
Garden Gifts
MIXED MEDIA

2
Bet Your Life
MIXED MEDIA

3
If the Wind Is Right
MIXED MEDIA

Amy Rice
UNITED STATES

SITE	amyrice.com
BLOG	egg-basket-full-of-hollyhock-dolls.blogspot.com
SHOP	etsy.com/shop/amyriceart

The joyful, bright, and nostalgic artwork of Amy Rice invites the viewer into her world with open arms. She's based in Minneapolis, Minnesota, and a Midwest character pervades her works. Rice uses a wealth of mixed-media art techniques: printmaking with Gocco and linocut, stencils, spray paint, acrylics, vintage ephemera, gouache, and inks.

"I've always made art and enjoyed learning new art-making techniques. I started cutting linoleum blocks fifteen years ago to give my hands something to do when I quit smoking cigarettes. It worked," says Rice.

"My work is most often reflective of my day-to-day life and the things going on that excite me. I bought some rural property last year, and my most recent work is documenting the plant species on it, beaver art (I have a resident beaver family!) and also prints for fabric.

"There was a long period of time when I stopped carving relief-print blocks because it was too hard on my wrists and hands. In the last few years, though, there have been a bunch of new products on the market that make it much easier, and I'm happy to get back at it.

"For me, the challenge is putting in so much time to cut a piece and not really knowing if it will be something I am happy with or I will ever use to print with more than a few times. The reward is having lots of copies to experiment with.

"All that fabric and faux textiles (like a 'braided rug' and 'patchwork' quilt) I've been printing—I plan to use them to refurbish furniture, make pillows, and tea towels. Someday those things will decorate a cute cabin in the woods full of all my own designs."

2

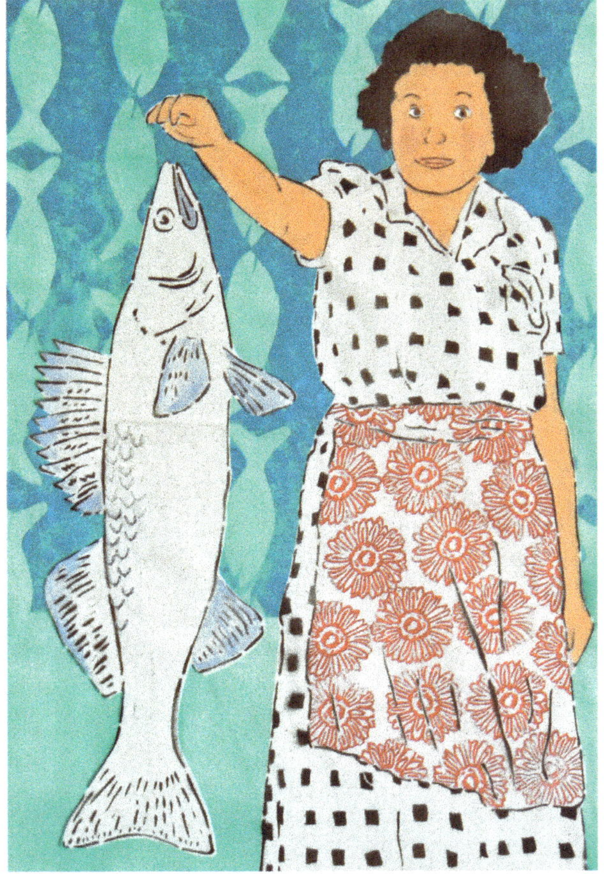

3

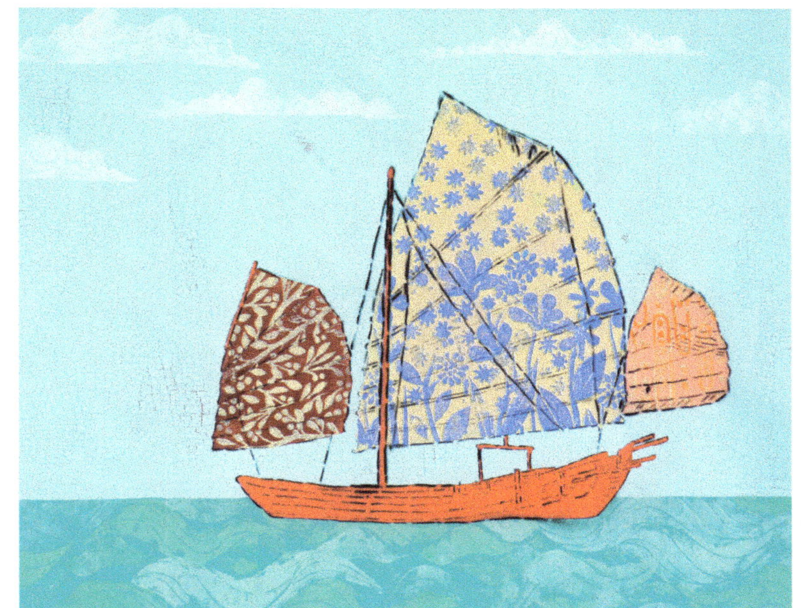

1

1
Snow Fox
LINOCUT

2
River Hare
LINOCUT

3
York Walls
LINOCUT

Giuliana Lazzerini

UNITED KINGDOM

SITE	giulianalazzerini.com
BLOG	http://giulianalazzerini.com/blog
SHOP	etsy.com/shop/thebluebirdgallery

The artistic journey of Giuliana Lazzerini is an exciting one to follow, right up to the present. Early inspiration by art in her father's studio in Tuscany, Italy, led to formal training and a master of arts degree from the Istituto d'Arte Stagio Stagi in Pietrasanta and a degree in painting from the Accademia di Belle Arti in Carrara. Even after moving to Yorkshire, England, in 1987, Lazzerini's native landscapes continued to inform her work. But, at the same time, her growing familiarity with the dramatic natural beauty of the northern English landscape began leaving its mark.

"I get inspiration from the natural world and wildlife that surrounds me in Yorkshire. I like simple, minimal images, which lend themselves to the linoprinting technique. I carve my linocuts and woodcuts by hand, then individually print them myself on a hand-operated press or sometimes burnish them by hand. This process is repeated for every color needed, which takes time as some prints are made from three or four printing plates. Some of the linocuts are also limited editions, usually small editions, and not mass produced.

Lazzerini relishes that special moment printmaking offers to the practitioner—the first lifting of the paper to discover the results. "I normally do a few artist's proofs before I start the edition, to try different options. In some cases, I mark some prints "E.V."—varied edition—so the total number stated will include different color variations.

"I'm now working on a lot of different projects. I'm excited by incorporating collage in the linocuts to give each print a unique feel. I'm also experimenting with the translucency of mosaic images: The way colors can vibrate against each other always fascinates me."

2

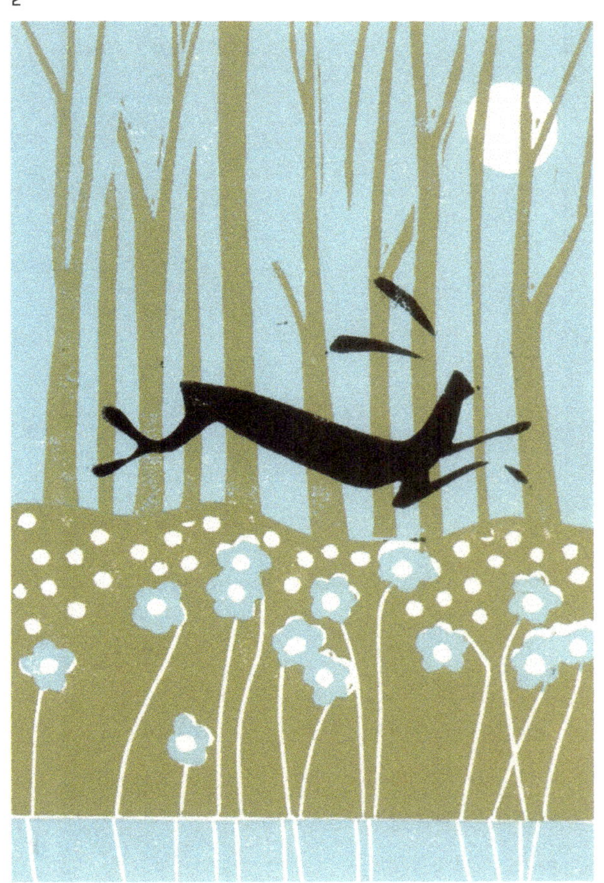

3

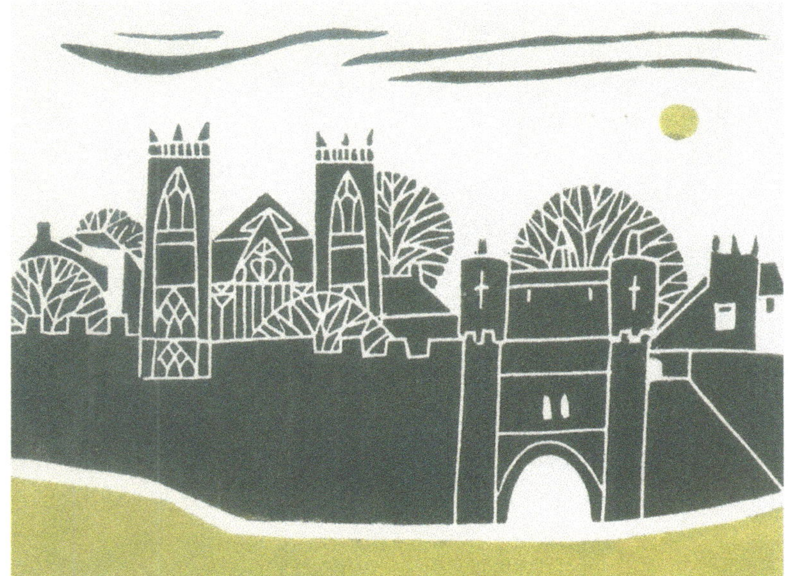

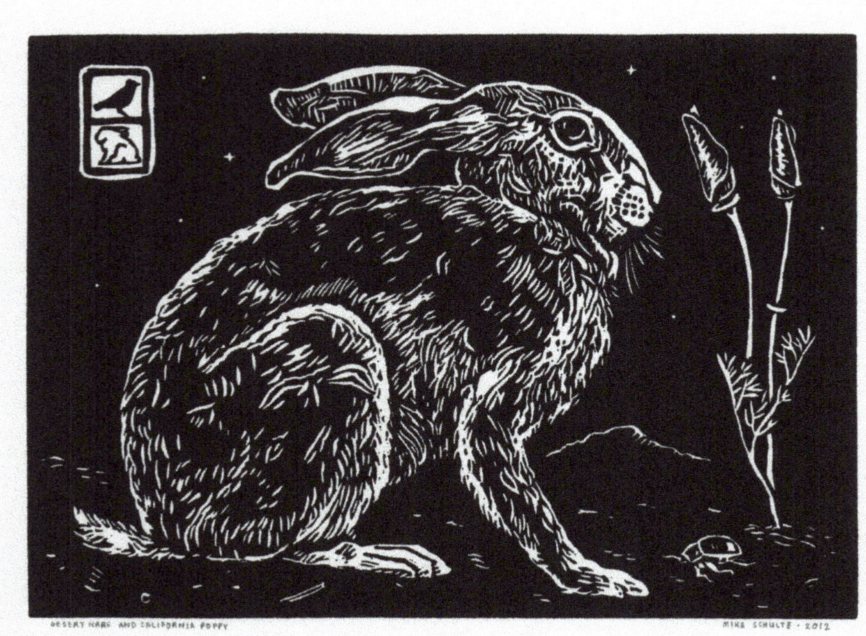

1

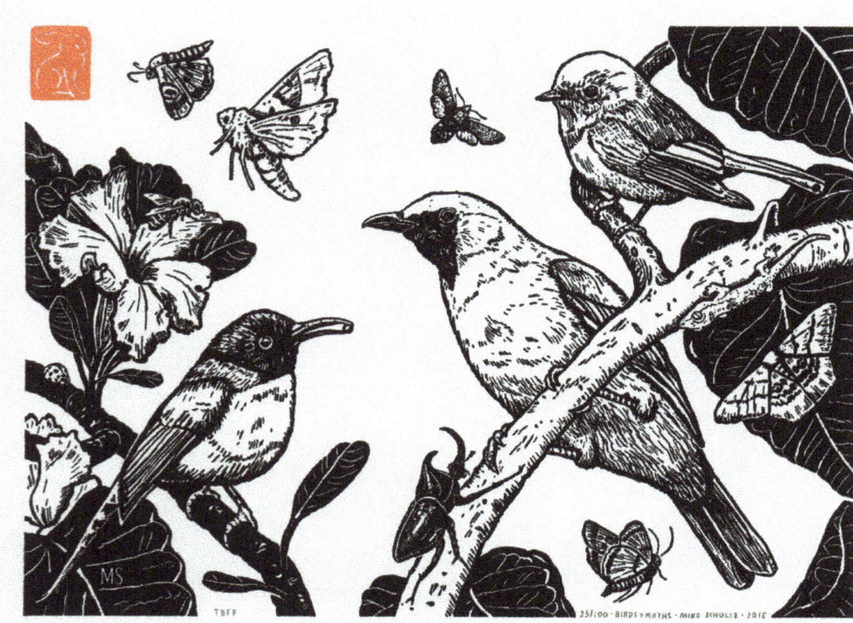

2

Mike Schultz

UNITED STATES

1
Desert Hare with Poppy and Mt. Shasta
LINOCUT
SERIES:
CALIFORNIA FLORA FAUNA

2
Birds and Moths (Featuring the Green Tailed Sunbird, the Blue Winged Leafbird, and the Sapphire Flycatcher with a Gecko, Rhinoceros Beetle, Asiatic Honeybees, and Various Moths)
LETTERPRESS
SERIES:
THAILAND BURMA FLORA FAUNA

3
Great Eastern Egret over Inle Lake
LETTERPRESS
SERIES:
THAILAND BURMA FLORA FAUNA

SITE	**mikeschultzstudio.com**
INSTAGRAM	**@mike_schultz_studio**
SHOP	**mikeschultz.etsy.com**

Printmaker Mike Schultz hails from Ithaca, New York, and currently lives and works in Portland, Oregon.

"In 1996, I learned the basics of printmaking at the Kansas City Art Institute, but it wasn't until 2007 when I was broke and living in Brooklyn that I really got into it. My sweet grandmother sent me a check for $100 along with her Christmas card. So, on Christmas Eve, I took the train into Manhattan and bought paper, a carving tool, a linoleum block, a brayer, a tin of black oil-based ink, and a can of mineral spirits. I spent all that night and Christmas Day carving and printing my first linocut edition, and have been hooked ever since!

"My work is largely about my experience living on the Thai-Burma border, where in 2010–2011 I coestablished a studio and taught various artisan skills to Burmese migrant youth living there in exile. I have a deep love of drawing plants, animals, and narratives involving the natural world, so I found printmaking to be a great way to talk about Burma and other things that are important to me without being too heavy handed. For example, I can depict and honor incredible creatures such as the Malayan tapir, sun bear, or golden cat without getting specific about their status as endangered species or about politics. My current printmaking project, Thailand Burma Flora Fauna, is a large body of drawings, linocuts, monotypes, and letterpress prints. This project enabled me to travel back to the Thai-Burma border to teach drawing classes to children and to lead higher-level, skill-specific workshops for young-adult art teachers.

"There is so much that I love about relief printmaking. Formally speaking, to me it seems to be an extension of drawing, and what I am most interested in is what I can do with the simplicity of a black-and-white image. For example, what kind of space can you create using only the inked block and the carved absence of the block? Depending on its weight and movement, a simple line can sufficiently describe a subject or create great depth, even on a small scale. This is endlessly fascinating to me. Relief printmaking appeals to my meticulous side, and I enjoy the meditative, process-oriented tasks that it presents. I like that the relative control that you may have with oil painting or drawing is further removed with printmaking. Often, there is unpredictable variation in the prints—unexpected textures, visual noise, and character that I feel adds humanity to the work, and therefore makes the prints more interesting."

3

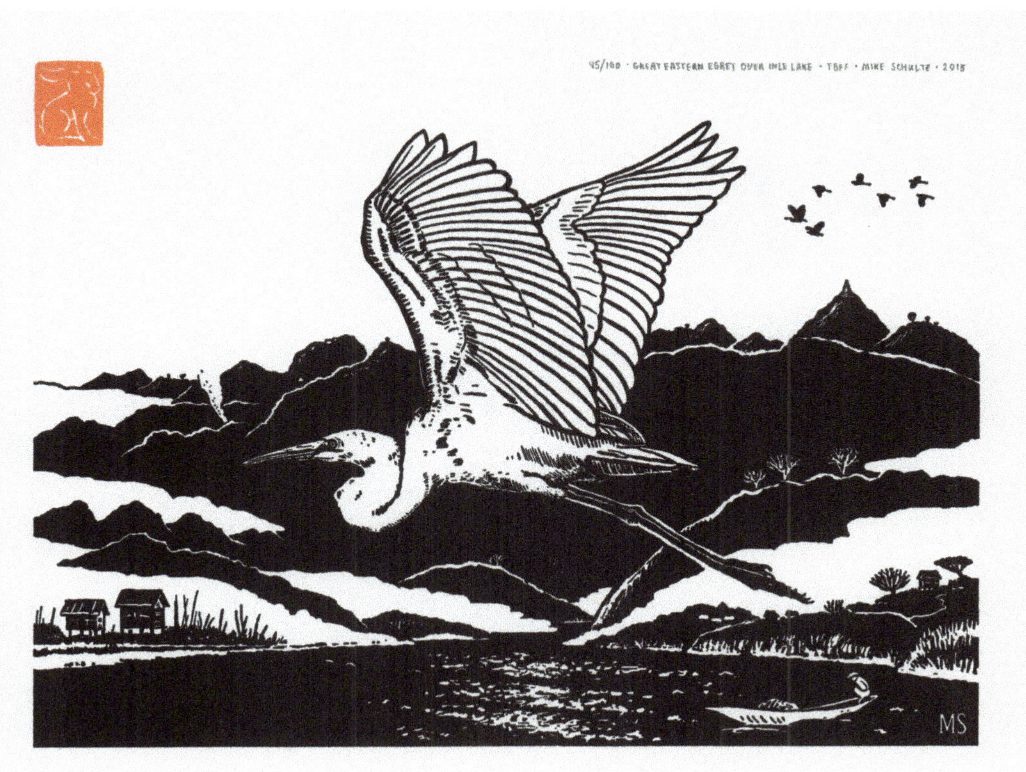

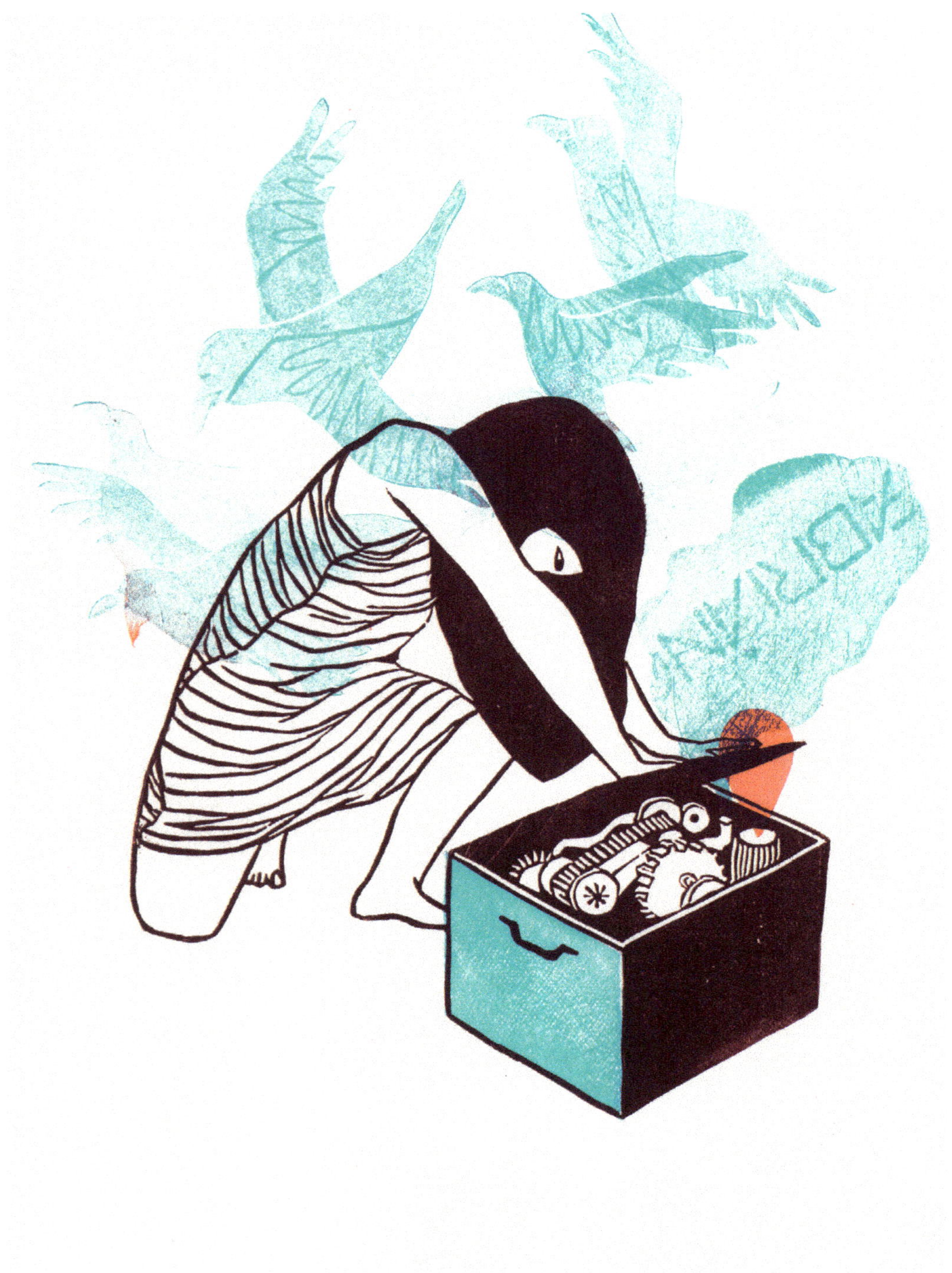

1

1
Les Oiseaux
LINOCUT

2
Trois Ours Blancs
LINOCUT

3
Chasseur-Loup
LINOCUT

Evelyne Mary
FRANCE

SITE	**evelynemary.fr**
BLOG	**evelynemary.blogspot.fr**
SHOP	**etsy.com/shop/evelynemary**

In a review of artist Evelyne Mary's work, journalist Dominique Thibaud says, "she creates pictures using a vocabulary of forms that she assembles in beautiful minimalist compositions: the white of the page vibrates next to intense colors, figures play with the background, the full with the vacuum, the masses with the lines."

Evelyne Mary says, "I discovered printmaking at school [École Estienne, National Applied Arts School, in Paris] but I didn't practice a lot during that period. One year later, I bought a little binding press at the flea market, and I started engraving at home with my companion. Then we started to recover old printing equipment and developed a workshop around letterpress and engraving. That's how I've practiced this technique for the last ten years. It let me experiment and develop my own way of engraving and printing.

"Now I work with a large number of matrices, such as lino and engravings, that I print and overprint. They are a kind of 'graphic vocabulary' that I use to create sense or graphic composition. This way of printing allows for the inclusion of accidents, chance, and sensitive material. I could say that I'm searching for happy plastic or semiotic accidents.

"Right now, I'm working on a lot of linocuts for cards and prints that are selling in a few galleries in Paris and illustrations for posters. Also, I am currently working on a children's book project entirely achieved with linocut."

2

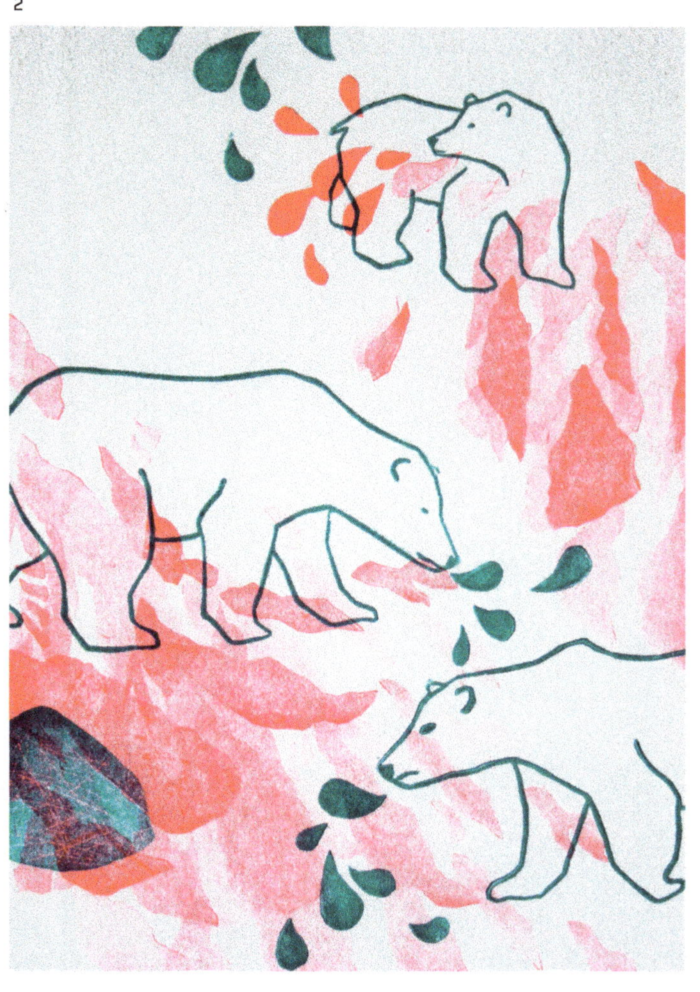

3

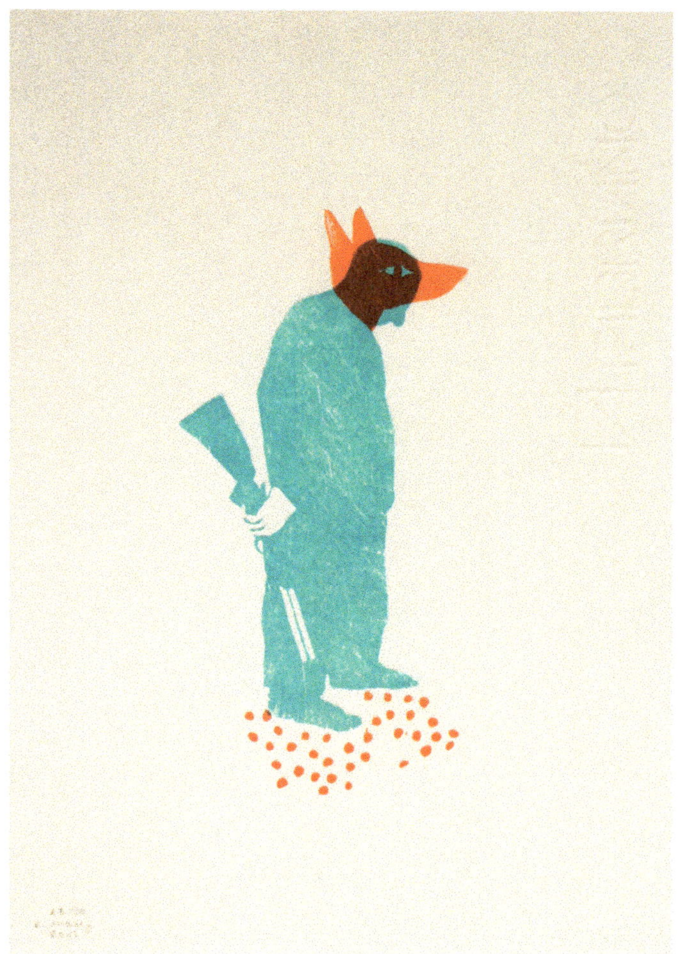

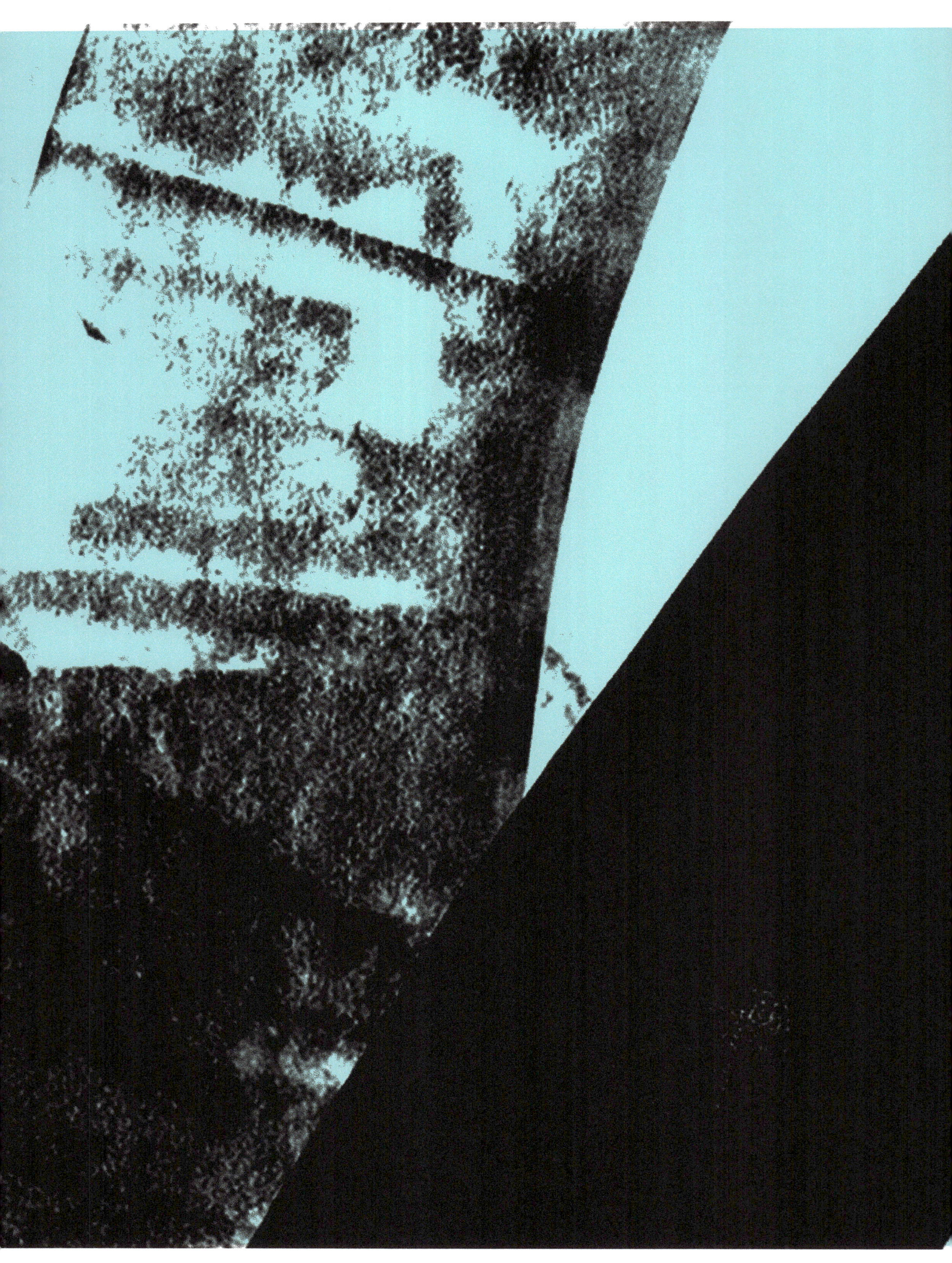

artist's proof or a.p. / The initial proofs or test prints pulled by the artist before the edition begins.

baren / A flat, circular disc from the Japanese printmaking tradition used to burnish the back of the paper when printing by hand.

block / Sometimes referred to as a plate, a block is the matrix in which the artist makes marks. In this book, we use linoleum and dense rubber blocks, all collectively referred to as blocks.

brayer / A hard rubber roller that works the ink on the platen and applies ink to the surface of the block.

burnish / To rub the back of printmaking paper in order to transfer the ink from the block onto the printmaking paper. This can be accomplished with numerous tools.

chine-collé / A print using a patterned, thin, tissue-like paper (originally Chinese paper, but now also made in India and Japan) adhered to the print during printing.

edition / The edition of prints is the number of identical prints the artist makes with the block. The artist then numbers each print as an original. An open-edition print means the block may be printed over and over again. A limited-edition print is only printed a set number of times.

ghost print / After finishing the standard inking and printing process, the block is used for a second print without re-inking.

gouges / Blades that the relief printer uses to carve away areas from the block, typically V and U shaped.

ink modifiers / Additives to printmaking ink that extend the open time or make the ink more transparent. There are many varieties of ink modifiers, each adjusting a specific quality of printmaking ink.

linocut / A relief print made from linoleum rather than wood. Linoleum, which has no grain, was popularized as an art material in the early 1900s. It gained recognition and acceptance in the art world when artists such as Matisse and Picasso experimented with the medium.

matrix / The block or plate that holds the image that will be printed.

monoprint / A one-of-a-kind print that is based on unique inking, placement, or other unreproducible printing techniques. Multiple monoprints are often made from the same block, but you cannot make an edition (identical prints) of monoprints.

open time / The time it takes ink to dry. Water-soluble inks dry quickly and thus have a short open time. Soy or oil-based inks take several days to dry and have a long open time. Open times can be drawn out with ink extenders.

overprint / Printing one image directly over another printed image.

plate / Also called a block, the matrix in which the artist makes impressions. In this book, we use linoleum and dense rubber blocks.

printing jig / A registration guide that can be customized to the dimensions of every block and printmaking paper.

printmaking paper or **washi /** Handmade or machine-made paper used in Japanese printmaking. Washi is most often made from long plant fibers such as kozo or mulberry.

proofs / The initial proofs or test prints pulled by the artist before the edition begins.

reduction printing / Multilayered prints printed from a single block. After one color is printed, more of the block is removed, and the printing process is repeated.

registration / The process of lining up blocks for exact placement in printing.

relief print / A surface print—such as a woodcut, linocut, wood engraving, or stamp—wherein the design is cut away and subtracted from the block. When inked, the ink lies only on the surface of the block. Cut-away areas do not receive ink and do not print. These types of prints are known for their high-contrast look.

PRINTMAKING BOOKS

The Complete Printmaker: Techniques, Traditions, Innovations, **Revised and Expanded Edition.** John Ross, Clare Romano, and Tim Ross. The Free Press, 1990.

Printmaking: A Complete Guide to Materials & Processes. Beth Grabowski and Bill Fick. Laurence King, 2009.

The Printmaking Bible: The Complete Guide to Materials and Techniques. Ann d'Arcy Hughes and Hebe Vernon-Morris. Chronicle Books, 2008.

Print Workshop: Hand-Printing Techniques and Truly Original Projects. Christine Schmidt. Potter Craft, 2010.

Japanese Woodblock Print Workshop: A Modern Guide to the Ancient Art of Mokuhanga. April Vollmer. Watson-Guptill, 2015.

Block Printing: Techniques for Linoleum and Wood. Sandy Allison and Robert Craig. Stackpole Books, 2011.

Learning Linocut: A Comprehensive Guide to the Art of Relief Printing through Linocut. Susan Yeates. New Generation Publishing, 2011.

The Woodcut Artist's Handbook: Techniques and Tools for Relief Printmaking, **Second Edition.** George Walker and Barry Moser. Firefly Books, 2010.

Wood Engraving and Linocutting. Anne Hayward. Crowwood Press, 2011.

Making an Impression: Designing & Creating Artful Stamps. Geninne Zlatkis. Lark Craft, 2012.

Printing by Hand: A Modern Guide to Printing with Handmade Stamps, Stencils, and Silk Screens. Lena Corwin and Thayer Allyson Gowdy. Stewart, Tabori, and Chang, 2008.

Printmaking Unleashed: More Than 50 Techniques for Expressive Mark Making. Traci Bautista. North Light Books, 2014.

Carve, Stamp, Play: Designing and Creating Custom Stamps. Julie Fei-Fan Balzer. Interweave, 2013.

Stamp It!: DIY Printing with Handmade Stamps. Jenny Doh. Lark Crafts, 2013.

Yellow Owl's Little Prints: Stamp, Stencil, and Print Projects to Make for Kids. Christine Schmidt. Potter Craft, 2013.

PRINTMAKING SOCIETIES AND COURSES

3 Fish Studios
3fishstudios.com

Birmingham Printmakers Workshop
birminghamprintmakers.org

California Society of Printmakers
caprintmakers.org

Center for Contemporary Printmaking
contemprints.org

Los Angeles Printmaking Society
laprintmaking.com

Lower East Side Printshop
printshop.org

Open Studio
openstudio.on.ca

Penland School of Crafts
penland.org

Printeresting
printeresting.org

Seattle Print Arts
seattleprintarts.org

Tamarind Institute
tamarind.unm.edu

Venice Printmaking Studio
veniceprintmaking.it

Warringah Printmakers Studio
printstudio.org.au

Zea Mays Printmaking
zeamaysprintmaking.com

PRINTING SUPPLIES

Most basic printmaking supplies can be found at art supply stores, but choices can be limited. Online art stores can be daunting at first if you are not quite sure what you are looking for. With a little guidance from this book and some research online, you should be able to find what you need and get started printing with only a few supplies. To begin, you will want one or two types of carving blocks, an inexpensive set of carving gouges, and a few colors of water-soluble block-printing ink. You will also need the appropriate thin, Japanese-style, printmaking paper; look for packs of mulberry or block-printing paper to get started.

Dick Blick Art Supplies
800.828.4548
dickblick.com

Dick Blick is the largest and oldest provider of art supplies in the United States. It carries a variety of supplies from student-grade through artist-grade materials. Explore the printmaking section on its website to find supplies such as mulberry papers and a variety of printing blocks, or visit one of the Dick Blick stores to get started.

McClain's Printmaking Supplies
15685 SW 116th Avenue, PMB 202
King City, OR 97224
800.832.4264
imcclains.com

Focused primarily on Japanese printmaking supplies, McClain's offers high-quality, professional printmaking materials for relief printmakers. Japanese barens and paper products are available.

Jackson's Art Supplies
1 Farleigh Place
London UK N16 7SX
+44 (0)207 254 0077
jacksonsart.com

UK-based Jackson's Art Supplies carries many brands of printmaking papers, inks, Pfeil-brand linoleum, and block cutters. Affordable and fast international shipping make this a valuable resource.

Speedball Art Supplies
800.898.7224
speedballart.com

Speedball produces many beginning printmaking materials, such as dense rubber blocks, carving gouge sets, and brayers. Visit the website to find a retailer near you.

The Japanese Paper Place
77 Brock Avenue
Toronto, Ontario
Canada M6K 2L3
416.538.9669
japanesepaperplace.com

There are many varieties of handmade and machine-made washi papers suitable for hand printing. This store specializes in Japanese-style printmaking paper. Email the helpful staff with questions about the papers in their catalog of offerings.

Akua Inks
800.898.7224
akuainks.com

Akua Inks are soy-based printmaking inks. They are an excellent choice for nontoxic printmaking in the home, and they produce the look and feel of traditional, oil-based, relief printing ink.

INDEX

Acknowledgments

Many thanks to the people who have lent their support and encouragement during the creation of this book. To Judith, my wonderful editor, who gave great advice, great notes, and made the process enjoyable; and, to Rockport Publishers, who made this book possible.

I'd like to thank my teachers in art and music who have enthusiastically supported me over the years, allowing me to become the artist and musician I am today. In particular, the art department and faculty at Teachers College, Columbia University, who allowed me to practice my technique in the art studios and with the printmaking presses.

Thanks to my mother, father, and sister for their never-ending love and support in life, and to my grandparents who encouraged my art and proudly displayed my creations.

Most importantly, thanks to my best friend and partner in life, art, and music, Paul, for his continual support and encouragement and his patience in assisting with this book, both in photography and writing—and, most importantly, printing.

About the Author

Andrea Lauren is a textile designer and printmaker born in Shepperton, England. She arrived in the United States as a teenager with her family, who settled in Florida. She spent her formative years making art and playing the cello. After graduating with an undergraduate degree in music performance, Andrea traveled around the United States playing music and making art in Chicago, Portland, New York City, and Asheville. Her relief prints for textiles as well as digital designs are sold internationally. Andrea is inspired by nature, music, and travel.

She shares her printmaking journey on her blog at **inkprintrepeat.com** and her Instagram account @inkprintrepeat.

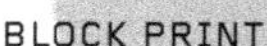

www.ingramcontent.com/pod-product-compliance
Lightning Source LLC
LaVergne TN
LVHW071344160126
829374LV00011B/23
* 9 7 8 1 6 3 1 5 9 1 1 3 6 *